Free Speech in the Digital Age

Free Speech in the Digital Age

Edited by Susan J. Brison
and
Katharine Gelber

OXFORD
UNIVERSITY PRESS

OXFORD
UNIVERSITY PRESS

Oxford University Press is a department of the University of Oxford. It furthers
the University's objective of excellence in research, scholarship, and education
by publishing worldwide. Oxford is a registered trade mark of Oxford University
Press in the UK and certain other countries.

Published in the United States of America by Oxford University Press
198 Madison Avenue, New York, NY 10016, United States of America.

CIP data is on file at the Library of Congress
ISBN 978-0-19-088360-7 (pbk.)
ISBN 978-0-19-088359-1 (hbk.)

9 8 7 6 5 4 3 2 1

Paperback printed by Sheridan Books, Inc., United States of America
Hardback printed by Bridgeport National Bindery, Inc., United States of America

For Tom and Gabriel

and for Lou and Simon

CONTENTS

ACKNOWLEDGMENTS

Our mutual engagement with the topic of free speech in the digital age was sparked when we met at a roundtable on "Freedom of Expression: Universal or Particular?" hosted by Adrienne Stone at the University of Melbourne Law School in December 2011. Out of that roundtable has grown a deep friendship, combined with ongoing scholarly collaboration.

Several of the chapters in this volume were first presented at a workshop on "Global Expressive Rights and the Internet" held at Dartmouth College in April 2015. We thank the Leslie Center for the Humanities, the Office of the Dean of the Faculty of Arts and Sciences, the Ethics Institute, the Gender Research Institute at Dartmouth, and the Department of Philosophy for funding the workshop. We also thank the participants in that workshop: Sonu Bedi, Alex Brown, Rafael Cohen-Almagor, Rae Langton, Ishani Maitra, Mary Kate McGowan, Frederick Schauer, Robert Mark Simpson, Natalie Stoljar, and Lynne Tirrell.

Katharine Gelber was a Visiting Scholar at the Global Freedom of Expression Project at Columbia University in December 2017 and would like to thank the Director, Agnès Callamard, and the Project Manager, Hawley Johnson, for providing a wonderful environment in which to complete this work. She is also grateful to the University of Queensland for a sabbatical leave and to Stephen Bell, Nicole George, Chris Reus-Smit, Alastair Stark, Adrienne Stone, Elizabeth Thurbon, and Ariadne Vromen for always being happy to debate ideas.

Susan J. Brison thanks the Princeton University Center for Human Values—especially Melissa Lane, Michael Smith, and Maureen Killeen— for providing a vibrant intellectual community when she was the 2016–17 Visiting Professor for Distinguished Teaching. She also thanks Karen Jones, Eva Feder Kittay, Margot Livesey, and Thomas Trezise, for invaluable feedback and support.

Finally, we are grateful to Peter Ohlin, at Oxford University Press, and to Samantha Koreman, who read chapter drafts and checked references while a Sophomore Research Scholar at Dartmouth College.

Susan J. Brison
Katharine Gelber
February 2018

CONTRIBUTORS

Diana L. Ascher is the director of the Information Studies Research Lab at UCLA, a cofounder of the Information Ethics & Equity Institute, and a cofounding partner at Stratelligence LLC. She studies how people seek, prioritize, and trust information, often using data visualization to reveal how power and information flow through social networks. She brings more than two decades of experience as an analyst, editor, media director, and information strategist to her work at the intersection of information studies and the fields of behavioral science, finance, higher education, journalism, law, leadership, management, medicine, and public policy. Dr. Ascher earned a PhD in the Department of Information Studies at the University of California, Los Angeles; an MBA at the Peter F. Drucker Graduate School of Management at Claremont Graduate University; and a BA in Public Policy from Duke University as a recipient of the Benjamin N. Duke Leadership Scholarship.

Sonu Bedi is Associate Professor of Government at Dartmouth College where he has been teaching since January 2007. He is the author of *Political Contingency* (NYU Press, 2007) (co-editor), *Rejecting Rights* (Cambridge University Press, 2009), and *Beyond Race, Sex, and Sexual Orientation: Legal Equality without Identity* (Cambridge University Press, 2013). He has published articles in the following peer-reviewed journals: *Political Theory; Journal of Political Philosophy; Studies in Law, Politics, and Society; Journal of Moral Philosophy; Criminal Law and Philosophy*; and *Polity*. He has published in the *Cleveland State Law Review* and has an article on equal protection theory in the *Georgia Law Review*. He was awarded the John M. Manley Huntington Award for newly tenured faculty in recognition of outstanding merit in 2013. He was also awarded the Jerome Goldstein Award for Distinguished Teaching (twice), by a vote of the classes of 2014 and 2017. His research interests are in the areas of contemporary political theory, constitutional law and theory, and race, law, and identity. He teaches courses on constitutional law, civil liberties, legal theory, freedom of speech, and theories of justice.

Ashutosh Bhagwat is Martin Luther King, Jr. Professor of Law at the UC Davis School of Law. Prior to joining UC Davis, he taught at UC Hastings College of the Law for seventeen years. Bhagwat is the author of *The Myth of Rights*, published by the Oxford University Press in 2010, as well as numerous books, articles, and book chapters on a wide variety of subjects, ranging from the structure of constitutional rights, to free speech law, to the

California Electricity Crisis. Journals his articles have appeared in include the *Yale Law Journal*, the *Supreme Court Review*, the *California Law Review*, the *Administrative Law Review*, and the *University of Illinois Law Review*. Bhagwat is a summa cum laude graduate of Yale University, where he received a BA with Honors in History. He is also an Honors graduate of The University of Chicago Law School, where he served as Articles Editor of the *University of Chicago Law Review*.

Susan J. Brison is Professor of Philosophy and Eunice and Julian Cohen Professor for the Study of Ethics and Human Values at Dartmouth College. She has held visiting positions at Tufts, New York University, and Princeton, where she was Visiting Professor for Distinguished Teaching at the University Center for Human Values in 2016–17 and Visiting Professor of Philosophy in 2018- 19. She has been a Mellon Fellow, a National Endowment for the Humanities Fellow, and a Member of the School of Social Science at the Institute for Advanced Study in Princeton, New Jersey. The author of *Aftermath: Violence and the Remaking of a Self* (Princeton University Press, 2002) and co-editor of *Contemporary Perspectives on Constitutional Interpretation* (Westview Press, 1993), she has also published numerous articles on gender-based violence and on free speech theory in scholarly journals and anthologies, as well as in more popular venues, such as the *New York Times*, the *Guardian*, *Time*, and the *Chronicle Review*.

Alexander Brown is Reader in Political and Legal Theory at the University of East Anglia (UEA). He has published articles in *Law and Philosophy, Canadian Journal of Law and Jurisprudence, Constitutional Commentary, and Ethnicities*. He is also the co-author of *The Politics of Hate Speech Laws* (Routledge, 2019), and the author of *A Theory of Legitimate Expectations for Public Administration* (OUP, 2017), *Hate Speech Law: A Philosophical Examination* (Routledge, 2015), *Ronald Dworkin's Theory of Equality: Domestic and Global Perspectives* (Palgrave, 2009), and *Personal Responsibility: Why It Matters* (Continuum, 2009).

Soraya Chemaly is a writer and activist whose work focuses on the role of gender in culture, politics, religion and media. She is the Director of the Women's Media Center Speech Project and organizer of the Safety and Free Speech Coalition, both of which are involved in curbing online abuse, media, and tech diversity, and expanding women's freedom of expression. In 1994 she helped launch the News and Media Division at Claritas, Inc. (now part of Nielsen, Inc.), a pioneer in consumer demography, database marketing, and data technology owned by VNU. She left the company after serving as Senior Vice President of Corporate Marketing, responsible for market development and marketing strategy. She returned to writing full time in 2011. Her work appears in the *Atlantic, Time*, the *Guardian*, the *New Statesman*, the *Nation*,

Huffington Post and Quartz, the *Verge*, and the *Washington Post*. Soraya serves on the boards of several organizations dedicated to diversity in media and technology, including Women, Action and The Media; In this Together Media, No Bully, and the Women's Media Center.

Danielle Keats Citron is the Morton & Sophia Macht Professor of Law at the University of Maryland Francis King Carey School of Law, an Affiliate Scholar at the Stanford Center on Internet and Society, Affiliate Fellow at the Yale Information Society Project, and Senior Fellow at the Future of Privacy. She is the author of *Hate Crimes in Cyberspace* (Harvard University Press, 2014), and has published numerous book chapters and law review articles, and her opinion pieces have appeared in such media outlets as *Forbes*, the *New York Times*, the *Atlantic, Slate, Time, CNN*, and the *Guardian*. In 2015, the UK's *Prospect Magazine* named Professor Citron one of the "Top 50 World Thinkers" and she is a frequent guest on National Public Radio shows. She has advised federal and state legislators, law enforcement, and international lawmakers on privacy issues and also works closely with companies on issues involving online safety and privacy. She serves on Twitter's Trust and Safety Council and has presented her research at Facebook, Google, and Microsoft. In addition, Professor Citron serves as an advisor to civil liberties and privacy organizations and is currently Chair of the Electronic Privacy Information Center's Board of Directors.

Mary Anne Franks is Professor of Law at the University of Miami. She graduated from Harvard Law School in 2007, having received her doctorate in 2004 and master's degree in 2001 in Modern Languages and Literature from Oxford University, where she studied on a Rhodes Scholarship. Before she began teaching at UM, Prof. Franks was a Bigelow Fellow and Lecturer in Law at the University of Chicago Law School. Prior to this, Prof. Franks taught social theory and philosophy at Harvard University. Professor Franks's research and teaching interests include cyberlaw, self-defense, discrimination, free speech, and privacy. Her academic scholarship has appeared in the *California Law Review*, the *UCLA Law Review, Illinois Law Review*, and *Columbia Journal of Law & Gender*, among others. Professor Franks also publishes articles in the popular press including the *Atlantic*, the *Guardian, Time*, and the *Huffington Post*. Professor Franks serves as the Legislative and Tech Policy Director and Vice-President of the Cyber Civil Rights Initiative, a nonprofit organization that raises awareness about online harassment and advocates for legal, technical, and social reform. Professor Franks has worked with both state and federal legislators on a variety of laws dealing with privacy and harassment, including the Intimate Privacy Protection Act, a bipartisan bill introduced in Congress in July 2016.

Katharine Gelber is Professor of Politics and Public Policy at the University of Queensland, a former Australian Research Council Future Fellow, and a Fellow of the Academy of Social Sciences Australia. In November–December 2017 she was a Visiting Scholar at Columbia University. She has expertise in freedom of speech, the regulation of hate speech, and the application of the capabilities approach to freedom of speech theory. She recently published *Free Speech after 9/11* (Oxford University Press, Oxford, 2016) and has also recently completed, with Luke McNamara, a project assessing the impact of hate speech laws on public discourse in Australia. She has articles published in *Political Studies, Parliamentary Affairs, Social Identities, Law and Society Review, Civil Justice Quarterly*, the *Australian Journal of Human Rights, Melbourne University Law Review*, and the *Australian Journal of Political Science*. In 2011 she was the Australian Expert Witness at a United Nations Asia Pacific regional meeting in Bangkok considering countries' responses to the free speech and hate speech provisions of international law.

Safiya Umoja Noble is an Associate Professor at the University of California, Los Angeles (UCLA) in the Departments of Information Studies and African American Studies, and is a visiting faculty member to the University of Southern California (USC) Annenberg School of Communication. Previously, she was Assistant Professor in the Institute for Communication Research at the University of Illinois at Urbana-Champaign. In 2019, she will join the Oxford Internet Institute at the University of Oxford as a Senior Research Fellow. Noble's academic research focuses on the design of digital media platforms on the internet and their impact on society, marking the ways that digital media impacts and intersects with issues of race, gender, culture, and technology design. Her monograph on racist and sexist algorithmic bias in commercial search engines is entitled *Algorithms of Oppression: How Search Engines Reinforce Racism* (NYU Press), and she is the co-editor of two volumes, *The Intersectional Internet: Race, Sex, Culture, and Class* and *Emotions, Technology & Design*.

Dinah PoKempner is General Counsel for Human Rights Watch. Her work has taken her to Cambodia, the Republic of Korea, Vietnam, the former Yugoslavia, and elsewhere to document and analyze war crimes and violations of civil and political rights and to monitor compliance with international humanitarian law. She has written on freedom of expression, peacekeeping operations, international tribunals, U.N. human rights mechanisms, cyberliberties and security, and refugee law, among other human rights topics, and she oversees the organization's positions on international law and policy. A graduate of Yale and Columbia University School of Law and a member of the Council on Foreign Relations, Ms. PoKempner also teaches at Columbia University.

Robert C. Post is a Sterling Professor of Law at Yale Law School, and served as the School's sixteenth dean, from 2009 until 2017. Before coming to Yale, he taught at the University of California at Berkeley School of Law. Post's subject areas are constitutional law, First Amendment, legal history, and equal protection. He has written and edited numerous books, including *Citizens Divided: A Constitutional Theory of Campaign Finance Reform* (Harvard University Press, 2014), which was originally delivered as the Tanner Lectures at Harvard in 2013. Other books include *Democracy, Expertise, Academic Freedom: A First Amendment Jurisprudence for the Modern State* (Yale University Press, 2012); *For the Common Good: Principles of American Academic Freedom* (with Matthew M. Finkin, Yale University Press, 2009); *Prejudicial Appearances: The Logic of American Antidiscrimination Law* (with K. Anthony Appiah, Judith Butler, Thomas C. Grey, and Reva Siegel, Duke University Press, 2001); and *Constitutional Domains: Democracy, Community, Management* (Harvard University Press, 1995).

Frederick Schauer is David and Mary Harrison Distinguished Professor of Law at the University of Virginia. He is also Frank Stanton Professor of the First Amendment, Emeritus, at the Kennedy School of Government, Harvard University. Previously, Schauer was Professor of Law at the University of Michigan, and has also been Visiting Professor of Law at the Columbia Law School, Fischel-Neil Distinguished Visiting Professor of Law at the University of Chicago, Morton Distinguished Visiting Professor of the Humanities at Dartmouth College, Distinguished Visiting Professor at the University of Toronto, Distinguished Visitor at New York University, and James Goold Cutler Professor of Law at the College of William and Mary. In 2007–2008, he was the Eastman Professor at Oxford University and a fellow of Balliol College. A fellow of the American Academy of Arts and Sciences and former holder of a Guggenheim Fellowship, Schauer is the author of *The Law of Obscenity* (BNA, 1976), *Free Speech: A Philosophical Enquiry* (Cambridge, 1982), *Playing by the Rules: A Philosophical Examination of Rule-Based Decision-Making in Law and in Life* (Oxford, 1991), *Profiles, Probabilities, and Stereotypes* (Harvard, 2003), *Thinking Like a Lawyer: A New Introduction to Legal Reasoning* (Harvard, 2009), and, most recently *The Force of Law* (Harvard, 2015). He is also the editor of *Karl Llewellyn, The Theory of Rules* (Chicago, 2011), and co-editor of *The Philosophy of Law* (Oxford, 1996) and *The First Amendment* (West, 1995).

Robert Mark Simpson is Lecturer in Philosophy at University College London, and was previously Lecturer in Philosophy at Monash University (2013–17), and Visiting Assistant Professor in the Law and Philosophy program at the University of Chicago (2015). His research interests are primarily in social and political philosophy; they include topics such as free speech, hate speech, the analysis of speech-harm, attributions of responsibility in law, the moral limits of the criminal law, the epistemology of disagreement, and philosophical issues around religious conflict.

James Weinstein is the Dan Cracchiolo Chair in Constitutional Law and Faculty Fellow, Center for Law, Science and Innovation at Arizona State University and Associate Fellow, Centre for Public Law at the University of Cambridge. His areas of academic interest are constitutional law, especially free speech, as well as jurisprudence and legal history. He is co- editor of *Extreme Speech and Democracy* (Oxford University Press, 2009) and the author of *Hate Speech, Pornography and the Radical Attack on Free Speech Doctrine* (Westview Press, 1999), and has written numerous articles in law review symposia on a variety of free speech topics including free speech theory, obscenity doctrine, institutional review boards, commercial speech, database protection, campaign finance reform, election lies, the relationship between free speech and constitutional rights, hate crimes, and campus speech codes. Professor Weinstein has litigated several significant free speech cases, primarily on behalf of the Arizona Civil Liberties Union.

Heather M. Whitney is a doctoral candidate in Philosophy at New York University. She earned a JD from Harvard Law School, *magna cum laude*, and a BA in Philosophy from UCLA, *summa cum laude*. Prior to law school she worked on Google's Global Ethics and Compliance team. After law school she clerked for the Honorable Chief Judge of the Seventh Circuit, Diane P. Wood. She was then Bigelow Fellow at the University of Chicago Law School and Faculty Affiliate at the Berkman Klein Center for Internet & Society (where she was previously a Fellow). Immediately prior to starting at NYU she was a Visiting Researcher at Harvard Law School. Her research interests are primarily in philosophy of law (public and private), moral, social, and political philosophy, and aesthetics.

Free Speech in the Digital Age

Introduction

Susan J. Brison and Katharine Gelber

Free speech is a value of paramount importance to liberal democracies and their citizens, with political leaders collectively and routinely declaring their fervent endorsement of it. Just what free speech is, however, and how and why it should be protected and fostered, are subjects of ongoing controversy and need to be examined anew in the digital age. This volume of thirteen new essays explores how the internet changes—or should change—our understanding of the right to freedom of expression, broadly understood in a global context.

Consistent with usage in the relevant literature, we use the terms "free speech" and "freedom of expression" interchangeably in this volume and we understand speech and expression to include not only spoken and written words, but also symbols, graphics, and many other forms of communication. Not all of what we call "speech" in ordinary language, however, is covered by a principle of free speech. Even in the United States, where the First Amendment to the Constitution declares that "Congress shall make no law . . . abridging the freedom of speech," much of what we would ordinarily call "speech" receives no First Amendment protection. Such speech includes perjury, insider trading, true threats, trade secrets, and, since the passage of the Patriot Act, speech that constitutes "material support" to terrorist groups.[1]

The word "speech," in the context of determining what is covered by a principle of free speech, is a term of art and is understood in different ways in different legal cultures. The massive, worldwide, and instantaneous reach of the internet has made for inevitable clashes among diverse free speech regimes, creating an urgent need for new ways of understanding free speech that might aid in resolving such conflicts.

The scale and pace at which the medium of expression is changing in the digital age are unprecedented. From 2000 to 2015, the number of people with access to the internet increased from 6.5 percent to 43 percent of the global population and, by January 2016, the number of people online exceeded 3.2 billion (Aiken 2016: 9). By 2020, another 1.5 billion people are expected to become connected (Aiken 2016: 302).

Concerns about how technological advances may affect human thought and communication, however, are by no means new. In the *Phaedrus*, for example, Plato details a conversation between Socrates and Phaedrus in which Socrates cites the story of the ancient Egyptian king Thamus's reaction to Theuth's invention of the art of letters. After Theuth claimed to "'have discovered a potion for memory and for wisdom,'" the king replied:

> "O most expert Theuth, one man can give birth to the elements of an art, but only another can judge how they can benefit or harm those who will use them. And now, since you are the father of writing, your affection for it has made you describe its effects as the opposite of what they really are. In fact, it will introduce forgetfulness into the soul of those who learn it: they will not practice using their memory because they will put their trust in writing . . . . [Y]ou provide your students with the appearance of wisdom, not with its reality. Your invention will enable them to hear many things without being properly taught, and they will imagine that they have come to know much while for the most part they will know nothing." (Plato *Phaedrus* 273e–275b 1997: 551–52).

Just as Thamus warned against the hazards to our abilities to think, know, and remember posed by the written word, critics of the internet have cautioned us that the current use of online technologies is diminishing our cognitive functions (Carr 2010) and leading to a dumbing down of individuals (Coopersmith 2016). But it is not only our cognitive capacities that may be altered by such technological developments; it is the very nature of freedom of expression itself—its definition, its rationales, its boundaries, and its applications—that the internet calls into question.

In 1992, as the radically new technology of the internet was just beginning to revolutionize global communication, Neil Postman began his book, *Technopoly: The Surrender of Culture to Technology*, by urging us to take to heart the cautionary tale in the legend of Thamus. He briefly noted an error in Thamus's judgment, which was "in his believing that writing will be a burden to society and *nothing but a burden*." As Postman observed, "it is mistake to suppose that any technological innovation has a one-sided effect. Every technology is both a burden and a blessing; not either-or, but this-and-that" (1992, 4–5). But the greater part of *Technopoly* takes the moral of Thamus's story as applied to the digital age to be that we need to be wary of the pernicious effects of computer technology, especially those that might otherwise escape our notice. According to Postman, "it is a certainty that radical technologies create new definitions of old terms, and that this process takes place without our being fully conscious of it. Thus, it is insidious and dangerous, quite different from the process whereby new technologies introduce new terms to the language." (1992, 8) He observed that we are not taken unawares by new words and phrases such as "VCR," "software," and "Walkman" or, one might add today, "Facebook," "Twitter," and "Snapchat." "New things require new words. But new things also modify old words, words that have deep-rooted meanings. The telegraph and the penny press changed what we once meant by 'information'. Television changes what we once meant by the terms 'political debate', 'news', and 'public opinion'. The computer changes 'information' once again. . . . The old words still look the same, are still used in the same kinds of sentences. But they do not have the same meanings; in some cases, they have opposite meanings. And this is what Thamus wishes to teach us—that technology imperiously commandeers our most important terminology. It redefines 'freedom', 'truth', 'intelligence', 'fact', 'wisdom', 'memory', 'history'—all the words we live by. And it does not pause to tell us. And we do not pause to ask" (1992: 8–9).

As Marshall McLuhan had already famously and persuasively argued in the early 1960s, technological advances in forms of communication directly influence the ways in which we understand our rights and freedoms. McLuhan argued that the development of mass, uniform printing both facilitated the development of conceptions of individual freedom and provided the means by which people could assert their right to expression against governmental authority. Mass printing meant books became portable and accessible to laypeople, no longer rare, precious objects in libraries seen by only a few. The use of typefaces made books easier to read and, in addition, people who were unable to read Latin could now read them in the vernacular. The principles of uniformity and accessibility central to mass printing came to be extended to social organization. They enabled the development of a technology of "homogenous citizens" upon which (counterintuitively) individualism could be developed, as individuals strove to differentiate themselves from the homogenous group (1962: 207–09).

The "vernacular in printed form" facilitated the assertion of individual rights, while at the same time enabling the emergence of nationalism, manifest in understandings of the uniformity of citizens within a nation state (1962: 218). Thus, "print created national uniformity and government centralism, but also individualism and opposition to government" (1962: 235). Likewise, the introduction and proliferation of new electronic media—telegraph, telephone, radio, films, television—transformed not only how we communicated with others, but also how we understood ourselves and our communities. McLuhan's own gloss on his most famous saying, "the medium is the message," was that it was "merely to say that the personal and social consequences of any medium—that is, of any extension of ourselves—result from the new scale that is introduced into our affairs by . . . any new technology" (1964: 7).

In today's world, the sending and receiving of information on the internet is a ubiquitous and, for many of us, unavoidable means of communication. Indeed, some argue that it will soon no longer make sense to differentiate our online from our offline lives, given the increasing extent to which they intersect and interact. According to Luciano Floridi, "[i]n the near future, the distinction between online and offline will become ever more blurred and then disappear. For example, it already makes little sense to ask whether one is online or offline when driving a car following the instructions of a navigation system that is updating its database in real time. The same question will be incomprehensible to someone checking her email while travelling inside a driverless car guided by a GPS" (Floridi 2014: 43–44).

The chapters in this volume examine whether, and, if so, how our ways of understanding, practicing, and regulating freedom of speech are changing in the digital age. It is undeniable that the internet has changed how we communicate. Given the interactive nature of the internet, the dissemination and reception of information (textual, visual, aural) have become dynamic and social media have facilitated new forms of networking and collaboration (Jones 2008; Oates 2008: 155–57). The roles of creator and user (and those of performer and audience, speaker and listener, writer and reader) have become less distinct in many online contexts, and when we engage in online communication we are, typically unwittingly, subject to surveillance and to having data about us extracted, stored, and used. These developments raise urgent questions about how this relatively new medium may call for the reconceptualization of the theory and practice of free speech.

Free speech theory and practice across the globe have been heavily influenced by First Amendment jurisprudence (Schauer 2005: 29–56), the exclusive focus of which is government regulation of speech. The extent to which governments may justifiably restrict speech is still a subject about which there is considerable disagreement and debate. To see this, we need only look at the German government's recent law that will fine social media companies who do not remove proscribed racist content (Eddy and Scott 2017). At the same time, the ubiquity and global reach of the internet require a new and different focus that examines the role played in speech regulation by nonstate actors, including social media companies and internet platform providers. This is because the nature of the internet means that nongovernment actors play vital roles in mediating online expression in ways that substantively affect people's freedom of speech, as, for example, when Facebook has the power and the technological capability to determine what users can read (Tufekci 2016) and which posts are removed by its moderation system (Levin 2017).

We acknowledge that some speech is capable of causing significant harms and several chapters in this volume provide evidence of it doing so. The chapters dealing with harmful online speech take as a given that speech *can* harm[2] and they go on to assess whether already acknowledged speech-based harms might differ in the context of online speech. They also discuss new forms of harmful speech that have come into existence as a result of recent advances in information technology.

Although some contributors to our volume focus on speech-based harms in the digital age, none of us would deny the unprecedented benefits that online speech has brought to people's lives. There is a tension, however, between the freedom-enhancing and democracy-enabling capacities of the internet and its freedom-infringing and democracy-undermining capacities. In some (particularly early) studies, the internet was posited as a site of freedom, a place where anyone and everyone could have their say, and thus a site of democratic—and democratizing—practice and engagement (Margetts 2013; Margolis and Moreno-Riaño 2009: 1–3), although others contested this claim (Sunstein 2007). There is increasing recognition of the potentially negative impacts of some expression online (Best and Wade 2009), including an understanding of how online communications can facilitate speech-based harms. This can occur through the instantaneous and global dissemination of previously recognized types of harmful speech, such as hate speech (Leets 2001). In addition, internet-based social media have given rise to new types of speech-based harms, such as the deliberate targeting of individuals, especially women, in, for example, cyber harassment, "revenge" porn, and cyberstalking (Citron 2014; Jane 2014a, 2014b; Levmore and Nussbaum 2011; Foxman and Wolf 2013).

Questions addressed by our contributors include the following: Should greater regulation be applied to online speech than is currently the case, and, if so, how can freedom of expression also be protected and enhanced? How can we assess different types of speech online for their contribution to genuine public discourse, the discourse that is at the heart of free speech protections in liberal democracies? Do people have a right to be forgotten? Should third-party hosts of online material be immune from prosecution for harms? Given that cyberspace is not delineated by national borders, is it possible to set standards for online discourse across the globe?

The volume begins with chapters that revisit free speech theory in light of internet speech. Some explicitly discuss First Amendment controversies, but all are applicable to global expressive rights in the digital age. First, in "Digital Dualism and the 'Speech as Thought' Paradox," Katharine Gelber and Susan J. Brison critique the view, expressed in the 1996 Barlow Declaration and elsewhere, that the digital realm—"cyberspace"—is a disembodied space for pure thought. They show that the view that speech online is distinct from the material world echoes the same idea in traditional free speech theory, which has long considered speech to be more akin to thought than to action. They conclude that it is incorrect to hold that online communications are, in their ontological status and causal capacity, more akin to thought than to conduct, just as it is incorrect to hold that offline communications are more akin to thought than to conduct.

In chapter 2, "Search Engines and Free Speech Coverage," Robert Mark Simpson and Heather Whitney investigate whether search engines and other new modes of online communication should be covered by free speech principles. They critique an argument given by some U.S. courts that analogizes the results of algorithms underpinning search engines to decisions made by newspaper editors. Pointing out dissimilarities between search engines and newspapers that undermine this analogy, they argue that an analogical approach to questions of free speech coverage is of limited use in this context and that, in order to decide how free speech principles apply to new modes of online communication, we need to re-evaluate the normative foundations of free speech.

Next, James Weinstein asks, in chapter 3, "Cyber Harassment and Free Speech: Drawing the Line Online," how we might address the harms of doxxing and cyber harassment with remedies that are compatible with First Amendment jurisprudence and doctrine. He argues against treating all online communications as deserving of protection, as the United States Supreme Court suggested in the recent *Packingham*[3] judgment, permitting restriction of only speech that falls within one of the limited and narrow traditional exceptions to First Amendment coverage, such as true threats, defamation, obscenity, or fighting words. A better approach, on Weinstein's view, would be to consider whether, and the extent to which, the speech at issue can fairly be considered part of public discourse.

A distinction that some free speech theorists and jurists have considered to be crucial to determining what speech should be regulated is that between speech that advocates a criminal action, which, it is argued, should be protected, and speech that provides people with instructions for performing such an action, which, on this view, is justifiably restricted. Frederick Schauer asks in chapter 4, "Recipes, Plans, Instructions, and the Free Speech Implications of Words That Are Tools," whether we can justify treating speech acts of urging and recommending, on the one hand, and those of instructing and informing, on the other, in different ways for the purposes of implementing a principle of free speech. On what basis might we consider some speech to be mere advocacy, and thus protected, while other speech is considered incitement or crime-facilitating and, thus, unprotected? This question has come to the fore in the digital age as the proliferation of new forms of social media has enabled the mass distribution of instructions for committing antisocial acts such as building dirty bombs and 3-D printing guns.

Modern free speech law in liberal democracies is oriented around some basic categorical distinctions, including: speech versus non-expressive conduct; public versus private actors; political versus commercial speech; and public discourse versus private gossip. In chapter 5, "Free Speech Categories in the Digital Age," Ashutosh Bhagwat argues that the evolution of the internet and social media into the primary platforms for commerce and expression has fundamentally destabilized these categories, undermining the distinction between the commercial and the political, as well as that between the public and the private. He concludes that, in order to construct new, more workable categories in the digital age, scholars and policymakers must begin by examining *why* free speech remains of paramount importance today.

In chapter 6, "Privacy, Speech, and the Digital Imagination," Robert Post considers the vexed issue of online privacy, revisiting the 2014 "*Google Spain*" decision by the Court of Justice of the European Union (CJEU) which is considered to have created an alleged "right to be forgotten." He argues against this decision, suggesting it misunderstands the nature of privacy, confusing the instrumental logic of data privacy with the concept of dignitary privacy, which, he claims, courts have applied to public discourse for more than a century. The CJEU's confusion between data privacy and dignitary privacy, he concludes, leads to logical deficiencies in its opinion.

Danielle Keats Citron's contribution, chapter 7, "Why Combating Online Abuse Is Good for Free Expression," traces a shift in public attitudes from an exclusive focus on the expressive rights of speakers to a concern for the safety, privacy, and free speech rights of the targets of cyber harassment and other abusive forms of online speech. She documents the ways the tech industry and various government agencies are responding to the need to protect the rights of victims of online abuse and applauds these developments as enhancing freedom of expression in the digital age.

In chapter 8, "'Not Where Bodies Live': The Abstraction of Internet Expression," Mary Anne Franks argues against the aggressively anti-regulatory approach to the internet encoded in U.S. federal law in Section 230 of the 1996 Communications Decency Act. Section 230 invokes free speech principles to provide broad immunity for online intermediaries against liability for the actions of those who use their services. This, Franks argues, encourages an abstract approach to online conduct that downplays its material conditions and impact, thereby allowing powerful internet corporations to profit from harmful online conduct while absorbing none of its costs.

Free speech policies in the United States have a disproportionate effect on global expressive rights today, not only because of the long and influential tradition of First Amendment jurisprudence, but also because so much information technology originated in the United States and continues to be developed in Silicon Valley. Soraya Chemaly examines how the toxicity of online interactions challenges traditional free speech norms in chapter 9, "Demographics, Design, and Free Speech: How Demographics Have Produced Social Media Optimized for Abuse and the Silencing of Marginalized Voices." She argues that the sex segregation and gender-based hierarchies in the tech sector's workforce result in harmful and unjust effects on women's safety and free expression around the world.

Diana Ascher and Safiya Noble also discuss the unjust effects of toxic online speech on marginalized groups in chapter 10, "Unmasking Hate on Twitter: Disrupting Anonymity by Tracking Trolls." They argue that corporate digital media platforms moderate and manage free speech in ways that provide greater protection for speakers of hate, while disproportionately harming vulnerable populations. After being targets of racist and misogynist trolling themselves, they investigated whether new modes of analysis could identify and strengthen the ties between the online personas of anonymous speakers of hate and their identities in real life, thereby providing victims and law enforcement agencies with opportunities for intervention.

In chapter 11, "Online Dating Sites as Public Accommodations: Facilitating Racial Discrimination," Sonu Bedi argues that parts of the internet are also social institutions that are within the scope of justice. In particular, he argues that online commercial dating services are public accommodations, providing their customers with an important public service—the ability to find romantic partners—and thus should not unjustly discriminate in providing their services. Even though racial preferences for romantic partners implicate rights to speech and association, Bedi argues, it is unjust for commercial online dating websites to enable and, thereby, on his view, explicitly endorse such preferences.

The question of whether some online speech constitutes a form of unjust discrimination is raised again by Alexander Brown in chapter 12, "The Meaning of Silence in Cyberspace: The Authority Problem and Online Hate Speech." In the literature on hate speech and pornography, some have argued that even ordinary speakers who are not authority figures in any conventional sense can possess the power to subordinate—that is, rank as inferior, deny rights and powers to, or authorize discrimination against—the targets of their hate speech when witnesses remain silent and thereby license or grant authority to the hate speaker (Maitra and McGowan 2012). An example of this is when a hate speaker targets a victim on public transport and other passengers remain silent. Brown explores whether the distinctive nature of online communication changes the meaning of silence such that it becomes difficult to interpret silence in cyberspace as licensing or granting authority.

In the final chapter, "Regulating Online Speech: Keeping Humans, and Human Rights, at the Core," Dinah PoKempner, drawing on her work as general counsel of Human Rights Watch, argues that we are at a difficult juncture in protecting online speech and privacy when states resist applying principles they have endorsed internationally to their own domestic legislation and practice. Although governments have welcomed the internet's globalizing effect on economic development, they now fear its ability to amplify speech, such as propaganda and advocacy of terrorism, capable of undermining domestic security. She warns against sacrificing basic freedoms and argues that how well we protect privacy and speech in the digital age will determine whether the internet liberates or enchains us.

McLuhan observed, in *Understanding Media: The Extensions of Man*, that we tend to get so caught up in the content conveyed by new media technologies that we neglect to examine the effects of the new technologies themselves (1964). In recent debates between internet enthusiasts and internet sceptics, what gets missed, as Nicholas Carr puts it, "is what McLuhan saw: that in the long run a medium's content matters less than the medium itself in influencing how we think and act. As our window onto the world, and onto ourselves, a popular medium molds what we see and how we see it—and, eventually, if we use it enough, it changes who we are, as individuals and as a society" (2010). In compiling this volume, we have not attempted to address all the ways in which the internet is transforming our conceptions of ourselves and the cultures in which we live, but we hope to have begun a lively and ongoing interdisciplinary conversation about our changing views of free speech in the digital age.

Notes

1. Holder v. Humanitarian Law Project, 561 U.S. 1 (2010).
2. Following, among others, Langton (1993); MacKinnon (1993); Matsuda et al. (1993); Brison (1998a, 1998b); Gelber (2002, 2010); Maitra and McGowan (2012).
3. Packingham v. North Carolina, 528 U.S. ___ (2017).

References

Aiken, Mary. 2016. *The Cyber Effect: A Pioneering Cyberpsychologist Explains How Human Behavior Changes Online*. New York: Spiegel and Grau.

Best, Michael and Keegan Wade. 2009. "The Internet and Democracy. Global Catalyst or Democratic Dud?" *Bulletin of Science, Technology and Society* 29(4): 255–71.

Brison, Susan J. 1998a. "The Autonomy Defense of Free Speech," *Ethics* 108: 312–39.

Brison, Susan J. 1998b. "Speech, Harm, and the Mind-Body Problem in First Amendment Jurisprudence," *Legal Theory* 4: 39–61.

Carr, Nicholas. 2010. *The Shallows: What the Internet Is Doing to Our Brains*. New York: W.W. Norton.

Citron, Danielle Keats. 2014. *Hate Crimes in Cyberspace*. Cambridge, MA: Harvard University Press.

Coopersmith, Jonathan. 2016. "Is Technology Making Us Dumber or Smarter? Yes." *The Conversation*. June 18. https://theconversation.com/is-technology-making-us-dumber-or-smarter-yes-58124.

Eddy, Melissa and Mark Scott. 2017. "Delete Hate Speech or Pay Up, Germany Tells Social Media Companies." *New York Times.* June 30. https://www.nytimes.com/2017/06/30/business/germany-facebook-google-twitter.html.

Floridi, Luciano. 2014. *The Fourth Revolution: How the Infosphere Is Reshaping Human Reality.* Oxford: Oxford University Press.

Foxman, Abraham and Christopher Wolf. 2013. *Viral Hate: Containing Its Spread on the Internet.* New York: Palgrave Macmillan.

Gelber, Katharine. 2002. *Speaking Back: The Free Speech versus Hate Speech Debate.* Amsterdam: John Benjamins.

Gelber, Katharine. 2010. "Freedom of Political Speech, Hate Speech, and the Argument from Democracy: The Transformative Contribution of Capabilities Theory." *Contemporary Political Theory* 9: 304–24.

Jane, Emma. 2014a. "Beyond Antifandom: Cheerleading, Textual Hate and New Media Ethics." *International Journal of Cultural Studies* 17(2): 175–90.

Jane, Emma. 2014b. "'Your a Ugly, Whorish, Slut'—Understanding e-bile." *Feminist Media Studies* 14(4): 531–46.

Jones, Bradley. 2008. *Web 2.0 Heroes: Interviews with 20 Web 2.0 Influencers.* Indianapolis, IN: Wiley.

Langton, Rae. 1993. "Speech Acts and Unspeakable Acts." *Philosophy and Public Affairs* 22(4): 293–330.

Leets, Laura. 2001. "Responses to Internet Hate Sites: Is Speech Too Free in Cyberspace?" *Communication Law and Policy* 6(2): 287–317.

Levin, Sam. 2017. "Civil Rights Groups Urge Facebook to Fix 'Racially Biased' Moderation System." *The Guardian.* January 18. https://www.theguardian.com/technology/2017/jan/18/facebook-moderation-racial-bias-black-lives-matter

Levmore, Saul and Martha Nussbaum (eds.) 2011. *The Offensive Internet: Speech, Privacy and Reputation.* Cambridge, MA: Harvard University Press.

MacKinnon, Catharine. 1993. *Only Words.* Cambridge, MA: Harvard University Press.

Maitra, Ishani and Mary Kate McGowan (eds.) 2012. *Speech & Harm: Controversies over Free Speech.* Oxford: Oxford University Press.

Margetts, Helen Margetts. 2013. "The Internet and Democracy" In: William Dutton (ed.) *The Oxford Handbook of Internet Studies.* Oxford: Oxford University Press.

Margolis, Michael and Gerson Moreno-Riaño. 2009. *The Prospect of Internet Democracy.* Surrey: Ashgate.

Matsuda, Mari, Charles R. Lawrence III, Richard Delgado, and Kimberlé Williams Crenshaw. 1993. *Words That Wound: Critical Race Theory, Assaultive Speech, and the First Amendment.* Boulder, CO: Westview Press.

McLuhan, Marshall. 1962. *The Gutenberg Galaxy: The Making of Typographic Man.* Toronto: University of Toronto Press.

McLuhan, Marshall. 1964. *Understanding Media: The Extensions of Man.* New York: McGraw-Hill.

Oates, Sarah. 2008. *Introduction to Media and Politics.* London: Sage.

Plato. 1997. *Complete Works.* John M. Cooper and D.S. Hutchinson (eds.). Indianapolis, IN.: Hackett.

Postman, Neil. 1992. *Technopoly: The Surrender of Culture to Technology.* New York: Knopf.

Schauer, Frederick. 2005. "The Exceptional First Amendment." In Michael Ignatieff (ed.) *American Exceptionalism and Human Rights.* Princeton< NJ: Princeton University Press, 29–56.

Sunstein, Cass. 2007. *Republic.com 2.0.* Princeton, NJ: Princeton University Press.

Tufekci, Zeynep. 2016. "The Real Bias Built in at Facebook." *New York Times.* May 19. https://www.nytimes.com/2016/05/19/opinion/the-real-bias-built-in-at-facebook.html.

1

Digital Dualism and the "Speech as Thought" Paradox

Katharine Gelber and Susan J. Brison

1. Introduction

Online communication is now a ubiquitous feature of billions of people's lives. In this context, some question how "real" online expression is, as compared with offline expression. The term "IRL"—"In Real Life"—is often used to distinguish what happens in the world from what happens online. Some users have claimed that what happens online is distinct and different from conduct offline that has equivalent effects. This claim has manifested in suggestions— both explicit and implicit—that speech online is more akin to thought than speech offline. In this chapter, we challenge this. We do this not because it no longer makes sense, as Floridi (2017) points out, to differentiate our online from our offline lives given that, for those of us with constant internet access, they are interwoven to such a degree as to be almost indistinguishable. Instead, we focus on the unsustainability of the philosophical underpinnings of the claim that speech online is more akin to thought than to non-speech conduct in its causal capacities, and we argue that that speech online is no different than speech offline in this respect.

To do this, we first outline key components of a free speech principle, showing how some defenses of this principle rely on a view that speech is more akin to thought than to non-speech conduct. We argue further that this view, when used as a premise in an argument for a free speech principle, leads to a paradox in which speech is treated as both special, unlike any non-speech conduct, in being causally inert and thus harmless; and yet still in need of special protection, justified by an independent free speech principle distinct from a general principle of liberty such as John Stuart Mill's harm to others principle. Those defending an independent free speech principle hold that there is a presumption against restricting speech, even if it causes harm that, if brought about by non-speech conduct, would justify restricting such conduct. If, however, speech is treated as harmless in the sense that—like thought—it is incapable of directly harming others and is, to that extent, distinct from action, then there would be no need to posit an independent free speech principle.

We detail claims as to the special nature of online speech, how in current debates about internet freedom, some proponents of freedom of expression are (re)asserting free speech principles through the prism of speech as more akin to thought than to conduct. We connect these claims to a long-standing underlying theme in free speech literature that upholds this same view. We show how this view has manifested in free speech scholarship and jurisprudence over time, and connect this view to the paradox we identify.

We then discuss, drawing on our earlier work, a theoretical defense of freedom of speech grounded in Amartya Sen's and Martha Nussbaum's capabilities approach that is not susceptible to this paradox. We argue this presents a good way of understanding what it is that speech does in and for people's lives, and therefore why it is important. It also overcomes the problem with viewing speech as especially deserving of protection compared with other political liberties. We argue, using a capabilities-informed approach, that freedom of speech warrants protection for the same reasons that other freedoms that are essential to the attainment of central human functional capabilities are worthy of protection. We posit that freedom of speech deserves no lesser or greater a degree of protection than other freedoms that are central to people's ability to choose what to do and who to be. We posit further that understanding freedom of speech in this way yields a nuanced argument for the robust protection of freedom of speech, one that also explains that a regulatory response to speech is justified when the speech hinders others' attainment of central human functional capabilities.

We conclude by drawing out the implications of understanding freedom of speech in this way for speech online, in particular by critiquing the alleged speech/conduct distinction that we are claiming has been entrenched and revitalized in debates about online speech. We argue that online speech is agent-driven, just as offline speech is, albeit in different ways; and that the materialities of the information technology that facilitates online speech also render it unlike thought, in much the same way as offline speech also requires materialities to ensure its communication. Those who claim a special sphere of speech online misconstrue the nature of speech itself and use unviable arguments for its protection.

2. Speech, Thought, and Conduct

Free speech theorists in the United States have tended to assume that (1) the U.S. legal system protects free speech in a way that other, less enlightened, countries would do well to emulate; and (2) there must be a sound philosophical basis for a fundamental human right to free speech, even if we do not (yet) know what that is. Both of these beliefs are held so fervently that those who are not true believers are at times not taken seriously in academic as well as popular debates about free speech controversies. But, as Kathleen Sullivan has pointed out, those who, in arguing for the regulation of harmful speech such as hate speech, question the foundation of the supposed right to freedom of expression, "deserve a response that goes beyond the rote and reflexive invocation of free speech as an article of faith. The appeal to the First Amendment as self-evident truth may be no more effective, as Professor Henry Louis Gates Jr. recently cautioned, than Samuel Johnson's attempt to refute Bishop Berkeley merely by kicking a stone" (Sullivan 1994: 213; citing Gates 1993: 37–38).

Views about free speech on the internet originated, as did the internet itself, in the United States and so have been heavily influenced by "First Amendment exceptionalism" (Schauer 1992, 2005). Current controversies over the alleged harms of online speech are reviving issues raised in the 1980s and 1990s. In some hate speech and pornography cases of that era, U.S. courts ruled that, even if speech causes harm (of the sort that constitutes a form of harassment, or race or sex discrimination), it is protected under the First Amendment.[1] In his opinion in *American Booksellers Ass'n v. Hudnut*[2] ruling unconstitutional an anti-pornography ordinance that had been adopted in Indianapolis, Judge Frank Easterbrook conceded the empirical claims made in the ordinance concerning the harmfulness of pornography. He wrote, "we accept the premises of this legislation. Depictions of subordination tend to perpetuate subordination. The subordinate status of women in turn leads to affront and lower pay at work, insult and injury at home, battery and rape on the streets." Easterbrook concluded, rather stunningly, given the nature of the harms catalogued, "Yet this simply demonstrates the power of pornography as speech,"[3] which, *because* it is speech, must be protected.

Likewise, in *John Doe v. University of Michigan*, an opinion ruling unconstitutional a University of Michigan policy on discrimination and discriminatory harassment, Judge Avern Cohn wrote, "It is an unfortunate fact of our constitutional system that the ideals of freedom and equality are often in conflict. The difficult and sometimes painful task of our political and legal institutions is to mediate the appropriate balance between these two competing values."[4] Judge Cohn concluded that, "While the Court is sympathetic to the University's obligation to ensure equal educational opportunities for all of its students, such efforts must not be at the expense of free speech."[5]

In the United States, not only jurists, but legal theorists as well, seemed to agree that free speech was, in such cases of conflict, not only paramount, but so obviously so that little or no argument was needed to support the claim. Many of those arguing against restrictions on even admittedly harmful speech, seemed to adhere to the First Amendment unthinkingly, as a dead dogma (to use a phrase of John Stuart Mill's), invoking it in a pragmatically self-defeating way, to cut off critical inquiry into its own foundations (or lack thereof).

Contemporary theorizing about free speech done by American scholars tends to take the free speech clause of the First Amendment of the U.S. Constitution to be the articulation of a legal right grounded in a fundamental human right, rather than a piece of positive law that may or may not be based on a moral imperative. Rather like warring countries that all claim to have God on their side, most contemporary U.S. legal theorists debating free speech issues argue that the First Amendment, when interpreted correctly, clearly supports their position. Virtually no theorists question whether the First Amendment is morally justified to begin with.[6] But if the right to free speech is to be considered as prior to and more fundamental than mere positive law, if it is, rather, the principle underlying the series of cases that the courts decided (or at least those that were decided correctly), then the right to free speech must be grounded in something *other* than this founding document and the precedents of earlier cases —it must have a foundation of some sort.

If the free speech clause of the First Amendment—"Congress shall make no law abridging the freedom of speech or of the press"—is interpreted to mean that speech is to be granted special protection not accorded to other forms of conduct, then a free speech principle, distinct from a principle of general liberty, must be posited and must receive a distinct justification. Such a principle must hold that speech is special, in the following way, as articulated by Frederick Schauer: "Under a Free Speech Principle, any governmental ac-tion to achieve a goal, whether that goal be positive or negative, must provide a stronger justification when the attainment of that goal requires the restric-tion of speech than when no limitations on speech are employed" (Schauer 1982: 7–8).[7]

It should be noted that a free speech principle understood in this way protects what we might call procedural free speech, not substantive free speech. It constrains state action, but not private action. So the right to free speech protected by the First Amendment is considered a right to be free from governmental interference of a certain sort, not (necessarily) a positive right actually to be able to speak and to have access to others' speech.

To hold that there is a right to free speech is not, however, to hold that it is absolute, and contemporary U.S. philosophers and legal theorists writing on free speech, like the U.S. courts, reject First Amendment absolutism.[8] Rather, they advocate some sort of balancing between free speech interests and other interests, for example, the interest in national security. The *value* of free speech, however, is taken to justify balancing interests with "a thumb on the scales" in favor of speech. As Thomas Scanlon notes, "on any strong version of the doctrine [of freedom of expression] there will be cases where protected acts are held to be immune from restriction despite the fact that they have as consequences harms which would normally be sufficient to justify the imposition of legal sanctions" (1972: 204). On Scanlon's view, *any* theory of free speech that counts as a "significant" one has this consequence, namely, that it considers immune from restriction not only offensive, or morally repugnant, speech, but also *harmful* speech, even where the resulting harms are so serious that the government would normally be justified in trying to prevent them.

Some jurists and legal theorists hold that speech simply cannot cause as much—or the same kind of—harm as non-speech conduct. Justice Scalia asserted such a view in oral arguments in *Schenck v. Pro-Choice Network* in stating "Sticks and stones will break my bones, but words can never hurt me. That's the First Amendment."[9] But, if it were really the case that words could never cause injury, a free speech principle would be otiose, adding nothing to a general principle of liberty grounded in the harm principle (Schauer 2015). Defenders of a robust, and not merely redundant, free speech principle must say why speech is deserving of heightened protection even when it is harmful.

But what justifies this tipping of the scales in favor of speech? Why should speech be considered so special as to be worthy of protection, even when it is conceded to cause real harms—harms that, if brought about by any other means, would be considered unjust and sanctionable?

Our legal systems, in the United States and Australia, are based, apart from a few unfortunate aberrations, on the view, articulated by Mill, that the government may justifiably exercise power over individuals, against their will, only to prevent harm to others (Mill 1978: 9). Mill considered his harm principle to apply equally to governmental regulation and to "the moral coercion of public opinion." Mill does not, however, specify what counts as harm. Following Joel Feinberg, we consider it to be a wrongful setback to (or invasion of) one's significant interests, so it encompasses much more than the hit-on-the-head sort of physical harm (see Feinberg 1984). Our legal systems already take into account harms understood in this way. Even in the case of physical injury, it is not merely the extent of the hurt—that is, the physical pain or damage—that is taken into account by the law, but also the harm, construed so as to include long-term financial and emotional damage.

A defense of a free speech principle must explain why the harm principle does not apply in the case of speech—or applies with less force than in the case of all other forms of human conduct. Many theorists have argued that one thing or another—the desirability of arriving at truth in the long run, say, or the need for a well-functioning democracy, or the fostering of individual autonomy—provides the foundation for a right to free speech. This kind of argument proceeds as follows: We value x. The right to free speech is essential for (or at least instrumental in) the achievement of x. Therefore, we must posit the right to free speech and design social structures (constitutions, laws, public policies) to protect and possibly even foster it.

As we, and others, have argued, however, such defenses of a free speech principle fail to show why speech that is as harmful as some regulable non-speech conduct must nevertheless be protected (Haworth 1998; Brison 1998a; Gelber 2002, 2010, 2012a, 2012b, 2012c). This lack of a coherent defense of the protection of harmful speech derives, we argue, from a deeper assumption underlying much political philosophy in this area. That is the assumption that speech deserves special protection because it is more like thought than like conduct.

In his 1996 "Declaration of the Independence of Cyberspace,"[10] John Perry Barlow, founder of the Electronic Frontier Foundation, considered to be "the leading nonprofit defending digital privacy, free speech, and inno-vation,"[11] declared the internet to be the "new home of Mind." Cyberspace was, on Barlow's view, a realm distinct from all of the countries on earth and "consist[ing] of transactions, relationships, and thought itself . . . ., a world that is both everywhere and nowhere, but . . . not where bodies live." He declared that governments had no sovereignty over cyberspace, and that its regulation was not welcome. He urged governments and people "of the past" to leave those in cyberspace alone—"You are not welcome among us. You have no sovereignty where we gather"—while also asserting that those in cyberspace were untouchable by law. "Your legal concepts of property, expression, iden-tity, movement, and context do not apply to us. They are all based on matter, and there is no matter here."[12]

As much as the Declaration was an assertion against government regula-tory power, it was simultaneously a statement about the ontological status of online speech and about the novel form of freedom of expression that cyber-space facilitates. And Barlow was not alone in holding this view of the oth-erworldliness of cyberspace. Not only is his declaration still featured on the Electronic Frontier Foundation's website, but others have invoked a kind of "digital dualism" in distinguishing cyberspace from the "real world."[13]

For example, some U.S. courts have grappled with this digital dualism in cases involving online expression, in which those accused of engaging in criminal speech online have declared that it is more difficult to understand what the expression in question did because it took place online. In an early U.S. case concerning online speech, *United States v Baker*,[14] a college student at the University of Michigan who was prosecuted for a criminal offense of "in-tent to communicate to injure or harm,"[15] successfully appealed the prosecu-tion in the Court of Appeals. He had written, and posted on a publicly available electronic bulletin board, a short story discussing the rape and mutilation of a woman with the name of one of his classmates. Investigations subsequently revealed private emails he had exchanged with a Canadian resident discussing sexual violence against women and girls in which he had stated he "wanted to do" such things, and fictional stories about abduction, rape, torture, mutilation, and murder posted to a specialist news group (Kelner 1998: 307). This case is considered to be one of the first to raise First Amendment issues in relation to the internet (Kelner 1998: 288).

More recently, the *Elonis* case concerned a man, Anthony Douglas Elonis, who had been convicted of violating a federal anti-threat statute, 18 U.S.C. 875(c), which makes it a crime to use interstate commerce to make a threat. Elonis appealed the district court decision and, although the U.S. Court of Appeals for the Third Circuit affirmed his conviction, the U.S. Supreme Court later held[16] that prosecutors had to show that he had intended to threaten, in a case which turned in part on the online nature of the threats. His conviction was subsequently upheld in a lower court.

Elonis had posted a photograph publicly on Facebook in which he held a toy knife to the neck of a former co-worker with the caption, "I wish," and had made public posts about his ex-wife including describing smothering, murdering and mutilating her, and how he would make his way to her house to commit these acts. He claimed in his defense that his words lacked an intent to threaten because they "echoed words by rapper Eminem" (Epps 2014), and that he had provided links on his Facebook page to other artistic expression, including a comedy sketch about the nature of threats, and rap songs (Totenberg 2014). He posted explicit disclaimers stating that the threatening posts were "fictitious lyrics," that he had posted them "for entertainment purposes only," that he "ain't a legitimate threat," and that he "would never hurt my wife" (Bazelon 2014; Levine and Elwood 2014: 7). He stated that the posts "do not reflect the views, values or beliefs of Anthony Elonis the person." His wife, however, testified she had never seen Elonis write rap lyrics, and that he had had little prior interest in rap music.[17]

In a third case, Gilberto Valle, a New York City police officer, was convicted in 2013 on a charge of "conspiracy to commit kidnapping"[18] after he posted to chat rooms and emailed another internet user with detailed plans to kidnap, rape, kill, and eat a number of named women, including his wife, friends, and acquaintances (Ek 2015: 902).[19] He was a member of the Dark Fetish Network online, and used an anonymous handle to post to it (Calvert 2015). The site contained pictures of severed feet, and discussions of tying women up, slitting their throats, and raping them.[20] Like Elonis, Valle argued that his online expression should not be interpreted in a threatening way, stating that, "I like to press the envelope, but no matter what I say, it is all fantasy."[21] Valle successfully appealed to the District Court, and then the U.S. Court of Appeals for the Second Circuit affirmed his acquittal (Mueller 2014; Jauregi 2015). The basis for his appeal was that the posts were mere fantasy, and that they did not amount to a true conspiracy to commit the crimes that he discussed. In his acquittal, the judge said that the "highly unusual facts of this case reflect the

Internet age in which we live."[22] In all these examples, the fact that the speech took place online influenced the protagonists', and in some cases the courts', reluctance to understand the meaning of the speech in the same way as it may have been viewed had it taken place offline.

The idea of cyberspace as an other-worldly realm where disembodied thinkers interact revisits a theme found in traditional arguments for free speech, namely the claim that speech is more akin to thought than to action. Theorists and judges arguing against governmental regulation of speech have often used rhetoric that detaches speech from speakers, and, even more implausibly, rhetoric that detaches thoughts from thinkers. In his 1644 treatise, *Areopagitica*, Milton argued that governments should not be motivated, by fear of the proliferation of pernicious falsehoods, to restrict speech, for, as he urged, "Let [Truth] and Falshood grapple, who ever knew Truth put to the wors, in a free and open encounter?" (Milton 1918 [1644]: 58).

Nearly three centuries later, Holmes wrote, in his famous dissent in *Abrams v. United States* (1919), that "when men have realized that time has upset many fighting faiths, they may come to believe even more than they believe the very foundations of their own conduct that the ultimate good desired is better reached by free trade in ideas—that the best test of truth is the power of the thought to get itself accepted in the competition of the market."[23] And, in his dissent in *United States v. Schwimmer* (1929), Holmes asserted, "If there is any principle of the Constitution that more imperatively calls for attachment than any other it is the principle of free thought—not free thought for those who agree with us but freedom for the thought that we hate."[24] This quote is notable not only for the uniquely high status attributed in it to the principle of free speech (taken to be identical to the principle of free thought), but also for the absence of any human agency implied by its formulation.

No one makes comparable claims about actions. We do not talk about "freedom for the action that we hate," and this is not simply because we do not subscribe to a general principle of freedom of action (unconstrained by something like Mill's harm-to-others principle). Rather, it does not even make sense to talk about actions without agents. Although we do speak of actions as being free or unfree, this is clearly elliptical for talk of actions performed by agents freely or under duress. And yet we do talk about thoughts—or ideas—without thinkers and words without speakers, as if they could exist without agents.

Perhaps this is because thoughts and words can be written down or recorded and thus detached from those who think them. But actions can be recorded (on film), digitized, described (in language), and notated in ways that makes them reproducible without the intervention of the original agent (as in music notation and Labanotation in ballet). A thought or idea has no more life while unthought, or unread in a book, or unheard on a tape, than does an action such as a dance when unperformed.[25]

If we attend more closely to what people *do* with words, we are less likely to see words as having a life of their own, free-floating in a realm in which truths grapple with falsehoods and words we like do battle with words we hate.[26] Although the phrase "freedom of speech" might seem to refer to a state of affairs consisting of unfettered words, pictures, and other symbols, detached from their makers, it is, insofar as it describes a constitutionally, or otherwise legally, protected right, a state of speakers and listeners, a liberty only *people* can enjoy.

Focusing on what people do with their speech makes it less plausible to assimilate speech to thought. Not surprisingly, those who do not want speech to be regulated assimilate it to thought and conscience, whereas those who focus on its harms and advocate its regulation assimilate it to action and look at what speech *does*. In response to attempts to restrict hate speech, U.S. jurists and legal theorists have argued that regulating speech is like regulating thought, and just as impermissible. In its judgment overturning a University of Wisconsin hate speech code, the district court stated, "the suppression of speech, even where the speech's content appears to have little value and great costs, amounts to governmental thought control."[27] And in arguing against hate crime sentencing enhancement laws, Martin Redish (who sees them as on a par with hate speech codes) asserts that, "[a]s dangerous and offensive as I find any expression of bigotry, I fear much more any attempt by government to control the minds of its citizens" (Redish 1992: 39).

Defenders of restrictions on harmful online speech, like earlier defenders of hate speech codes and anti-pornography ordinances, argue that they are targeting, not (mere) speech, but rather discrimination and expressive behavior. In arguing for the Stanford code prohibiting discriminatory harassment, for example, Charles Lawrence cites "the inseparability of racist speech and discriminatory conduct," arguing that "[r]acism is both 100% speech and 100% conduct" (1993: 61; see also Citron 2014).

The prophets of the internet utopia (such as Barlow) correctly predicted the good that would come from the internet, but failed to take into account that speech—on or off the internet—while, often, a force for good, can also be a source of serious harms. Today, some recognize the error of this assumption. For example, Rick Webb, in "My Internet Mea Culpa," confesses "I'm sorry I was wrong. We all were." He recently tweeted, "Have any of those 90s/00s Internet utopians . . . written a 'hey sorry I was wrong the place turned out to be a terrordome' mea culpa essay? *Any* of them?" (Webb 2017)

Webb notes that "we *have* seen some of the good of this revolution . . . What we *didn't* expect—what we weren't told by our prophets—is that for all of this progress, there could well be a diametrically opposed force hindering progress, or even forcing its retreat on other fronts. I don't think anyone saw coming that we'd have to actually be explaining to American children why racism and fascism are bad in the 21st century. Our digital prophets certainly left that bit out." (Webb 2017).

In the recent *Packingham* judgment, the U.S. Supreme Court declared that "[w]hile in the past there may have been difficulty in identifying the most important places (in a spatial sense) for the exchange of views, today the answer is clear. It is cyberspace—the 'vast democratic forums of the Internet' in general,[28] and social media in particular."[29] And, yet, *Packingham* also acknowledged that online speech can cause (significant) harm. In his opinion concurring with the judgment, but disagreeing with "its undisciplined dicta," Justice Alito expressed concern that the Court's rationale might leave states with "little ability to restrict the sites that may be visited by even the most dangerous sex offenders. May a state preclude an adult previously convicted of molesting children from visiting a dating site for teenagers?"[30]

This recognition of the potential conduct-like harms of speech online has been expressed in other fora. A debate took place recently between Alexis Ohanian, cofounder of Reddit, and Rick Webb about Reddit's hosting of racist and misogynistic content. Ohanian had defended Reddit's hosting of the material on the ground that "more speech," not regulation, was the appropriate remedy. This led to an exchange on Twitter, shown in Figure 1.1:

A free speech theory that subscribes to the idea that the justification for the protection of freedom of speech is its special nature as more akin to thought than action exhibits a paradox: it treats speech as being as causally inefficacious as a person's private thoughts, yet, at the same time, considers it to require protection above and beyond the protection afforded to other liberties by a general harm-to-others principle (Brison 1998b). In earlier work, Brison has critiqued the inherent tension between these two views. She has shown that they can be shown to be compatible only if one accepts the implausible claim that any direct injury that may result from speech is under the control of the victim and, thus, could have been avoided by that person (Brison 1998b; see also Schauer 1993: 642–46). Both views—that speech is costless and that it is priceless—misconstrue not only the harms of assaultive speech, but also the harms of physical assaults with which speech-caused harms are typically contrasted. Brison has argued that these harms have been misunderstood because of the implicit and unexamined acceptance, primarily but not exclusively in First Amendment jurisprudence, of mind-body dualism—a view widely rejected by contemporary philosophers of mind (see, e.g., Rosenthal ed. 1991, Warner and Szubka eds. 1994).

On our view, all speech is conduct, involving an agent, and all conduct, being intentional action, expresses the agent's intention to engage in it. Speech does not differ from other conduct in being context-dependent and subject to interpretation. Speech is a physical phenomenon, being instigated by agents, expressed by agents, and having physical effects on its listeners, effects that can be caused by the content of the speech. For these (and other) reasons,

Alexis Ohanian Sr. @ @alexisohanian · 16 Mar 2015
One day, I won't need to tweet this. #RecognizetheGenocide
4   42   55

Rick Webb @RickWebb · 16 Mar 2015
@alexisohanian you could kick the racists off of reddit. That might help.
1   4

Alexis Ohanian Sr. @ @alexisohanian · 16 Mar 2015
@RickWebb If armenian genocide deniers want to use my platform to deny facts, counterspeech (truth) will prevail.
1   3

Rick Webb @RickWebb · 16 Mar 2015
@alexisohanian the truth would prevail in an argument in my living room, too. But I'd still ask them to leave.
1   1

Alexis Ohanian Sr. @ @alexisohanian · 16 Mar 2015
@RickWebb a living room of 200M people is going to have crazies, but more speech not less is the answer #RecognizeArmenianGenocide
2   2

Rick Webb
@RickWebb

Replying to @alexisohanian

@alexisohanian the implications of us kicking pedophiles off because of the law but not racists cuz no ones making us are embarrassing

1:34 PM - 16 Mar 2015

FIGURE 1.1 Twitter exchange between Reddit cofounder Alexis Ohanian and Rick Webb.

Brison has argued that the attempt to assimilate freedom of speech to freedom of thought, and in that way distinguishes it from freedom of action, fails (Brison 1998b: 61). The view, therefore, that online speech is akin to thought is susceptible to an established critique, including of the mind-body dualism underpinning it.

Furthermore, the attempt to define speech (that is protected by a free speech principle) in a way that distinguishes it from non-speech conduct has not succeeded. Charles Collier has asserted, in response to Brison (1998b), that, although "[t]he term 'speech' in the First Amendment . . . is a term of art, . . . one possibility can be rejected at the outset: that there is no constitutionally significant difference between speech and any other form of intentional action. As the U.S. Supreme Court has recently noted: "To hold otherwise would be to create a rule that all conduct is presumptively expressive" (Collier 2001: 204). This *is* the U.S. Supreme Court's stated position, but we do not agree that it is correct.

As others, for example, Robert Post, have argued, it has proven to be notoriously difficult—some would say impossible—for the Court to distinguish speech from other forms of intentional action (Post 1995). Collier cites *Spence v. Washington*, a flag-desecration case in which the Court's analysis began with an inquiry into whether the defendant's "activity was sufficiently imbued with elements of communication to fall within the scope of the First and Fourteenth Amendments."[31] The test used by the Court, which has come to be known as the Spence test, was whether "an intent to convey a particularized message was present and [whether] the likelihood was great that the message would be understood by those who viewed it."[32] The Spence test, however, does not succeed in distinguishing speech from non-speech conduct, as Robert Post has persuasively argued:

> A small but telling example plainly demonstrates the problem with the Spence test. Consider laws imposing criminal sanctions for the defacement of public property. Such laws do not "bring the First Amendment into play"; a defendant accused of defacing a city bus would not have a First Amendment defense. This would be true regardless of whether the defacement took the form of random blotches of color spray-painted onto the walls, or the form of words like "Down with Clinton" or "Eric is Cool" carved into the seats. Although in the latter case the defendant has satisfied the Spence test—his words carry a particularized message that is likely to be understood by his audience—no court in the country would consider the case as raising a First Amendment question. This example can be multiplied indefinitely, for any action can at any time be made communicative in a manner that satisfies the Spence test. (Post 1995: 1252)

As Post notes, "[i]f the Spence test were to describe actual judicial practice, we would expect criminals routinely to attempt to immunize their crimes by endowing them with particular messages" (1995: 1252).

3. A Capabilities-Informed Defense of Free Speech

We have shown that, and how, in current debates about digital speech, some are (re)asserting that speech is deserving of greater protection than non-speech conduct because it is akin to thought. We have also shown that, and how, this reproduces a paradox, common in some free speech arguments, that speech conceived in this way is at once assumed to be both powerful—and worthy of special protection—and powerless to cause harm. In this section, we propose a theoretical defense of freedom of speech that is capable of overcoming this paradox by recognizing the power of speech to do things in and for people's lives. This capabilities-informed view provides a framework for the robust protection of freedom of speech, one that acknowledges the power of speech to do both good and harm.

Gelber has elaborated in previous work (2010, 2012a, 2012b, 2012c) how a Nussbaumian capabilities approach implies the robust protection of freedom of speech. She has extrapolated from Nussbaum's often implicit discussion of polit-ical liberties, how free speech can be understood as a component of the central political liberties needed for individuals to be able to participate meaningfully in the activities that will develop their central human functional capabilities, and thereby enable them to choose how to live and function well (Nussbaum 1988, 1990, 1993, 2000). It is the responsibility of policymakers in this framework to provide an entire set of conditions that will enable individuals to become capable of choosing how to live well, and who to be (Nussbaum 2006: 7, 70).

Nussbaum's approach protects the core "political liberties" that are essen-tial to the attainment of central human functional capabilities (2006: 766–78, 2000: 231–33). Although they have often not been prominent in her work, these liberties include freedom of speech, freedom of association, and freedom of conscience (Gelber 2012a: 41). Gelber has elaborated on the role freedom of speech plays in Nussbaum's approach, showing that it plays a constitutive and facilitative role in developing and enabling the capabilities of "senses, im-agination and thought," "affiliation," and "control over one's environment," all of which are essential to being able to make meaningful choices in how to live well. Speech, meaning both the freedom to speak and the actual ability to participate meaningfully in communications with others, is essential to being able to think and reason, to engage in meaningful social interaction, and to "participate effectively in political choices that govern one's life" (Nussbaum 2006: 76–77).

The attainment of a capabilities threshold, at which one becomes capable of choosing how to live and who to be requires both internal conditions (such as the capacity for complex thought) and external conditions to be realized. Among the latter are measures that effectively enable people to engage in speech affecting their lives (Gelber 2012a: 42), measures that are understood as including "affirmative task[s]" (Nussbaum 2006: 287). Affirmative tasks in-clude policymakers thinking "from the start about what obstacles there are to full and effective empowerment for all citizens, and . . . devis[ing] measures that address these obstacles" (Nussbaum 2006: 288).

Gelber's elaboration has shown that when this perspective is applied to freedom of speech, it provides a strong and robust ground for the protection of freedom of speech due to the central role it, along with other core political liberties, plays in allowing individuals to attain a capabilities threshold that enables them to make decisions as to how to live well.

Importantly, this justification for freedom of speech does not rest on an assumption that speech is powerless. On the contrary, it recognizes the essential role that speech plays in human flourishing, providing a mandate for its protection and enablement. Also importantly, this justification for protecting freedom of speech does not rely on a view of speech as akin to thought, or more akin to thought than non-speech conduct. On the contrary, speech is understood as distinct from a right to conscience or freedom of thought; all are important to the development of human functional capabilities, but in different ways and via distinct mechanisms. Engaging in speech is a discrete mechanism by which individuals are able to learn, and to exercise, their human functional capabilities in utilizing their senses, imagination, thought, affiliation, control over their environment and choices, and participation in the deliberation essential to self-governance. Engaging in thought may also assist in the development of these, and other, human functional capabilities as does exercising one's conscience. But each is a distinct human activity, which contributes uniquely to the attainment of the capabilities threshold.

Indeed, this approach does not mandate the protection of *all* capabilities, but only those that assist in the attainment of a capabilities threshold by all individuals, so that they become capable of choosing how to live well. Nussbaum gives the example of the capability to discriminate on the ground of race, gender, or sexuality, which she argues ought to be prevented because the exercise of that capability by one person prohibits others from attaining her own capabilities threshold (2006: 166). Gelber has developed this insight further in arguing that a capabilities-informed approach to freedom of speech permits the regulation of harmful speech, on the ground that there is sufficient evidence to substantiate the claim that hate speech can harm the attainment of capabilities in its direct targets, and, by extension, in other members of the targeted group. Additionally, a capabilities approach recognizes the harm of some capabilities, for example, discrimination on the ground of race or gender or sexuality. There are human activities that some people might claim as a capability—such as the capability of engaging in hate speech—that, to the extent that they hinder the attainment of capabilities in others, are justifiably regulable. Harmful speech, conceptualized as speech that is capable of hindering the attainment of central human functional capabilities in others, is therefore justifiably susceptible to regulation to ensure that the external conditions are provided for all individuals to achieve the capabilities threshold.[33]

4. Free Speech Online

A capabilities-informed approach takes the view that speech *is* powerful, and that *this* is the strongest reason for its protection. A robust protection for freedom of speech is essential so that speech can play its crucial role in the development of individual capabilities that is required for human flourishing, and, through that, the legitimizing role of speech in democratic deliberation. This is because people *do* the work of democracy by engaging in speech, and, through that, democracy is legitimized by the participation of citizens in self-governance and deliberation over issues affecting their lives (Gelber 2012a).

What effects does the fact of speech taking place online have on this argument? We argue here that speech online is no more or less akin to thought than speech offline, since in both instances speech is agent-driven and in both cases it has material effects on its listeners, targets, and bystanders. This therefore answers the question with which this chapter began— namely, ought online speech to be considered more akin to thought than to action—clearly in the negative. Online speech ought to be assessed for what the speech does in and for people's lives, just as offline speech ought to be assessed in this way.

The internet is certainly viewed as a particularly efficacious medium for the exchange of ideas, as emphasized in the *Packingham* judgment dealing with online speech, in which the internet was viewed as inherently and importantly facilitative of communication:

> One of the most important places to exchange views is cyberspace, particularly social media, which offers "relatively unlimited, low-cost capacity for communication of all kinds."[34]

The relative ease with which a range of speakers can access widely broadcast communications via the internet, however, does not change the character of speech as conduct affecting speakers, listeners, targets, and bystanders, who are all agents. Even social media bots are programmed to engage in communication by a human creator.

There is, furthermore, a discrete argument concerning the materiality of the internet itself. Real human beings are involved in the mining, installation, and recycling of the components of the technology required for the internet to exist, which imposes high health risks on workers and communities (Shinder 2008). There are additional risks to health and safety from working in the industry. Workers in poor countries, for example, are employed by Facebook to moderate its content, being paid as little as $1.00 per hour (Barnett and Hollingshead 2012), while dealing with obscene and harmful images and text on a daily basis (Roberts 2016). The internet is a place of material reality, not ethereal thought that is impervious to concrete consequences for those involved in using it, maintaining its platforms, or working in the industry surrounding it. This material reality stands in direct contradiction to Barlow's assertions in his Declaration.

For example, there is clear evidence now of the poisoning of workers who make smartphones by benzene and other carcinogens in the factories that make the products that facilitate online speech (Turk 2017). The rate at which phones and other technological products become obsolete is so fast that it is estimated that over 40 million metric tons of electronic waste is produced each year (McAllister 2013), with serious social, health, and environmental costs for the workers who recycle their components (Herat 2011).

In addition, the material harms caused by online speech are invisible to users of the internet. Notes attached to emails urging recipients to think twice before printing messages and attachments can make it seem as if there is no environmental cost to online communications. But it takes 70 billion kilowatt hours per year to operate the server farms and data centers used in online communication. To generate that much power requires the equivalent of about eight large nuclear reactors or twice the output of all the solar panels in the United States. The average American's internet use is responsible for about 300 pounds of carbon dioxide emissions per year (Helman 2016).

We advocate taking into account the circumstances of the world when thinking about freedom of speech—online and off. The view put forward by Barlow and others that online speech is akin to thought is wrong. It is empirically incorrect, as our explanation of the materialities of the internet has shown. It is theoretically incorrect, because it rests on a paradox, in which speech is conceptualized as both harmless, because causally inert, *and* capable of causing harms and so warranting protection not provided by a general harm-to-others principle. In fact, it is arguable that the internet exacerbates these problems compared with offline speech.[35]

The internet is a site in which structural inequalities play a significant role in affecting its users' ability to exercise their freedom of speech. It is not a disembodied space in which thought can travel freely—it is a material entity that is so entwined in our daily activities that, for millions of people, it is now inseparable from our daily lives. The machinery and technology that underpin it have real consequences for workers in its industry, as well as online users. The speech that takes place in it has real consequences for speakers, listeners, targets, audiences, and bystanders and through these for democracy itself. Regulations ought to be based on a theoretical understanding that recognizes these realities, taking into account the actual experiences of all its users. When viewed in this way, certain regulations of online speech may be seen to enhance, not hinder, speech freedoms.

Notes

1. Doe v. Univ. of Mich., 721 F. Supp. 852 (E.D. Mich. 1989), UWM Post v. Bd. of Regents of the University of Wisconsin, 774 F. Supp. 1163 (E.D. Wis. 1991).

2. For the U.S. Court of Appeals, Seventh Circuit, 771 F.2d 323 (7th Cir. 1985).

3. Ibid. p. 329. One does not, however, hear the courts declaring that if segregation harms minorities' opportunities for equal rights this simply demonstrates the power of freedom of association.

4. 721 F. Supp. 852 (E.D. Mich. 1989), p. 853.

5. Ibid., p. 863.

6. Rare exceptions are Robin L. West (1993), and Mary E. Becker (1992).

7. To state what a free speech principle requires is not to state that such a principle is justified. Elsewhere, Schauer has evinced a certain amount of skepticism about whether a distinct principle of free speech can be defended. For example, he notes that his conclusion, viz. that we should reject the hypothesis that speech, as a class, causes less harm than non-speech conduct, "puts more pressure on the positive arguments for a free speech principle, and perhaps no such argument will turn out to be sound" (Schauer 1993: 653). For insightful arguments against the existence of *any* justifiable general principle of free speech see Alexander and Horton (1983), Fish (1994), and Alexander (2005).

8. By "free speech absolutism" we mean the view that all speech is protected. The U.S. Supreme Court has not followed the absolutist interpretation of the First Amendment that one might have thought could be read off its straightforward wording. In spite of Justice Black's famous statement—"I read 'no law abridging' to mean no law abridging . . . ", the courts have considered many categories of speech to be unprotected. Justice Hugo L. Black, Smith v. California, 361 U.S. 147, 157 (1959). See also Black (1960).

9. Paul Schenck and Dwight Saunders, Petitioners v. Pro-Choice Network of Western New York, et al. No. 95-1065. United States Supreme Court Official Transcript. Wednesday, October 16, 1996. 1996 LW 608239 (U.S.Oral.Arg.), at 23.

10. https://www.eff.org/cyberspace-independence.

11. https://www.eff.org/.

12. https://www.eff.org/cyberspace-independence.

13. Tufekci notes that Barlow's "Cyberspace Independence Declaration" "reflects a profound digital dualism, with the expectation that people typing words would somehow remain isolated on the internet, with no consequences for our corporeal presence." Barlow was not alone in holding this view. Tufekci continues: "It may be tempting to dismiss this as merely one poetic statement, but this approach of assuming novel social dynamics on the internet (people being judged on the merits of their ideas regardless of status dynamics, for example), isolated from the rest of the world or its materiality, has influenced both scholarship and public commentary on the internet's effects." (Tufekci 2017: 130).

14. United States v. Alkhabaz (aka Jake Baker), 104 F.3d 1492 (6th Cir. 1997).

15. 18 U.S.C. § 875(c) (1994).

16. Elonis v. United States, 575 U.S. ___ (2015).

17. United States v. Elonis, 730 F.3d 321, 327 (3rd Cir. 2013), p. 7.

18. 18 U.S.C. § 1201 (1932).

19. Valle was also charged with improperly accessing a computer, because he used police databases to locate a woman he subsequently named in his chats as a potential victim.

20. USA v. Valle et al., New York Southern District Court, Case No. 1:12-cr-00847, document 343, pp. 11–12.

21. Ibid., p. 2.

22. Ibid., p. 1.

23. Oliver Wendell Holmes, dissenting, in Abrams v. United States 250 U.S. 616, 630 (1919).

24. United States v. Schwimmer, 279 U.S. 644, 654–55 (1929).

25. We are influenced here by the nominalism of Nelson Goodman and others, but even platonists should agree that if ideas can exist unthought as platonic forms, so can actions such as dances.

26. We are indebted here to, among others, J. L. Austin (1975), MacKinnon (1987,1993, 2017), Langton (1993), Hornsby (1995), and Matsuda, Lawrence, Delgado and Crenshaw (1993).

27. UWM Post v. Board of Regents of Univ. of Wisconsin, 774 F. Supp. 1163, 1174 n.9 (E.D. Wis. 1991).

28. Citing Reno v. ACLU, 521 U.S. 844, 868 (1997).

29. Packingham v. North Carolina, 582 U.S. ___ (2017), syllabus at 4–5, citing *Reno, supra* note 27, at 870.

30. Ibid., Alito J concurring, at 1.

31. Spence v. Washington, 418 U.S. 405, 409 (1974).

32. Ibid., pp. 410–11.

33. Brison in her earlier work (2000) has reached similar conclusions. Using Amartya Sen's account of capability, she has argued that a capabilities approach shows why the government must protect and foster some political and legal rights. Among them is the right to free speech, because freedom of speech plays an important part in the development of relationally autonomous persons. However, in making this argument, she has pointed out that the role of freedom of speech in this conception is no more significant than that of a number of other freedoms essential for enabling central human capabilities.

34. Packingham v. North Carolina, 582 U.S. ___ (2017), syllabus at p. 1, citing Reno v. ACLU, 521 U. S. 844, 870 (1997).

35. Balkin (2004), for example, argues that the focus of free speech theory needs to include paying attention to technological design and regulation that will enhance the possibilities for participation in speech.

References

Alexander, L. 2005. *Is There a Right of Freedom of Expression?* New York: Cambridge University Press.

Alexander, L and P Horton. 1983. "The Impossibility of a Free Speech Principle." *Northwestern University Law Review* 78: 1319–57.

Austin, J. L. 1975. *How To Do Things with Words*. Oxford, Sbisa Clarendon Press.

Balkin, J. 2004. "Digital Speech and Democratic Culture: A Theory of Freedom of Expression for the Information Society." *New York University Law Review* 79: 1–55.

Barnett, E and I. Hollingshead. 2012. "The Dark Side of Facebook." *The Telegraph*, March 2, http://www.telegraph.co.uk/technology/facebook/9118778/The-dark-side-of-Facebook.html.

Bazelon, E. 2014. "Do Online Death Threats Count as Free Speech?" *New York Times Magazine*, November 25. https://www.nytimes.com/2014/11/30/magazine/do-online-death-threats-count-as-free-speech.html (accessed February 15, 2018).

Becker, M. E. 1992. "The Politics of Women's Wrongs and the Bill of Rights: A Bicentennial Perspective." In G. Stone, R. Epstein and C. Sunstein (eds.) *The Bill of Rights in the Modern State*. Chicago, University of Chicago Press: 453–517.

Black, H. J. 1960. "The Bill of Rights." *New York University Law Review* 35: 865–81.

Brison, S. 1998a. "The Autonomy Defense of Free Speech." *Ethics* 108(2): 312–39.

Brison, S. 1998b. "Speech, Harm, and the Mind-Body Problem in First Amendment Jurisprudence." *Legal Theory* 4(1): 39–61.

Brison, S. J. 2000. "Relational Autonomy and Freedom of Expression." In C. MacKenzie and N. Stoljar (eds.) *Relational Autonomy: Feminist Perspectives on Autonomy, Agency, and the Social Self*. New York: Oxford University Press: 280–99.

Calvert, C. 2015. "Humanizing Cannibal Cop on Eve of Appeal: 'Thought Crimes' Doc Reveals Unseen Side of Gilberto Valle." *Huffington Post*, June 20, http://www.huffingtonpost.com/clay-calvert/humanizing-cannibal-cop-0_b_7102972.html (accessed December 12, 2016).

Citron, D. 2014. *Hate Crimes in Cyberspace*. Cambridge, MA, Harvard University Press.

Collier, C. W. 2001. "Hate Speech and the Mind-Body Problem: A Critique of Postmodern Censorship Theory." *Legal Theory* 7 (2): 203–34.

Ek, K. 2015. "Conspiracy and the Fantasy Defense: The Strange Case of the Cannibal Cop." *Duke Law Journal* 64: 901–45.

Epps, G. 2014. "When Does the First Amendment Protect Threat?" *The Atlantic*, November 29, http://www.theatlantic.com/politics/archive/2014/11/when-does-the-first-amendment-protect-threats-elonis-united-states-supreme-court-free-speech/383255/ (accessed March 20, 2015).

Feinberg, J. 1984. *The Moral Limits of the Criminal Law, Vol. 1: Harm to Others*. New York, Oxford University Press.

Fish, S. 1994. *There's No Such Thing as Free Speech—And It's a Good Thing, Too*. New York: Oxford University Press.

Floridi, L. 2017. What Kind of Society Should the Information Society Be? *Public Lecture*, Princeton University, October 5.

Gates, H. L. 1993. "Let Them Talk." *New Republic*. September 20 & 27: 37–49.

Gelber, K. 2002. *Speaking Back: The Free Speech versus Hate Speech Debate*. Amsterdam: John Benjamins.

Gelber, K. 2010. "Freedom of Political Speech, Hate Speech and the Argument from Democracy: The Transformative Contribution of Capabilities Theory." *Contemporary Political Theory* 9(3): 304–24.

Gelber, K. 2012a. "Nussbaum's Capabilities Approach and Freedom of Speech." In F. Panzironi and K. Gelber (eds.) *The Capability Approach: Development Practice and Public Policy in the Asia-Pacific Region*. Abingdon: Routledge: 38–52.

Gelber, K. 2012b. "'Speaking Back': The Likely Fate of Hate Speech Policy in the United States and Australia." In I. Maitra and M. K. McGowan (eds.) *Speech and Harm: Controversies over Free Speech*. Oxford: Oxford University Press: 50–71.

Gelber, K. 2012c. "Reconceptualizing Counterspeech in Hate Speech Policy (with a Focus on Australia)." In M. Herz and P. Molnar (eds.) *The Content and Context of Hate Speech*. New York: Cambridge University Press: 198–216.

Haworth, A. 1998. *Free Speech*. London, Routledge.

Helman, C. 2016. "Berkeley Lab: It Takes 70 Billion Kilowatt Hours to Run the Internet." *Forbes*, June 28, https://www.forbes.com/sites/christopherhelman/2016/06/28/how-much-electricity-does-it-take-to-run-the-internet/#62fc38981fff (accessed February 18, 2018).

Herat, S. 2011. "E-waste: the High Cost of High-Tech." *The Conversation*, December 12, https://theconversation.com/e-waste-the-high-cost-of-high-tech-4378.

Hornsby, J. 1995. "Speech Acts and Pornography." In S. Dwyer (ed.) *The Problem of Pornography*. Belmont, MA: Wadsworth: 220–32.

Jauregi, A. 2015. "Cannibal Cop's Online Dating Profile Seeks 'Non-Judgmental' Woman with 'Kinky' Tastes.'" *Huffington Post*, January 21, http://www.huffingtonpost.com/2015/01/21/cannibal-cop-online-dating-profile_n_6517282.html (accessed April 15, 2015).

Kelner, R. 1998. "*United States v. Jake Baker*: Revisiting Threats and the First Amendment." *Virginia Law Review* 84: 287–313.

Langton, R. 1993. "Speech Acts and Unspeakable Acts." *Philosophy and Public Affairs* 19: 293–330.

Lawrence, C. R. 1993. "If He Hollers Let Him Go: Regulating Racist Speech on Campus." In M. Matsuda, C. Lawrence, R. Delgado and K. Crenshaw (eds.) *Words That Wound: Critical Race Theory, Assaultive Speech, and the First Amendment*. Boulder, CO: Westview Press: 53–88.

Levine, R. and J. Elwood. 2014. *Brief for the Petitioner in the Supreme Court of the United States*, No. 13-983, http://www.americanbar.org/content/dam/aba/publications/supreme_court_preview/BriefsV4/13-983_pet.authcheckdam.pdf (accessed March 20, 2015).

MacKinnon, C. 1987. *Feminism Unmodified: Discourses on Life and Law*. Cambridge, MA: Harvard University Press.

MacKinnon, C. 1993. *Only Words*. Cambridge, MA: Harvard University Press.

MacKinnon, C. 2017. *Butterfly Politics*. Cambridge, MA: Belknap Press.

McAllister, L. 2013. The Human and Environmental Effects of E-Waste. *Population Reference Bureau*, April, http://www.prb.org/Publications/Articles/2013/e-waste.aspx.

Mill, J. S. 1978. *On Liberty*. Indianapolis, IN, Hackett.

Milton, J. 1918 [1644]. Areopagitica, *with a Commentary by Sir Richard C. Webb and with Supplementary Material*. Cambridge, MA: Cambridge University Press.

Mueller, B. 2014. "No More Jail Time in New York Cannibal Case." *New York Times*, November 12, http://www.nytimes.com/2014/11/13/nyregion/no-more-jail-time-in-new-york-cannibal-case.html (accessed March 19, 2015).

Nussbaum, M. 1988. "Nature, Function and Capability: Aristotle on Political Distribution." *Oxford Studies in Ancient Philosophy* Suppl: 145–84.

Nussbaum, M. 1990. "Aristotelian Social Democracy." In R. Douglass and G. Mara (eds.) *Liberalism and the Good*. New York: Routledge.

Nussbaum, M. 1993. "Non-Relative Virtues: An Aristotelian Approach." In M. Nussbaum and A. Sen (eds.) *Quality of Life*. Oxford: Clarendon Press.

Nussbaum, M. 2000. "Women's Capabilities and Social Justice." *Journal of Human Development* 1(2): 219–47.

Nussbaum, M. 2006. *Frontiers of Justice: Disability, Nationality, Species Membership.* Cambridge, MA: Belknap Press.

Post, R. 1995. "Recuperating First Amendment Doctrine." *Stanford Law Review* 47(6): 1249–81.

Redish, M. 1992. "Freedom of Thought as Freedom of Expression: Hate Crime Sentencing Enhancement and First Amendment Theory." *Criminal Justice Ethics* 11(2): 29–42.

Roberts, S. T. 2016. "Commercial Content Moderation: Digital Laborers' Dirty Work." In S. U. Noble and B. M. Tynes (eds.) *The Intersectional Internet: Race, Sex, Class, and Culture Online.* New York: Peter Lang.

Rosenthal, D. (ed.) 1991. *The Nature of Mind.* New York: Oxford University Press.

Scanlon, T. 1972. "A Theory of Freedom of Expression." *Philosophy and Public Affairs* 1(2): 204–26.

Schauer, F. 1982. *Free Speech: A Philosophical Enquiry.* New York: Cambridge University Press.

Schauer, F. 1992. "The First Amendment as Ideology." *William and Mary Law Review* 33: 853–69.

Schauer, F. 1993. "The Phenomenology of Speech and Harm." *Ethics* 103: 635–53.

Schauer, F. 2005. "The Exceptional First Amendment." In M. Ignatieff (ed.) *American Exceptionalism and Human Rights.* Princeton, NJ: Princeton University Press.

Schauer, F. 2015. "Free Speech on Tuesdays." *Law and Philosophy* 34: 119–40.

Shinder, D. 2008. "What IT Pros Should Know about Exposure to Hazardous Materials." *Tech Republic*, August 25, https://www.techrepublic.com/blog/data-center/what-it-pros-should-know-about-exposure-to-hazardous-materials/.

Sullivan, K. M. 1994. "Free Speech Wars." *SMU Law Review* 48: 203–16.

Totenberg, N. 2014. "Is a Threat Posted on Facebook Really a Threat?" *NPR*, December 1, http://www.npr.org/2014/12/01/366534452/is-a-threat-posted-on-facebook-really-a-threat (accessed March 20, 2015).

Tufekci, Z. 2017. *Twitter and Tear Gas: The Power and Fragility of Networked Protest.* New Haven, CT: Yale University Press.

Turk, V. 2017. "China's Workers Need Help to Fight Factories' Toxic Practices." *New Scientist*, March 22, https://www.newscientist.com/article/2125546-chinas-workers-need-help-to-fight-factories-toxic-practices/.

Warner, R. and T. Szubka (eds.) 1994. *The Mind-Body Problem: A Guide to the Current Debate.* Cambridge, MA: Blackwell.

Webb, R. 2017 "My Internet Mea Culpa," *New Co.*, December 25, https://shift.newco.co/my-internet-mea-culpa-f3ba77ac3eed (accessed February 18, 2018).

West, R. L. 1993. "Constitutional Scepticism." In S. Brison and W. Sinnott-Armstrong (eds.) *Contemporary Perspectives on Constitutional Interpretation.* Boulder, CO: Westview Press: 234–58.

2

Search Engines and Free Speech Coverage

Heather M. Whitney and Robert Mark Simpson[*]

1. Introduction

The idea at the heart of liberal political theory is that everyone should be free to live according to their own ideals, so far as this does not unduly interfere with other people's ability to do likewise. The government can only legitimately restrict people's freedom where this is necessary to prevent harm to others or to secure the demands of justice. The idea at the heart of free speech theory is that when it comes to communicative acts, a commitment to individual freedom isn't enough, and must be bolstered by extra protections that make harmful speech less liable to regulation than other similarly harmful forms of conduct.

Because free speech principles assign extra protection to a specially nominated class of communicative acts, they need to come packaged with an account that specifies which communicative acts warrant this protection. Following Frederick Schauer (1982), we call this the question of free speech *coverage*. Policy outcomes in a system based on free speech principles aren't fully dictated by how we address questions of coverage. (This is because not all conduct that is covered by free speech principles will be immune to regulation, once all relevant factors are considered, including degrees of harm and government interest.) But questions of coverage are important all the same, because stricter standards must be met before acts that are covered by free speech principles can justifiably be regulated.

* Heather M. Whitney; PhD Candidate in Philosophy at New York University; Visiting Researcher, Harvard Law School (2017); Bigelow Fellow and Lecturer in Law at the University of Chicago Law School (2014–16); Robert Mark Simpson, Lecturer in Philosophy, University College London, Monash University. For helpful comments, we thank Will Baude, Genevieve Lakier, Richard McAdams, Jim Weinstein, and participants at the 2016 Yale Law School Freedom of Expression Scholars Conference and 2016 Australian Society for Legal Philosophy Conference.

In this chapter we ask whether new modes of online communication should be covered by free speech principles. We'll focus on the outputs of programs that synthesize, organize, and transmit third-party communication to users. Search engine results are the most familiar example of this. Another notable example is Facebook's "Trending News" section. Whether these things should be covered by free speech principles is an important problem. The US Supreme Court recently declared cyberspace "the most important place . . . for the exchange of views" and social media sites "the modern public square."[1] Major tech companies increasingly control our channels of communication and access to information. If search results and the like are specially protected against regulation, this makes it harder for governments and other actors to counteract that control for the sake of goals or ideals that are in the wider public interest. Beside these implications, our question is also a kind of test case for examining the methods employed in debates over free speech coverage. Part of our aim in the chapter is to show certain limitations in addressing such debates using analogical reasoning.

In sections 2–3 we discuss the small body of US case law and related scholarship that deals with this issue. Most discussion in these contexts subscribes to an editorial analogy that likens search results to traditional editorial publications. We find this analogical reasoning tenuous at best. We argue that search engines are unlike traditional editorial publications in several important ways, and that there are other analogical frameworks that offer rival characterizations of the function of search engines, and which suggest different treatment. As for the more general methodological issues, we argue that although analogical inference is often seen as an essential element in common law legal reasoning, at best only certain forms of analogical inference are essential, and the form used by US courts and legal scholars in cases relating to search engines is not one of them. Building on these critical points, in sections 4–5 we argue that any credible judgment about whether search engines and the like should qualify as "speech" will need to be grounded in an account of free speech's normative purposes. We focus on two normative theories of free speech—democratic participation, and Shiffrin's thinker-based approach— and explain why, under either theory, only a subset of search engine results and similar communication should be accorded free speech coverage.

2. Recent Cases

Of the few US courts to address the question of whether search engine outputs qualify as "speech" for free speech purposes, *Zhang v. Baidu* offers the most thorough analysis.[2] The facts in *Zhang* are as follows. The plaintiffs, self-described as "promoters of democracy in China," alleged that Baidu.com (a Chinese search engine) intentionally delisted their pro-democracy websites at the behest of the Chinese government, and that this violated, inter alia, several of their rights.[3] In reply Baidu argued that its listings were protected speech, and the court agreed, finding that "First Amendment jurisprudence all but compels the conclusion that Plaintiff's suit must be dismissed."[4] The court saw the relevant precedent as *Miami Herald Publishing v. Tornillo*, in which a statute forcing newspapers to provide political candidates a right of reply to critical editorials was deemed unconstitutional, on free speech grounds.[5] The *Zhang* court also found *Hurley v. Irish-American Gay, Lesbian, and Bisexual Group of Boston* to be an extension of *Tornillo*, and equally applicable to Baidu.[6] In *Hurley* the Court held that compelling parade organizers to include a group that promoted a message with which they disagreed violated the organizers' First Amendment rights because "a speaker has the autonomy to choose the content of his own message."[7] The *Zhang* court's application of *Tornillo* and *Hurley* followed directly from its analogical reasoning. The court saw the purpose of search engines as organizing information, which requires judgments about what information to include and how to present it, and it found that this was relevantly similar to a "newspaper editor's judgment of which . . . stories to run."[8]

The editorial analogy also won out in the case of *E-ventures Worldwide v. Google* (Cushing 2017; Goldman 2016; Masnick 2016).[9] E-ventures is a search engine optimization (or SEO) firm. SEO firms seek to improve the visibility of client websites in organic (i.e., unpaid) search results, in order to increase the client's web traffic from search engines and enable them to sell advertising space at higher rates (DeMers 2016). SEO firms are engaged in an ongoing "cat-and-mouse game" with search engine companies such as Google because as the firms devise new tactics to improve their client's visibility, Google tries to prevent these firms from (as they see it) gaming the system for unpaid rankings. When SEO firms get the upper hand advertisers are more likely to spend their advertising budget with SEO firms, instead of paying Google for paid placement in search results (Tsotsis 2011). In *E-ventures* specifically, Google had manually manipulated their search results in order to delist 231 websites belonging to E-ventures's clients.[10] After reaching out to Google through a number of channels in the hope of getting these sites relisted, E-ventures filed suit, at which point Google relisted the sites. In its suit E-ventures alleged that Google's statements about its search results—for instance: "Google search results are a reflection of the content publically available on the web"; and "It is Google's policy not to censor search results"—were false and deceptive.[11] It also alleged that Google's delisting of its clients' sites constituted unfair competition under the Lanham Act, tortious interference with business relations, and violations of Florida's Deceptive and Unfair Trade Practices Act. Google responded by asserting, *inter alia*, that its search results were its editorial judgments and protected opinions, and thus, E-ventures's claims were overridden by the First Amendment.

In originally denying in part Google's Motion to Dismiss, the district court said it had "little quarrel with the cases cited by Google for the proposition that search engine outputs are protected by the First Amendment."[12] The court accepted the editorial analogy in general, but found that "while publishers are entitled to discretion for editorial judgment decisions" in this case the allegation was that such decisions were not the result of editorial judgments but anticompetitive motives.[13] Additionally, the court noted that facts published maliciously with knowledge of their falsity or serious doubt about their truth can overcome editorial judgment protection. Given these reasons, the court denied in part Google's Motion to Dismiss. However, at Summary Judgment Google's First Amendment arguments proved decisive. There the court cited *Baidu* for the proposition that search results are protected speech under the First Amendment.[14] Then, citing *Tornillo*, it found that a "search engine is akin to a publisher, whose judgments about what to publish and what not to publish are absolutely protected by the First Amendment."[15] Free speech overrides E-ventures' claims, the court said, because Google's determination of its rankings, and of which sites violated its guidelines and were subject to removal, were "*the same as* decisions by a newspaper editor regarding . . . which article belongs on the front page, and which article is unworthy of publication."[16] In short, the court said that free speech rights should protect such decisions "whether they are fair or unfair, or motivated by profit or altruism."[17]

The image of the search engine company as editor, with its publication and delisting choices (for paid and organic results alike) viewed as subjective editorial opinion, has been successfully invoked in several other cases as well.[18] A clear trend has emerged in US legal practice around this issue. Courts treat search engine results and advertisements like editorial judgments and extend free speech coverage to them accordingly.

That said, there are reasons to doubt that these rulings are settled constitutional doctrine. First, the Supreme Court has yet to weigh in on the matter. Second, plaintiffs in these cases were modestly resourced compared to the companies they were opposing (some plaintiffs proceeded *pro se*). Consequently, the courts were under little pressure to interrogate the cursory analogical rationales that favored the defendants. There may be conflicts involving better-resourced plaintiffs in the future. Indeed, one case like this is already brewing. Yelp and TripAdvisor have argued that Google deliberately diverts users searching for their sites to Google-owned alternatives. Google has said that some such results are due to software bugs, but its competitors have rejected this and lobbied in support of European antitrust investigations against Google (Bergen 2015; Kanter and Scott 2015; European Commission 2015). Given this, it's possible that a major lawsuit in the United States—and with it, a vigorous battle over First Amendment coverage—may yet materialize.

3. The Limits of Analogical Reasoning

In this section we explain why the analogical reasoning that has guided these cases doesn't offer adequate support for the view that search engine outputs should in fact receive free speech coverage. There are shortcomings with these analogies on their own terms, rival analogical frameworks with which to contend, and deeper limitations in the use of this form of analogical reasoning.

3.1 INTERNAL WEAKNESSES OF THE EDITORIAL ANALOGY

The strongest defense of the editorial analogy invoked in the cases discussed in section 2 comes in a white paper commissioned by Google on search engines and free speech, authored by Volokh and Falk (2012). In that paper the authors argue that companies such as Google are "analogous to newspapers and book publishers," since they "convey a wide range of information" (Volokh and Falk 2012, 27). More specifically, they say editorial publications and search results are alike since they both involve choices about "how to rank and organize content," "what should be presented to users," and "what constitutes useful information" (Volokh and Falk 2012, 11).

This is all correct as far as it goes, but it does not substantiate the claim that search engines are relevantly similar to editorial publications for purposes of free speech. Consider the layout of a retail outlet such as Target. Target selects "content" to present to customers and organizes it to convey information, for example, using store layouts to promote discounts. If *any* organization of content to convey information to users is deemed relevantly similar to editing, then store layouts would qualify, *ceteris paribus*, as speech. But this cannot be right. This way of thinking about the defining characteristics of "speech" transforms the idea that we need to institute additional protections for a special subset of communicative action into something hopelessly broad. Volokh and Falk may say that the organization of content to convey information counts as "speech" so long as it organizes things that are also *themselves* "speech," but this is similarly implausible. Whether a news article that ranks the top restaurants in a city qualifies as "speech" doesn't hinge on whether the things being ranked (restaurants) are themselves "speech." Nor will it do to say that it is only in the search engine and newspaper cases that the organization of content conveys a message. Google's message in its search results is that these websites are useful or relevant. But Target's store layout conveys a similar message about its products. In short, organizing things to convey information or judgments of usefulness isn't a function that's distinctive of newspapers and search engines.

Convincing analogies are not just based on relevant similarities, they are also based on the absence of relevant *dissimilarities*, so we need to consider how search engines and editorial publications are dissimilar. One difference that has figured prominently in the literature to date is the involvement of algorithms. While editorial publications reflect the conscious choices of specific individuals, search engines use algorithmic processing to index a massive, ever-increasing volume of material, and the staff responsible for them often cannot know what their outputs will be. In Oren Bracha and Frank Pasquale's (2008) terms, search engines produce *functional* rather than *dialogical* expression, and thus they are essentially unlike editorial publishing. Against these claims, Volokh and Falk maintain that search engines do in fact incorporate people's judgments, namely, the judgments of staff members who determine how their underlying algorithms will function (2012). Both sides are partially right on this point. Bracha and Pasquale are wrong to suggest that algorithmically encoded judgments are *necessarily* functional and not dialogical. At least some dialogical expression can be conveyed via the use of algorithms (Benjamin 2011). And this undermines the claim that algorithmically mediated speech *necessarily* lacks the dialogical nature that would make free speech coverage appropriate. But this is consistent with the plausible view, contra Volokh and Falk, that many instances of algorithmically mediated communication, including most search results, aren't dialogical, and thus differ from editorial communication.

There are other points of dissimilarity too. Newspapers generally avow their editorial content. By contrast, search engine companies sometimes explicitly disavow the content of their results. Benjamin (2013) describes a case in which Google's top result for the term "Jew" was an anti-Semitic site called "Jew Watch." When anti-Semitism groups pressured Google to delist the site, Google instead posted a note stating that their results rely on "algorithms using thousands of factors to calculate a page's relevance to a given query" and that they don't reflect "the beliefs and preferences of those who work at Google" (Benjamin 2013, 1469). Google thus presented itself as a mere conduit for others parties' content. Newspapers generally take the opposite stance. In *Tornillo*, the newspaper was so intimately tied to the content it published that a mere right of reply was thought to compel the *newspaper* to speak.

The recent controversy around Facebook's Trending News section (see Nunez 2016; GOP 2016; Oremus 2016; Hunt 2016) sheds further light on the ways companies tactically disavow authorship of the outputs of programs that synthesize and transmit third-party content to users. While this controversy was partly driven by partisan politics, it was also a reaction to the duplicity of Facebook's self-presentation. Facebook styled itself as a neutral conduit of information. It sought to "foster the illusion of a bias-free news ranking process," and it obscured its workers' involvement in curating Trending News content because otherwise it risked "losing its image as a non-partisan player in the media industry," as opposed to an "inherently flawed curator" (Nunez 2016). As with search engine results, this was a context in which the tech company synthesizing and transmitting third-party content was trying to have it both ways: posing as a neutral conduit where taking ownership for the outputs of its programs would be costly, but simultaneously seeking the special legal privileges of editorial speech.[19] Whatever may be said in defense of this balancing act, the crucial point for our purposes is that this is generally not what editorial publications do, nor how they are perceived by their users. Whereas users generally believe that search engines "provide *open conduits* to others' content" (Zittrain 2014), and whereas users typically do not "associate website content with the search engine that guided the user" (Bracha and Pasquale 2008, 1197), newspaper readers, by contrast, generally regard the newspaper's content as representative of the writers' and publishing company's editorial point of view (Spayd 2016).

We should acknowledge that search engines outputs, like editorial publications, come in different forms. Some search engine results are ostensibly paid advertising, and of those that *aren't*, some are produced by algorithms alone, while others result from the manual gerrymandering of algorithmic outputs. The debate around search engines and free speech coverage should be sensitive to this variety (Ballanco 2013). But recognition of this variety doesn't undermine the critical points we're making about the adequacy of the editorial analogy. Rather, it undermines any across-the-board analogical reasoning that tries to extend free speech coverage to all search engines and the like, based on partial similarities between search engines and newspapers. This analogy is much less compelling than recent First Amendment case law would suggest. The observed similarities that it rests on are overly broad, and there are dissimilarities that the analogy doesn't accommodate.

3.2 ALTERNATIVE ANALOGIES

Further to these problems, we can also offer rival analogies that favor the view that search engines *should not* receive free speech coverage. We will discuss two such analogies, focusing on search engines and likening them to (i) shopping malls and (ii) fiduciaries.

In *Pruneyard Shopping Center v. Robins*, the appellees, a group of high school students, set up a stand gathering signatures for a petition in a privately owned shopping center.[20] Security guards forced the students to leave, and the students sued, claiming their right to solicit signatures on the premises under the California Constitution. The California Supreme Court ruled in their favor, but the center appealed, claiming a violation under the federal Constitution of their speech rights, and—like the companies in section 2— cited *Tornillo* to argue that they were being compelled to endorse a message they opposed.[21] The court rejected this argument, finding that the center *was not* compelled to endorse any message, and was free to dissociate itself from the appellees' views. The court also offered an account of the reasoning behind *Tornillo*. The state cannot force newspapers to publish right of reply articles as this would deter editors "from publishing controversial political statements," and thus limit the "vigor" and "variety" of public debate.[22] That combination of factors did not obtain in the case of Pruneyard, and so the court ruled that the appellants' First Amendment rights were not infringed by a state-protected right of expression and petition on their property.

There is an analogy that can be drawn between *Pruneyard* and Google's search engine results, which has at least some prima facie appeal. Google, like the center, is not literally a newspaper. Google's homepage, like the shopping center, is accessible to the general public. Google, like the center, can and does publicly dissociate itself from views expressed by people who, so to speak, set up a table on their sites. And like in *Pruneyard*, preventing Google from ejecting (i.e., delisting) speakers won't do anything to limit the vigor or variety of public debate. If we liken search engines to the center in *Pruneyard*, a prohibition on delisting speakers and content does not look a First Amendment problem after all.

An alternative analogical approach conceives of major tech companies as information fiduciaries (Balkin 2016; Grimmelmann 2014). This is similar to how the court reasoned in imposing the Fairness Doctrine in *Red Lion v. Federal Communications Commission*,[23] and it also accords with the Court's recognition in *Packingham* of cyberspace as "the most important place" for the exchange of views. The law routinely regulates the speech of fiduciary actors such as lawyers or doctors, so there is ample case law to support the regulation of the online behavior of tech companies if the general thrust of the analogy holds.

Naturally, as with the editorial analogy, the analogization of search engine results to shopping malls, or of search companies to fiduciaries, requires us to assert the importance of the similarities that the analogies rest on, and to argue that there are no decisive countervailing dissimilarities. Others have discussed some limitations of these rival analogies (Bambauer 2016). The crucial point for our purposes is simply that all three analogies have some prima facie purchase. When it comes to programs that organize, rank, and transmit third-party communication to users, some of what they do is similar, *in some respects*, to some of what publishers or editors do; some of what they do is similar, *in some respects*, to some fiduciary services; and some of their functions are similar, *in some respects*, to the function of general public spaces in shopping malls. The question that everything hinges on is: Which similarities and dissimilarities are the ones that matter from the point of view of free speech principles? In the First Amendment context, to invoke compelled speech doctrine and cite *Tornillo* as the relevant precedent—simply based on the mere fact that both search engines and newspapers rank and organize content— is to beg this question, instead of properly addressing it. In asking which similarities and dissimilarities matter from the perspective of free speech principles, we are posing a question whose answer cannot but reside in normative considerations. Analogical methods that respond to questions of free speech coverage by noting similarities between different types of communication, but without examining these underlying normative concerns, are at best limited and at worst misleading.

3.3 THE LIMITS OF ANALOGICAL REASONING

The utility of analogical reasoning in law is contested, with some finding it to be the "cornerstone of common law reasoning" and others seeing it as "mere window-dressing, without normative force" (Lamond 2014; see also, Sunstein 1992; Alexander 1996; Sherwin 1999; Posner 2008; Alexander and Sherwin 2008; Lamond 2014). Our view is that, while there are reasons to reject the use of analogical reasoning in particular contexts, it doesn't make sense to either endorse *or* reject analogical legal reasoning wholesale. In short, although some forms of analogical reasoning are illuminating in some legal contexts, the analogical reasoning used in recent debates about search engines and free speech coverage is not such a case.

Grant Lamond (2014) distinguishes three types of analogies in legal reasoning: Classificatory, Close, and Distant. Classificatory Analogies are based on similarities between the facts of the two cases and are used to help determine the legal characterizations of those facts. Close Analogies help to settle novel legal issues raised by a case where there is no directly applicable legal authority. Judges identify a related case and consider whether the rationale that underlies its resolution is applicable to the one before it. Lamond gives the example of *D v. NSPCC*, in which the plaintiff sought to force a private charity to disclose the identity of its informant. Settled law had it that *the police* could not be forced to disclose informants' identities, but no law spoke to the issue of compelling a private charity vested with statutory power to disclose the identity of its informants. The House of Lords saw a Close Analogy in the offing. It looked at the law governing compelled disclosure of police informants, and concluded that the reasons behind the nondisclosure immunity were equally applicable to charities. Close Analogies are thus tools that help courts uncover the reasons that should guide them when no directly applicable authority is available. The analogy as such does little work.

Lamond's third category is Distant Analogies, which differ from Close Analogies by matter of degree. Like Close Analogies, Distant Analogies are raised when there is no binding authority. The difference is how far afield courts must look to find helpful cases. Lamond gives the example of the development of oil and gas rights in the United States. The novel question courts faced was whether land owners had property rights to oil or gas reservoirs that lay underneath their land. Early American courts were "captured" by the law of capture analogy. But as Posner (2008) points out, courts in the grip of this analogy failed to see the relevant dissimilarities between the cases. The identification of the purportedly relevant-yet-distant case is also "haphazard," which increases the risk that a court will not have "all possible (and possibly conflicting) analogies before it" (Lamond 2014, 583). And partly as a consequence of this haphazardness, prior cases are more likely to be invoked without adequate consideration of the reasons that underpinned the original judgment.

With these three types of analogical reasoning distinguished, we are faced with our own classificatory puzzle: where to place the analogical reasoning used in the search engine cases. In light of the points already discussed, we believe this to be an instance of Distant analogical reasoning. Although there are prima facie similarities between search engines and traditional editorial publications, there are also prima facie similarities between search engines and other kinds of entities, and this is the result of the fact that they are complex entities, which do not neatly correspond with any of our preexisting categories of communicative practice. Whether search engine results and similar forms of communication qualify as "speech" for the purposes of free speech principles is a genuinely novel and genuinely difficult question. To reiterate our earlier point, when analogical reasoning is brought in to try to address this question, everything then hinges on our judgments about which similarities really matter from the point of view of free speech. And this question forces us to reflect on the deeper aims or ideals that underpin free speech principles, and how those aims or ideals would be affected by expanding the scope of free speech principles to encompass search engines.

4. The Stakes of Coverage

To see how different normative concerns are implicated in a debate over free speech coverage, we need to clarify what practical consequences hinge on the debate and, unsurprisingly, for the questions of coverage that we are examining here, this is complicated. The types of communication that we are considering are relatively new and still evolving. Their functions now and their functions in the future may be different. But some insight is possible nonetheless. We approach the question of the stakes by considering some results that may ensue depending on whether free speech protections are extended to these entities.

Let us start by considering some implications for business practices. If search engines are covered by the First Amendment in the United States it will be easier for them to bury their competitors' websites without fear of consumer protection or unfair competition lawsuits. Note that Google seeks free speech protection for its search results *for this very reason*. For instance, in its briefs in *KinderStart.com*, Google argued that "because the actions on which KinderStart premises liability are protected by the First Amendment, they certainly cannot be 'unfair' under the UCL [Unfair Competition Law]."[24] Google used similar arguments in *E-Ventures*.[25] Note also that the court's response in *E-Ventures* suggests that how questions of coverage are decided may not fully dictate how unfair competition law applies. The court found Google's results to be fully protected opinion, but it also said that Google could be liable for anticompetitive conduct despite this finding, if Google's claims about *why* it delisted the plaintiff's site were found to be untrue. It is also notable that the California Attorney General's office has looked for ways to expose Google's search results around shopping to antitrust scrutiny, consistently with these results being covered by First Amendment doctrine (Gibson 2014). These developments indicate that free speech coverage would not necessarily result in full immunity from regulation or liability in this space. However, it is compatible with all this to recognize that the characterization of search engines and the like as protected speech would be, all things considered, a significant strategic victory for these companies.

Complex political implications might also hinge on how questions of coverage are resolved. The most obvious concern is that failure to grant free speech coverage to search engines and the like will allow the state to use its regulatory powers to enact a repressive political agenda. Governments in many parts of the world already do this (Goldsmith and Wu 2006; MacKinnon 2012). In the United States one might worry that an authoritarian president could use regulatory codes as a way to pressure online companies to obstruct the public's access to political dissent (Bambauer 2012; Bambauer 2015). Where such fears are overtly tied to questions of free speech coverage, however, they should be tempered by a recognition that actions in this vein can be and have been struck down on First Amendment grounds, even in cases in which they have not been deemed to infringe the free speech rights of distributors.[26] The withholding of coverage might be a more determinative factor if governments are trying to compel companies to include, rather than remove, content. For instance, if a state wanted specific health advice to be prominently displayed, and if First Amendment constraints were out of the picture, then legislation compelling this would quite probably pass constitutional muster, provided that the government did not exact unconstitutional takings.

In sum, confining our attention to the US context, there are certain areas where non-coverage could enable states to regulate sites that organize and transmit third-party content, and other areas where this would have minimal impact. It is not unreasonable to worry about how, without special protection for online programs, liberal states might be susceptible to authoritarian acts by governments. But in recognizing these fears we shouldn't downplay the ways in which anti-authoritarian ideals are already embedded in protections for the individuals using these sites. A commitment to a free press is generally compatible with the state imposing various forms of regulatory oversight on ISPs that mediate communication and the flow of data. The differences in how these organizations and types of content are liable to regulation owe to differences in the kinds of work they do, and the social functions they fulfill. So while it is prudent to worry about government overreach, it is also reasonable, given the increasing social dominance of the tech sector, to worry about tech companies using their market power to advance their own interests at the expense of the public interest.

5. Normative Theories of Free Speech

Against this mostly descriptive backdrop we are now in a position to ask whether search engine outputs should receive free speech coverage in view of the normative purposes of free speech principles. This of course requires us to specify what our reasons are for protecting a privileged subset of communicative activities in the first place. In what follows we will work through the question of coverage for online programs that rank and organize content, using two prominent normative theories of free speech as reference points, namely, the democratic participation theory and Seana Shiffrin's thinker-based theory.

Democratic ideals are invoked by a number of influential First Amendment scholars to explain and defend US free speech doctrine (e.g., Meiklejohn 1948; Post 1990). Building on this tradition, the democratic participation theory of free speech says that speech must be protected in order to ensure "the opportunity for individuals to participate in the speech by which we govern ourselves" (Weinstein 2011, 491). How do we decide what counts as "speech" using democratic participation as our normative reference point? We cannot construe the ideal too broadly, such that all parts of social life are seen as a part of the project of self-government, since, in encompassing everything, the ideal would prioritize nothing. Instead, the ideal of democratic participation requires us to conceptually divide society into two domains: public life, where we act as citizens cooperating in collective self-governance; and private life, where we act independently in the service of our own projects. For free speech principles grounded in democratic participation, "speech" denotes whatever forms of communication are integral to collective self-governance. Of course there will be complications at the margins, but the basic implications of the democratic participation theory are discernible all the same. Free speech principles are not meant to immunize all communication against legitimate regulatory aims. They are meant to support the project of collective self-government, by safeguarding the communicative conduct that is essential to that project's realization.

With those clarifications in place, the pertinent question for our purposes is whether the outputs of online programs that organize, synthesize, and transmit third-party communication to users are integral to democratic self-governance. We can gain a useful perspective on this by seeing how proponents of this theory of free speech assess questions of coverage in other areas. One prominent advocate of a democratic participation theory of the

First Amendment spells out the theory's implications for questions of coverage as follows.

> When allegedly defamatory speech concerns a public official, stringent First Amendment protection applies. . . . But if the speech addresses a purely private concern, then no First Amendment limitations restrain the normal operation of defamation law. . . . A lawyer has a First Amendment right to solicit clients when "seeking to further political and ideological goals" through litigation, but not for ordinary economic reasons (Weinstein 2011, 494).

For each of these pairs we see that communication primarily related to matters of public interest *is* covered by free speech, but communication primarily related to economic and personal matters *is not*. And notice that there is no requirement—in the theory, or in the doctrine it explains—that all instances of a communication-type receive the same coverage.

Now consider search engines. From one perspective, they are commercial entities, plain and simple. They organize content in a way that's enmeshed with the commercial practices of companies, they mediate people's access to sites of online commerce, and in these services they constitute a commercial enterprise of their own, built around advertising sales and data acquisition. But of course they are not *wholly* commercial. Search engines also fulfill important communicative functions related to matters of political concern, for example, by mediating access to information and opinions created by third-party speakers. As explained in section 4, questions of coverage could have implications for tech industry practices on both commercial and political fronts. On top of all this we should also note that search engines facilitate much in the way of purely private communication, for example, by making things such as personal blogs accessible to readers. In view of this diversity, the most reasonable way to set the scope of free speech coverage, under the democratic participation theory, would be to mirror this diversity by saying that search engines *are* covered by free speech principles in their functions related to matters of political concern, but *not* where they are primarily carrying out commercial functions or facilitating private communication. In relation to cases such as *E-Ventures*, or in relation to skirmishes between companies such as Google and Yelp, the main upshot of withholding universal free speech coverage from search engines would be that anticompetitive practices within this domain lose any de facto immunities against unfair competition laws. If we are being guided by a reasonable interpretation of the democratic participation theory of free speech, it would be a mistake to oppose that conclusion on free speech grounds. And this is a mistake that existing First Amendment doctrine makes it relatively easy to avoid, simply by drawing distinctions such as those that Weinstein mentions, which allow us to square the protection of *political* defamation with the restriction of *private* defamation.[27]

We will keep our discussion of our second normative theory of free speech brief, as our key points structurally resemble our remarks about the participatory democracy theory. The "thinker-based" theory of free speech, recently developed by Shiffrin, identifies "the individual agent's interest in the protection of the free development and operation of her mind" as its normative keystone (Shiffrin 2011, 287; 2014).[28] Whereas other theories situate the value of the thinker in relation to extrinsic ideals or desiderata, Shiffrin's theory identifies a direct and non-contingent link between the value of mental autonomy and the justification for the protected status of communicative conduct. Again, however, not all communication is privileged under such a theory. If we prioritize the "fundamental function of allowing an agent to transmit . . . the contents of her mind to others and to externalize her mental content" (Shiffrin 2011, 295), then we will need to have special protections for people expressing their thoughts on any matter under the sun. This is part of what makes Shiffrin's theory distinctive: the expression of thoughts about politics and government does not occupy an exalted position relative to the expression of thoughts about everyday life. But crucially, what is specially protected on this theory is not communication as such, but the communication of *the thought of individuals*. And this will tend to assign a less privileged status to much commercial communication. So when we revisit our key question—whether programs that synthesize and transmit third-party communication to users are implicated in "the fundamental function of allowing an agent to transmit the contents of her mind to others" (Shiffrin 2011, 295)—the diagnosis is mixed, as in the previous case. One interesting consequence of the thinker-based theory is that, unlike the democratic participation theory, it suggests that facilitation of everyday online chatter by search engines and social networks may be as much a part of the case for protecting (some of) their operations as their role in facilitating political discourse. But as with the democratic participation theory, much of what these programs do—and in particular, their functions that are primarily commercial in nature—will likely fall outside the scope of free speech coverage by the lights of this normative theory.

6. Conclusion: Similarity, Coverage, and Expansion

Nelson Goodman (1972) suggested that "similarity" is a near-useless concept. For any pair of things we can find *some* resemblance or shared feature, in view of which we can say that the things are in some sense alike. In most everyday settings Goodman's skepticism sounds over the top. If you pick up an apple that is the same color and complexion as the rotten one you bit into earlier, you do well to throw it away. Judgments based on observed similarity are, likewise, part of the law's everyday business. If a publisher launches a periodical printed in purple ink, the judge need not re-excavate the normative grounds of press freedom and compelled speech doctrine before deciding that a purple-ink newspaper merits the same protection as normal black-ink newspapers. The differences reside in peripheral and accidental properties, not central and essential ones. But as judgments of this sort progress along a spectrum in the comparisons they're dealing with—from simple to complex entities, from low-stakes to high-stakes decisions—the force of Goodman's skepticism becomes evident, and we lose confidence in saying which of a thing's properties are the ones that matter.

Or we should, at any rate. In debates over search engines and free speech coverage, neither the gravity of the policy stakes, nor the complexity of the things being compared, has dampened the willingness of courts and scholars to use tenuous analogies in charting the way forward. Everyone can agree that search engines and the like should be covered by principles of a free press, *if* and *to the extent that* they occupy a similar cultural position to the press (Tutt 2012). The point is that casual analogical methods—observing that both types of things "convey a wide range of information" or "rank and organize content"—do not tell us whether these things are similarly culturally positioned in the ways that really matter, given the ideals underlying the principles whose scope of application we are trying to determine. The only way to answer that question is to articulate what the consequences are likely to be if we do or do not extend free speech coverage (section 4), to review our most appealing or credible accounts of the underlying aims or purposes which are in play (section 5), and then to extend coverage where the likely consequences of doing so support the relevant aims. In applying this method we find that, contrary to the currently prevailing view, only a subset of search engine results and similar communication should receive free speech coverage.

The problems with analogical methods for addressing questions around free speech coverage are not peculiar to the specific debate that we have examined. In recent American free speech jurisprudence there has been steady outward pressure on the scope of free speech coverage. This is partly because novel arguments that drive in this direction have a recent track record as a winning strategy (Schauer 2015).[29] It may also reflect some sort of predilection in the underlying architecture of categorical legal rules, which in borderline cases tilts the scales in favor of encompassing a case under the rule rather than excluding it (Kendrick 2015). Regardless of what is driving it, the expansion of free speech coverage runs the risk of changing free speech from a precision instrument that warrants the support of liberals of all stripes, into a blunt deregulatory cudgel that only appeals to strident antigovernment types. Simple analogical approaches to questions of free speech coverage, which pay no attention to free speech's normative foundations, assist in that transformation. An approach to free speech coverage that is focused on normative theories of free speech will not deliver tidy verdicts about where and how free speech principles should apply. But all the same, it is one way to keep free speech coverage from expanding past the point of credibility.

Notes

1. Packingham v. North Carolina, 582 U.S. ___ (2017).
2. Zhang v. Baidu, 10 F. Supp. 3d 433 (S.D.N.Y. 2014).
3. *Zhang*, 10 F. Supp. 3d at 435.
4. *Zhang*, 10 F. Supp. 3d at 436.
5. *Zhang*, 10 F. Supp. 3d at 436 (citing Miami Herald Publishing Co. v. Tornillo, 418 U.S. 241 (1974)).
6. *Zhang*, 10 F. Supp. 3d at 437 (citing Hurley v. Irish American Gay, Lesbian, and Bisexual Group of Boston, 515 U.S. 557 (1995)).
7. Hurley v. Irish American Gay, Lesbian, and Bisexual Group of Boston, 515 US 557, 558 (1995).
8. *Zhang*, 10 F. Supp. 3d at 438.
9. E-ventures Worldwide v. Google, Inc., 2:14-cv-00646-PAM-CM at 3, 8 (M.D. Fla. Feb. 8, 2017).
10. "Delisting" means that the sites were removed from Google's search results such that no subsequent search query would bring up an E-ventures site.
11. Complaint, E-ventures Worldwide v. Google, Inc., 2:14-cv-00646-JES-CM (M.D. Fla. Nov. 4, 2014).
12. E-ventures Worldwide v. Google, Case No. 2:14-cv-646-FtM-29CM, 2016 WL 2758889 at 15 (M.D. Fla. May 12, 2016).
13. *E-ventures*, 2016 WL 2758889 at 16.
14. E-ventures Worldwide v. Google, Inc., 2:14-cv-00646-PAM-CM at 8–9 (M.D. Fla. Feb. 8, 2017).
15. *E-ventures*, 2:14-cv-00646-PAM-CM at 8.
16. *E-ventures*, 2:14-cv-00646-PAM-CM at 9 (emphasis added).
17. *E-ventures*, 2:14-cv-00646-PAM-CM at 9.
18. E.g., S. Louis Martin v. Google, Case No. 14-539972 (N.D. Cal. Nov. 13, 2014), Langdon v. Google, 474 F. Supp. 2d 622 (D. Del. 2007), Search King Inc. v. Google, 2003 WL 21464568 (W.D. Okla. 2003).
19. In response to this one might argue that search engines and Facebook newsfeeds cannot ever be purely neutral conduits of content, and that they cannot avoid embedding decisions about how to rank and organize content. That's right, but it doesn't follow that free speech protections are warranted for any and every method that a company might use to rank and organize content. Google supports network neutrality rules which prevent internet service providers (ISPs) from blocking or prioritizing content (Brodkin 2015; Benjamin 2011). Google thus endorses regulations that compel other companies to act like the sort of impartial conduits that it and Facebook present themselves as (McKinnon and Kendall 2016). This indicates that, by these companies' own lights, a commitment to free speech is compatible in principle with regulatory controls on companies that purport to supply users with neutral or open access to third-party sources of information and communication. See United States Telecom Ass'n v. FCC, 825 F.3d 674 (D.C. Cir. 2016).

20. Pruneyard Shopping Ctr. v. Robins, 447 U.S. 74 (1980).

21. Id. at 87–88.

22. Id. at 88.

23. Red Lion v. FCC, 395 U.S. 367 (1969).

24. Kinderstart.com, LLC v. Google Inc. 2006 WL 1786956 (N.D. Cal., filed May 2, 2006) (defendant's notice of motion and motion to dismiss the first amended complaint; memorandum of points and authorities).

25. E-Ventures Worldwide, LLC v. Google, Inc., No. 2:14-CV-646-FTM-29CM, 2016 WL 2758889 (M.D. Fla. May 12, 2016), *reconsideration denied,* No. 2:14-CV-646-FTM-29CM, 2016 WL 4409338 (M.D. Fla. Aug. 19, 2016), and *motion to certify appeal denied,* No. 2:14-CV-646-FTM-29CM, 2016 WL 4409339 (M.D. Fla. Aug. 19, 2016).

26. E.g., Bantam Books, Inc. v. Sullivan, 372 U.S. 58 (1963).

27. In contemporary US constitutional law an appeal to expansive interpretations of free speech to strike down commercial and economic regulation isn't unusual. It's a development—sometimes called "the Lochnerization of the First Amendment"—that's occurred on many fronts (Wu 2013; Kendrick 2015; Shanor 2016).

28. The antecedents of her theory in the free speech literature are diverse. Her emphasis on the individual's self-realization as an end in itself is reminiscent of certain themes from Mill (1859). Her theory characterizes the individual thinker as one who bears responsibility for her mental life, which is an idea stressed in influential work by Thomas Scanlon (1972) and David Strauss (1991). And the articulation of the interests of "the thinker" relating to expressive liberties is a part of Joshua Cohen's (1993) work on free speech, although it is merely one element among others. Bambauer (2014) also endorses a version of this theory, arguing for a thinker-centered First Amendment and corollary right to learn new things.

29. Although as our discussion of *Pruneyard* in section 3.2 shows, attempts to aggressively broaden the boundaries of what qualifies as "speech" needn't always succeed.

References

Alexander, L. and Sherwin, E. 2008. *Demystifying Legal Reasoning.* Cambridge: Cambridge University Press.

Alexander, L. 1996. "Bad Beginnings." *University of Pennsylvania Law Review* 145: 57–87.

Balkin, J. 2016. "Information Fiduciaries and the First Amendment." *University of California Davis Law Review* 49 (4): 1183–234.

Ballanco, M. 2013. "Comment: Searching for the First Amendment: An Inquisitive Free Speech Approach to Search Engine Rankings." *George Mason University Civil Rights Law Journal* 24 (1): 89–111.

Bambauer, J. 2014. "Is Data Speech?" *Stanford Law Review* 66 (1): 57–120.

Bambauer, J. 2016. "Response: The Relationships between Speech and Conduct." *University of California Davis Law Review* 49(4): 1941–53.

Bambauer, D. 2012. "Orwell's Armchair." *University of Chicago Law Review* 79 (3): 863–944.

Bambauer, D. 2015. "Against Jawboning." *Minnesota Law Review* 100 (1): 51–126.

Benjamin, S. 2013. "Algorithms and Speech." *University of Pennsylvania Law Review* 161 (6): 1445–94.

Benjamin, S. 2011. "Transmitting, Editing, and Communicating: Determining What 'the Freedom of Speech' Encompasses." *Duke Law Journal* 60(8): 1673–713.

Bergen, M. 2015. "Google Says Local Search Results That Buried
Rivals Yelp, Tripadvisor Is Just a Bug." *Re/Code*, November 24, 2015.

Bracha, O. and Pasquale, F. 2008. "Federal Search Commission? Access, Fairness and Accountability in the Law of Search." *Cornell Law Review* 93 (6): 1149–209.

Brodkin, J. 2015. "How Net Neutrality Violates the First Amendment (according to One ISP): Broadband Providers Exercise 'Editorial Discretion' over Internet, ISP Says." *Ars Technica*, October 6.

Cohen, J. 1993. "Freedom of Expression." *Philosophy & Public Affairs* 22 (3): 207–63.

Cushing, T. 2017. "Court Says Google Has a First Amendment Right to Delist Competitors." *TechDirt*, February 17.

DeMers, J. 2016. "The SEO Industry Is Worth $65 Billion; Will It Ever Stop Growing?" *Search Engine Land*, May 9, 2016.

European Commission Memo. 2015. "Antitrust: Commission Sends Statement of Objections to Google on Comparison Shopping Service, Case No. 39740." April 15.

Gibson, P. 2014. "Does the First Amendment Immunize Google's Search Engine Search Results from Government Antitrust Scrutiny?" *Competition: Journal of Antitrust & Unfair Competition Law, State Bar of California*, 23 (1): 125–41.

Goldman, E. 2016. "Google Must Answer Lawsuit for Manually Removing Websites from Its Search Results." *Forbes*, May 17.

Goldsmith, J. and T. Wu. 2006. *Who Controls the Internet? Illusions of a Borderless World.* Oxford: Oxford University Press.

Goodman, N. 1972. *Problems and Projects.* New York: Bobbs-Merrill: 22–32.

GOP. 2016. "#MakeThisTrend: Facebook Must Answer for Conservative Censorship." *GOP website*, May 9, 2016.

Grimmelmann, J. 2014. "Speech Engines." *Minnesota Law Review* 98 (3): 868–952.

Hunt, E. 2016. "Facebook to Change Trending Topics after Investigation into Bias Claims." *The Guardian*, May 23, 2016.

Kanter, J. and Scott, M. 2015. "European Challenges Google, Seeing Violations of Its Antitrust Laws." *New York Times*, April 15.

Kendrick, L. 2015. "First Amendment Expansionism." *William & Mary Law Review* 56 (4): 1199–219.

Lamond, G. 2014. "Analogical Reasoning in the Common Law." *Oxford Journal of Legal Studies* 34 (3): 567–588.

MacKinnon, R. 2012. *Consent of the Networked: The Worldwide Struggle for Internet Freedom.* New York: Basic Books.

Masnick, M. 2016. "Court Says Google Doesn't Have a First Amendment Right to Drop a Site from Its Search Results." *TechDirt*, May 20, 2016.

McKinnon, J. and B. Kendall. 2016. "FCC's Net-Neutrality Rules Upheld by Appeals Court." *Wall Street Journal*, June 14.

Meiklejohn, A. 1948. *Free Speech and Its Relation to Self-Government.* New York: Harper & Brothers.

Mill, J. S. 1859. *On Liberty.* Republished London: Penguin Books, 1985.

Nunez, M. 2016. "Former Facebook Workers: We Routinely Suppressed Conservative News." *Gizmodo*, May 9.

Oremus, W. 2016. "What the Facebook 'Liberal Bias' Controversy Is Really About." *Slate*, May 17.

Posner, R. 2008. *How Judges Think*. Cambridge, MA: Harvard University Press.

Post, R. 1990. "The Constitutional Conception of Public Discourse: Outrageous Opinion, Democratic Deliberation, and *Hustler Magazine v. Falwell.*" *Harvard Law Review* 103 (3): 601–86.

Scanlon, T. 1972. "A Theory of Freedom of Expression." *Philosophy & Public Affairs* 1 (2): 204–26.

Schauer, F. 1982. *Free Speech: A Philosophical Inquiry*. Cambridge: Cambridge University Press.

Schauer, F. 2015. "The Politics and Incentives of First Amendment Coverage." *William & Mary Law Review* 56 (4): 1613–36.

Shanor, A. 2016. "The New *Lochner.*" *Wisconsin Law Review* 2016(1): 133–208.

Sherwin, E. 1999. "A Defense of Analogical Reasoning in Law." *University of Chicago Law Review* 66: 1179–97.

Shiffrin, S. V. 2011. "A Thinker-Based Approach to Freedom of Speech." *Constitutional Commentary* 27 (2): 283–307.

Shiffrin, S. V. 2014. *Speech Matters: On Lying, Morality, and the Law*. Princeton, NJ: Princeton University Press.

Spayd, L. 2016. "Why Readers See The Times as Liberal." *The Times*, July 23, 2016.

Strauss, D.A. 1991. "Persuasion, Autonomy, and Freedom of Expression." *Columbia Law Review* 91 (2): 334–71.

Sunstein, C. 1992. "On Analogical Reasoning." *Harvard Law Review* 106 (3): 741–91.

Tsotsis, A. 2011. "Google's Algorithmic Cat and Mouse Game [Infographic]." *TechCrunch*, March 23, 2011.

Tutt, A. 2012. "Software Speech." *Stanford Law Review* 65: 73–78.

Volokh, E. and Falk, D. M. 2012. "First Amendment Protection for Search Engine Search Results." White Paper, April 20.

Weinstein, J. 2011. "Participatory Democracy as the Central Value of American Free Speech Doctrine." *Virginia Law Review* 97 (3): 491–514.

Wu, T. 2013. "Machine Speech." *University of Pennsylvania Law Review* 161 (6): 1495–533.

Zittrain, J. 2014. "Facebook Could Decide an Election without Anyone Ever Finding Out." *The New Republic*. June 21. https://newrepublic.com/article/117878/information-fiduciary-solution-facebook-digital-gerrymandering

3

Cyber Harassment and Free Speech

DRAWING THE LINE ONLINE

James Weinstein*

1. Introduction

An exceedingly difficult challenge facing contemporary liberal democracies is
how to effectively combat cyber harassment in ways that comport with basic
free speech principles. The types of harm inflicted by cyber harassment are
no strangers to the law, many of them potentially actionable, for instance, as
defamation, invasion of privacy, or intentional infliction of emotional distress.
Several features of the online environment, however, conspire both to magnify
this harm and to make it difficult either to prevent or to remedy. First, unlike
traditional mass media where the content of speech is tightly controlled by
publishers and editors, speech on the internet is largely unmediated (Leiter
2016, 428; Lidsky 2011, 149). As a result, unlike with newspapers, radio, and
television, there is often no effective check on individuals engaging in irre-
sponsible personal attacks.[1] In addition, the internet is a particularly pervasive medium, allowing "cyber-attackers . . . to harass their victims on a scale
never before possible because of both the immediate effect of their conduct,
and the speed and ease of the global dissemination of online information," a
harm exacerbated by the permanence of online content (Lipton 2011, 1112).
Finally, the anonymity typically available to online speakers fosters harassment by removing the social cost of making outrageous personal attacks, as
well as usually shielding the attackers from legal liability (Citron 2009a, 80).

Despite the magnitude of the problem, cyber harassment for far too long
remained a largely invisible phenomenon (Citron 2009b). It took pioneering

* I would like to thank Danielle Citron, Kath Gelber, and Eugene Volokh for their helpful
suggestions and Gus Cinquino, Luci Davis, Ryan Hogan, and Jesse Ritchey for their research assistance.

work by authors such as Danielle Citron to demonstrate that cyber harassment is a widespread practice that can have devastating consequence for people's lives, including extreme emotional distress and even suicide, as well as loss of employment or employment opportunities (Hua 2017). Moreover, cyber harassment disproportionately victimizes women, often driving them from online participation, including blogging (Sweeney 2017, 655; Franks 2012, 657–59, 667). Still, as obnoxious, harmful, and discriminatory as cyber harassment may be, it nonetheless constitutes expression. In addition, this expression occurs on the internet, a medium that in contemporary society is an essential medium for democratic self-governance. The challenge, then, is to find effective legal remedies for cyber harassment that will not unduly burden individual expression in "the vast democratic forums of the Internet."[2]

2. A Cyber Harassment Exemplar: "Nancy Andrews" and AutoAdmit

In a highly acclaimed book, Danielle Citron describes a case of cyber harassment that is emblematic of this behavior and the harm it can cause its victims. A first year student at Yale Law School, whom Citron refers to by the pseudonym "Nancy Andrews," became a topic of discussion on AutoAdmit, a discussion board for students. In connection with a contest called "T14talent—the Most Appealing Women@Top Law Schools," the site "began hosting discussions about female law students from various [top] schools." "STANFORDtroll," who Andrews believes was a college classmate whose sexual advances she rejected, started the attack on Andrews in a thread entitled "Stupid Bitch to Attend Yale Law" by warning her Yale classmates to "stay away from her." This led to an attack by a cyber mob, including threats of sodomy, rape, accusations of sexually transmitted disease, and videos depicting her as bloodied and shot (Citron 2014, 39–40). The attacks falsely claimed that Andrews had a middling LSAT score and therefore was not qualified to attend Yale Law School, and urged readers to inform top law firms about this before they made her an offer of employment. Another poster said the only reason that she got into Yale Law School was "because she was a 'nigger'" and yet another claimed she was admitted because she had a lesbian affair with the dean of admissions. These attacks likely had a devastating effect on Andrews's ability to find employment with a law firm during the summer between her second and third years as a law student. Although she was an editor of the *Yale Law Journal* and had sixteen job interviews, she was not offered employment, most likely because a routine internet search by potential employers revealed these allegations (Citron 2014, 40).

The posts also had a devastating impact on her law school experience. Because several posters suggested that they were her classmates by describing, for instance, the clothing she wore, Andrews could not "dismiss the posts as rants of strangers." As a result, Andrews at first did not attend class, concerned that "anything she said or did would be posted online." After she decided to again attend class, she avoided speaking in class and did not attend law school events. In addition, she suffered emotional distress, anxiety, and insomnia (Citron 2014, 40–41).

In 2007, represented pro bono by two law professors, Andrews sued thirty-nine pseudonymous AutoAdmit posters for defamation, invasion of privacy, and intentional infliction of emotional distress, among other claims. Andrews' lawyers obtained subpoenas compelling AutoAdmit to disclose information that revealed the identity of five of the posters. Two others voluntarily identified themselves but the rest could not be identified. In 2009, Andrews and the seven identified posters reached a confidential settlement (Citron 2014, 41–42).

The online expression to which Andrews was subject, and the lawsuit she filed but settled before trial, acutely raise the question of what legal remedies are, or could be made available, to combat such harassment consistent with First Amendment limitations. The answer to this question largely depends on the scope of a bedrock feature of contemporary American free speech jurisprudence: the rule against content regulation. If, as some believe, the rule extends to all speech with the exception of a few, narrow categories of expression that government has traditionally been allowed to regulate, then tort remedies or cyber harassment remedies that prohibit speech not falling within these few categories are presumptively unconstitutional. In an influential article, Eugene Volokh forcefully defends this view (Volokh 2013). If, in contrast, the rule against content discrimination applies primarily to expression related to democratic self-governance, as I believe it should, then the government has greater leeway to regulate online harassment.

Despite the focus on American free speech doctrine, this inquiry will be relevant to the question of appropriate legal remedies in other liberal democracies. This is because, properly understood, the First Amendment is primarily concerned with the right of individuals to participate in the democratic process, a vital concern of all liberal democracies.

3. American Free Speech Doctrine and the Rule against Content Discrimination

The cornerstone of contemporary American free speech doctrine is the rule against content regulation.[3] While government has a great deal of leeway to regulate speech for reasons unrelated to its message, such as the time, place, or manner of the speech,[4] the rule against content discrimination disables government from regulating speech because it fears the speech will persuade people to engage in some harmful activity; because it will upset, offend, or shock the audience; or for any other reason involving the message the speech conveys. The injuries inflicted by cyber harassment flow from the message such expression conveys directly to the victim, causing her emotional distress and similar harms, as well as by the message it conveys to others, besmirching the victim's reputation or revealing intensely private matters about her. Accordingly, in order to assess the constitutionality of laws remedying cyber harassment, it is first necessary to examine the rule against content discrimination in detail, as well as the free speech values that underlie it.

(I) THE DISPUTE CONCERNING THE SCOPE OF THE RULE AGAINST CONTENT DISCRIMINATION

While there can be no dispute that the rule against content discrimination is a central feature of contemporary American free speech doctrine, there is sharp disagreement about the scope of this rule. There are two competing views about the breadth of this rule, one named the "All-Inclusive Approach" (McDonald 2005, 1009) and another which I shall call the "Democratic Participation Model."

The All-Inclusive Approach posits that "all speech receives First Amendment protection unless it falls with[in] certain narrow categories of expression . . . such as incitement of imminent illegal conduct, intentional libel, obscenity, child pornography, fighting words, and true threats" (McDonald 2005, 1009). On this view, unless speech falls into one of these categories, any regulation of the content of speech will be subject to "strict scrutiny," a rigorous test that warrants "near-automatic condemnation."[5] This supposed general prohibition against content regulation is supported both by Supreme Court dicta[6] and by prominent commentators (e.g., Nowak and Rotunda 2004, 1226; Volokh 2013, 751). In my view, however, any such rule is inconsistent with both the scope and level of constitutional protection actually provided to speech in American society.

In addition to the "narrow categories of expression" that the proponents of the "All-Inclusive Approach" acknowledge can be prohibited because of their content, there is in fact an enormous range of speech routinely regulated on account of its content, all without a hint of interference from the First Amendment. This includes expression regulated by securities, antitrust, labor, copyright, food and drug, and health and safety laws, together with that regulated by the common law of contract, negligence, and fraud (Schauer 2003, 1768–69, 1778–84; Weinstein 2004, 1097–98). In addition, there are numerous Supreme Court holdings providing less than strict scrutiny to content regulation of speech beyond the "narrow" exceptions recognized by the All-Inclusive Approach, including speech in a nonpublic forum or in the government workplace, as well as commercial speech, and sexually explicit but non-obscene speech (Weinstein 2011a, 492). Contrary to the All-Inclusive Approach, then, there is no general rule against content regulation of speech.

The Democratic Participation Model, in contrast, readily accounts for these examples of permissible content regulation. It postulates that the prohibition against content regulation is primarily confined to expression essential to democratic self-governance, expression which the Supreme Court and commentators often refer to as "public discourse" (Post 1990).[7] However, since this democratic expression is not always aimed at the public but also includes informal conversations, I prefer to use the term "democratic discourse" (Weinstein 2011b, 639–42). There is no simple algorithm for determining whether expression qualifies as democratic discourse entitled to rigorous protection from content discrimination. It is possible nonetheless to identify two factors that are crucial to making this determination: (1) whether the speech is about a matter of public concern, and (2) whether the expression occurs in settings dedicated or essential to democratic self-governance, such as books, magazines, films, the internet, or in public forums such as the speaker's corner of the park.

(II) THE RULE AGAINST CONTENT DISCRIMINATION AND THE LESSONS OF *SNYDER V. PHELPS*

Snyder v. Phelps,[8] a United States Supreme Court decision nullifying on First Amendment grounds a large monetary judgment for intentional infliction of emotional distress, demonstrates the centrality of these two factors in determining whether speech is protected from content regulation. The defendants in *Snyder* were members of the Westboro Baptist Church, which had for decades publically expressed the view that God kills American soldiers as punishment for the country's tolerance of homosexuality, particularly in the military. In this case, church members picketed on public land near a Catholic church where the funeral of Matthew Snyder, a Marine corporal killed in the line of duty in Iraq, was being held. The picketers carried signs which included the following messages: "God Hates the USA/Thank God for 9/11," "America is Doomed," "Don't Pray for the USA, "Thank God for IEDs," "Thank God for Dead Soldiers," "Pope in Hell," "Priests Rape Boys," "God Hates Fags," "You're Going to Hell," and "God Hates You." Albert Snyder, Matthew's father, sued the protestors for intentional infliction of emotional distress. He won a five million dollar judgment in the trial court but an appellate court reversed on First Amendment grounds.[9]

Affirming the appellate court's decision, the United States Supreme Court noted that "[s]peech on matters of public concern . . . is at the heart of the First Amendment's protection." Chief Justice Roberts's opinion for the Court accordingly explained that whether "the First Amendment prohibits holding [the church] liable for its speech in this case turns largely on whether that speech is of public or private concern." He found that the expression at issue "plainly relates to broad issues of interest to society at large," such as homosexuality in the military and the moral conduct of the United States, "rather than matters of purely private concern."[10] The Court also emphasized that the protest occurred at a "public place adjacent to a public street," a "space [that] occupies a 'special position in terms of First Amendment protection.'" It noted further that the emotional distress occasioned by Westboro's picketing "turned on the content and viewpoint of the message conveyed," and not on some content-neutral rationale such as interference with the funeral itself. Because "Westboro's speech was at a public place on a matter of public concern," the Court found that the expression was "entitled to 'special protection' under the First Amendment." For this reason, it concluded that speech could not constitutionally form the basis of an intentional infliction of emotional distress suit.[11]

But what would have been the result if the expression were not a matter of public concern? What if, for instance, a family involved in a bitter personal dispute with Albert Snyder had carried signs on the public street near Matthew's funeral reading "Thank God for Killing Matthew," "Matthew is Going to Hell," and "Matthew was a Fag." Crucially for our inquiry, the Court in *Snyder* indicated that such expression might not be immune from a suit for intentional infliction of emotional distress. The Court noted that "not all speech is of equal First Amendment importance," and that "where matters of purely private significance are at issue, First Amendment protections are often less rigorous." This is because restricting speech "on purely private matters does not implicate the same constitutional concerns as limiting speech on matters of public interest," posing "no threat to the free and robust debate of public issues" or "interference with a meaningful dialogue of ideas."[12]

Whether the Court would have allowed recovery if the church members' speech had been on a matter of private concern is a difficult question and one of particular importance to our inquiry about the constitutionality of cyber harassment prohibition. The actual *Snyder* case was relatively easy in that both factors pointed toward protection: the speech was on a matter of public concern and it was in a setting essential to democratic self-governance. A similarly easy case would have been presented, I submit, if both factors had indicated lack of protection. This would have been the case, for instance, if Albert Snyder's enemy had handed him a note with these statements about Matthew as Albert was leaving his house for his son's funeral. But in the scenario I imagined, the two factors pull in opposite directions. On the one hand, the expression involves speech on a matter of purely private concern but, on the other hand, it occurred in a "public place adjacent to a public street," which like the internet, "occupies a 'special position in terms of First Amendment protection.'"[13] As I will discuss in detail, this scenario is analogous to much cyber harassment, which typically involves matters of purely private concern, often material posted by a jilted lover, but in a medium that "occupies a special position in terms of First Amendment protection."

Despite the relative lack of emphasis in the Court's decisions on the nature of the medium as compared to whether the speech is on a matter of public or private concern, the democratic nature of the settings in which the speech at issue occurs is crucial to the determination whether it is entitled to "special protection" under the First Amendment. As Robert Post has explained, in modern democratic societies, certain modes of communication form "a structural skeleton that is necessary . . . for public discourse to serve the constitutional value of democracy" (Post 1995, 1276). For this reason, if speech occurs in a setting essential to democratic self-governance, then regardless of the content of the expression, it will be presumed that the expression is protected (Weinstein 2007, 874). Since the Court has expressly deemed the internet to be a medium essential to democratic self-governance,[14] the presumption of protection afforded any instance of expression in that medium has particular significance to our ultimate inquiry into whether cyber harassment laws comport with the First Amendment.

(III) DEFINING THE SCOPE OF THE RULE AGAINST CONTENT DISCRIMINATION ACCORDING TO FIRST AMENDMENT VALUES

While vigorous disagreement persists about what other values might also be central to the First Amendment, there is "practically universal agreement" that at least one core norm is democratic self-governance.[15] And it is this norm that best explains the special protection afforded speech on matters of public concern occurring in settings essential to democratic self-governance.

The opportunity to freely express one's views on matters of public concern in these settings promotes vital democratic interests of both speakers and audience. Like voting, the opportunity to participate in this democratic discourse is essential to the legitimacy of the legal system in that it allows individuals to have their say about laws that bind them (Weinstein 2017; Scanlon 1972, 214). There may be no fully satisfactory answer to the age-old question of what justifies the state using force to make free and autonomous people obey laws with which they reasonably disagree. But the democratic process, which includes not just the ability to vote for representatives who enact the laws, but also the opportunity of individuals to freely criticize or support laws and government policies, is perhaps "arguably the best that can be done . . . for justifying the legitimacy of the social order" (Baker 2011, 262–63). In addition to promoting legitimacy in this crucial normative sense, the opportunity to participate in democratic discourse contributes to "the descriptive conditions necessary for a diverse and heterogeneous population to live together in a relatively peaceable manner under a common system of governance and politics" (Post 2017, 651). In addition to these key speaker interests, there is also an important democratic audience interest in receiving information and perspectives needed by citizens to "effectively participate in and contribute to our republican system of self-government."[16]

We are now in a position to consider how possible legal responses to cyber harassment comport with First Amendment doctrine and the core democratic values underlying the First Amendment. I will first consider civil remedies, primarily the application of traditional tort law. I then turn to criminal prohibitions, both general provisions such as laws forbidding threats as well as laws specifically prohibiting cyber harassment.

3. Civil Remedies and the First Amendment

(I) DEFAMATION

As exemplified by the attack on law student "Nancy Andrews," cyber harassment often includes false statements of fact damaging to the reputation of the person attacked online. As such, this expression potentially constitutes actionable libel. In almost any context, the false accusation that someone has a sexually transmitted disease is defamatory. The same is true with respect to a false claim that someone gained admission to a university program because of an affair with an admissions officer. And in some special contexts, such as a discussion board involving law students, even a false statement about a student's entry scores might be defamatory.

Defamation is among those "narrow categories of expression" that government has traditionally been allowed to regulate on the basis of its content,[17] and thus may be subject to liability consistent with the First Amendment. Beginning with its landmark decision in *New York Times Co. v. Sullivan*, [18] however, the United States Supreme Court has in several circumstances extended First Amendment immunity to defamatory expression in order to assure that the "debate on public issues remain uninhibited, robust, and wide-open."[19] So it would be extremely difficult, and properly so in light of the First Amendment's core democratic concern, for a public official to recover for defamatory statements on an internet discussion board. And even where a private person has been defamed, the First Amendment sets limitations on recovery if the false statement was on a matter of public concern.[20] But consistent with the previous discussion about the reservation of special First Amendment protection for matters of public concern, the Court to date has not extended any constitutional protection to defamatory speech about a private person on a matter of private concern.[21]

So in a situation such as the cyber harassment of Andrews involving an attack on a private person not involving a matter of public concern, the First Amendment would not bar recovery for defamatory expression. But not all cyber harassment necessarily involves false factual statements. For instance, what if the attack contained embarrassing revelations that were true? This brings us to one of most vexed issues in American constitutional law: whether the First Amendment permits the imposition of liability for invasion of privacy for public disclosure of private facts.

(II) INVASION OF PRIVACY

Under American tort law, a person is subject to liability for publicizing "a matter concerning the private life of another" if the matter publicized is "of a kind that (a) would be highly offensive to reasonable person, and (b) is not of legitimate concern to the public."[22] Note that consistent with the Democratic Participation Model, the tort applies only to disclosures that are not on a matter of public concern. Any attempt to extend liability for disclosure of private facts about a person on a matter of public concern would in almost any circumstance violate the First Amendment.[23] Whether the First Amendment similarly bars the imposition of liability for the publication of "highly offensive" (or perhaps more aptly, "intensely private" and "embarrassing"[24]) private facts *not* on a matter of public concern is a daunting question.

To date, the Court has addressed First Amendment constraints on invasion of privacy actions only in cases involving disclosure of the names of juveniles accused of a crime or victims of sexual assault.[25] In each case the Court held that imposition of liability for publishing the name of the juvenile already available to the public was unconstitutional. The Supreme Court, however, has never suggested that the First Amendment forbids all recovery for invasion of privacy. Indeed, in the last of the series of cases on the subject, the Court emphasized that "[w]e do not hold that truthful publication is automatically constitutionally protected, or that there is no zone of personal privacy within which the State may protect the individual from intrusion by the press . . . ."[26] And as has been observed, "[t]he 'disclosure of private facts' tort remains recognized by most lower courts" (Volokh 2013, 758).

Suppose that on a discussion board geared to the concerns of first year law students, a poster anonymously revealed that his ex-girlfriend, whom he identifies by name and law school, was unfaithful to him and contracted herpes. Unlike imposing liability on someone for posting this same information *on his own Facebook page*, liability for invasion of privacy in this context would not unduly impinge a speaker's important First Amendment interest, correctly defended by Volokh, to discuss *his own life* with *his* circle of friends (Volokh 2013, 761). The only arguably significant interest that the anonymously posted speech in this scenario serves is to warn others in the law student's professional and social circle that she "is untrustworthy and even dangerous" (Volokh 2013, 758). But in this case, the law student's interest in preventing this egregious "intrusion" into her "zone of personal privacy"[27] would seem to greatly outweigh any legitimate interest that the relevant community might have about the law student's character. Of course, in other cases the balance of interests may be different, either because the intrusion on privacy is not as serious or because the relevant community has a greater interest in being warned one of its members is untrustworthy or dangerous. But unlike in ideological contexts, in the typical disclosure of intimate information case, courts can be trusted to identify "extreme cases" in which it is "constitutionally permissible for a governmental entity to regulate the public disclosure of facts about a private individual."[28]

Finally, I want to briefly discuss "doxing"—the online release of "personally identifiable information" harvested from an internet search (MacAllister 2017, 2455–56; McIntyre 2016, 113–14)—such as a person's home address, telephone number, social security number, children's name, or the schools they attend. Doxing is sometimes referred to as an invasion of privacy, which in some sense it is. It does not, however, typically involve disclosure of "intensely private" or "embarrassing" information or factual revelations that a reasonable person would find "highly offensive." The typical "dox," therefore, would not be actionable under the traditional tort of invasion of privacy for disclosure of private facts. Indeed, viewed in isolation, revelation of publicly available information would ordinarily be protected speech. Nonetheless, when such disclosure of personal information is combined, for instance, with lurid descriptions of the sexual acts that the poster would like to engage in with the person whose personal information he publicizes, such disclosures might lose their protection. It is important to note, though, that this loss of First Amendment protection would not be because the disclosure invades the target's "zone of personal privacy." Rather, it is because the disclosure is part of a pattern or course of expression on purely private matters that inflicts substantial emotional distress on the subject.

(III) INTENTIONAL INFLICTION OF EMOTIONAL DISTRESS

All too common features of cyber harassment are graphic descriptions of sexual acts that the poster wants to perform with the victim or statements that the victim should be raped. In another example of cyber harassment featured in Citron's book, a tech blogger named Kathy Sierra received frightening emails and posts on her blog, including one stating: "Fuck off you boring slut . . . I hope someone slits your throat and cums down your gob."[29] As just discussed, the emotional distress that such expression inflicts can be exacerbated by the disclosure of personal information that informs the victim of the cyberattack that the poster, or other members of a hostile cyber mob, knows where she lives or where her children go to school. As will be discussed shortly, these statements most likely do not qualify as "true threats" categorically unprotected by the First Amendment, though the added doxxing element makes it a closer question. Such expression is, however, likely actionable as intentional infliction of emotional distress.

The Restatement (Second) of Torts provides: "One who by extreme and outrageous conduct intentionally or recklessly causes severe emotional distress to another is subject to liability for such emotional distress."[30] There is an argument that "when one-to-many speech about a person falls outside [recognized First Amendment] exceptions, it *should* be constitutionally protected" (Volokh 2013, 751, emphasis added). Nonetheless, even this argument concedes that the Court in *Snyder v. Phelps* "suggested that statements on matters of purely private concern could lead to liability under the intentional infliction of emotional distress tort" (Volokh 2013, 783). Lower court decisions support the conclusion that the First Amendment does not bar imposition of liability for even one-to-many speech about a person on a purely private matter.[31]

(IV) INADEQUACY OF CIVIL REMEDIES

Before discussing the constitutionality of criminal sanctions for cyber harassment, it is important to briefly note some inherent limitations on the effectiveness of civil remedies to combat this behavior. First, for many victims of cyber harassment the cost of bringing a claim against the perpetrator will be prohibitive. Prosecuting such a lawsuit will ordinarily require paying for the services of a lawyer knowledgeable about cyber law, torts, and freedom of expression. Relatedly, even if the perpetrators of cyber harassment can be identified and held liable, they will often not have the resources to pay the judgment. In other contexts, the problem of a "judgment proof" speaker is mitigated because in most jurisdictions the publisher as well as the author of tortious speech is liable for damages caused by such expression. In the United States, however, federal law immunizes internet providers from liability as publishers or speakers.[32] For all these reasons, the availability of civil remedies for cyber harassment, properly confined by the First Amendment, is alone unlikely either to effectively deter such conduct or adequately redress the harm it causes.

4. Criminal Sanctions

(I) THREATS

A category of expression that both proponents of the All-Inclusive Approach and the Democratic Participation model agree is, and should be, beyond the scope of First Amendment protection is "true threats."[33] Speech falling within this category may therefore be criminally punished consistent with the First Amendment. But as the modifier "true" signifies, not all expression that in some sense is threatening to listeners is punishable. Like other categories of speech categorically beyond the scope of the First Amendment, "true threats" has been narrowly confined by the Supreme Court in order to provide breathing space for valuable expression.[34]

Regrettably, the Court has offered little specific guidance on how to distinguish true threats from protected speech (Rothman 2001, 288). Despite this doctrinal uncertainty, however, online expression remains unproblematically punishable in cases where the threat to kill or injure another is unequivocal.[35] In contrast, the statement on AutoAdmit that "[c]learly [Andrews] deserves to be raped" or even the email stating that "I hope someone slits your throat and cums down your gob," would, considered in isolation, probably not constitute a true threat under the Supreme Court's jurisprudence. If, however, such statements were combined, say, with a photograph of the bedroom window of the home of the subject, or with video of her driving her car into her garage, the totality of the expression might qualify as a true threat.

(II) INCITEMENT TO CRIMINAL ACTIVITY

Another type of expression that the Supreme Court has listed as categorically without First Amendment protection is incitement to unlawful activity.[36] Here, the Court has attempted to define with some precision the boundaries of this exception from First Amendment protection. "[T]he constitutional guarantees of free speech and free press," the Court declared in *Brandenburg v. Ohio*,[37] "do not permit a State to forbid or proscribe advocacy of the use of force or of law violation except where such advocacy is directed to inciting or producing imminent lawless action and is likely to incite or produce such action." The *Brandenburg* test, requiring both advocacy of imminent lawless action *and* the likelihood that such conduct will result, severely limits the government's ability to punish speech urging criminal activity.

A comment on a discussion board urging the other participants to attack another poster would usually not qualify either as advocating *imminent* lawless action or as likely to produce an attack, let alone to do so imminently. This does not mean, however, that all online speech advocating criminal activity is constitutionally immune from punishment.[38] It does mean though that the typical cyber-harassment rant expressing the view that someone should be raped or murdered cannot be punished consistent with the stringent limitations imposed by *Brandenburg*. The narrow confines imposed by the true threats and incitement standards thus raise the crucial question whether cyber harassment not falling within any of the categorical exceptions to First Amendment protection may constitutionally be punished.

(III) CRIMINAL PROHIBITION OF CYBER HARASSMENT

The federal anti-stalking law, 18 U.S.C. Section 2261A, makes it a crime for anyone "with the intent to . . . harass . . . another person" to use an interactive computer service "to engage in a course of conduct that . . . causes, attempts to cause, or would be reasonably expected to cause substantial emotional distress" to that person.[39] Several state laws similarly criminalize online harassment causing emotional distress.[40] As we have seen, criminal punishment can constitutionally be imposed for cyber harassment consisting of true threats or incitement to criminal conduct. Moreover, as was also discussed, the Supreme Court has strongly suggested that *civil* liability can constitutionally be imposed for cyber harassment constituting intentional infliction of emotional distress regarding a matter of purely private concern. The question raised by the federal anti-stalking law and similar state legislation is whether imposing *criminal* liability on a person for engaging in such expression similarly comports with the First Amendment.

In my view, if interpreted narrowly to apply only to speech on purely private concern, laws imposing criminal liability for cyber harassment are constitutional, even when applied to one-to-many speech (*contra* Volokh 2013: 783–86). In American jurisprudence, the key question is not the nature of the penalty imposed upon expression, but rather whether the speech in question is protected by the First Amendment. If protected, then the speech cannot be subjected to either civil or criminal penalties. Conversely, if it is constitutionally unprotected expression, then it can ordinarily be punished either civilly or criminally. For instance, the Supreme Court has held that unprotected defamation can constitutionally be subject to criminal as well as civil penalties.[41]

In deciding whether the First Amendment should offer protection against tort liability, the Court has inquired whether operation of the law in question provided adequate "breathing space" for the public discussion "essential to enlightened opinion and right conduct on the part of the citizens of a democracy."[42] The Court has thus interpreted the First Amendment to offer qualified immunity from tort liability for speech about public officials or public figures, or even about private individuals involving speech on matters of public concern.[43] In contrast, where tort law does not threaten to interfere with these values, which will ordinarily be the case with imposition of liability for harm caused by speech on matters of purely private concern, the Court has not imposed constraints on the ordinary operation of tort law.[44]

The Court has taken a similar approach towards First Amendment constraints on criminal law. Thus in limiting the operation of the law punishing threats against the President,[45] the Court explicitly adopted the prophylactic approach from *New York Times v. Sullivan*, explaining that "we must interpret the language Congress chose 'against the background of a profound national commitment to the principle that debate on public issues should be uninhibited, robust, and wide-open . . . .' "[46] In extending such protection to "political hyperbole" to protect First Amendment values, the Court made clear, however, that this did not prevent the punishment of "true threats."[47] Similarly, to protect First Amendment values, the Supreme Court has sharply curtailed the government's ability to outlaw sexually explicit material, by affording First Amendment protection to sexually graphic expression that, taken as a whole, has "serious literary, artistic, political, or scientific value."[48] Yet, the Court has afforded no First Amendment protection to "hard core" pornography lacking such value.[49] More recently, the Court held that it would be unconstitutional to impose either civil or criminal liability for publishing "truthful information of public concern" that had been illegally intercepted by someone other than the publisher.[50] In doing so, however, a majority of the justices indicated that such immunity would not have been available if the information published had been a matter of private concern.[51]

I suggest that a similar approach be taken with respect to cyber harassment laws. If the speech is on a matter of public concern, then statutes such as Section 2261A should be interpreted as not applying to harassment causing emotional distress. And if such a statute is interpreted to apply to such speech, then the application should be deemed to violate the First Amendment. By the same token, if the speech is on a matter of purely private concern, then there should ordinarily be no First Amendment immunity from criminal liability available to someone who with "the intent to . . . harass . . . another person" has engaged "in a course of conduct that . . . causes, attempts to cause, or would be reasonably expected to cause substantial emotional distress." Along with confinement to speech on purely private matters, the intent requirement and the requirement that the defendant has engaged in a "course of conduct"[52] should keep the application of this law within constitutional bounds.

What of the objection that the distinction between public and private concern, while "perhaps" acceptable for imposition of civil liability for intentional infliction of emotional distress (Volokh 2013, 788), is too vague to be used in criminal cases? I agree that in the civil context the "public concern/private concern line" has "never [been] defined clearly" and "has often been applied in surprising ways. . . ." (Volokh 2013, 785). But the appropriate solution to this problem is not to entirely disallow criminal prosecutions for all cyber harassment involving one-to-many speech that inflicts serious emotional distress. Rather, in accord with the description that the expression be "purely" of private concern, the better approach is to narrowly confine the type of speech which can be criminally prosecuted. Doing so would, for instance, bar imposition of criminal liability on a blogger for inflicting emotional distress on a feminist media critic for complaining about sexist stereotypes in video games.[53] At the same time, this approach would leave open the availability of criminal prosecution for expression whose suppression would not implicate any significant free speech values, as would usually be the case, for instance, in prosecutions for egregious cases of cyber harassment targeting former lovers.

(III) CRIMINAL CYBER HARASSMENT CASE LAW

The case law supports the view that the First Amendment bars the application of cyber harassment laws to speech on matters of public concern but not to speech on purely private matters. For instance, in *United States v. Cassidy*,[54] after being fired as an employee of a Buddhist sect, William Cassidy engaged in a barrage of often extremely vulgar, and in some instances threatening[55] statements on Twitter and his blog that viciously attacked Alyce Zeoli, a well-known and controversial leader of the sect. Based on this online expression, Cassidy was indicted under Section 2261A. The United States District Court found that application of Section 2261A to Cassidy violated the First Amendment and dismissed the indictment. Although agreeing that the tweets and blog posts may have inflicted substantial emotional distress to Zeoli, the court held the indictment was "directed squarely at protected speech: anonymous, uncomfortable Internet speech addressing religious matters." The court also observed that "Zeoli is not merely a private individual but rather an easily identifiable public figure that leads a religious sect and that many of the [Cassidy's] statements related to [the sect's] beliefs and [Zeoli's] qualifications as a leader." Citing *New York Times v. Sullivan*, the court then correctly concluded that this is "the type of expression that the Supreme Court has consistently tried to protect."[56] Other decisions similarly have found application of criminal harassment laws unconstitutional as applied to online speech on matters of public concern.[57]

In contrast, as exemplified in *United States v. Osinger*,[58] courts have consistently upheld the constitutionality of Section 2261A as applied to speech on matters of purely private concern. Christopher Osinger was involved in a nine-month relationship with V.B., which ended when V.B. discovered that Osinger was married. After V.B. moved out of the apartment they had shared, Osinger contacted V.B.'s sister-in-law and told her he still wanted to be with V.B. V.B. then telephoned Osinger because she "wanted him to stop looking for her family or friends, and she wanted to hear what he had to say." Osinger then came to V.B.'s new residence late at night on several occasions in an attempt at reconciliation, but V.B. did not answer when he knocked on the door and window. He also came to her place of work several times. After moving to another neighborhood to avoid his unwanted visits, V.B. eventually agreed to meet with Osinger. They reconciled briefly until V.B. discovered that the divorce papers Osinger had shown her were fraudulent and that he was seeing other women. V.B. told Osinger that she was not interested in continuing the relationship and moved in with her sister. Nevertheless, Osinger continued to call and to text V.B. And although she did not give him her sister's address, Osinger found it out and eventually came to her sister's house. V.B. again told him that she was not interested in continuing the relationship.[59]

After V.B. received a job offer in California, she informed Osinger that she was leaving Illinois but did not give him her address in California. Months after relocating and not hearing from Osinger, V.B. received a spate of text messages from Osinger that "started out with declarations of love, but . . . quickly turned nasty." And when V.B. made clear that she was not interested in giving Osinger another chance, "the messages took on a threatening tone," for example "am about to pull the rug rite under ur sexxy lil feet!!!"[60] Soon thereafter V.B. was informed by a friend about what appeared to him to be a fake Facebook account set up under V.B.'s name with sexually explicit pictures of V.B. and claims she wanted sex. V.B. recognized the photographs as ones that Osinger had taken of her during their relationship. Crying hysterically, V.B. called her supervisor for help in removing the Facebook page. The supervisor did so but informed V.B. that he had been contacted by another employee who had received an email at work through the company's webmail with many of these pictures. In addition, one of V.B.'s former co-workers in Chicago received a similar email.[61]

Based upon emails sent to V.B. and her co-workers and the postings on the fake Facebook page, Osinger was found guilty of engaging in a course of harassing conduct causing substantial emotional distress in violation of Section 2261A. Osinger appealed the conviction, claiming that this expression was protected by the First Amendment. Adopting the All-Inclusive Approach, the United States Court of Appeals for the Ninth Circuit explained that "[t]he First Amendment prohibits any law abridging the freedom of speech," with the exception of "some limited categories of unprotected speech" including the "speech integral to criminal conduct" exception. It then held that "[a] ny expressive aspects of Osinger's speech were not protected under the First Amendment because they were 'integral to criminal conduct' in intentionally harassing, intimidating or causing substantial emotional distress to V.B."[62]

A concurring opinion also relied on the "speech integral to criminal conduct" exception. It more forthrightly acknowledged, however, that Osinger's "text messages, emails, and Facebook page constitute speech that, considered in isolation, might have been entitled to First Amendment protection." The deciding factor for the concurring judge was that Osinger committed the offense by engaging in both speech and "unprotected non-speech conduct," namely, numerous in-person unwanted contacts, including knocking on her door or window late at night.[63]

The court was correct in concluding that the application of Section 2261A to Osinger's online expression did not violate the First Amendment. Unlike the prosecution of online harassment aimed at a well-known and controversial religious figure, punishment of Osinger's expression did not threaten any significant free speech value. It was very problematic, however, to reach this conclusion by invoking the "speech integral to criminal conduct" exception. Unfortunately, other decisions rejecting First Amendment challenges to Section 2261A have also taken this wrong turn.[64]

(IV) ESCHEWING THE "SPEECH INTEGRAL TO
CRIMINAL CONDUCT" EXCEPTION

The "speech integral to criminal conduct" exception has been condemned as "indeterminate, dangerous, and inconsistent with more recent cases" (Volokh 2005, 1285). This criticism is apt, for this exception would allow the government vast authority to punish speech that must be allowed in a free and democratic society. It would, for instance, justify punishing speech decrying the morality of a nation's war effort as expression "integral to the crime" of draft resistance if it could be shown that this expression led people to resist the draft.

What then should judges do when faced with a case like *Osinger* involving expression which they intuitively know should not be protected under a proper understanding of the First Amendment? One possibility is to try to uphold the application of the law under the "strict scrutiny" standard applicable to content regulation of protected speech. The Supreme Court, however, has rarely found a speech regulation to pass this extremely rigorous test, and for this reason lower courts wanting to uphold applications of cyber harassment laws will correctly want to avoid this standard of review. The better approach, in my view, is for courts to look to the Supreme Court's decisions regarding sexual harassment in the workplace.

As the concurring judge in *Osinger* correctly noted, "there is no categorical exception to the First Amendment for harassing . . . speech."[65] Yet, on two occasions the Supreme Court has held that "discriminatory intimidation, ridicule, and insult" can violate Title VII of the Civil Rights Act of 1964, if "sufficiently severe or pervasive to alter the conditions of the victim's employment and create an abusive working environment."[66] While the Court did not in either of these cases expressly hold that this restriction on harassing workplace speech is consistent with the First Amendment, there can be little doubt that the Court formulated this standard to comport with the First Amendment.[67] In this regard, it is noteworthy that no opinion in either case suggests that this standard affronts the First Amendment.

To be sure, Section 2261A is a criminal prohibition that can have a significantly greater "chilling" effect on speech than does the civil liability Title VII imposes. In addition, the internet is an essential medium for democratic communication in a way that the workplace is not. For these reasons, I am not suggesting that the Court's standard for what constitutes actionable workplace harassment is a good guide to the specific limitations that courts should impose on the application of criminal bans on cyber harassment. To the contrary, First Amendment constraints on the application of criminal cyber harassment laws should be more extensive than those limiting bans on sexual harassment in the workplace. Still, the Court's decisions on sexual harassment in the workplace show that despite the All-Inclusive Approach mythology, bans on harassing speech can comport with the First Amendment if properly confined. In accord with these decisions, lower courts faced with First Amendment challenges to cyber harassment laws should similarly eschew trying to force these laws into some First Amendment "exception" and instead construe these laws to cohere with free speech values.

5. Conclusion

In a recent case striking down a North Carolina law imposing extensive restrictions on registered sex offenders' ability to legally access commercial websites, the Supreme Court declared that cyberspace was now the "most important place[] . . . for the exchange of ideas." At the same time, the Court also recognized that "advances in human progress have been exploited by the criminal mind . . . to commit serious crimes" and that "[s]o it will be with the Internet and social media."[68] This observation neatly underscores the challenge to combating cyber harassment in a way consistent with the basic liberal democratic commitment to free speech: how, on the one hand, to prohibit online expression intended to inflict substantial emotional distress on an individual, without, on the other hand, impairing people's ability to "debate religion or politics with their friends and neighbors," or "petition their elected representatives."[69]

In this chapter I have suggested that the basic criterion for properly drawing the line online between protected speech and expression which may constitutionally form the basis of liability for cyber harassment is whether the speech at issue is on a matter of public or private concern. To mitigate any chilling effect from the uncertainty that might otherwise exist in applying such a standard, I suggest that courts, especially in criminal cases, tightly confine the category of actionable expression to matters of *purely* private concern, such as the speech typically involved in the all too frequent cyber harassment of a former romantic partner. Combined with the requirement of most criminal prohibitions that the defendant have engaged in a course of conduct intended to inflict emotional distress, limiting punishment to expression on matters of purely private concern would allow punishment of the most egregious cases of cyber harassment while safeguarding the proper functioning of the "vast democratic forums of the Internet."[70]

Notes

1. Expression on the internet is not entirely unmediated. Social media (e.g., Facebook, Instagram, Twitter, YouTube) and search engines (e.g., Google, AOL, Bing, Yahoo) have the ability to control the content of speech and to some extent do so. However, they have little incentive to regulate the content they host (Leiter 2016, 166). In the United States, the

most significant disincentive is s 230 of the Communications Decency Act, which insulates intermediaries from liability for any content that they host on their websites.

2. Reno v. ACLU, 521 U.S. 844, 868 (1997).

3. See, e.g., Arkansas Writers' Project, Inc. v. Ragland, 481 U.S. 221, 229 (1987); Hudgens v. NLRB, 424 U.S. 507, 520 (1976); Erznoznik v. City of Jacksonville, 422 U.S. 205, 215 (1975), quoting Police Dept. of City of Chicago v. Mosley, 408 U.S. 92, 95 (1972).

4. See, e.g., Ward v. Rock Against Racism, 491 U.S. 781 (1989).

5. United States v. Alvarez, 567 U.S. 709, 731 (2012) (Breyer, J., concurring).

6. See, e.g., *Alvarez*, 547 U.S. at 717 (plurality opinion); United States v. Stevens, 559 U.S. 460, 468 (2010); R.A.V. v. City of St. Paul, 505 U.S. 377, 383 (1992).

7. See, e.g., Cohen v. California, 403 U.S. 15, 22 (1971).

8. 562 U.S. 443 (2011).

9. *Snyder*, 562 U.S. at 448–50.

10. *Snyder*, 562 U.S. at 451–53.

11. *Snyder*, 562 U.S. at 456–59.

12. *Snyder*, 562 U.S. at 452. Supporting the suggestion in *Snyder* that the First Amendment would permit recovery for intentional infliction of emotional distress caused by speech on matters of purely private concern, the Court has on several occasions declined to provide protection for speech on matters of private concern while doing so for expression of the same ilk on matters of public concern. See Weinstein (2011, 494–95).

13. *Synder*, 562 U.S. at 455, quoting United States v. Grace, 461 U. S. 171, 180 (1983).

14. See, e.g., Packingham v. North Carolina, 137 S. Ct. 1730, 1735-36 (2017); Reno v. ACLU, 521 U.S. 844, 868 (1997).

15. See Mills v. Alabama, 384 U.S. 214, 218 (1966); Stromberg v. California, 283 U.S. 359, 369 (1931). Other contenders as a core norm include search for truth and individual autonomy (Sullivan and Feldman 2016, 935–40).

16. Globe Newspaper Co. v. Superior Court, 457 U.S. 596, 604 (1982). This view was famously expounded by Alexander Meiklejohn (1948, 25).

17. See note 6, *supra*.

18. New York Times Co. v. Sullivan, 376 U.S. 254 (1964).

19. *New York Times Co.*, 376 U.S. at 270.

20. Gertz v. Robert Welch, Inc., 418 U.S. 323 (1974).

21. See Dun & Bradstreet, Inc. v. Greenmoss Builders, Inc., 472 U.S. 749, 760–61 (1985) (plurality opinion); *Greenmoss Builders*, 472 U.S. at 764 (Burger, C.J., concurring in judgment); *Greenmoss Builders*, 472 U.S. at 774 (White, J., concurring in judgment). See also Phila. Newspapers v. Hepps, 475 U.S. 767, 775 (1986); Snead v. Redlands Aggregates Ltd., 998 F.2d 1325, 1333 (5th Cir. 1993); Ross v. Bricker, 770 F. Supp. 1038 (D.VI. 1991).

22. RESTATEMENT (SECOND) OF TORTS, § 652 D (AM. LAW INST. 1977).

23. See generally Bartnicki v. Vopper, 532 U.S. 514 (2001).

24. See United States v. Petrovic, 701 F.3d 849, 855–56 (8th Cir. 2012).

25. Florida Star v. B.J.F., 491 U.S. 524 (1989); Smith v. Daily Mail Publ'g Co., 443 U.S. 97 (1979); Oklahoma Publ'g Co. v. Dist. Court in & for Okla. Cty., 430 U.S. 308 (1977); Cox Broad. Corp. v. Cohn, 420 U.S. 469 (1975).

26. *Florida Star*, 491 U.S. at 524.

27. *Florida Star*, 491 U.S. at 524.

28. *Petrovic*, 701 F.3d at 855, *quoting* Coplin v. Fairfield Pub. Access Television Comm., 111 F.3d 1395, 1404 (8th Cir. 1977).

29. While typical of the speech constituting cyber harassment of women, lurid sexual expression is of course not the only type of expression that can inflict severe emotional distress on its victims.

30. RESTATEMENT (SECOND) OF TORTS, §46 (AM. LAW INST. 1977).

31. See, e.g., Armstrong v. Shirvell, 596 F. App'x 433, 453 (6th Cir. 2015); Esposito-Hilder v. SFX Broad., 236 A.D.2d 186, 191 (N.Y. App. Div. 1997).

32. Communications Decency Act 1996 (47 U.S.C. § 230). See the chapter by Mary Anne Franks in this volume.

33. See Virginia v. Black, 538 U. S. 343, 359–60 (2003); R. A. V. v. St. Paul, 505 U. S. 377, 388 (1992). Threats in interstate or foreign commerce on proscribed by 18 U.S.C. § 875 (2012). Online threats are specifically addressed in 18 U.S.C. §2261A(2)(A) (2015).

34. United States v. Watts, 394 U.S. 705, 706, 708 (1969); NAACP v. Claiborne Hardware, 458 U.S. 886, 902, 928, n.71 citing *Watts* (1982).

35. See, e.g., People v. Chase, 2013 WL 979519 (2013).

36. See, e.g., United States v. Stevens, 559 U.S. 460 (2010).

37. 395 U.S. 444, 447 (1969).

38. See, e.g., Planned Parenthood of the Columbia/Willamette, Inc. v. Am. Coalition of Life Activists, 290 F.3d 1058 (9th Cir. 2002).

39. 18 U.S. Code § 2261A(2)(B) (2015). "Course of conduct" is defined as "a pattern of conduct composed of 2 or more acts, evidencing a continuity of purpose." § 2266 (2).

40. See, e.g., N.J. Stat. Ann. § 2C:33-4.1 (West 2014). A.R.S. § 13-2921 (2008) (harassment); Md. Code Ann., Crim. Law § 3-805 (2013) (misuse of electronic mail); 2017 Oregon Laws Ch. 430 (H.B. 2988) (harassment) (Hazelwood and Koon-Magnin 2013: 160).

41. See Garrison v. Louisiana, 379 U.S. 64 (1964).

42. New York Times v. Sullivan, 376 U.S. 254, 271–72 (1964).

43. See *New York Times*, 376 U.S. at 271–72; Curtis Publ'g Co. v. Butts, 388 U.S. 130 (1967); Hustler Magazine, Inc. v. Falwell, 485 U.S. 46 (1988); Gertz v. Robert Welch, Inc., 418 U.S. 323, 346 (1974); Snyder v. Phelps, 562 U.S. 443 (2011). See also note 12, *supra*.

44. See Dun & Bradstreet, Inc. v. Greenmoss Builders, Inc., 472 U.S. 749, 759, 763 (1985); *Snyder*, 562 U.S. at 452 (dicta). See also Phila. Newspapers v. Hepps, 475 U.S. 767, 775 (1986).

45. See Watts v. United States, 394 U.S. 705 (1969).

46. *Watts*, 394 U.S. at 708, *quoting* New York Times v. Sullivan Co., 376 U. S. 254, 270 (1964).

47. *Watts*, 394 U.S. at 708, *quoting* New York Times v. Sullivan Co., 376 U. S. 254, 270 (1964).

48. Miller v. California, 413 U.S. 15, 24 (1973).

49. *Miller*, 314 U.S. at 27.

50. Bartnicki v. Vopper, 532 U.S. 514 (2001).

51. *Bartnicki*, 532 U.S. at 535–36 (Breyer, J., concurring, joined by O'Connor, J.) (emphasizing that the "narrow" holding that he joined involved "a matter of unusual public concern"); *Bartnicki*, 532 U.S at 541. (Rehnquist, C.J., dissenting joined by Thomas and Scalia, J.J.)

52. *Supra* note 39.

53. https://en.wikipedia.org/wiki/Anita_Sarkeesian.

54. 814 F. Supp. 2d. 574 (D. Md. 2011).

55. The court noted that although "true threats" are not protected speech, the government did not seek an indictment under the portion of the federal anti-stalking law dealing with threats (see note 33, *supra*) but rather under the provisions dealing with emotional distress. *Cassidy*, 814 F. Supp. at 583 n.11.

56. *Cassidy*, 814 F. Supp. at 583, 586.

57. See, e.g., Publius v. Boyer-Vine, 237 F. Supp. 3d 997, 1005 (E.D. Cal. 2017).

58. 753 F.3d 939 (9th Cir. 2014).

59. *Osinger*, 753 F.3d at 941–42, 951–52 (Watford, J., concurring).

60. *Osinger*, 753 F.3d at 952 (Watford, J., concurring).

61. *Osinger*, 753 F.3d at 952 (Watford, J., concurring).

62. *Osinger*, 753 F.3d at 947.

63. *Osinger*, 753 F.3d at 953.

64. See, e.g., United States v. Petrovic, 701 F.3d 849, 854–55 (8th Cir. 2012).

65. *Osinger*, 753 F.3d at 953 (Watford, J., concurring).

66. Harris v. Forklift Sys. Inc., 510 U.S. 17, 21 (1993), *quoting* Meritor Savings Bank v. Vinson, 477 U.S. 57, 65 (1986).

67. "After *Harris*, . . . it is virtually inconceivable that the Supreme Court might hold that the First Amendment forbids the imposition of Title VII liability for a broad category of sexually harassing speech." (Fallon 1994:14)

68. Packingham v. North Carolina, 137 S. Ct. 1730, 1736 (2017).

69. *Packingham*, 137 S. Ct. at 1735–36.

70. Reno v. ACLU, 521 U.S. 844, 868 (1997).

References

Baker, E. C. 2011. "Autonomy and Free Speech." *Constitutional Commentary* 27: 251–82.

Citron, D. K. 2009a. "Cyber Civil Rights." *Boston University Law Review* 89: 61–125.

Citron, D. K. 2009b. "Law's Expressive Value in Combating Cyber Gender Harassment." *Michigan Law Review* 108: 373–415.

Citron, D. K. 2014. *Hate Crimes in Cyberspace*. Cambridge, MA: Harvard University Press.

Fallon, R. H. 1994. "Sexual Harassment, Content Neutrality, and the First Amendment Dog That Didn't Bark." *The Supreme Court Review*, 1–56. doi:10.1086/scr.1994.3109644.

Franks, M. A. 2012. "Sexual Harassment 2.0." *Maryland Law Review*, 71: 655–704.

Hazelwood, S. D. and S. Koon-Magnin. 2013. "Cyber Stalking and Cyber Harassment Legislation in the United States: A Qualitative Analysis." *International Journal of Cyber Criminology* 7: 155–68.

Hua, W. 2017. "Cybermobs, Civil Conspiracy, and Tort Liability." *Fordham Urban Law Journal* 44: 1217–66.

Leiter, B. 2016. "The Case against Free Speech." *Sydney Law Review* 38: 407–39.

Lidsky, L. B. 2011. "Incendiary Speech and Social Media." *Texas Tech Law Journal* 44 (1): 1–18.

Lipton, J. D. 2011. "Combating Cyber-Victimization." *Berkeley Technology Law Review* 26 (2): 1103–56.

McAllister, J. M. 2017. "The Doxing Dilemma: Seeking a Remedy for the Malicious Publication of Personal Information." *Fordham Law Review* 85: 2451–83.

McDonald, B. P. 2005. "Government Regulation or Other 'Abridgments' of Scientific Research: The Proper Scope of Judicial Review under the First Amendment." *Emory Law Journal* 54: 979–1092.

McIntyre, V. 2016. "Do(x) You Really Want to Hurt Me?: Adapting IIED as a Solution to Doxing by Reshaping Intent." *Tulane Journal of Technology & Intellectual Property* 19: 111–34.

Meiklejohn, A. 1948. *Free Speech and Its Relation to Self-Government*. New York: Harper.

Nowak, J. E. and Rotunda, D. 2004. *Constitutional Law*. 7th ed. St. Paul, MN: Thomson/West.

Post, R. C. 1990. "The Constitutional Concept of Public Discourse: Outrageous Opinion, Democratic Deliberation, and *Hustler Magazine v. Falwell*." *Harvard Law Review* 103: 601–86.

Post, R. C. 1995. "Recuperating the First Amendment Doctrine." *Stanford Law Review* 47: 1249–81.

Post, R. C. 2017. "Legitimacy and Hate Speech." *Constitutional Commentary* 32: 651–59.

Rothman, J. 2001. "Freedom of Speech and True Threats." *Harvard Journal of Law and Public Policy* 25: 283–367.

Scanlon, T. 1972. "A Theory of Freedom of Expression." *Philosophy and Public Affairs* 1: 204–26.

Schauer, F. 2003. "The Boundaries of the First Amendment: A Preliminary Exploration of Constitutional Salience." *Harvard Law Review* 117: 1765–809.

Sullivan, K. and N. Feldman. 2016. *Constitutional Law*. 19th ed. St. Paul, MN: Foundation Press.

Sweeney, J. 2017. "Trapped in Public: The Regulation of Street Harassment and Cyber-Harassment under the Captive Audience Doctrine." *Nevada Law Journal* 17: 651–66.

Volokh, E. 2005. "Speech as Conduct: Generally Applicable Laws, Illegal Courses of Conduct, Situation-Altering Utterances, and the Uncharted Zones." *Cornell Law Review* 90: 1277–348.

Volokh, E. 2013. "One-to-One Speech vs. One-to-Many Speech, Criminal Harassment Laws, and 'Cyber-Stalking.'" *Northwestern University Law Review* 107: 731–94.

Weinstein, J. 2007. "Democracy, Sex and the First Amendment." *New York University Review of Law & Social Change* 31: 865–98.

Weinstein, J. 2011a. "Participatory Democracy as the Central Value of American Free Speech Doctrine." *Virginia Law Review* 97: 491–514.

Weinstein, J. 2011b. "Participatory Democracy as the Basis of American Free Speech Doctrine: A Reply." *Virginia Law Review* 97: 633–80.

Weinstein, J. 2004. "Speech Categorization and the Limits of First Amendment Formalism: Lessons from *Nike v. Kasky*." *Case Western Reserve Law Review* 54(4): 1091–142.

Weinstein, J. 2017. "Hate Speech Bans, Democracy, and Political Legitimacy." *Constitutional Commentary* 32: 527–83.

4

Recipes, Plans, Instructions, and the Free Speech Implications of Words That Are Tools

Frederick Schauer*

1. Introduction

Jay tells Stanley that it is imperative that the tools of capitalist imperialism be destroyed. Nikki tells Stanley that he ought to rob the First National Bank on Main Street as a blow against capitalist fascism. Barbara, who works at the First National Bank, tells Stanley that she has seen the night schedule for the bank guards, and it shows that there is a shift change at 2 a.m., often producing a five-minute interval during which no guard is on duty. And Betty, who is an electronics engineer, gives Stanley a twenty-seven character alphanumeric code, accompanied by the advice that if he transmits this number in a certain way on a certain frequency with a certain device, the bank's electronic security system will be disabled for two hours.

In this scenario Jay, Nikki, Barbara, and Betty have each committed speech acts, and they have done nothing else. That is, none of them have engaged in any physical behavior other than that necessary to utter words—to speak. But although the acts in which they are engaged are all speech acts, they are speech acts of different types. In this collection of speech acts we see urging, advising, recommending, instructing, and informing, among others. The question I address here is whether all of these speech acts should be treated in the same way for purposes of implementing a principle of freedom of speech, and, if not, then why not. More specifically, should instructing and informing occupy a different category from urging, advising, and recommending? And if

---

* David and Mary Harrison Distinguished Professor of Law, University of Virginia. This chapter was prepared for presentation to the Department of Philosophy, Dartmouth College, on April 18, 2015, in connection with the conference on Global Expressive Rights and the Internet.

the answer to that question is in the affirmative, how do we explain the difference? Is it that instructing and informing are more causally efficacious than advising, urging, and recommending in producing some socially detrimental consequence— here, bank robbery? Or is there a deeper difference, such that the contingent and non-universal causal superiority of informing and instructing is of less importance, or at least of less free speech importance, than something about the very nature of the speech acts in the two categories?

This is the problem I seek to address in this chapter. The problem is, arguably, more pressing than it has been in the past, as the internet and various forms of social media have seemingly facilitated the mass distribution of instructions for committing antisocial acts, or have helped to propagate the factual information that will assist in the commission of such acts. Anyone who can search the internet and not find instructions for blowing up a building or a railroad station is simply not looking hard enough. But the problem is not new, as I shall show, even if its manifestation in the internet age is now more widespread and its consequences accordingly more grave. And even thinking about whether it is a problem at all, and what kind of a problem it is, will take us into some potentially new domains for thinking about freedom of speech[1] more generally.[2]

2. Three Examples

In a 1972 article of enduring philosophical importance,[3] T. M. Scanlon asked his readers, almost as an aside to his main argument, to imagine the publication of instructions that would enable an individual to manufacture nerve gas in his kitchen using only a mixture of gasoline, urine, and table salt (Scanlon 1972, 211). Scanlon took it as self-evident that such speech would not be protected even under the extremely strong free speech principle he was advocating, but he was unclear about the reasoning behind that conclusion. Is it that the potential harm is so obvious (and so likely) that it should override the force of even an extremely strong but non-absolute free speech principle? Or is it that an instruction or recipe of this type is different in kind from the type of normative argument that Scanlon sought to protect, such that the nerve gas recipe was not even covered by the principle at all?[4] We cannot be sure what Scanlon had in mind, and although his imagination and prescience should be applauded, his example goes only so far in helping us to deal with such problems in today's world.

Seven years after Scanlon published his article, the left-of-center and militantly antiwar magazine *The Progressive* obtained and made arrangements to publish the plans and instructions for manufacturing a hydrogen bomb.[5] Having been informed of *The Progressive*'s intentions, the United States sought and obtained an injunction against publication, with the trial judge agreeing with the government that the nature of the potential danger was so great that this potential publication represented one of the extraordinarily rare instances in which a prior restraint on a publication would be allowed.[6] And although the United States discontinued the action after it became clear that much of the information was available in the nonclassified public domain,[7] the events present a remarkably clear real world example, and one whose importance is plainly magnified in the era of the internet, of what Scanlon had imagined to be purely hypothetical.

A third example is presented by a case involving a publisher named Paladin Enterprises, which in 1983 published a book entitled *Hit Man: A Technical Manual for Independent Contractors*, and another with the title *How to Make a Disposable Silencer*. Between them, the two books provided their readers with more than one hundred pages of detailed information and instructions about how to embark on a career as a contract killer, and even more detail about how the reader should perform the killings in order to assure maximum effectiveness and minimize the likelihood of apprehension. In 1992, a man named James Earl Perry, who had purchased and read both books, murdered Mildred Horn; her disabled child, Trevor; and the child's nurse, Janice Saunders. Perry had been hired by Horn's estranged husband Lawrence Horn to commit the murders, largely with the goal of securing for himself the two-million dollar insurance settlement that the accident that produced Trevor's disability had produced. And having secured the "contract" largely in the manner explicitly recommended by the book, Perry then committed the murders in more or less exact compliance with the instructions in the two books. Perry was apprehended, convicted of murder, convicted again on retrial after a successful appeal, and subsequently died in prison in 2010 while serving three life sentences. Lawrence Horn was also convicted of murder, similarly sentenced, and remains in prison to this day.

Although Perry and Horn were convicted of murder, the victims' families brought a civil lawsuit against Paladin Press, seeking to hold it jointly accountable for Perry's act in accordance with more or less standard tort law principles of causation. Against Paladin's First Amendment defense, which was accepted on a motion to dismiss at the trial level,[8] the United States Court of Appeals for the Fourth Circuit allowed the case to go forward,[9] after which it was settled on undisclosed terms prior to trial.[10]

These three examples, and I shall add additional ones presently, offer a series of vivid illustrations of the way in which, increasingly, free speech controversies and litigation involve publications whose argued liability to restriction stems not from advocacy or argument, nor from harm or offense to viewers or readers, but rather from the publication of instructions and plans in sufficient detail to facilitate a reader or user in using those instructions and plans to commit crimes in ways that, it is argued, would otherwise have been beyond the knowledge or the abilities of the ultimate perpetrator. This is the issue I address here, and this is the issue that these three examples present so clearly.

3. Just Enough History

The modern history of freedom of speech is substantially a history of advocacy. Advocacy is not the entire story, of course. There is a long history of censorship of books, magazines, and movies, among other media, on grounds of their alleged immorality, indecency, or obscenity, and a not insignificant amount of free speech law and theory has developed in response to this history.[11] Other dimensions of free speech law and theory have been focused on the question of insults and other uses of language whose very hearing (or reading) causes pain, anguish, psychic harm, and related forms of distress.[12] And still other issues have persistently arisen in the context of defamation and privacy, where the harms are harms that arise from the ways in which others think about us or from the things that others know about us.[13]

But although all of these topics are important ones in the history, the law, and the theory of free speech, much of that history, law, and theory has been about the use of language (or pictures, symbols, etc.) that is alleged to have a causal effect on the likelihood of commission of some act that is considered wrong or otherwise regulable in its own right. Thus, when I say that much of the history of free speech is a history of advocacy, I am referring to issues arising out of the explicit or implicit advocacy (which includes glorification, even when unaccompanied by specifically prescriptive language) of revolution,[14] murder,[15] sexual violence,[16] resistance to conscription,[17] racial violence, and racial discrimination,[18] and many other acts whose ontology is analytically distinct from the question of which preliminary or causal or preparatory acts might increase the likelihood that such subsequent acts will occur.

Not all such preliminary, preparatory, or causal acts are speech acts. Indeed, most are not, and thus it is not surprising that those who provide guns to murderers, explosives to safecrackers, and alcohol to inebriated drivers are sometimes held criminally or civilly liable along with the ultimate perpetrators for the acts that those perpetrators have committed, but which the preparatory or preliminary acts have in some way facilitated.[19] But sometimes such preliminary acts are acts of speech—they are speech acts that will in the same or analogous ways plausibly increase the likelihood that the subsequent unlawful acts will ensue. When that is the case, much of free speech thinking has been about the standards to be applied when *A* urges—explicitly or implicitly—that *B* engage in such an illegal and antisocial act. The formative American free speech cases of the 1910s and 1920s were about people who advocated draft resistance or advocated revolution,[20] and the ensuing landmarks of the American free speech tradition were again about advocates of revolution, as well as advocates of racial and other forms of violence.[21]

In all of these cases, as well as many more of the same variety in the lower courts, the question was about the causal relationship between A's advocacy and B's potential crime. When Oliver Wendell Holmes memorably (mis)applied the "clear and present danger" standard to such utterances,[22] he is best understood as having held that, although in the normal course the government is free to deal with perceived dangers that are speculative and possibly remote,[23] when the object of control is speech, speculative and remote dangers are insufficient to justify the control, with "clear" being understood as in contrast to speculative and "present" as in contrast to remote or distant.

A similar focus on likelihood is present even when the standards are more relaxed. The now rejected idea of regulation under the so-called "bad tendency" test[24] lowers the necessary temporal and probabilistic connection between the advocacy and the advocated act, and the (possibly) also rejected idea of the "gravity of the evil discounted by its improbability"[25] is another articulation of the standard to be applied to the same relationship. But even under such lower thresholds, the basic idea is one of attempting to specify the necessary relationship between the existence of a speech act and some subsequent non-speech danger, consequence, or crime allegedly assisted or caused (in the probabilistic sense of causation) by the speech act.

Under current American law, the connection between the advocacy and the occurrence must be especially close. As articulated in *Brandenburg v. Ohio* in 1969,[26] advocacy of unlawful acts cannot be prohibited unless the advocacy explicitly urges the unlawful acts, unless the advocacy urges that those unlawful acts are to be committed imminently, and unless it is actually likely that the unlawful acts will occur imminently because of the advocacy. As a result, not only is non-explicit advocacy (as in Marc Antony's oration over the body of Caesar) constitutionally protected, but so too is explicit advocacy in which what is advocated is illegality to occur at some uncertain future time. To urge in general that police officers be killed, or that public buildings be bombed, is, under current American law, constitutionally protected. And although the purpose of this chapter is not to provide an exposition of American constitutional doctrine, and although the standards in much of the rest of the world are somewhat more relaxed, the basic idea is the same—accepting a principle of freedom of speech entails accepting that advocacy of unlawful acts is to be protected unless the causal connection between the advocacy and the acts satisfies a higher standard than that which would otherwise be applied to preliminary or preparatory non-speech acts alleged to have a causal relationship to subsequent criminal behavior.

4. Are Facts Different?

Consider again Scanlon's example of publishing the recipe for manufacturing nerve gas in a household kitchen from gasoline, urine, and table salt.[27] Scanlon takes it as plain that such an act would be punishable even under a strong free speech principle, and he says that this is because that act would cause a "drastic" decrease in personal safety by "radically increasing" the likelihood that such an act would ensue, such that distribution of the recipe should be considered akin to actually selling the nerve gas in an aerosol can.

But what is it that leads Scanlon to believe that such a "radical" or "drastic" increase in the act would occur? After all, my kitchen is full of recipes that have yet to produce finished (or even started) dishes. So why should a recipe for nerve gas be very much different? Compare, for example, John Stuart Mill's famous example of telling an angry mob in front of the house of a corn dealer that corn dealers are starvers of the poor (Mill [1859] 2001, 52–53). Like Scanlon, Mill took the example to represent an obvious limiting example, but Mill's example is different from Scanlon's. As most plausibly understood, Mill's example is not one that involves a speaker who provides previously unknown facts to his listeners. One strongly suspects that the angry mob in front of the corn dealer's house is composed of people already predisposed to dislike corn dealers. Rather, Mill's example appears to be one of advocacy, although it is the extreme form of advocacy that we tend to refer to as "incitement." Still, Mill appears to believe that this variety of advocacy can, under certain circumstances of preexisting audience ire,[28] be so certain (or at least highly likely) to cause unlawful acts that it should be excluded from his protection of the liberty of thought and discussion. And Scanlon believes that providing instructions of a certain kind can produce the same consequences. The question, then, is about precisely which dimensions or components of the two scenarios produce the probabilistic and temporal increase that for both Scanlon and Mill justify restriction even in the face of a strong free speech principle. And, more particularly, is there something about providing instructions, plans, recipes, or facts that has an effect that is different from pure advocacy, such that we can attribute to instructions, plans, recipes, and facts a degree of causality not present in mere advocacy? Scanlon, after all, did not include in his example anything about the susceptibility or proximity of the audience, and thus it appears that he attributes the causal increase in the likelihood of the recipe producing nerve gas proliferation to the power of the facts and the instructions, and not, as Mill did, to the particular circumstances and susceptibility of the audience.

In considering these questions, three other well-known examples may be of some assistance. First is a case from the state courts of California called *Olivia N. v. National Broadcasting Co.*[29] The case arose out of a made-for-television film entitled *Born Innocent*, which centered around a rape of a teenage girl by a group of girls in a group home, the rape being committed in a particularly gruesome manner with the use of a household plunger—a plumber's helper.[30] Shortly thereafter a nine-year-old girl was raped by a group of teenage boys who had earlier discussed the film among themselves, the rape bearing a strong similarity, although different in some respects,[31] to the one portrayed on television. The victim proceeded to sue the National Broadcasting Company, arguing that NBC was responsible for having caused the rape. The trial judge granted a motion to dismiss, and the appellate court upheld the dismissal on the ground that the strong free speech protections applicable to advocacy (specifically, *Brandenburg v. Ohio*[32]) controlled the case. In the view of both the trial and appellate courts, the absence of explicit advocacy, as well as the lack of imminence and likelihood, made imposing liability on NBC constitutionally impermissible no matter how foreseeable, on the basis of social science evidence, the ensuing event was, and no matter therefore how much NBC should reasonably have expected such consequences to ensue as a result of the broadcast.

Somewhat similar is a slightly more recent case of the same vintage—*Herceg v. Hustler Magazine, Inc.*[33] This case arose out of *Hustler's* publication of an article dealing with autoerotic asphyxiation, accompanied by the standard (and numerous) "Do not attempt" and "Don't try this at home" warnings. A fourteen-year-old boy did try it at home, and was found dead by hanging, with a copy of the magazine, open to the aforesaid article, lying below his feet. As in *Olivia N.*, a civil lawsuit[34] against the publisher ensued, and again an appellate court—the United States Court of Appeals for the Fifth Circuit—reversed a jury verdict of $169,000, again holding that no amount of foreseeability and no amount of negligence under common law tort standards could counteract the absence of intent by the publisher that such an event actually take place, as well as the absence of any explicit words of advocacy of imminent lawless action.

Finally, consider the issues involved in a website called *The Nuremburg Files*, which listed the names, addresses, and telephone numbers of abortion providers, accompanied by the not-very-veiled suggestion that it would be good if those providers were to wind up dead. The actual court case arising out of the website turned heavily on the issue whether the website could be considered a "true threat," which implicates a different category of First Amendment analysis,[35] but the court's conclusion also turned on the view that the detail of the facts on the website contributed heavily to a finding that subsequent violence was both imminent and likely.

The *Nuremburg Files* example is especially important, because the appearance of the information on a website, as opposed to in a book, a magazine, or even on television, increases exponentially the number of likely recipients of the information, and increases as well the duration of the information's availability. But even without the difference in degree, if not in kind, brought about by the internet, it is still the case that many of the foregoing examples focus on a common question: Is there a degree of factual detail and/or detailed instructional content that moves these cases into a different category from that occupied by the largely fact-free and instruction-free normative argument or pure prescription that has dominated the legal and philosophical history of freedom of speech? Neither Charles Schenck nor Benjamin Spock[36] offered any instructions on how the targets of their urgings might actually go about resisting the draft, or about how they might avoid apprehension once having resisted. Nor did those who have advocated communist or socialist or anarchist revolution typically provide any detail or concrete advice about how actually to go about launching such a revolution or even about what the post-revolutionary state would look like. All that the defendants have done in these and other cases is to have told people what they ought to do, but they have not told people how to do it.

To the extent that there is a difference between the six cases I have described, on the one hand, and the more traditional advocacy cases that inspire standard free speech rhetoric and doctrine, on the other, there are a number of hypotheses that might explain the difference. First, consider the cases in which the hearers or readers might plausibly be understood as not having been particularly predisposed to commit the crimes they turned out to commit. It is unlikely, for example, that the deceased fourteen-year-old in *Herceg* had ever even *heard* of autoerotic asphyxiation, let alone thought about engaging in it. And although I do not wish to underestimate the general receptiveness of adolescent males to all things sexual, nor their proclivity to risk-taking compared to other population groups, it is at least plausible that the *Hustler* article was, to use the language of tort law, the "but for" cause of his asphyxiation. Moreover, it is also plausible that had the same boy simply read about the practice but with less detail and no instructions, he might have been titillated but no more. Indeed, it is also plausible that even an article strongly recommending autoerotic asphyxiation, if unaccompanied by instructions or detail, would again have produced some interest and titillation but probably nothing in the way of actual action.

So too with the rape of Olivia N. Again, it is hardly controversial that teenage boys in packs are more likely than a randomly selected group of the population to commit dangerous (to themselves and others), abusive, and illegal acts. But it is unlikely that, absent the television film, this group of boys would have committed an act this abusive, this violent, or this appalling. And it is possible that even diffuse advocacy of sexual assault on minors, but without this degree of specificity of target or method, would have produced far less of an increase in the likelihood of an act of this type.

At least one hypothesis is thus before us: It can be hypothesized that the link between words and action, for a generally susceptible audience, will be substantially greater when the words provide instructions, and substantially greater when the words give explicit examples of possible subsequent acts, and substantially greater still when the two are combined—when detailed instructions are conjoined with detailed or concrete descriptions of possible outcomes. And the stronger hypothesis, over a large range of events, is that, especially for a generally susceptible audience, instructional content and factual detail will generally produce more of an increase in causal likelihood than will non-instructional advocacy of acts of a certain broad type, but without factual detail about specific acts falling within that type. Thus, an interesting aspect of *Brandenburg v. Ohio*[37] is that there is no indication that any of the Ku Klux Klan members who comprised Clarence Brandenburg's audience when he urged acts of "revengeance" against African Americans[38] and Jews actually committed such acts, at least not in any way attributable to Brandenburg's advocacy. The question, and it is only a question, is whether some such acts would have been committed had Brandenburg given this plainly predisposed[39] audience instructions on how to commit such acts or concrete examples of the kinds of acts he had in mind. The court dealing with the *Nuremburg Files* situation plainly thought that the answer to a question of this type was in the affirmative, for here the detail and the implicit instructions were plainly directed at an audience likely already predisposed to committing acts of the very type that the publication is thought to have been likely to facilitate. And thus the *Nuremburg Files* situation, involving as it did a website as opposed to a book or magazine, might again be especially relevant insofar as one important feature of the internet is that it allows and encourages "narrowcasting," the targeting of a niche market or audience likely to seek out exactly the variety of content that the speaker is offering.

The difference between the *Brandenburg* scenario and the events in the *Herceg* and *Olivia N.* cases thus suggests that the degree of predisposition might matter. If there is a strongly predisposed target audience, will providing instructions and concrete detail substantially increase the probability that at least some members of the strongly predisposed target audience will commit the acts that are the subject of the instructions and/or the concrete detail? Probably yes. But at lower levels of predisposition the effect is likely much less. Still, the question, or at least the question most relevant to free speech theory and doctrine, is about the comparative causal effect of instructions, of concrete detail, and of argument or advocacy. Implicit in the appeal of Scanlon's example, and in the troubling dimensions of the other examples I have described, is the belief that instructional content and concrete detail will provide a degree of causal inflation that even the most persuasive advocacy and argument are unlikely to give. It is not so much that the implicit urgings of facts, recipes, and instructions represent a speech act of a different kind than explicit urgings with arguments and prescriptions. The pragmatics of Mill's corn dealer example are such that he seems to want us to understand this as a form of advocacy and not just as the provision of information. And thus it is not that we should understand that facts, recipes, and instructions are in the normal free speech scenario speech acts of a different kind. Rather, they are often tools of advocacy, or, as in *Olivia N.* and *Herceg*, tools of irresponsibility, tools whose very effectiveness might, as a quantitative matter and not because of differences in kind, lead to the instincts to push certain speech acts across the line from the protected to the unprotected. And much the same can be said about the effect of the internet, social media, and other forms of modern electronic communication. At least when we think about questions of freedom of expression and the causation of antisocial acts, social media and the internet are not different in kind from traditional print and broadcast media. But differences of degree matter, and insofar as any calculation about the appropriate legal response to causal speech will inevitably involve considering both the extent of the consequences and the degree of causation—the expected danger, in the statistical sense of "expected"—then the quantitative differences wrought by the forms of modern communication cannot help but be part of the calculation.

5. The Nature of the Questions

As with many questions in the law and theory of freedom of speech,[40] these issues are as much if not more social scientific as they are purely philosophical or conceptual. There is a vast amount of research, for example, mostly conducted by social psychologists, on the psychology of persuasion.[41] Does factual detail actually increase persuasiveness? And, if so, for which topics, and for which groups, and under what conditions? When are instructions effective in producing successful action and when not? And under what conditions does pure advocacy change minds and increase the likelihood of action? In his memorable dissent in *Gitlow v. People of New York*, Oliver Wendell Holmes observed that "[e]very idea is an incitement."[42] Insofar as he is understood to have been observing that offering an idea, even without explicitly prescriptive language, has the potential of increasing the receptivity to that idea, then he was plainly correct. But insofar as the word "incitement" suggests a closer connection between the words and action than when we use words such as "advocate" or "urge," then it is an open empirical question whether and when certain words and certain arguments and certain prescriptions do or do not increase the likelihood of certain actions. It all depends on the audience, the topic, the consequences, and much, much else. Every idea is a potential incitement, but every idea is also potentially just so much ineffectual hot air.

Thus, the normative and philosophical questions about the relationship between freedom of speech and the provision of instructions, plans, recipes, and detailed facts are in the final analysis less philosophical than they are empirical and social scientific. And, as empirical social scientific questions, the answers to them are plainly influenced by the nature of the communicative method as well as by the nature of the content, the nature of the speaker, and the nature of the audience. Insofar as social media and the internet present quantitatively different communicative methods, they present quantitatively different dimensions of the inquiry into the effect of instructions, plans, recipes, and facts on the expected consequences and expected harms of various speech acts. And thus insofar as genuine social scientific research yet to be performed may suggest that the causal consequences of providing hard facts and detailed instructions are substantially different from the causal consequences of mere advocacy, it may turn out that Scanlon's intuitions were indeed correct, and, in the internet era, in ways that are much more important than he could have anticipated in 1972.

Notes

1. I will continue to use "freedom of speech" in this chapter, with the understanding that "speech" is functioning here as a term of art. In much of the world, especially the world outside the United States, and indeed in much of the philosophical literature, the preferred phrase is "freedom of expression." Substituting "freedom of expression" for "freedom of speech," however, creates as many problems as it solves. Although "freedom of expression" has the advantages of distinguishing the topic (and the right) from specific questions under the American First Amendment, and of emphasizing that the right includes communicative acts (such as flag waving, flag burning, armband wearing, parading, picketing, demonstrating, and kneeling in protest) that are not "speech" in any literal sense of that word, it introduces a new confusion because there are many acts of expression that are in no way communicative. The substitution, therefore, risks shifting the conversation to one about general liberty and away from the specific topic conventionally designated by "freedom of speech." See Schauer (2015). The phrase "freedom of communication" is perhaps most accurate, but again with the understanding that "communication" is still a term of art, for few would contend that even the right as so specified has anything to do with, for example, the communication of an offer as a matter of contract law, or the communication of an acceptance by the recipient of the offer. See Schauer (2004).

2. In this chapter, I rely almost exclusively on American judicial opinions, on the American literature, and on American legal doctrine, but I do not intend the chapter to be about American law or the American First Amendment. American courts and scholars have been more focused (or obsessed, if you will) with free speech questions for a longer time than their counterparts elsewhere, and thus the United States offers a wealth of examples and a huge and relevant academic literature. But in this chapter, American examples notwithstanding, my goal is to engage in theoretical questions that have no particular American dimension.

3. Although Scanlon now believes that the highly influential account he offered in 1972 is "mistaken in important respects," his subsequent narrowing of his earlier position, however relevant it may be to taking his earlier article as a self-standing contribution usable or not on its own terms, does not touch his basic argument for a free speech

principle, nor the role of the nerve gas example in clarifying and limiting it (Scanlon 2011; Scanlon 1979).

4. I distinguish here, as I have done previously (see Schauer 1982; Schauer 2015; Schauer 2004; Schauer 1993) between the behavior to which a right, a rule, or a principle is applicable at all—coverage—and the question whether the behavior winds up being protected after the approach mandated by inclusion within the coverage is applied.

5. United States v. Progressive, Inc., 467 F. Supp. 990 (W.D. Wis. 1979), appeal dismissed, 610 F.2d 819 (7th Cir. 1979), motion to dissolve injunction denied, 486 F. Supp. 5 (W.D. Wis. 1979).

6. On the virtually but not quite absolute aversion to prior restraints in American free speech doctrine, see the *Pentagon Papers* case, *United States v. New York Times Co.*, 403 U.S. 713 (1971). Blackstone famously opined that the principle of freedom of the press encompassed *only* what he referred to as "previous restraints," but even as the principle has become understood to include subsequent punishment as well as prior restraint by licensing or injunction, the special aversion to prior restraints remains (Blackstone 1766, 151). See Near v. Minnesota, 283 U.S. 697 (1931).

7. Putting aside the specific context of the *Progressive* case, and putting aside any issues about the incentives or disincentives provided by restricting the distribution of non-classified material, it is far from obvious that the fact of classification (or not) is of substantial free speech importance. If the publication of certain information will, by virtue of that publication, increase the likelihood of some regulable action by the requisite (which is what this chapter is about) amount, the fact that some recipient might have obtained the same information by other means is largely beside the point.

8. Rice v. Paladin Enters., Inc., 940 F. Supp. 836 (D. Md. 1996).

9. Rice v. Paladin Enters., Inc., 128 F.3d 233 (4th Cir. 1997).

10. The Supreme Court of the United States has never decided a case in which a victim of a murder or other violent act brought suit against a publication for having indirectly caused that act. Indeed, the Supreme Court has never decided a case involving instructions, plans, recipes, or advocacy with detailed facts. Because the facts of *Rice v. Paladin* are so sympathetic to the plaintiffs claim and so unsympathetic to the publisher's, it is possible that the settlement was urged (or forced) on the defendant by various publishers' associations and/or insurers in order to prevent the first case on this issue to go to the Supreme Court to be one with such an unappealing, from the publishers' and insurers' perspective, set of facts.

11. See, in the American context, Miller v. California, 413 U.S. 49 (1973); Paris Adult Theatre I v. Slaton, 413 U.S. 15 (1973); Roth v. United States, 354 U.S. 476 (1957). See generally Schauer (1976).

12. See Snyder v. Phelps, 562 U.S. 443 (2011); Virginia v. Black, 538 U.S. 343 (2003); R.A.V. v. City of St. Paul, 505 U.S. 377 (1992); Cohen v. California, 403 U.S. 15 (1971); Chaplinsky v. New Hampshire, 315 U.S. 568 (1942)

13. Florida Star v. B.J.F., 491 U.S. 524 (1989) (privacy); New York Times Co. v. Sullivan, 376 U.S. 254 (1964) (libel).

14. Debs v. United States, 249 U.S. 211 (1919).

15. Brown v. Entm't Merchants Ass'n, 131 S. Ct. 2729 (2011).

16. Brown v. Entm't Merchants Ass'n, 131 S. Ct. 2729 (2011); Am. Booksellers Ass'n, Inc. v. Hudnut, 771 F.2d 323 (7th Cir. 1985).

17. Schenck v. United States, 249 U.S. 47 (1919); United States v. Spock, 416 F.2d 165 (1st Cir. 1969).

18. Brandenburg v. Ohio, 395 U.S. 444 (1969).

19. Jeremy Bentham discusses preparatory offenses under the general heading of accessory offenses (not all of which are preparatory) in (Bentham 1914, 4–8). A good discussion is in Ashworth, Dolinko, and Deigh (2011: 127–31).

20. Schenck v. United States, 249 U.S. 47 (1919).

21. E.g., Brandenburg v. Ohio, 395 U.S. 444 (1969)

22. Schenck v. United States, 249 U.S. 47 (1919). I refer to this as a misapplication because it is almost certain that the antiwar, anti-capitalism, and anti-conscription utterances of Charles Schenck created little clear and present danger of anything, and that Holmes reached his conclusion by virtue of a degree of deference to military or official judgment that would almost certainly no longer hold sway in American law, at least in a free speech context.

23. Consider, for example, legislation dealing with climate change, or, far more speculatively and far more remotely, legislation that might regulate the use and sale of Genetically Modified Organisms. In these and other instances, the general assumption is that a legislature or other governmental body may permissibly deal with dangers that may not be present and may not even be clear. Indeed, a good contrast is provided by the difference between the idea of clear and present danger and what in environmental and related contexts is often referred to as the "precautionary principle." According to that principle, there are circumstances in which the default rule for regulation under conditions of scientific uncertainty is to regulate under what we might think of as a "better safe than sorry" rule. But it is plain that the idea of clear and present danger is in direct contrast to the precautionary principle, accordingly insisting that under conditions of uncertainty about the effects of speech the default rule is not to regulate. See Schauer (2009).

24. Gitlow v. New York, 268 U.S. 652 (1925).

25. Dennis v. United States, 341 U.S. 494 (1951).

26. 395 U.S. 444 (1969).

27. Scanlon (1972, 211).

28. As noted later on in this section 4, the circumstances under which a speaker through advocacy or argument alone might incite a previously non-disposed audience seem at best highly remote.

29. 178 Cal. Rptr. 888 (Cal. Ct. App. 1981).

30. The court uses the term "artificial rape." I don't.

31. The instrument in the real event was a bottle and not a plumber's helper.

32. Brandenburg v. Ohio, 395 U.S. 444 (1969).

33. 814 F.2d 1017 (5th Cir. 1987).

34. For wrongful death, brought by the victim's mother.

35. See Virginia v. Black, 538 U.S. 343 (2003); **Watts v. United States**, 394 U.S. 705 (1969); Schauer (2003). In *Elonis v. United States of America*, No. 13-983 (2015), the court held that "requiring only negligence with respect to the communication of a threat . . . is not sufficient to support a conviction under Section 875(c)," reversing Elonis's conviction on the grounds that mens rea is required to prove that a crime was committed.

36. Schenck v. United States, 249 U.S. 47 (1919); United States v. Spock, 416 F.2d 165 (1st Cir. 1969).

37. Brandenburg v. Ohio, 395 U.S. 444 (1969).

38. Not the word he used.

39. At least to racial hatred, even if not necessarily to violent manifestation of that hatred.

40. The standard marketplace of ideas/search for truth arguments for a free speech principle are typically treated as philosophical claims to be discussed in the philosophical literature, but the arguments are in fact contingent empirical claims. Whether a particular form of institutional design will or will not increase the number of truths located or errors identified, or the amount of knowledge gained, is in the final analysis an empirical question. The identification of such arguments with prominent poets, philosophers, and jurists such as John Milton, John Stuart Mill, and Oliver Wendell Holmes has produced an environment in which such matters are more often discussed in legal and philosophical circles than in social scientific ones, but the question is, primarily, one of empirical social science.

41. The classic overview is Cialdini (2006).

42. Gitlow v. People of New York 268 U.S. 652, 673 (1925), (Holmes, J., dissenting).

References

Ashworth, A., D. Dolinko and J. Deigh. 2011. "Attempts." In J. Deigh and D. Dolinko (eds.) *Oxford Handbook of the Philosophy of Criminal Law*. Oxford: Oxford University Press: 125–46.

Bentham, J. 1914. *Principles of the Penal Code*. Translated by Charles Miller Atkinson. Oxford: Oxford University Press.

Blackstone, W. 1766. *Commentaries on the Laws of England*. Vol. 4. Chicago: University of Chicago Press.

Cialdini, Robert B. 2006. *Influence: The Psychology of Persuasion*. New York: Harper Business.

Mill, John Stuart. 1859. *On Liberty*. London: Longman, Roberts and Green.

Scanlon, T.M. 1972. "A Theory of Freedom of Expression." *Philosophy and Public Affairs* 1: 204–26.

Scanlon, T. M. 2011. "Comment on Baker's Autonomy and Free Speech." *Constitutional Commentary* 27: 319–25.

Scanlon, T. M. 1979. "Freedom of Expression and Categories of Expression." *University of Pittsburgh Law Review* 40: 519–50.

Schauer, Frederick. (1976). *The Law of Obscenity*. Washington, DC: BNA Books.

Schauer, F. 1982. *Free Speech: A Philosophical Enquiry*. Cambridge: Cambridge University Press.

Schauer, F. 1993. "A Comment on the Structure of Rights." *Georgia Law Review* 27: 427–54.

Schauer, F. 2003. "Intentions, Conventions, and the First Amendment: The Case of Cross-Burning." *The Supreme Court Review*: 197–231.

Schauer, F. 2004. "The Boundaries of the First Amendment: A Preliminary Exploration of Constitutional Salience." *Harvard Law Review* 117: 1765–809.

Schauer, F. 2009. "Is It Better to Be Safe than Sorry?: Free Speech and the Precautionary Principle." *Pepperdine Law Review* 36: 301–15.

Schauer, F. 2015. "Free Speech on Tuesdays." *Law and Philosophy* 34: 427–54.

5

Free Speech Categories in the Digital Age

Ashutosh Bhagwat

1. Introduction

Almost every written constitution in the world contains provisions guaranteeing the freedom of speech.[1] Such provisions are often, though not always, written in nearly absolute terms and do not typically qualify the sorts of speech that are protected (Bhagwat 2015). If there is any topic on which societies across the globe purport to agree, it seems it is the importance of providing strong protections for freedom of expression. Yet obviously, no society could or does provide absolute protection against regulation or punishment to all forms of expression. There is thus an inevitable tension between written law and actual legal practice. In nations with authoritarian constitutions—which are perhaps the majority in the world—the issue simply does not arise, because their written constitutional protections are not enforced (Elkins, Ginsburg & Melton 2014). But in legal regimes that do seek to provide meaningful protections for freedom of expression, the problem is pervasive. Indeed, the main task of free speech law and theory in such societies has been to determine what the acceptable limits on free speech should be.

One set of tools for determining the legitimacy of such limits has been judicial doctrines, such as proportionality analysis in Europe and strict or intermediate scrutiny in the United States, which determine whether social interests are strong enough to justify restrictions on speech. But such analyses are truly only the tip of the iceberg in terms of how societies limit the scope of seemingly absolute protections for freedom of expression or speech. And this is as it must be, because in reality limitations on speech are ubiquitous, even in the freest of societies, and every such restriction cannot possibly be subject to searching judicial oversight. No one believes that the state must justify a ban on solicitation of murder via "proportionality" analysis or strict scrutiny. Nor does anyone believe that subjecting doctors to professional sanctions or malpractice liability for negligent medical advice poses any constitutional concerns. Those are of course easy examples. But even in more nuanced areas of speech, where most observers would think that *some* constitutional concerns are implicated, legal systems regularly restrict or sanction speech without much hesitation. How is that so?

The short answer is that much of the work of distinguishing troublesome from routine restrictions on free expression is done through the use of categorical analysis, albeit sometimes the categories of free speech being employed are not explicitly or even consciously identified. I will argue in this chapter, however, that many of the basic categorical distinctions that have sustained essentially all systems of free expression to date are being systematically undermined by the growth of the internet, including social media, and the digital economy. The question that such legal regimes must confront (though few have seriously attempted to do so yet) is what comes next in a free speech world without firm categories.

2. The Speech/Conduct Distinction

One of the key elements of the postwar liberal consensus has been the understanding that given the complexities of modern economies, the State must enjoy broad authority to regulate economic conduct for the common good. In the United States, this development is reflected in the abandonment in 1937 of the so-called *Lochner* doctrine,[2] but the growth of the modern regulatory state occurred in the rest of the industrial world at approximately the same time. In addition, during approximately the same time frame a separate consensus emerged that basic political liberties such as freedom of expression, assembly, and association required special protections as a safeguard against the rise of the kinds of totalitarianism that produced World War II. Thus in the United States, the Supreme Court for the first time in the 1930s and 1940s began to aggressively enforce the Free Speech Clause of the First Amendment;[3] and in Europe the Council of Europe agreed in 1950 to the terms of the European Convention on Human Rights, with its Articles 10 and 11 providing robust protections for freedom of expression, assembly, and association.[4] These two contrasting commitments—the primacy of the State in the economic sphere, and the primacy of private parties in the sphere of political rights—did not create any serious conflicts until recently. After all, if the state regulates the quality or price of footwear, no issue of political rights is raised; and at the same time, restrictions on the content of political expression were not seen as being in the realm of legitimate *economic* regulation.[5] Today, however, these different commitments are on a collision course.

The source of the conflict here is quite simple: one of the primary commodities traded and sold in private markets in the modern digital economy is information in the form of electronic data. As Jane Bamberger among others has pointed out, however, data is speech (Bamberger 2014).[6] Under any plausible theory of free expression, the transmission of at least some forms of information must be considered a form of protected expression because factual information undergirds most political discourse. As such, certain kinds of information sit at the core of what is protected under any plausible theory of free speech. Put differently, if information was not protected the State would enjoy a monopoly on defining factual truths, a result completely at odds with the basic structure of liberal democracy—consider, for example, how political debate over climate change policy would be distorted if the government controlled access to all climate data. Moreover, even if the State chooses to regulate only the *sale* of information/data, that too cannot alleviate concerns since many crucial forms of factual discourse, from newspapers to scientific journals, are sold in the market.

This is not to say, of course, that free speech theory requires an absolutely laissez-faire approach to data regulation—for example, surely some regulation of data transfers in order to protect, for example, personal privacy, must be permissible because not all information is as relevant to political discourse as, say, climate data, and some may not be relevant at all. But the traditional economic conduct/free expression dichotomy is no longer useful in defining the lines between permissible and impermissible regulation. Clearly some forms of regulation, such as prohibiting the disclosure or sale of the shopping or video streaming habits of private individuals, will be tolerated in most if not all liberal democracies even if such data has some political applications in the microtargeting of potential voters (though the existence of such political applications further undermines the distinction between data-as-commodity and data-as-political-input)[7] (Hersh 2015). But what about similar data with regards to public officials, or candidates for public office? Here, clear answers and, one suspects, consensus disappear. And even with respect to unqualifiedly private individuals, what about regulations restricting the use or sale of data regarding individual voters' party registrations and/or voting turnout histories? Such data is quite personal, but obviously highly relevant to political expression and activities such as get-out-the-vote efforts. To restrict access to or use of such data is to interfere with political processes, but at the same time the state may have legitimate, privacy-related reasons for doing so given the possibility, in this hyper-partisan era, that an individual's party affiliation might open her up to economic retaliation. In addition, as Abby Wood and my colleague Chris Elmendorf argue, there may be sound reasons grounded in democratic theory for denying politicians access to voter-specific data (Elmendorf & Wood 2017). Hence the dilemma. As before, there is no "correct" answer to how this conflict should be resolved, and one suspects again that different societies will reach different, permissible solutions.

The fundamental problem in this area is that traditional free-speech theory provides little guidance on how to resolve such conflicts because it provides few objective means to evaluate the relative significance of speech and non-speech interests. The general tendency has been to simply describe regulated activities as "conduct" unworthy of constitutional protection, and so uphold regulation without further analysis. The difficulty is that if data is speech, then applying the "conduct" label to sales or usage of data is quite unconvincing (which is not to say that litigants, and courts, have not tried to do so[8]).

3. Public Censors and Private Speakers

Another basic, categorical distinction undergirding *all* systems of free expression in functioning democracies has been the public/private divide. The function of free speech protections has always been understood to be to restrict the power of the State to regulate expression, especially political expression, by private entities, including citizens and the media. In other words, the very concept of free expression assumes that private entities act as protected speakers, and public entities act as potential censors. Private actors cannot be censors by definition, because they lack the coercive powers of the State. To the contrary, we protect the right of private parties to control their own speech, and that of others utilizing their property, through concepts such as editorial discretion[9] and compelled speech.[10] The traditional paradigm, then, envisioned a sphere of private speech controlled by private actors, which the government should generally not interfere in.

To be fair, the simple public/private distinction described in the previous paragraph has always been incomplete since it ignores the role of the government itself as a speaker, and often a rather loud one. And even before the spread of the internet, the phenomenon of state-owned electronic media complicated the picture because of disputes—which have arisen even in that paradigm of private ownership, the United States[11]—over access to those media outlets. But the electronic media was the exception rather than the rule, and rarely has the concept of a *private* censor who must be subjected to constitutional restrictions gained much traction. Indeed, when faced with such an argument the United States Supreme Court explicitly rejected it.[12]

It should be perfectly obvious to even the most casual observer, however, that the simple distinctions of an earlier age can no longer be sustained. In particular, the growing dominance of privately owned social media platforms such as Facebook and Twitter as the sites of political discourse and dialogue make nonsense of the traditional public/private paradigm. This breakdown of traditional categories is especially well illustrated by a recent United States Supreme Court decision in which the Court described modern social media—citing the examples of Facebook and Twitter in particular—as the "the most important places . . . for the exchange of views," and analogized them to traditional public forums such as streets and parks.[13] The difficulty with this analogy, completely ignored by the Court, is the fact that streets and parks are generally government property, while Facebook and Twitter are entirely privately owned. As a consequence, in the modern world a handful of private entities are effectively the gatekeepers of political discourse, yet operate completely free of constitutional restraints. The ramifications of that reality remained entirely unexplored by the Court, thereby eliding a fundamental, underlying problem.

The problem, of course, is that legal principles such as the public forum doctrine in the United States—the set of legal rules governing the circumstances in which the government must grant, or may limit, citizens' access to public property for expressive purposes—do not apply to social media. To the contrary, current law in some countries may well protect a right of social media entities to exclude individuals from their platforms (so long as they do not do so on impermissible grounds such as race or gender), and may well also protect the platform-owners' rights to control the content of what materials are available on their platforms. Social media companies such as Facebook are not, after all, common carriers,[14] and so presumably have some editorial discretion to control the content that appears on their platforms. The United States Supreme Court has held that in the case of newspaper editors and cable television providers, such editorial discretion is entitled to constitutional protection.[15] It is hard to see why social media platforms are any different— certainly, the fact that social media typically carry the speech of others does not distinguish them from cable television providers or the advertising content of print newspapers.

Nor are these editorial rights merely theoretical. Facebook, to use the most prominent example, engages in pervasive censorship of content carried on its platform through its Community Standards, which ban, among other things, nudity, hate speech, and graphic violence.[16] The process through which such standards are set, and then enforced, has an enormous impact on political and other dialogue throughout the world, and yet the process is both opaque and entirely independent of any constitutional control (Ammori 2014; Klonick 2018). Consider for example the public commitment in the wake of the 2016 American elections by Mark Zuckerberg, the founder and CEO of Facebook, to combat so-called "fake news" on Facebook.[17] If and how Facebook identifies and removes content it identifies as "fake" from its platform could easily have a major impact on public debate in many countries—Facebook, after all, has 2 *billion* monthly users worldwide.[18] If a government (or at least a non-authoritarian government) undertook to suppress "fake news," free-expression alarm bells would begin ringing immediately, and in the United States it is questionable whether such an undertaking would be constitutional even if directed only at demonstrably false factual statements.[19] Are there really no free expression concerns raised by similar efforts by Facebook, which after all would affect *far* more individuals' access to information than the actions of any nation-state? And to be clear, while I am using Facebook as an example, exactly the same concerns are raised by content restrictions imposed by other social media firms such as Twitter, or search engines such as Google.

Nor do the concerns stop with facially laudable goals such as controlling fake news. If social media and other internet firms really do have a right to exercise editorial control over content on their websites, then presumably that power could be used to skew debate in explicitly political ways—after all, in every other context the *purpose* of editorial control is to enable editors to pursue ideological ends. Indeed, Facebook was accused of precisely such political (anti-conservative) bias during the 2016 American election cycle, albeit the firm denied the allegations.[20] Given the concentration of debate onto a handful of platforms in the internet era, the potential damage that such ideological skewing could do to democratic debate is difficult to understate. After all, as Cass Sunstein has argued, there are good reasons to think that democratic discourse has already been distorted by the growth of online echo chambers. (Sunstein 2017). And there is growing evidence that during the 2016 U.S. elections, foreign (in particular Russian) actors exploited this phenomenon to manipulate public opinion. (Shane & Goel 2017). Imagine how much worse such problems could be if the owners of social media platforms assisted efforts to shape political discourse.

In short, the internet has transformed the nature of public discourse, concentrating it onto a handful of privately owned platforms whose owners have no constitutional obligations to grant nondiscriminatory access to their platforms, and who regularly exercise authority to control the content of expression on their platforms. Calls have begun to emerge for regulations that would restrict the power of internet firms to control content on their platforms (Langvardt 2018). But would such regulations be consistent with free speech law or theory? The answer is far from clear. Indeed, these firms have a nontrivial argument that free-expression principles *guarantee* their right to exercise control, including ideological control, over content on their private property on the grounds that they should enjoy the same rights of editorial discretion as owners of older forms of media. But what is the nature and extent of these editorial rights, if they exist? And concomitantly, to what extent may the State require, restrict, or otherwise control Facebook's exercise of its "editorial discretion"? These are questions that are notable mainly for their opacity, and the lack of any sound basis in current theory for resolving them. Would it be acceptable, for example, for the State to impose quasi-common carrier obligations on social media firms, and so substantially reduce their control over content on their platforms by banning such firms from discriminating amongst customers or content for any other than technological reasons? Current law and theory give remarkably little guidance on how to even approach such questions, much less answer them (Bhagwat 2017). Once again, then, the internet has broken down a fundamental category of free expression theory, and we are struggling to figure out what to replace it with.

4. Political versus Commercial Speech

A recurring free speech issue that arises across jurisdictions is whether, and to what extent, commercial advertising—what in the United States is called "commercial speech"—constitutes protected expression. In the United States, prior to 1976 commercial speech received no constitutional protection;[21] but in 1976 the Supreme Court held that commercial speech did fall within the First Amendment, and since then it has received increasingly robust protection.[22] In Europe, by contrast, the European Court of Human Rights has consistently considered commercial advertising to fall within the scope of the right to "receive and impart information" protected by Article 10 of the European Convention on Human Rights (Rich 1998; Johnson & Youm 2009). However, both jurisdictions also agree that commercial advertising is generally entitled to less protection than speech on political or cultural topics. Or put differently, both jurisdictions permit greater regulations of commercial advertising than of political speech. Thus in the United States, regulations of commercial speech are subject only to a form of intermediate scrutiny, permitting regulations which advance a "substantial" governmental interest.[23] Content-based regulations of political or cultural speech, on the other hand, are permissible only if necessary to advance a "compelling" governmental interest, a standard almost impossible to satisfy.[24] And while the European Court of Human Rights does not apply a different standard in evaluating restrictions on commercial advertising, commentators agree that the Court grants national governments far more leeway to regulate advertising than political speech (Johnson & Youm 2009; Rich 1998; Gassy-Wright 2005). Indeed, in 1994 the European Court went so far as to uphold an almost total ban on professional advertising by lawyers.[25] Such a restriction certainly would not have been permitted in the United States at that time or since.[26]

The distinction between "commercial" and "political" speech thus has important implications for the scope of regulatory authority in many legal regimes. And this is as one would expect, given the close links between free expression and democracy (hence the strong protection for political speech), and the obvious social harms that can result from commercial advertising (hence the greater need to regulate). In most cases, the line between commercial and political speech has in the past been relatively clear—though there are of course always difficult cases.[27] But today, as a result of social and cultural changes in the nature of public discourse generated by the spread of social media, the line is increasingly threatened.

There is of course no doubt that even in the internet era, there is a core category of commercial speech that can be identified as such. A picture of a shampoo bottle accompanied by the statement "Buy Acme Shampoo— Your Hair Will Be Cleaner than Clean" constitutes commercial advertising whether it appears in a newspaper, on television, or on the internet. But corporations are increasingly being forced to participate in public debates that are far afield from simple commercial transactions. Thus in the face of U.S. president Trump's equivocal response to a march by white supremacists in Charlottesville, Virginia, a number of major corporations immediately issued statements denouncing the march and several corporate CEOs resigned from various White House advisory councils (Gelles 2017). Similarly, when President Trump announced the end of the Deferred Action for Childhood Arrivals (DACA) immigration program, a number of corporate CEOs, including notably the leaders of the largest technology companies, immediately condemned the decision (Wichter 2017). Such public statements straddle the line between political and commercial speech because while on the one hand they are clearly statements on highly political topics, the underlying motive for the statements is undoubtedly to maintain the reputations of the corporations expressing the views with their customer base, and so ultimately to enhance the corporations' commercial earnings. This relationship is demonstrated by the fact that corporations that do not sell directly to consumers appear to feel less pressure to step into these political disputes (Gelles 2017). But at least one significant American court—the California Supreme Court—has held that speech on even political topics constitutes commercial speech when the statements are made "for the purpose of promoting sales of [the corporation's] products."[28] The consequence is that there remains grave ambiguity about the State's power to regulate or impose liability upon such speech.

The blurring of the commercial and political described above is undoubtedly a new and important phenomenon. One might reasonably question, however, whether it has any causal relationship to the spread of the internet and social media (as opposed to, say, unprecedented political developments in the form of Brexit and the election of Donald Trump). I would argue, however, that social media in particular has a direct, causal connection to the politicization of commerce. The reason is that social media has fundamentally changed the nature of the relationship between consumers and corporations. Prior to social media, consumers were largely passive purchasers and corporations were viewed as primarily economic actors, who participated minimally in the realm of public discourse. Certainly in most instances consumers did not pay much attention to the political actions or stances (if any) of the corporate entities that made the products they purchased. There was always, of course, some political pressure on corporations, as reflected in the Corporate Social Responsibility movement and the South African Divestment campaigns of the apartheid era. But these pressures were generally marginal, and the traditional media paid little attention to the political roles of corporations (perhaps in part because of their own corporate ownership). Social media, however, has turned this dynamic upside down. Today, if any major consumer corporation takes any potentially controversial actions or stances, news of it spreads like wildfire on social media, and the spread is driven not by institutional media but rather by private individuals. The result is immediate consumer pressure on the corporation to change course, often accompanied by the threat of a consumer boycott. Examples include a boycott campaign organized via Facebook after the retailer Target donated money to a political candidate known for his antigay stances (Montpoli 2010), and a protest campaign against the fast food chain Chick-fil-A after its president stated in an interview that his (privately held) company opposed same-sex marriage (Severson 2012). It is hard to imagine how such mass consumer movements could have been organized so quickly and widely prior to the age of social media. And while the examples just given involve consumer pressure *against* political stances by corporations, more recently (as illustrated by the Charlottesville and DACA examples) the pressure has been for corporations to take positive steps to clarify their political stances. The result is a persistent blurring of the political/commercial line.

In short, corporate speech is another area, like the commodification of data and the privatization of censorship, where the internet and social media have upended conventional approaches to free expression. When private consumers can quickly become mass-movement activists, corporations feel an obligation to respond to such activism. And while that pressure might sometimes lead them to eschew politics, in the modern era consumer activists more and more insist on political engagement by corporations. Such engagement, however, raises obvious and persistent concerns about the proper role of corporations in democratic politics and public discourse.[29] And consequently, it also raises pressure on national governments to regulate political speech by corporations. The legitimacy of such regulation will surely turn, at least in part, on whether the targeted speech is considered "commercial" because it is in furtherance of corporate economic interests, or "political" because it is a contribution to public discourse. But for all the reasons noted, our ability to draw that distinction is increasingly threatened.

5. Domestic Gossip and Public Discourse

Finally, we come to a distinction that in the internet era is likely to be of singular importance: the line between speech on purely personal, private matters and speech that contributes to public discourse on matters of general import. Speech that contributes to public discourse must of course be at the center of any system of free expression within democratic societies, given the close connection between free speech and democracy (Post 1990; Sunstein 1993). On the other hand, if personal privacy is to receive any form of legal protection—a rather pressing public policy concern in the internet era—even truthful speech about private individuals *must* be susceptible to regulation. Indeed this insight, that private gossip can be subjected to regulation without impinging on a system of free expression, can be traced back at least as far as Louis Brandeis and Samuel Warren's pathbreaking article on "The Right to Privacy" published in 1890 (Brandeis & Warren 1890). Brandeis's position is particularly noteworthy given that he later, as a Supreme Court justice, authored probably the most articulate and effective defense of freedom of political discourse in American history.[30]

Not surprisingly, the preferred position of public discourse over speech on purely personal topics has received strong judicial endorsement. The United States Supreme Court has distinguished clearly between "domestic gossip" and speech "on a matter of public concern," according far stronger protection to the latter.[31] And the European Court of Human Rights has similarly indicated clearly that speech on issues relevant to democracy sits at the pinnacle of Art. 10 protections for free expression (Johnson & Youm 2009). Finally, and notably, in 2014 the European Court of Justice recognized a "right to be forgotten" which entitled private figures to force search engines to remove links to truthful but no longer relevant information which is harmful to that individual.[32] By distinguishing between public and private figures in defining the scope of this new right, the Court unambiguously indicated that while with respect to purely personal facts about private individuals privacy concerns can trump principles of free expression, the same would not be true with respect to public figures—presumably because even personal facts about the past conduct of such individuals can be relevant to public discourse.

It would be easy to point to any number of further examples of courts and regulators treating personal facts differently from public discourse.[33] But the basic line of argument is neither obscure nor controversial—if privacy is to be maintained without harming public debate some distinction between personal facts and public discourse must be drawn. Furthermore, this need has become particularly urgent and important in the internet era, because of the profound implications of the internet for personal privacy. Before the internet, when the primary forms of mass communication were the print and broadcast media, invasions of privacy, while undoubtedly painful to individuals in the moment, had a spatial and time-limited quality to them. Thus when in 1983 the newspaper *The Florida Star* published the name of a rape survivor in violation of state law, an action the United States Supreme Court held the paper had a First Amendment right to do,[34] the victim undoubtedly suffered an immediate invasion of privacy within her community of Jacksonville, where the paper circulated. But her name would not have been exposed to many people outside that immediate community (especially because she litigated her case anonymously), and there would have been no easy way for people outside the community to even look up the article without digging through the newspapers' archives. Even within the community the information would fade over time, and people who came to know her after 1983 would have no reason to connect her to the story. Finally, if she truly wished to leave the episode behind her, she could simply move to another reasonably distant community (an admittedly not costless alternative, but an alternative nonetheless). Contrast the situation today. Even if published in a print newspaper, the story identifying B.J.F. by name would immediately appear on the internet on the paper's website, in fully searchable form. And it would remain available indefinitely, since the implication of the Supreme Court decision is that B.J.F. would have no right to force the newspaper to scrub its website. The result is that a simple Google search of B.J.F.'s name, conducted anywhere in the world, would immediately yield this information. Such searches are today standard practice for potential employers, and are often conducted by individuals about their new friends because of the quick and costless nature of Google searches. Therefore, the reality is that today, B.J.F. simply could not escape the invasion of privacy she had suffered unless she were to change her name and refuse to disclose her original name, a step with huge costs in terms of loss of educational and employment history. It is precisely this phenomenon, of course, that led the European Court of Justice to recognize a "right to be forgotten" applicable to Google searches; but such a holding was only made possible by drawing a distinction between the personal and the public, since a right to scrub matters relevant to public discourse from the internet would obviously be a democratic catastrophe (not least because it would permit public officials and political candidates to hide their pasts from citizens).

The difficulty is that the precise same phenomenon that drives the urgency of maintaining the distinction between personal facts and public discourse— the internet—also tends to undermine it. In the predigital era, public discourse was dominated by a few media outlets and public opinion tended to be shaped by the views of a relatively small, identifiable group of speakers who included both public officials and "opinion makers." The rest of us were "private" and our personal lives were our own. But in the age of self-created YouTube stars (McAlone 2017) and ever-proliferating bloggers and social media sensations, the universe of opinion-makers has exploded. Is an individual with several hundred or several thousand social media followers who regularly posts on cultural or political topics a "public" or a "private" figure? Surely when someone aims to shape public opinion on an issue, his or her past activities can be relevant to judging their credibility—I would certainly want to know about David Duke's affiliation with the Ku Klux Klan when assessing a blog posting by him concerning race issues. But where to draw the line between private people entitled to keep their pasts private, and public individuals with no such entitlement? There are no easy answers here, as elsewhere.

As always, I do not mean to imply here that answers to these questions ultimately cannot be arrived at, or that the answers will be the same across different societies. Consider for example the remarkable decision of the Chilean Supreme Court in *Graziani Le-Fort, Albo v. Empresa El Mercurio S.A.P.* (Ramirez 2017; Callamard 2017). There, the court held that an individual and his family had a right to require a newspaper to delete references to the individual's 10-year-old trial for sexual abuse of a minor, even though the individual was a relatively senior retired police officer. The contrast between this decision and the *Florida Star* case in the United States is quite striking. My own instinct is that that both decisions are incorrect. The *Florida Star* case probably was wrong when decided, but certainly is indefensible in the digital era given the harm such invasions of privacy can cause. And while the *Graziani* case is closer, it too seems wrong given the public character of the claimant seeking to bury the past. But regardless, the key point is that neither court appears to have asked the relevant, hard questions about whether the personal information at issue was relevant to public discourse in a meaningful way, a question all the more pressing given the magnified privacy harms associated with the internet. And again, some overarching, cross-societal theory of free expression must be developed which can yield consistent and rational answers to this exceedingly difficult class of questions.

6. Conclusion

Given the ubiquity of free-expression constitutional guaranties across the world, and the relatively robust protections generally accorded free expression in most functioning democracies, it is remarkable how little underlying theoretical consensus exists regarding the purposes of free speech law. In the United States the courts (and scholars) have advanced a hodgepodge of vague and mutually inconsistent "theories" for why free speech matters. And in much of the rest of the world broad references to free expression as a "human right" similarly obfuscate rather than advance debate. The purpose of this chapter is to suggest that this way of doing business must come to an end. The lack of a theoretical framework underlying free speech law has until now been if not acceptable, then not fatal, because of a series of generally agreed-upon distinctions that have permitted courts to protect speech without sacrificing vital social interests. I have identified here four such categorical distinctions. And crucially, I have argued that the viability of these distinctions, as traditionally defined, has been seriously threatened in recent years by the spread of the internet and social media. I would add that there are many other areas of free-speech law, not addressed here in detail, facing similar problems.[35]

The task ahead is then clear—to identify specific principles that will permit courts to distinguish between speech that must be protected under all circumstances, and other speech that may be regulated to ward off the expanded set of social harms that the internet can create. I do not here aspire to develop such a theory, but from my discussion above it should be clear what I believe the starting point must be: identifying clearly and in a straightforward way what forms of speech are a necessary part of the public discourse that undergirds all democratic societies, and what forms of speech are not. Both the United States Supreme Court and the major European courts have already begun exploring these ideas, but only in the vaguest, most skeletal fashion. It is time now for scholars to begin the work needed to put meat on those bare bones.

Notes

1. The database "Constitute" attempts to collect all of the world's written, national constitutions. *See* https://constituteproject.org/?lang=en (last visited August 31, 2017). Use of the database's filter for "freedom of expression" suggests that 180 of the 190 constitutions included in the database provide protection for freedom of speech (by contrast, the "freedom of press" filter produces 150 constitutions, and the "right to bear arms" filter only 6 constitutions).

2. *See* Lochner v. New York, 198 U.S. 45 (1905) (holding that the due process clause of the Fourteenth Amendment forbids states from imposing economic regulations which unreasonable interfere with freedom of contract); West Coast Hotel Co. v. Parrish, 300 U.S. 379 (1937) (holding that the Constitution does not provide special protections to the freedom of contract, and therefore overruling *Lochner* and its progeny cases).

3. *See, e.g.,* De Jonge v. Oregon, 299 U.S. 353 (1937); Lovell v. Griffin, 303 U.S. 444 (1938); Cantwell v. Connecticut, 310 U.S. 296 (1940).

4. *European Convention on Human Rights, available at* http://www.echr.coe.int/Documents/Convention_ENG.pdf (last visited September 1, 2017).

5. The primary tension between the spheres of economic regulation and political freedoms during the early postwar era arose when the State sought to regulate or nationalize the new electronic mass media. Different societies chose vastly different strategies to resolve this tension, from predominantly public ownership in some countries such as Great Britain, to a generally autonomous private media in the United States.

6. *See also* Sorrell v. IMS Health Inc., 564 U.S. 552, 570 (2011) ("the creation and dissemination of information are speech within the meaning of the First Amendment").

7. I qualify this statement because of the uncertainty regarding, as always, the United States, whose Supreme Court has extended free-speech protections into the commercial sphere far more than most of its peer societies.

8. *Cf. Sorrell*, 564 U.S. at 570–71 (rejecting argument made by State of Vermont that "transfer, and use of [data] are conduct, not speech"); IMS Health Inc. v. Ayotte, 550 F.3d 42, 52–53 (1st Cir. 2008) (accepting argument that restriction on data usage regulated only conduct, and so was indistinguishable from a regulation of "beef jerky").

9. *See, e.g.,* Turner Broadcasting v. FCC, 512 U.S. 622, 636–37 (1994) (recognizing that the First Amendment protects the "editorial discretion" of cable television operators as to which channels they transmit to their customers).

10. *See, e.g.,* Hurley v Irish-American Gay, Lesbian and Bisexual Group of Boston, 515 U.S. 557 (1995) (upholding First Amendment right of parade organizers to exclude LGBT group from parade).

11. Arkansas Educational Television Comm'n v. Forbes, 523 U.S. 666 (1998).

12. Columbia Broadcasting Sys. Inc. v. Democratic Nat'l Comm., 412 U.S. 94 (1973).

13. Packingham v. North Carolina, 137 S. Ct. 1730, 1735–36 (2017).

14. *See* U.S. Telecom Ass'n v. FCC, 825 F.3d 674, 740 (D.C. Cir. 2016) (holding that broadband Internet Service Providers lacked editorial rights, because they were regulated as common carriers).

15. Miami Herald Publ'g Co. v. Tornillo, 418 U.S. 241, 254–57 (1974) (newspapers); Turner Broad. *v. FCC*, 512 U.S. 622, 636–37 (1994) (cable television providers). *See also* the chapter by Simpson and Whitney in this volume.

16. *Facebook Community Standards, available at* https://www.facebook.com/communitystandards (accessed September 5, 2017).

17. https://www.facebook.com/zuck/posts/10103253901916271.

18. https://newsroom.fb.com/company-info/.

19. *See* United States v. Alvarez, 567 U.S. 709 (2012) (extending constitutional protection to intentional falsehoods).

20. "Facebook to Change Trending Topics after Investigation into Bias Claims," *The Guardian* (May 23, 2016), *available at* https://www.theguardian.com/technology/2016/may/24/facebook-changes-trending-topics-anti-conservative-bias (accessed September 5, 2017).

21. Valentine v. Chrestensen, 316 U.S. 52 (1942).

22. Va. State Bd. of Pharmacy v. Va. Citizens Consumer Council, Inc., 425 U.S. 748 (1976); *Lorillard Tobacco Co. v. Reilly*, 533 U.S. 525 (2001).

23. Central Hudson Gas & Electric Corp. v. Public Servs. Comm'n, 447 U.S. 557, 566 (1980).

24. Brown v. Entm't Merchants Ass'n, 564 U.S. 786, 799 (2011).

25. Casado Coca v. Spain, 18 Eur. Ct. H.R. 1 (ser. A) (1994).

26. Bates v. State Bar of Arizona, 433 U.S. 350 (1977).

27. *See, e.g.,* Bolger v. Youngs Drug Prods. Corp., 463 U.S. 60 (1983); Nike, Inc. v. Kasky, 539 U.S. 654 (2003).

28. Kasky v. Nike, Inc., 27 Cal.4th 939, 946 (2002).

29. *Cf.* Citizens United v. FEC, 558 U.S. 310 (2010) (holding that corporations enjoy a broad constitutional right to engage in independent expenditures funding political speech).

30. Whitney v. California, 274 U.S. 357, 375–77 (1927) (Brandeis, J., concurring).

31. Bartnicki v. Vopper, 532 U.S. 514, 533, 535 (2001); Snyder v. Phelps, 562 U.S. 443, 452 (2011).

32. Google Spain v. Agencia Espanola de Proteccion de Datos, Mario Costeja Gonzalez, C-131/12. ECLI:EU:C:2014:317 (May 13, 2014). *See* the chapter by Robert Post in this volume.

33. *See, e.g.,* Dun & Bradstreet v. Greenmoss Builders, 472 U.S. 749 (1985).

34. The Florida Star v. B.J.F., 491 U.S. 524 (1989).

35. A good example would be the distinction, drawn in the United States, between protected abstract advocacy of violence, and unprotected "incitement" which must be "directed to inciting or producing imminent lawless action and is likely to incite or produce such action." Brandenburg v. Ohio, 395 U.S. 444, 447 (1969) (per curiam). In recent years,

several prominent academics have questioned whether this distinction is sustainable in an era of domestic terrorism and online radicalization (Posner 2015, Sunstein 2015).

References

Ammori, M. 2014. "The 'New' *New York Times*: Free Speech Lawyering in the Age of Google and Twitter." *Harvard Law Review* 127(8): 2259–95.

Bamberger, J. 2014. "Is Data Speech?" *Stanford Law Review* 66(1): 57–120.

Bhagwat, A. 2015. "Free Speech without Democracy." *U.C. Davis Law Review* 49(1): 59–121.

Bhagwat, A. 2017. "When Speech Is Not 'Speech.'" *Ohio State Law Journal* 78(4): 839–85.

Brandeis, L and S. Warren 1890. "The Right to Privacy." *Harvard Law Review* 4(5): 193–220.

Callamard, A. 2017. "Are Courts Re-inventing Internet Regulation?" *International Review of Law, Computers & Technology*, DOI: 10.1080/13600869.2017.1304603.

Elkins, Z., T. Ginsburg, and J. Melton. 2014. "The Content of Authoritarian Constitutions." In T. Ginsburg and A. Simpser (eds.) *Constitutions in Authoritarian Regimes.* New York: Cambridge University Press: 141–64.

Elmendorf, C. and A. Wood. 2017. "Elite Political Ignorance: Law, Data and the Representation of (Mis)Perceived Electorates." UC Davis Legal Studies Research Paper Series, https://papers.ssrn.com/sol3/papers.cfm?abstract_id=3034685.

Gassy-Wright, O. 2005. "Commercial Speech in the United States and Europe." *LLM Theses and Essays*. Paper 13. http://digitalcommons.law.uga.edu/stu_llm/13.

Gelles, D. 2017. "The Moral Voice of Corporate America." *New York Times*, August 19, https://www.nytimes.com/2017/08/19/business/moral-voice-ceos.html?_r=0 (accessed September 8, 2017).

Hersh, E. 2015. *Hacking the Electorate: How Campaigns Perceive Voters.* New York: Cambridge University Press.

Johnson, B. and K. Youm. 2009. "Commercial Speech and Free Expression: The United States and Europe Compared." *Journal of International Media & Entertainment Law* 2(2): 159–98.

Klonick, K. 2018. "The New Governors: The People, Rules, and Processes Governing Online Speech." *Harvard Law Review* 131(6): 1598-1670.

Langvardt, K. 2018. "Regulating Online Content Moderation." *Georgetown Law Journal* 106(5): 1353-1388.

McAlone, N. 2017. "These Are the 18 Most Popular YouTube Stars in the World—and Some Are Making Millions." *Business Insider*, March 7, http://www.businessinsider.com/most-popular-youtuber-stars-salaries-2017/#no-18-epic-rap-battles-erb-142-million-subscribers-1 (accessed September 12, 2017).

Montpoli, B. 2010. "Target Boycott Movement Grows Following Donation to Support 'Antigay' Candidate." *CBS News*, July 28, https://www.cbsnews.com/news/target-boycott-movement-grows-following-donation-to-support-antigay-candidate/ (accessed September 8, 2017).

Posner, E. 2015. "ISIS Gives Us No Choice but to Consider Limits on Speech." *Slate.com*, December 15, http://www.slate.com/articles/news_and_politics/view_from_chicago/2015/12/isis_s_online_radicalization_efforts_present_an_unprecedented_danger.html (accessed September 12, 2017).

Post, R. 1990. "The Constitutional Concept of Public Discourse: Outrageous Opinion, Democratic Deliberation, and *Hustler Magazine v. Falwell.*" *Harvard Law Review* 103(3): 603–86.

Ramirez, P. 2017. "The Right to Be Forgotten in Chile: Doctrine and Jurisprudence." *E-Conference Right to Be Forgotten in Europe and Beyond.* June 2017, https://blogdroiteuropeen.files.wordpress.com/2017/06/article-pedro-chile-final-version.pdf (accessed September 12, 2017).

Rich, J. 1998. "Commercial Speech in the Law of the European Union: Lessons for the United States?" *Federal Communications Journal* 51(1): 263–79.

Severson, K. 2012. "Chick-fil-A Thrust Back into Spotlight on Gay Rights." *New York Times*, July 25 http://www.nytimes.com/2012/07/26/us/gay-rights-uproar-over-chick-fil-a-widens.html?mcubz=0 (accessed September 8, 2017).

Shane, S. and V. Goel. "Fake Russian Facebook Accounts Bought $100,000 in Political Ads." *New York Times*, September 6 https://www.nytimes.com/2017/09/06/technology/facebook-russian-political-ads.html (accessed October 24, 2017).

Sunstein, C. 1993. *Democracy and the Problem of Free Speech.* New York: Free Press.

Sunstein, C. 2015. "Islamic State's Challenge to Free Speech." *Bloomberg View*, November 23, https://www.bloomberg.com/view/articles/2015-11-23/islamic-state-s-challenge-to-free-speech (accessed September 12, 2017).

Sunstein, C. 2017. *#republic: Divided Democracy in the Age of Social Media.* Princeton, NJ: Princeton University Press.

Wichter, Z. 2017. "C.E.O.s See a 'Sad Day' after Trump's DACA Decision." *New York Times*, September 5, https://www.nytimes.com/2017/09/05/business/chief-executives-see-a-sad-day-after-trumps-daca-decision.html?mcubz=0 (accessed September 8, 2017).

6

Privacy, Speech, and the Digital Imagination
Robert C. Post

Specifying the value of privacy is notoriously difficult. We often resort to ideal concepts such as "dignity" or "control" or "autonomy," concepts that obscure as much as they reveal. At root this is because the value of privacy does not inhere in abstractions, but in lived experience. We enjoy the goods of privacy by participating in the forms of sociality that make these goods immanent (Post 1989, 9; Hirshleifer 1980, 649).

Forms of sociality lie at the intersection of the material and the imaginary. They exist as real and entrenched social structures insofar as we share a commitment to their importance and worth (Searle 2006). These commitments in turn arise out of and are sustained by the fulfillment and nourishment we derive from the forms of life they inspire. This virtuous cycle is pervasive in ordinary life, but it is rare in the digital world. Virtual reality is evolving so rapidly that it lacks the settled forms of life necessary to underwrite shared commitments. It should come as no surprise, therefore, that our digital imagination has yet to settle on a coherent account of the value of privacy. The confusion is especially important when government seeks to restrain digital expression in order to protect the value of privacy.

That digital expression is somehow important to the traditional democratic value of freedom of speech is widely accepted. It is commonly agreed that "in light of its accessibility and its capacity to store and communicate vast amounts of information, the internet plays an important role in enhancing the public's access to news and facilitating the dissemination of information in general."[1] As the United States Supreme Court recently opined:

> A fundamental principle of the First Amendment is that all persons have access to places where they can speak and listen, and then, after reflection, speak and listen once more. The Court has sought to protect the right to speak in this spatial context. A basic rule, for example, is that a street

or a park is a quintessential forum for the exercise of First Amendment rights. . . . Even in the modern era, these places are still essential venues for public gatherings to celebrate some views, to protest others, or simply to learn and inquire.

While in the past there may have been difficulty in identifying the most important places (in a spatial sense) for the exchange of views, today the answer is clear. It is cyberspace—the "vast democratic forums of the Internet" in general, . . . and social media in particular.[2]

At a minimum, the traditional democratic value of freedom of speech requires that digital expression should be curtailed only if necessary to achieve specific goods that we hold to be more important than the contribution of expression to the digital public sphere. If we wish to constrain expression to protect digital privacy, and if at the same time we have no very firm or clear conception of the nature of digital privacy, we face a serious challenge. The conundrum is unfortunately not theoretical, for we have recently witnessed powerful legal encroachments on communication that seem fundamentally confused in their apprehension of digital privacy.

I am referring to what has become known as the "right to be forgotten." The right became internationally prominent in 2014 when the Court of Justice of the European Union (CJEU) decided the monumental case of *Google Spain SL v. Agencia Española de Protección de Datos (AEPD)* ("*Google Spain*").[3] *Google Spain* sought to interpret Directive 95/46/EC[4] ("Directive"), which "is probably the most influential data privacy text in the world" (Kulk and Zuidvereen Borgesius, forthcoming, 14). The Directive contains comprehensive rules for processing the "personal data" of "data subjects"; it seeks to ensure that such personal data be used only for the "specified purposes"[5] for which they have been properly acquired.[6] The Directive protects what we may call "data privacy" by establishing "fair information practices" to assure the accuracy, transparency, and instrumental rationality of data processing (Flaherty 1986, 8). The point of these practices is to give data subjects "control," or "informational self-determination," over the use of their personal data.[7]

In essence, *Google Spain* held that the Google search engine ("Google") processed personal data whenever it performed a search of internet sites for the name of a data subject. Applying the criteria of the Directive, the CJEU held that a data subject could ask Google to remove search results that produced personal data that were "inadequate, irrelevant or no longer relevant, or excessive in relation to the purposes of the processing at issue carried out by the operator of the search engine."[8] *Google Spain* concluded that a data subject could "require the operator of a search engine to remove from the list of results displayed following a search made on the basis of his name links to web pages published lawfully by third parties and containing true information relating to him, on the ground that . . . he wishes it to be 'forgotten' after a certain time."[9]

Following *Google Spain,* the European Union doubled down on the right to be forgotten by enacting the General Data Protection Regulation (GDPR),[10] which subsequently became the law of all EU member states and which contains a right to be forgotten that will likely be interpreted in light of *Google Spain.*[11] The GDPR marks the legislative triumph of a distinctive EU variant of the right to be forgotten that can be expected massively to constrain the international digital public sphere of the internet.

The tension between the right to be forgotten and digital freedom of speech is palpable. By the beginning of 2017, the *Google Spain* decision had required Google to process 703,910 requests to remove 1,948,737 URLs from its search engine; some 43.2% of these URLs were erased from searches made under the name of the person requesting removal.[12] In the past several years, the right to be forgotten has been asserted by a vicar who resigned after villagers accused him of standing naked at a vicarage window and swearing at children; by a doctor convicted of attempting to spike his pregnant mistress' drinks with drugs to cause a miscarriage of their son; and by a butcher convicted of blackmail for threatening to send his estranged wife's wealthy parents videos of her participating in group sex (Williams 2015). The right to be forgotten has even been asserted against articles about the right to be forgotten (Peguera 2015).

The Index on Censorship denounced *Google Spain* as "akin to marching into a library and forcing it to pulp books" (Index on Censorship 2014). The European Union Committee of the British House of Lords responded to *Google Spain* by concluding (in bold-faced type) that "**the 'right to be forgotten' . . . must go. It is misguided in principle and unworkable in practice**" (House of Lords EU Committee 2014). Jimmy Wales, the cofounder of Wikipedia, condemned the right to be forgotten as "deeply immoral" because "history is a human right" (Curtis and Philipson 2014). The American legal scholar Jeffrey Rosen has observed that *Google Spain* and the GDPR portend a "titanic clash" with American free-speech principles (Rosen 2012).

The clash between the right to be forgotten and freedom of expression ultimately derives from the fact that the latter presupposes a form of sociality in which personal information is seamlessly integrated into intersubjective communication between persons, whereas the right to be forgotten presupposes that such information consists of compilations of data that persons control and manipulate. The right to be forgotten protects the right of persons autonomously to control information that pertains to them; the right to freedom of expression protects forms of communication that transpire in a common and shared world.

Data privacy conceptualizes personal data as something which persons use by gathering, storing, accessing, combining, analyzing, transmitting, or obliterating. Information is conceived as a kind of "thing" that is controlled by one agent or another. Fair information practices specify who can "own" personal data, as well as the purposes for which such data can be used. Fair information practices create accountability procedures to ensure that personal data are used only to serve specified purposes. The point of data privacy is to endow data subjects with the appropriate level of control over the use of their personal data. It is irrelevant whether data subjects suffer material or psychological harm from failure to comply with fair information practices,[13] because damage is conceptualized as losing control to which data subjects are otherwise entitled.

The Directive (and the GDPR) are quite ambitious. EU data privacy seeks to apply fair information practices to the "processing" of "personal data," which is defined as all information "relating" to an identifiable person.[14] There is no requirement that "personal data" be limited to private information or that it be limited to information that, if released, would be harmful to a data subject.[15] Taken literally, personal data seems to include even "very innocuous published information such as the name of an author coupled with a book title" (Erdos 2015, 122). The Directive defines "processing" in equally expansive terms, as "any operation or set of operations which is performed upon personal data, whether or not by automatic means, such as collection, recording, organization, storage, adaptation or alteration, retrieval, consultation, use, disclosure by transmission, dissemination or otherwise making available, alignment or combination, blocking, erasure or destruction."[16] Under this definition, every transmission of information over the internet constitutes the "processing" of data.[17]

In applying the right to be forgotten to Google, therefore, the CJEU asked whether Google's processing of personal data was "inadequate, irrelevant or no longer relevant, or excessive in relation to the purposes of the processing at issue carried out by the operator of the search engine."[18] This question presupposes a social world in which persons use Google searches for specific purposes, and in which the necessity of such searches can be assessed by the criteria of instrumental reason. The presupposition reflects the ways in which large corporations and organizations gather and use personal data. Large institutions acquire data in order to achieve specific ends—to allocate welfare benefits or to determine the creditworthiness of debtors or to increase the effectiveness of healthcare. In such situations, it may make perfect sense to restrict the manipulation of data to particular purposes and to maximize the control of data subjects over the use of their personal data.

Yet all would agree that there are vast stretches of life in which this kind of instrumental reason is out of place. Friendship is not instrumental, nor is love, nor is play, nor is much of common human expression. Suppose, for example, that I write a blog about your birthday party, which I have just attended. I am processing your personal data, but I am not doing it for a "specific" purpose. I am most likely engaging in what Habermas might call communicative action, which is expression designed to coordinate and affirm social understandings with friends and readers (Habermas 1972; Habermas 1971).[19]

Someone who would ask whether my processing personal data about your birthday party has become "irrelevant" or "excessive" with respect to the purposes of my blog shows that they do not understand the social practice of writing a blog. The personal data in my blog are not connected to the purpose for which I am writing the blog in the same way that a "means" is connected to an "end." When fair information practices are applied to communications such as my blog, they advance criteria for assessing the legitimacy of processing personal data that are literally unintelligible. The criteria presuppose forms of sociality that have nothing to do with the relevant form of life in which my blog participates.

The same is true of the virtual public sphere, which is also characterized by communicative action rather than instrumental reason. Persons express themselves in the public sphere in order to engage in a dialogue that they hope will forge shared values and commitments. The metaphor of "control" is incompatible with the intersubjective nature of this dialogue (Schwartz 2000, 760–61). Consider public discussion of Hillary Clinton's emails or of Donald Trump's "university." Although such discussions will include a great deal of "personal data," it makes little sense to ask who "controls" those data. In matters of legitimate public concern, we wish to promote an ongoing public dialogue that involves a common search for meaning in light of shared facts. To assert individual agential "control" of these facts is to shut down the exchange. In the context of the virtual public sphere, information is a public good.

We protect communicative exchange within the public sphere in order to sustain democracy. We can roughly define democracy as "'government by public opinion'" (Schmitt [1928] 2008, 275). It is for this reason that democracy requires the freedom of speech necessary to form public opinion (Post 2012, 13–21). I use the term "public discourse" to refer to the set of communications constitutionally deemed necessary to form a democratic public opinion (Post 2012, 15).[20] Democracy presupposes that dialogue within public discourse is intersubjective rather than instrumental (Michelman 1988, 1526–27). Public conversation must be permitted to allow the free play of public interest and attention; it cannot be bureaucratically organized to achieve specific purposes.[21] For this reason, information within public discourse is (typically) not "owned" by one person or another; it is a common good that facilitates communal communicative exchange.[22]

Google is essential to the infrastructure that sustains the virtual public sphere. It connects persons who wish to communicate with each other. It creates a moving archive that corresponds to the internet itself.[23] The purpose of such an archive is comparable to the purpose of traditional library archives, which are dedicated to providing "the public the means of acquiring information, knowledge, education, aesthetic experience, and entertainment" (Molz and Dain 1990, 2). Such archives sustain "democratic" culture[24] by "recapturing and extending democratic processes and potential" through linking persons to "the public sphere" (Buschman 2003, 175). The "allure of the archives," writes Arlette Farge, is the anticipation of a "roaming voyage through the words of others," so that we might "enter into an unending conversation about humanity" and about "the debates that surround us" (Farge 2013, 123–24). When might it be said that the processing of personal data necessary to populate such archives is "inadequate, irrelevant or no longer relevant, or excessive in relation to" this social purpose?[25]

There is no answer to this question. If we wish to use archives to produce shared understandings, we cannot accept the right to be forgotten, which is why even one of the GDPR's most passionate advocates has observed:

> The right to be forgotten is of course not an absolute right. There are cases where there is a legitimate and legally justified interest to keep data in a data base. The archives of a newspaper are a good example. It is clear that the right to be forgotten cannot amount to a right of the total erasure of history (Reding 2012, emphasis omitted).

History is produced by a form of sociality that regards personal data as a communal good, rather than as a "thing" that is under the "control"[26] of any single data subject. Data privacy would unravel the fabric of history itself. It would authorize me to prevent you from narrating your account of historical events if it included information "relating to"[27] me, and vice versa. Yet history can be constructed only from the interplay of such perspectives, including the personal data contained within them. That is why "[i]t is not the role of judicial authorities to engage in rewriting history by ordering the removal from the public domain of all traces of" past publications.[28]

This same need for communal information applies when personal data are communicated in the public sphere, which is where our understandings of history are forged. Public discourse would collapse if individuals were authorized to withdraw from circulation all information "relating to" themselves.[29] The pressing importance of self-governance gives us good constitutional reasons to release public discourse from the grip of data privacy. Fair information practices would in effect cede power to create public opinion to those entitled to control the circulation of personal data in the public sphere.

This tension is so obvious that both the Directive and the GDPR acknowledge forms of public communication that should be exempt from the reach of data privacy.[30] The Directive provides that "Member States shall provide for exemptions or derogations from the [Directive] for the processing of personal data carried out solely for journalistic purposes or the purpose of artistic or literary expression only if they are necessary to reconcile the right to privacy with the rules governing freedom of expression."[31] The GDPR more capaciously provides that "Member States shall by law reconcile the right to the protection of personal data pursuant to this Regulation with the right to freedom of expression and information, including processing for journalistic purposes and the purposes of academic, artistic or literary expression."[32]

The important theoretical question, then, is how "freedom of expression and information"[33] can be *reconciled* with the regime of instrumental reason that structures data privacy. Neither the Directive nor the GDPR offers so much as a hint. When pressed, reconciliation is explained through the metaphor of striking "a balance between [data] privacy and freedom of expression" (EC 1997, 5).[34] But it is hard to understand how the image of balancing makes sense when data privacy and freedom of expression presuppose mutually exclusive social domains. The possibility of public discourse is foreclosed if personal data must be processed according to the managerial logic of data privacy, but fair information practices are eliminated if public discourse is exempted from this logic to allow for the free play of common information. How data privacy might be safeguarded *within* public discourse is unexplained, because data privacy exists in a bureaucratic universe that is incompatible with the communicative action constitutive of the public sphere.

Within the world of print or broadcast media, very few would dare to claim that persons should have the right to "control" the dissemination of any information "relating" to them, however innocuous. The need for information as a public good, the necessity for common discussion, are just too obvious. But by creating the right to be forgotten, the CJEU seemingly accepts the validity of such a claim with respect to Google, even though Google plays as important a role in the virtual public sphere as do the print or broadcast media in the traditional public sphere (Post 2018). How could the CJEU have made such a categorical mistake?

I suggest that the CJEU's confusion reflects our uncertainty in the face of digital social practices. In the traditional press, no one would think to categorize Beyoncé's birthday (September 4, 1981) as a "thing" that she can control. Yet if information identifying her birthday is collected in digital form, available for processing for various purposes, we may become unsure how to characterize it. We might well conclude that Beyoncé should be able to control the dissemination of her birthdate if it is stored within the databank of a large organization to serve managerial purposes. In creating the right to be forgotten, the CJEU generalized from this intuition.

The fallacy of the CJEU was to focus on the digital form of information, rather than on the human relationships in which information was embedded. Information that is incorporated into managerial regimes ought to be regulated according to the technocratic logic of such domains. But information that is constitutive of communication action ought to be regulated in ways that are compatible with communicative action. It does not matter how information is stored, whether digitally or in print. What matters are the forms of sociality that we wish information to serve. It is possible that the CJEU failed to grasp this fundamental insight because it was blinded by Google's digital character.

The CJEU seems to have imagined that the mere fact of digitization produces its own form of sociality. But this is manifestly not the case.

Data privacy arose out of the need to control the large-scale accumulation of personal data by organizations that created intolerable imbalances of power and information. This implies that fair information practices can and should apply to the personal data that Google gathers on its customers to effect "massive online captures of everydayness," which Shoshana Zuboff has labeled "surveillance capitalism" (Constantiou and Kallinnikos 2015, 55; Zuboff 2015, 75).[35] Such personal data is gathered and used for instrumental purposes. But it also implies that data privacy principles should not be applied to the vast stretches of digital communication that have nothing to do with the bureaucratic accumulation and manipulation of data.

Ordinary Google searches, from the perspective of Google's customers, underwrite the structure of the virtual public sphere. They create a web of communications that connects us each to the other as we participate in a public conversation out of which public opinion emerges. "Google and similar search engines are . . . increasingly becoming our windows to the world" (de Mars and O'Callaghan 2016, 267). The spell of the digital blinded the CJEU to the vital distinction between these two distinct forms of sociality within which digital information is embedded.

Does this imply that privacy cannot be protected within the virtual public sphere? Not at all. It implies that privacy should be protected in the virtual public sphere in the same way that it is protected within the traditional public sphere. For more than a century, legal systems around the world have imposed legal restrictions upon the press and media that protect privacy by seeking to preserve the dignity of persons rather than informational self-determination. Let us call the telos of such restrictions "dignitary privacy." It is sometimes said that "two of the most prominent conceptions of privacy are the control-based and the dignitarian" (O'Callaghan 2018, 160).

To various degrees in various countries, law has proscribed the dissemination within public discourse of "personal information which individuals can legitimately expect should not be published without their consent"[36] because it would damage their "honour" or "psychological or moral integrity"[37] or "prejudice" their "personal enjoyment of the right to respect for private life."[38] When communications disrespectfully dredge up old events that compromise the dignity of a person, a version of the right to be forgotten can exist within the framework of dignitary privacy (Franz 2009; Werro 2009).

In the law of France, as well as that of "other European countries," (Mantelero 2013) the latter version of the right to be forgotten is known as "le Droit à l'Oubli," which places "a time limit on the publication of information: the press . . . cannot continue to publicize matters that are no longer in the public interest" and that can "relentlessly harm" persons "beyond a period of newsworthy relevancy" (Mantelero 2013, 229; LoCascio 2015, 299).[39]

American courts have also sought to protect dignitary privacy. They have asked whether particular communications have become so offensive as defined by "community mores" that they cause "humiliation and mortification"[40] and cannot be justified by "a legitimate interest or curiosity"[41] of the public.[42] This can include dredging up old and offensive information.[43]

Almost all legal systems determine violations of dignitary privacy by balancing the "seriousness" of harms caused by a communication against the communication's "contribution . . . to a debate of general interest."[44] Protections of data privacy cannot analogously weigh harm to personality against the legitimate interests of the public, because data privacy does not contain within it any analogous concept of harm to personality. It instead imagines persons as autonomous agents who control information. Within the context of dignitary privacy, by contrast, "harm" is determined on the premise that the well-being of persons depends upon compliance with intersubjective norms of respect, which are embodied by rules of civil communication.[45]

Dignitary and data privacy differ in essential respects. Dignitary privacy does not focus on personal data per se, but instead seeks to ascertain whether specific communications are consistent with civility rules that reciprocally define both individual and community identity (Post 1989, 978–87). It asks whether communications are *appropriate*, meaning in accordance with "finely calibrated systems of social norms, or rules . . . [that] define and sustain essential activities and key relationships and interests" (Nissenbaum 2010, 2–3). Communications that are sufficiently outrageous are conceived as damaging human personality.

If data privacy follows an instrumental logic of rationality, dignitary privacy follows a hermeneutic logic of social norms. Data privacy focuses on the manipulation of data; dignitary privacy focuses instead on acts of communication. Dignitary privacy protects the human personality understood as embedded in social norms; data privacy protects the capacity of autonomous human agents to exercise control. Damage to personality, which is essential to dignitary privacy, is irrelevant to data privacy, which focuses purely on the scope of control. Dignitary privacy turns on the legitimate interests of the public, whereas the data privacy is indifferent to those interests.

Most importantly, data privacy presupposes a form of sociality that is fundamentally incompatible with the public discourse, whereas dignitary privacy does not. Freedom of speech is generally regarded as essential to democracy because it empowers persons to participate in the formation of public opinion and hence to experience the state as potentially responsive to them (Post 2014, 39–42). But if public discourse becomes sufficiently abusive and alienating, persons are unlikely to experience it as a medium through which they might influence the construction of public opinion. In such circumstances, public discourse will no longer serve the purpose of democratic legitimation, and the democratic justification for freedom of speech will pro tanto diminish.

This creates what I have elsewhere called "the paradox of public discourse": Although public discourse can sustain democratic legitimation only if it is conducted with a modicum of civility, the enforcement of civility restricts freedom of speech (Post 1990, 601, 640–44, 680–84). The existence of the paradox demonstrates that dignitary privacy can be compatible with the democratic function of public discourse in ways that data privacy cannot. The genuine conundrum of the paradox means that different legal systems can resolve the balance between freedom of expression and dignitary privacy in different ways.

The extreme cultural diversity of the United States makes American courts loath to restrict public curiosity in the name of intersubjective norms.[46] American law characteristically regards "the interest of the public in the free dissemination of the truth and unimpeded access to news" as "so broad, so difficult to define and so dangerous to circumscribe," that they "have been reluctant to make . . . factually accurate public disclosures tortious, except where the lack of any meritorious public interest in the disclosure is very clear and its offensiveness to ordinary sensibilities is equally clear."[47] The suppression of public discourse in the interests of dignitary privacy is thus rare and plausible only in exceptionally outrageous cases as measured by the extraordinary offensiveness of a publication (Barbas 2010, 172–73; Sterne 2016). In Europe, by contrast, courts are far less deferential to the curiosity of the public[48] and far more sympathetic to the authoritative enforcement of social norms considered indispensable to dignitary privacy.[49]

These differences result from distinctive historical traditions that have produced divergent forms of elite control over social norms, divergent needs to appeal to democratic legitimation to justify state action, divergent commitments to cultural individualism (Post 1988), and so on. Such differences suggest that distinct legal systems can differently resolve the paradox of public discourse and yet nevertheless retain the benefits of democratic legitimation (Post 2009). It is not possible, however, to eliminate the incompatibility between data privacy and public discourse. The bureaucratic domain of data privacy is fundamentally irreconcilable with the shared and open communicative space required by public discourse.

The CJEU in *Google Spain* must ultimately have realized this fact. It is noteworthy that although the decision purports to apply the instrumental logic of the Directive, it nevertheless negotiates a series of murky legal maneuvers that seem to point to the conclusion that the right to be forgotten can be successfully asserted only if the "harm" to a data subject is balanced against the "interest of the general public" (Post 2018).[50] Yet this balance is the precise legal form assumed by protections for dignitary privacy, which weigh damage to personality (a concept that does not exist within data privacy) against the legitimate concerns of the public. But the CJEU reached this conclusion in such an obscure and labyrinthine way that it is hard to be confident what *Google Spain* actually means.

It is certain, however, that by focusing primarily on data privacy and the Directive, and by obscurely invoking considerations appropriate to dignitary privacy only when backed into a conceptual corner,[51] the CJEU failed to articulate a sophisticated or even adequate account of how dignity might be weighed against the public's need to know. (Kulk and Borgesius 2015, 123). This failure might have been avoided had the CJEU not been so distracted by the digital nature of the information at issue. *Google Spain* illustrates how difficult it is for courts to grasp in the digital world the same forms of ordinary sociality that are so salient elsewhere in constitutional doctrine.

Perhaps the digital world is as yet too shapeless to sustain the creation of sound principles of jurisprudential order. The legal anthropologist Paul Bohannan once defined law as the "double institutionalization" of norms (Bohannan 1965, 35–36). Law functions well when it can take norms that society has already institutionalized and re-institutionalize them to serve the specific needs of the legal system. But if society lacks such norms, as seems to be the case within the digital world, legal regulation becomes destabilized and uncertain.[52]

It is common ground, however, that in the context of regulating public discourse "[p]recision of regulation must be the touchstone in an area so closely touching our most precious freedoms."[53] The consequences of conceptual confusion when the legitimacy of democratic self-governance is itself at stake can be quite significant, as the example of *Google Spain* well illustrates. Certainly we owe it to ourselves to try to see more clearly into the digital abyss.

Notes

1. *Case of Magyar Tartalomszolgáltatók Egyesülete and Index.hu Zrt v. Hungary*, ECtHR (Application no. 22947/13) (February 2, 2016), at ¶ 56.

2. Packingham v. North Carolina, 137 S. Ct. 1730, 1735 (2017).

3. Case C-131/12 (May 13, 2014), available at http://curia.europa.eu/juris/document/document_print.jsf?doclang=EN&docid=152065.

4. Directive 95/46/EC On the Protection of Individuals with Regard to the Processing of Personal Data and on the Free Movement of such Data (October 24, 1995), available at http://eur-lex.europa.eu/LexUriServ/LexUriServ.do?uri=CELEX:31995L0046:en:HTML.

5. *See* Article 8 of the Charter of Fundamental Rights of the European Union ("Protection of Personal Data"), Section 2, available at http://eur-lex.europa.eu/legal-content/EN/TXT/PDF/?uri=CELEX:12012P/TXT&from=EN.

6. Directive, Article 6(1).

7. "Generally, the 'privacy-as-control' approach has manifested in the area of personal information protection as a call for awarding individuals the greatest control possible over their personal information. This is reflected in what are commonly referred to as Fair

Information Practices." (Levin and Abril 2009, 1009). "The right to be forgotten represents 'informational self-determination' as well as the control-based definition of privacy and attempts to migrate personal information from a public sphere to a private sphere." (Jones 2016, 94). In this context, the right to "control" the manipulation of existing personal data should be distinguished from the right to prevent surveillance, which is the right to prevent the augmentation of existing personal data.

8. *Google Spain* at ¶ 94.

9. *Google Spain,* ¶ 89.

10. Regulation (EU) 2016/679 of the European Parliament and of the Council of 27 April 2016, available at http://eur-lex.europa.eu/legal-content/EN/TXT/PDF/ ?uri=CELEX:32016R0679&from=EN. The GDPR went into effect on May 25, 2018. It repealed the Directive. Article 17 of the GDPR, which is entitled "Right to Erasure ('Right to be Forgotten')," is an explicit gesture toward the holding of *Google Spain.*

11. GDPR, Art. 17.

12. https://www.google.com/transparencyreport/removals/europeprivacy/?hl=en (accessed March 17, 2017). For examples of sites that Google has and has not removed in response to *Google Spain, see* https://www.google.com/transparencyreport/removals/ europeprivacy/.

13. *Google Spain,* at ¶ 96. *See* The Advisory Council to Google on the Right to Be Forgotten (February 6, 2015), available at http://docs.dpaq.de/8527-report_of_the_ advisory_committee_to_google_on_the_right_to_be_forgotten.pdf, at 5 ("The right to object to and require cessation of the processing of data about himself or herself . . . exists regardless of whether the processing at issue causes harm or is prejudicial in some way to the data subject.").

14. *Google Spain,* at ¶ 4. Directive, Article 2(a).

15. *Google Spain.* at ¶ 96.

16. Directive, Article 2(b). The GDPR defines "processing" in virtually the same way. *See* GDPR, Article 4(2).

17. Reference to the CJEU for a preliminary ruling in the criminal proceedings against Bodil Lindqvist, Case C-101/01 (November 6, 2003) ¶ 27, available at http://curia.europa. eu/juris/document/document.jsf?docid=48382&doclang=en.

18. *Google Spain,* ¶ 94.

19. *See, e.g.,* Habermas ([1962] 1970, 81–122); [1968] 1972).

20. In this chapter, I am *not* using the term "public discourse" to refer to those speech acts that in American constitutional law would create the value of democratic legitimation for individual human beings. *Compare* Post (2014, 71–74).

21. For this reason, speech within managerial spaces is differently protected than speech within public discourse. *See* Post (1987); Post (1993).

22. The law of intellectual property, of course, represents an awkward exception to this generalization.

23. In *Case of Times Newspapers Ltd (nos 1 and 2) v. The United Kingdom,* Applications nos 3002/03 and 23676/03, ECtHR (October 6, 2009), the ECtHR acknowledged "the substantial contribution made by Internet archives to preserving and making available news and information. Such archives constitute an important source for education and historical research, particularly as they are readily accessible to the public and are generally free. The Court therefore considers that, while the primary function of the press in a

democracy is to act as a 'public watchdog', it has a valuable secondary role in maintaining and making available to the public archives containing news which has previously been reported." *Id.* at 45, available at http://hudoc.echr.coe.int/eng#{"dmdocnumber":["848220"]," itemid":["001-91706"]}.

24. The 1979 White House Conference on Library and Information Services affirmed that "publicly-supported libraries are institutions of education for democratic living." *Resolutions of the White House Conference on Library and Information Services 1979*, at 42 (March 1980).

25. *Google Spain.* at ¶ 93; For a fascinating if unsuccessful effort to wrestle with this question, see Szekely (2014).

26. GDPR, recital 7.

27. Directive, Article 2(a). Article GDPR, Article 4(1).

28. Węgrzynowski and Smolczewski v. Poland, ECtHR (Application No. 33846/07), July 16, 2013, at ¶ 65.

29. *See, e.g.,* Dresbach v. Doubleday & Co., Inc., 518 F. Supp. 1285, 1289–91 (D.C. 1981); Bonome v. Kaysen, 17 Mass. L. Rptr. 695 (2004); Anonsen v. Donahue, 857 S.W.2d 700 (Tex. Ct. App. 1993).

30. Both the Directive and GDPR permit the processing of personal data that is used "purely" for personal or household activities. *See* Directive, Article 3(2), Recital 12; GDPR, Article 2(2)(c); Recital 18. But the dissemination of information to the general public through the internet is not considered a personal or household activity. *See* Opinion 5/2009 of the Article 29 Data Protection Working Party (*On Online Social Networking*) (June 12, 2009), available at http://ec.europa.eu/justice/data-protection/article-29/documentation/opinion-recommendation/files/2009/wp163_en.pdf.

31. Directive, Article 9. For an exhaustive and disquieting study of how the national law of EU member states seeks (or does not seek) to reconcile the Directive with journalistic freedom, *see* Erdos 2016a, 2016b, 2016c.

32. GDPR, Article 85(1).

33. In the European context, the "right of . . . information" focuses on the right of the public to *receive* information. *See* Charter, Article 11, available at http://eur-lex.europa.eu/legal-content/EN/TXT/PDF/?uri=CELEX:12012P/TXT&from=EN (emphasis added).

34. *See Google Spain,* ¶ 81; Directive, Recital 37.

35. On Google's acquisition of data, see Jones and Jones (2010); Van der Sloot, Boresius, and Taurrella (2012).

36. *Case of Axel Springer AG v. Germany,* (7 February 2012) (Application no. 39954/08), ¶ 83.

37. *Case of A. v. Norway* (9 April 2009)) (Application no. 28070/06), ¶ 63.

38. *Case of Axel Springer AG v. Germany,* (7 February 2012) (Application no. 39954/08), ¶ 83.

39. "In Continental Europe, the right to be forgotten can be considered as being contained in the right of the personality, encompassing several elements such as dignity, honor, and the right to private life. Manifold terminologies are used in the context of the right of personality—mainly the right for the (moral and legal) integrity of a person not to be infringed and for a sphere of privacy to be maintained and distinguished" (Weber 2011).

40. Pavesich v. New England Life Ins. Co. 50 S.E. 68, 79 (Ga. 1905). "There must be . . . some reasonable and plausible ground for the existence of this mental distress and

injury. It must not be the creation of mere caprice nor of pure fancy, nor the result of a supersensitive and morbid mental organization, dwelling with undue emphasis upon the exclusive and sacred character of this right of privacy. . . . [A] violation of a legal right must . . . be of such a nature as a reasonable man can see might and probably would cause mental distress and injury to any one possessed of ordinary feeling and intelligence." Schuyler v. Curtis, 147 N.Y. 434, 448 (1895). For a discussion of the sociological interconnection between community mores and emotional damage, see Post (1989).

41. Virgil v. Time, Inc., 527 F.2d 1122, 1131 (9th Cir. 1975), *cert. denied*, 425 U.S. 998 (1976).

42. Haynes v. Alfred A. Knopf, Inc., 8 F.3d 1222, 1232 (7th Cir. 1993). When the first *Restatement of Torts* recognized the tort of invasion of privacy in 1939, it explicitly observed that the protection of privacy must be "relative to the customs of the time and place and to the habits and occupation of the plaintiff." RESTATEMENT (FIRST) OF TORTS, § 867, comment c(1939).

43. *See, e.g.,* Melvin v. Reid, 297 P. 91 (Cal. App. 1931); Briscoe v. Reader's Digest Ass'n, 483 P.2d 34 (Cal. 1971).

44. *Case of Axel Springer AG v. Germany,* (7 February 2012) (Application no. 39954/08), ¶¶ 83, 89, 90. *Compare* RESTATEMENT (SECOND) OF TORTS § 652D (1977): "One who gives publicity to a matter concerning the private life of another is subject to liability to the other for invasion of his privacy, if the matter publicized is of a kind that (a) would be highly offensive to a reasonable person, and (b) is not of legitimate concern to the public."

45. *See* Post (1989).

46. In a nation as diverse as the United States, "what is 'private' so as to make its publication offensive likely differs among communities, between generations, and among ethnic, religious, or other social groups, as well as among individuals. Likewise, one reader's or viewer's 'news' is another's tedium or trivia." Anderson v. Fisher Broad. Cos., 300 Or. 452, 461 (1986).

47. Jenkins v. Dell Pub. Co., 251 F.2d 447, 450 (3d Cir. 1958).

48. *See, e.g.,* Alesey Ovchinnikov v. Russia, No. 24061/04 ECtHR (December 16, 2010), at ¶ 50, available at http://www.google.com/url?sa=t&rct=j&q=&esrc=s&source=web&cd=1&ved=0ahUKEwjk1Zq_gKnPAhUm5oMKHeA3BGwQFggcMAA&url=http%3A%2F%2Fhudoc.echr.coe.int%2Fapp%2Fconversion%2Fpdf%2F%3Flibrary%3DECHR%26id%3D001-102322%26filename%3D001-102322.pdf&usg=AFQjCNFWIMDcEbeo7clqXiU MwpoghhqFgg; Case of Hanover v. Germany, ECtHR (Application no. 59320/00) (24 June 2004), at 65; Spanish Supreme Court Judgment n. 545/2015, October 15, 2015, at 6.

49. Biriuk v. Lithuana, App no. 23373/03 ECtHR (November 25, 2008), at 38, available at http://en.tm.lt/dok/Biriuk_v__Lithuania.pdf; Tammer v. Estonia, App. no. 41205/98 (6 February 2001), at ¶¶ 64–69. On the confidence of European courts to balance dignity and privacy against freedom of speech, *see* Ronald J. Krotoszynski Jr., *Reconciling Privacy and Speech in the Era of Big Data: A Comparative Analysis,* 56 WM. & MY. L. REV. 1279, 1314–26 (2015).

50. *Google Spain,* ¶¶ 81, 99.

51. The CJEU could appeal to those considerations insofar as Article 7 of the Charter, which provides that "[e]veryone has the right to respect for his or her private and family life, home and communications," available at http://eur-lex.europa.eu/legal-content/EN/TXT/PDF/?uri=CELEX:12012P/TXT&from=EN, was also involved in the *Google Spain* case.

Free Speech in the Digital Age

Article 7 refers to dignitary privacy, *see* Post 2018, *supra* note 54, and was specifically (if obscurely) mentioned by the CJEU in its *Google Spain* opinion as relevant to its decision. *Google Spain,* ¶ 99.

52. As Justice Harlan Fiske Stone once put it, "moral standards must become generally settled and accepted by society before they can find expression in law as an established rule of conduct. The moral rule must be a settled principle of social conduct before the law can or should attempt to make that principle mandatory upon all members of the community" (Stone 1915, 34).

53. NAACP v. Button, 371 U.S. 415, 438 (1963).

References

Barbas, S. 2010. "The Death of the Public Disclosure Tort: A Historical Perspective." *Yale Journal of Law and Humanities* 22 (171). doi:10.5040/9781474200974.ch-002.

Bohannan, P. 1965. "The Differing Realms of the Law." *American Anthropologist* 67 (6): 33–42. doi:10.1525/aa.1965.67.6.02a00930.

Buschman, J. 2003. *Dismantling The Public Sphere: Situating and Sustaining Librarianship in the Age of the New Public Philosophy.* Westport, CT: Libraries Unlimited.

Constantiou, I. D. and J. Kallinikos. 2014. "New Games, New Rules: Big Data and the Changing Context of Strategy." *Journal of Information Technology* 30 (1): 44–57. doi:10.1057/jit.2015.17.

Curtis, S. and A. Philipson. 2014. "Wikipedia Founder: EU's Right to Be Forgotten Is 'Deeply Immoral.'" *The Telegraph.* August 6. http://www.telegraph.co.uk/technology/wikipedia/11015901/EU-ruling-on-link-removal-   deeply-immoral-says-Wikipedia-founder.html.

Erdos, D. 2015. "From the Scylla of Restriction to the Charybdis of License? Exploring the Scope of the 'Special Purposes' Freedom of Expression Shield in European Data Protection." *Common Market Law Review,* April: 119–54.

Erdos, D. 2016a. "European Regulatory Interpretation of the Interface between Data Protection and Journalistic Freedom: An Incomplete and Imperfect Balancing Act?" *Public Law:* 631–50. doi:10.2139/ssrn.2683471.

Erdos, D. 2016b. "Fundamentally Off Balance: European Union Data Protection Law and Media Expression." *International and Comparative Law Quarterly* 65: 139–83. doi:10.2139/ssrn.2471531.

Erdos, D. 2016c. "Statutory Regulation of Professional Journalism Under European Data Protection: Down But Not Out?" *Journal of Media Law* 8 (2): 229–65. doi:10.2139/ssrn.2817823.

Farge, A. 2013. *The Allure of the Archives,* Translated by T. Scott-Railton. New Haven: Yale University Press.

Flaherty, D. H. 1986. "Governmental Surveillance and Bureaucratic Accountability: Data Protection Agencies in Western Societies." *Science, Technology, & Human Values* 11 (1): 7–18. doi:10.1177/027046768601100102.

Franz, W. 2009. "The Right to Inform v. the Right to Be Forgotten: A Transatlantic Clash." In A. Colombie Ciacchi, C. Godt, P. Rott, and L J. Smith (eds.) *Haftungsrecht Im Dritten Millennium—Liability in the Third Millennium: Liber Amicorum Gert Brüggemeier.* Baden-Baden: Nomos Verlag.

Google. 2017. *Transparency Report.* https://www.google.com/transparencyreport/ removals/europeprivacy.com/transparencyreport/removals/europeprivacy/.

Habermas, J. 1971. *Toward a Rational Society: Student Protest, Science, and Politics.* Translated by Jeremy J. Shapiro. Boston: Beacon Press.

Habermas, J. 1972. *Knowledge and Human Interests.* Translated by Jeremy J. Shapiro. Boston: Beacon Press.

Hirshleifer, J. 1980. "Privacy: Its Origin, Function, and Future." *Journal of Legal Studies* 9 (4): 649–64.

House of Lords EU Committeee. 2014. *2nd Report of Session 2014–15: EU Data Protection Law: a "Right to Be Forgotten"?* July 23. http://www.publications.parliament.uk/pa/ld201415/ldselect/ldeucom/40/40.pdf.

Index on Censorship. 2014. "Index Blasts EU Court Ruling on 'Right to Be Forgotten'. . . " May 13. indexoncensorship.org%2f2014%2f05%2findex-blasts-eu-court-ruling-right-forgotten%2f&p=DevEx,5063.1

Jones, E. A. and J. W. Janes. 2010. "Anonymity in a World of Digital Books: Google Books, Privacy, and the Freedom to Read." *Policy & Internet* 2 (4): 42–74. doi:10.2202/1944-2866.1072.

Jones, M. L. 2016. *Ctrl Z: The Right to Be Forgotten.* New York: New York University Press.

Kulk, S. and F. Zuiderveen Borgesius. Forthcoming. "Privacy, Freedom of Expression, and Right to Be Forgotten in Europe." In J. Polonetsky, O. Ten, and E. Selinger (eds.) *Cambridge Handbook of Consumer Privacy.* Cambridge: Cambridge University Press.

Kulk, S. and F. Zuiderveen Borgesius. 2015. "Freedom of Expression and 'Right to Be Forgotten' Cases in the Netherlands after *Google Spain*." *European Data Protection Law Review* 1 (2): 113–24. doi:10.21552/edpl/2015/2/5.

Levin, A. and P. Sánchez Abril. 2009. "Two Notions of Privacy Online." *Vanderbilt Journal of Entertainment & Technology Law* 11 (4): 1001–51.

LoCascio, S. M. 2015. "Forcing Europe to Wear Rose-Colored Google Glass: The 'Right to Be Forgotten' and the Struggle to Manage Compliance Post *Google Spain*." *Columbia Journal of Transnational Law* 54 (1): 296–331.

Mantelero, A. 2013. "The EU Proposal for a General Data Protection Regulation and the Roots of the 'Right to Be Forgotten.'" *Computer Law & Security Review* 29 (3): 229–35. doi:10.1016/j.clsr.2013.03.010.

Michelman, F. 1988. "Law's Republic." *Yale Law Journal* 97: 1493–537.

Molz, R. K. and P. Dain. 1999. *Civic Space/Cyberspace: The American Public Library in the Information Age.* Cambridge, MA: MIT Press

De Mars, S. and P. O'Callaghan, P. 2016. "Privacy and Search Engines: Forgetting or Contextualizing?" *Journal of Law and Society* 43 (2): 257–84. doi:10.1111/j.1467-6478.2016.00751.x.

Nissenbaum, H. 2010. *Privacy in Context: Technology, Policy, and the Integrity of Social Life.* Stanford: Stanford University Press.

O'Callaghan, P. 2018. "The Chance 'to Melt into the Shadows of Obscurity'. Developing a Right to Be Forgotten in the United States." In A. Cudd and M. Navin (eds.) *Privacy: Core Concepts and Contemporary Issues.* Cham: Springer.

Peguera, M. 2015. "No More Right-to-Be-Forgotten for Mr. Costeja, Says Spanish Data Protection Authority." *Center for Internet and Society.* Stanford University. October 3. https://cyberlaw.stanford.edu/blog/2015/10/no-more-right-be-forgotten-mr-costeja-says-spanish-data-protection-authority.

Post, R. C. 1987. "Between Governance and Management: The History and Theory of the Public Forum." *UCLA Law Review* 34: 1713–835.

Post, R. C. 1988. "Cultural Heterogeneity and Law: Pornography, Blasphemy, and the First Amendment." *California Law Review* 76 (2): 297–335. doi:10.2307/3480615.

Post, R. C. 1989. "The Social Foundations of Privacy: Community and Self in the Common Law Tort." *California Law Review* 77 (5): 957–1010. doi:10.2307/3480641.

Post, R. C. 1990. "The Constitutional Concept of Public Discourse: Outrageous Opinion, Democratic Deliberation, and Hustler Magazine v. Falwell." *Harvard Law Review* 103: 601–86.

Post, R. C. 1993 "Meiklejohn's Mistake: Individual Autonomy and the Reform of Public Discourse." *University of Colorado Law Review* 64: 1109–38.

Post, R. C. 2009. "Hate Speech." In I. Hare and J. Weinstein (eds.) *Extreme Speech and Democracy.* New York: Oxford University Press.

Post, R. C. 2012. *Democracy, Expertise, Academic Freedom: A First Amendment Jurisprudence for the Modern State.* New Haven, CT: Yale University Press.

Post, R. C. 2014. *Citizens Divided: Campaign Finance Reform and the Constitution.* Cambridge, MA: Harvard University Press.

Post, R. C. 2018. "Data Privacy and Dignitary Privacy: *Google Spain*, the Right to Be Forgotten, and the Construction of the Public Sphere." *Duke Law Journal.* doi:10.2139/ssrn.2953468.

Reding, V. 2012. "The EU Data Protection Reform 2012: Making Europe the Standard Setter for Modern Data Protection Rules in the Digital Age." *Address at the Innovation Conference Digital, Life, Design,* January 22. http://europa.eu/rapid/press-release_SPEECH-12-26_en.htm.

Rosen, J. 2012. "The Right to Be Forgotten." *The Atlantic,* October 6. http://www.theatlantic.com/magazine/archive/2012/07/the-right-to-be-forgotten/309044/.

Schmitt, C. 2008. *Constitutional Theory.* Translated by Jeffrey Seitzer. Durham, NC: Duke University Press.

Schwartz, P. M. 2000. "Beyond Lessig's Code for Internet Privacy: Cyberspace Filters, Privacy Control and Fair Information Practices." *Wisconsin Law Review:* 743–88. doi:10.2139/ssrn.254849.

Searle, J. R. 2006. "Social Ontology: Some Basic Principles." *Anthropological* Theory 6 (1): 12–29.

Szekely, I. 2014. "The Right to Be Forgotten and the New Archival Paradigm." In A. Ghezzi, A Guimares Pareira, and L. Vesnic-Alujevic (eds.) *The Ethics of Memory in a Digital Age: Interrogating the Right to Be Forgotten.* London: Palgrave Macmillan: 28–49.

Sterne, P. 2016. "Jury Awards Hulk Hogan $115 Million as Gawker Looks to Appeal." *Politico Media,* March 18. http://www.politico.com/media/story/2016/03/jury-awards-hulk-hogan-115-million-as-gawker-looks-to-appeal-004433.

Stone, H. F. 1915. *Law and Its Administration.* New York: Columbia University Press.

van der Sloot, B., F Zuiderveen Boresius, and A. Lopez-Tarruella. 2012. "Google and Personal Data Protection." In A. Lopez-Tarruella (ed.) *Google and the Law: Empirical Approaches to Legal Aspects of Knowledge-Economy Business Models.* The Hague: Springer: 75–112.

Weber, R. H. 2011. "The Right to Be Forgotten: More than a Pandora's Box?" *Journal of Intellectual Property, Information Technology and Electronic Commerce Law* 2: 120–30.

Werro, F. 2009. "The Right to Inform v. the Right to Be Forgotten: A Transatlantic Clash." In A. Colombie Ciacchi, C. Godt, P. Rott, and L J. Smith (eds.) *Haftungsrecht Im Dritten Millennium—Liability in the Third Millennium: Liber Amicorum Gert Brüggemeier.* Baden-Baden, Nomos Verlag: 285–300.

Williams, R. 2015. "Telegraph Stories Affected by EU 'Right to be Forgotten." *Telegraph,* September 3. https://www.telegraph.co.uk/technology/google/11036257/Telegraph-stories-affected-by-EU-right-to-be-forgotten.html.

Zuboff, S. 2015. "Big Other: Surveillance, Capitalism and the Prospects of an Information Civilization." *Journal of Information Technology* 75: 75–89.

7

Restricting Speech to Protect It

Danielle Keats Citron

1. Introduction

A decade ago, online abuse was routinely dismissed as "no big deal." Activities that would have ordinarily been viewed as violations of the law if perpetrated in physical space were viewed as deserving of special protection because they occurred in "cyberspace." The "internet" deserved special protection because it was a unique zone of public discourse. No matter that targeted individuals (who were more often women and minorities) were being terrorized and silenced with rape threats, defamation, and invasions of sexual privacy. The common refrain was that the abuse had to be tolerated, lest we endanger speech online.

Much has changed in the past ten years. Social attitudes have evolved to recognize the expressive interests of victims as well as those of the perpetrators. Cyber harassment is now widely understood as profoundly damaging to victims' expressive and privacy interests. Law and corporate practices have been developed and increasingly enforced to protect those interests. As this chapter contends, this development is for the good of free expression in the digital age.

2. Early Attitudes about Online Abuse

When the media started covering the phenomenon of online abuse in 2007, the public's reaction was disheartening (Valenti 2007). Cyber harassment was viewed as part of the bargain of online life. This was true even though individuals were targeted with a perfect storm of abuse. Harassers terrorized victims by threatening to rape them or by impersonating them in online ads suggesting their interest in sex. Falsehoods accusing victims of having sexually transmitted infections appeared prominently in searches of their names. Victims' nude photos were posted for the world to see. Sometimes, harassers used technology, including distributed denial-of-service attacks that make a victim's website unavailable by overwhelming it with traffic from multiple sources, to knock people offline (Citron 2014).

No matter, victims were told that if they wanted to enjoy the benefits of online engagement, they had to accept its risks. Victims were advised to stop "whining." Commentators dismissed online abuse as "no big deal" (Citron 2009a, 2009b). Cyber harassment was deemed an uneventful part of online life that was at least partially the victims' fault. What did victims expect when they took intimate photos of themselves (McDonough 2013)? If victims were not ready for "heat" in their Twitter feed, they should not have used the service (Citron 2014). Victims had chosen to "go online" so they should toughen up or plug out. They were advised to ignore abusers' "juvenile antics," an impossible task because search results of victims' names were saturated with nude photos, lies, and rape threats (Citron 2014, 19).

3. Don't Ruin the Internet

A decade ago, any suggestion that law should be brought to bear against cyber harassment was met with hostility. Commentators argued that people should be allowed to say anything they wanted online because their comments constituted speech. A common view was that the internet would cease to foster expression if law intervened. Law would jeopardize the internet's role as a special forum for public discourse. The internet constituted the "equivalent of the public square" so hands off. The message to lawmakers was "Don't wreck our virtual town meetings" (Citron 2014, 280). The benefits of legal action were far outweighed by the costs to free expression. For the good of free speech, abusers needed to be let alone (Citron 2014, 39–45).[1]

Absent from discussions about the internet's speech-facilitating role was individuals' difficulty expressing themselves in the face of online assaults (Citron 2015c). In response to cyber harassment, individuals often withdrew from online discourse. They shut down their blogs, sites, and social network profiles not because they tired of them, but because they hoped to avoid provoking their attackers. Little attention, however, was paid to the silencing of victims (Citron 2009b).

Several faulty assumptions plagued public attitudes. The first concerned the way online platforms were conceptualized. Without doubt, online platforms played a key role in public dialogue about issues large and small. In theory, people could reach a national and possibly global audience. But those opportunities were not guaranteed. Powerful private entities mediated the dialogue, which meant that they controlled the extent to which users' speech was highlighted or alternatively hidden. Public conversation also was not the only thing happening online. Online platforms hosted a dizzying array of activities. Some sites were hybrid workplaces, schools, social clubs, and town squares. Blogs, for instance, helped establish the author's professional expertise and attract clients while hosting a public conversation. Then, as now, online platforms were crucial speech platforms, but they were not just speech platforms (Citron 2014, 192). They were far more than that.

The second faulty assumption was connected to the first. It presumed that if networked platforms served as public forums like public parks and streets, then special free-speech protections were in order. If that were true, regulation would endanger indispensable channels of public discourse. Although online sites facilitated expression, they did not warrant special protection—certainly no more and no less than speech occurring in other platforms with diverse opportunities for work, play, and expression. Workplaces, schools, homes, professional conferences, and coffee shops are zones of conversations, but they are not exempt from legal norms. Civil rights, criminal, and tort laws have not destroyed workplaces, homes, and social venues. Rather, they have made those spaces available to all on equal terms.

4. Changing Social Attitudes: Victims Tell Their Stories

Over the years, public attitudes toward cyber harassment evolved. Change occurred slowly but steadily, the result of several converging trends. Crucially, victims began sharing their experiences with the press. Members of the media wrote about their own experiences with online abuse. Female journalists discussed the rape and death threats filling their email inboxes and Twitter feeds. In an award-winning article, writer Amanda Hess described law enforcement's refusal to help her in the face of online threats. As Hess poignantly noted, rape threats made all women feel unwelcome online (Hess 2014, 42–47).

Then too, individuals whose nude photos had been posted online without consent started to talk publicly about their suffering. That was true for Holly Jacobs. After Jacobs graduated from Boston College, she returned home to Florida to start graduate school. At that time, she was in a long distance relationship. She and her ex shared nude images with each other on the understanding that the photos were for their eyes only. After their breakup, Jacobs started receiving emails and texts from strangers who said they saw her advertisements and were interested in sex. After Googling herself, she found hundreds of posts with her nude photos, including fake ads suggesting her interest in anonymous sex. Her dean received calls accusing her of sleeping with undergraduate students. Although her dean was sympathetic to her struggles, she advised Jacobs to change her name (which she did—to Jacobs) (Citron 2014, 48).

In 2013, Jacobs started an organization called the *Cyber Civil Rights Initiative* (CCRI) devoted to combating cyber harassment. She received hundreds of emails and comments on her site. Although some accused her of being responsible for her predicament (didn't she know better than to share nude photos with a guy?), far more praised her for bravely speaking out about the abuse. CCRI and *Without My Consent* (WMC), an anti-harassment group started by attorneys Colette Vogel and Erica Johnstone, have made significant strides in educating the public about cyber harassment and in spearheading reform (Cyber Civil Rights Initiative).

After a phishing attack led to the viral spread of female celebrities' nude photos in 2014, actress Jennifer Lawrence condemned the gawking as an invasion of sexual privacy. As she wrote in *Vanity Fair*, the disclosure of her nude photos was humiliating and destructive. Her message was clear—the invasion of her privacy was a "sex crime." To those who looked at those pictures, she said: "'you're perpetuating a sexual offense. You should cower with shame . . . I didn't tell you that you could look at my naked body'" (2014).

Women in the video-gaming industry spoke out about being targeted with threats, doxxing (the publication of personal information online), impersonations, and defamation at the hands of cyber mobs. Consider Anita Sarkeesian's experience. In 2012, Sarkeesian announced that she was starting a campaign to raise money on Kickstarter to fund a documentary series about sexism in video games. In short order, a cyber mob tried to hijack her efforts by falsely reporting that her fundraising was fraudulent. She was inundated with rape and death threats on her blog, on her Twitter feed, and in her email inbox. A game appeared called *Beat Up Anita Sarkeesian*—with each keystroke, her face appeared increasingly bloodied and swollen. Twitter and Facebook got hundreds of false reports that her accounts constituted hate speech, spam, and terrorism in violation of terms of service. In 2014, Sarkeesian was scheduled to give a talk at Utah State University. After the Dean's Office received threats that if she spoke, there would be a school shooting worse than Columbine and Newtown combined, Sarkeesian canceled the engagement (Wingfield 2014).

Although the abuse was relentless, Sarkeesian refused to remain silent. She explained, "I am certainly not the first woman to suffer this kind of harassment and sadly, I won't be the last. But I'd just like to reiterate that this is not a trivial issue. It can not and should not be brushed off by saying 'oh well that's YouTube for you', 'trolls will be trolls', or 'it's to be expected on the internet'. These are serious threats of violence, harassment and slander across many online platforms meant to intimidate and silence. And it's not okay. Again, don't worry, this harassment will never stop me from making my videos" (Lewis 2012).

Victims and advocates helped contribute to a shift in our cultural attitudes. Through their public accounts of their experiences and the efforts of anti-harassment advocacy groups such as CCRI and WMC, the public, lawmakers, and law enforcers began to recognize the harm of cyber harassment. They increasingly understood that online abuse interfered with victims' ability to take advantage of life's crucial opportunities, including the ability to speak and engage with others online (Citron 2014).

5. Changing Legal Practices

Cyber stalking, harassment, and threat laws have been on the books at the federal level and in half of the states since 2006 (Citron 2014). At the state level, those laws were too often under-enforced, and victims were turned away because officers lacked training in the law and with the technology. Whereas law enforcement had expertise in street crimes, they lacked the investigative know-how necessary to pursue cyber harassers. Officers would take reports, but their investigations routinely went nowhere. Sometimes, social attitudes were the problem. Some officers refused to help victims because they believed the abuse was just "boys being boys." At the federal level, investigators often turned away victims due to the scarcity of resources. Complicating some cases, scant law punished the publication of someone's nude photo without consent (Citron 2014, 33).

Significant progress has been made in recent years. Gaps in the law have been filled in important areas. Whereas in 2014 only two states criminalized nonconsensual pornography, today, 40 states and the District of Columbia have laws criminalizing the practice (Goldberg 2017; Franks and Citron 2014). This is in large part thanks to the advocacy of Professor Mary Anne Franks who serves as CCRI's Legislative Director. Professor Franks has advised state lawmakers across the country on how to craft a well-designed bill to criminalize non-consensual pornography (Franks 2016). Franks and I worked together advising the Maryland legislature in its effort to criminalize the practice. In 2016, Congresswoman Jackie Speier proposed a bill that would make non-consensual pornography a federal crime. In 2017, Senator Kamala Harris proposed her own version of the bill. Because the Senate and House bills enjoy bipartisan support and because they have much in common, a federal bill may become a reality in the near future.

The next important step involved the training of officers to handle online abuse cases. State attorneys general have spearheaded efforts to ensure that law enforcement personnel have the tools and training they need to pursue investigations. In 2014, U.S. senator Kamala Harris, then the California attorney general (AG), established a Cyber Exploitation Task Force made up of victim advocates, 50 major technology companies, law enforcement representatives, and experts (Mullin 2015). Under Harris's leadership, California created an online hub providing resources for law enforcement investigating invasions of sexual privacy, harassment, and stalking.[2]

In turn, there has been an increase in criminal enforcement. The California AG's office prosecuted operators of revenge porn websites for engaging in extortion and other crimes. In those cases, site operators were convicted of, or pleaded guilty to, encouraging users to post nude photos of their exes and charging hundreds of dollars for the photos to be removed (California Office of the Attorney General 2015). For instance, the operator of UGotPosted, Kevin Bollaert, faced charges of extortion, conspiracy, and identity theft for allegedly urging users to post their ex-lovers' nude photos and then demanding up to $350 for the removal of each photo (Citron 2015a). Bollaert's conviction signaled that extorting money from individuals whose confidential nude images were posted without permission is an illegal enterprise (Citron and Hartzog 2015). The Department of Justice's Computer Crimes and Intellectual Property section has prosecutors such as Mona Sedky who have developed an expertise in cyber stalking, cyber harassment, and sextortion.[3]

The Federal Trade Commission (FTC) followed California's lead by bringing an enforcement action against revenge porn site operator Craig Brittain. The FTC's charges focused on the site's solicitation of individuals' nude photos and contact information and the disclosure of that information to the public (Federal Trade Commission 2015). The FTC argued that it was unfair for Brittain to exploit nude images shared in confidence for commercial gain (Federal Trade Commission 2015). In the consent decree, Brittain pledged not to disclose anyone's nude images online without first getting their express written consent (Federal Trade Commission 2015).

We have seen important progress in the civil arena. Victims always had the option of suing their harassers for defamation, public disclosure of private facts, and intentional infliction of emotional distress. But victims often lacked the funds to bring lawsuits (Citron 2014, 122–23). The good news is that law firms are increasingly volunteering to help victims. K&L Gates founded the *Cyber Civil Rights Legal Project* to provide pro bono counsel for cyber harassment victims (Cyber Civil Rights Legal Project). In the fall of 2016, New York Law School opened the first ever law clinic devoted to representing victims of online abuse (New York Law School Cyberharassment Clinic 2017).

6. Crucial Step Forward: Civil Liberties Groups Join the Fight

Thanks to these efforts, cyber harassment's harms are now part of the national conversation. The public is more aware of victims' suffering—including their difficulty in getting and keeping jobs, increased risk of physical attack, and emotional distress. It is now uncontroversial to suggest that cyber harassment interferes with expression, even as it is perpetrated via expression.

In January 2015, the esteemed civil liberties group, the Electronic Frontier Foundation (EFF), put its reputation behind efforts to combat cyber harassment. EFF wrote an article highlighting online harassment as a pressing "digital rights issue" (Kayyali and O'Brien 2015). It was a big deal for a civil liberties group to recognize that speech can silence speech. (Civil liberties groups have long resisted that argument.) EFF said to the public that cyber harassment wasn't a niche issue—it wasn't a small problem that could be ignored. Instead, EFF made clear that cyber harassment was "profoundly damaging to the free speech and privacy rights of the people targeted" (Kayyali and O'Brien 2015). It was crucial for the public's understanding of online abuse for a civil liberties organization to contend that online abuse silences people, especially women and minorities who enjoy "less political or social power" (Kayyali and O'Brien 2015).

As EFF's blog post made clear, we have come a long way in our understanding of cyber harassment in fairly short order. No longer are we focusing on the speech interests of online harassers to the exclusion of the speech interests of victims. No longer are we ignoring the fact that harassers deprive victims of the ability to engage in life's important opportunities, including the ability to speak and interact with others. Victims' expressive interests are attracting concern, and rightly so.

7. First Amendment and Free Speech Values

What we have come to understand is that First Amendment protections and free speech values do not work as absolutes. There are speech interests beyond those of the harassers to consider. Rather than working against speech interests, intervention against online abuse would secure the necessary preconditions for free expression while safeguarding the equality of opportunity in the digital age (Citron 2009b, 96).

We can square the enforcement of criminal, tort, and civil rights laws with both First Amendment doctrine and free speech values. The First Amendment does not operate in absolutes. Certain categories of speech can be regulated because they contribute so little to cultural and political conversations and inflict grave harm (Citron 2009b, 96–97). Cyber harassment involves categories of speech that enjoy little to no protection. It typically involves true threats, defamation of private individuals, and crime-facilitating speech such as extortion, solicitation, and blackmail (Citron 2014, 3). It also includes speech that enjoys less rigorous protection—such as the disclosure of private communications about purely private matters such as nude photos posted without consent (Citron 2015b).

Crucially, regulating cyber harassment is important for the protection of free expression. While online abuse contributes little to cultural, social, or political conversations, it is costly to public discourse. Having the opportunity to engage as a citizen and to participate in the creation of culture is one of the central reasons why we protect free speech. As Professor Neil Richards argues in his book *Intellectual Privacy: Civil Liberties and Information in the Digital Age,* "we need free speech if we are to govern ourselves" (2015). Much inspiration for the self-governance theory of the First Amendment comes from Supreme Court Justice Louis Brandeis. In his concurrence in *Whitney v. California,* Justice Brandeis argued that "the freedom to think as you will and to speak as you think are means indispensable to the discovery and spread of political truth; that, without free speech and assembly, discussion would be futile; that, with them, discussion affords ordinarily adequate protection against the dissemination of noxious doctrine."[4] Citizens, not the government, must determine what is a fit subject for public debate.

The self-governance theory is based on the idea that individuals who can freely speak and listen to others make more informed decisions about the kind of society they want to live in (Richards 2015). Civic virtue comes from "discussion and education, not by lazy and impatient reliance on the coercive authority of the state." Professor Jack Balkin powerfully argues that free speech promotes "democracy in the widest possible sense, not merely at the level of governance, or at the level of deliberation, but at the level of culture, where we interact, create, build communities, and build ourselves" (2004, 32).

Online speech is crucial for self-government and cultural engagement. Networked spaces host expression that is explicitly political and speech that is less so but that nonetheless is key to civic and cultural engagement (Putnam 2007, 338). Blogs about food, software design, body image, and sex may explore political issues, or they may not; in either case, they contribute to the exchange of ideas and the building of online communities. Online engagement can reinforce the skills of discourse, just as Justice Brandeis contemplated. The internet holds great promise for *digital citizenship,* by which I mean the various ways online activities deepen civic engagement, political and cultural participation, and public conversation (Citron and Norton 2011).

Cyber harassment does little to enhance self-governance and does much to destroy it. Its contribution to public conversation is negligible. Cyber harassers are not engaged in political, cultural, or social discourse. Lies about targeted individuals (such as accusing a victim of having herpes) do not address individuals' ideas. Rape threats have no connection to a debate about cultural concerns. Nude photos posted without consent contribute nothing to conversations about social issues. Harassment of private individuals does not advance public discussion. Listeners learn nothing about social, cultural, and political concerns.

Cyber harassment destroys victims' ability to interact in ways that are essential to self-governance. Online abuse prevents targeted individuals from realizing their full potential as digital citizens. Victims cannot participate in online networks if they are under assault. Rape threats, defamatory lies, the non-consensual disclosure of nude photos, and technological attacks destroy victims' ability to interact with others. They sever a victim's connections with people engaged in similar pursuits.

Robust democratic discourse cannot be achieved if cyber harassers drive victims away from it. Victims are unable to engage in public dialogue if they are under assault (Citron 2009a, 2009b). Defeating online aggressions that deny victims their ability to engage with others as citizens outweighs the negligible contribution that cyber harassment makes to cultural interaction and expression.

What about the theory that free speech matters for the marketplace of ideas and that truth will make itself known? Justice Oliver Wendell Holmes drew on notions about truths and falsehoods when arguing that "[t]he best test of truth is the power of the thought to get itself accepted in the competition of the market."[5] A popular account of free speech is that truths will emerge if ideas are subjected to strenuous challenge. In this vein, hateful views should be aired so that they can be refuted. As John Stuart Mill argued in *On Liberty*, the best protection against prejudice is open debate and strong counterarguments (Durham Peters 2005, 132). According to Mill, citizens should work to persuade others of the truth.

An extreme version of the truth-seeking theory might insist that listeners sort out cyber harassers' deceptions and assaults. To do so, however, the theory has to assume that we could have an open, rigorous, and rational discourse about rape threats, social security numbers, nude photos posted without the subject's consent, technological attacks, and impersonations suggesting someone's interest in sex. A more plausible vision of truth-seeking theory suggests that no truths are contested in these cases. Threats, for instance, tell us nothing about victims. Threats are not ideas that can be refuted, unless responding that someone should not be raped amounts to a meaningful counterpoint.

Posts with a woman's nude photo, home address, and supposed interest in sex are not facts or ideas to be debated in the service of truth. When dealing with falsehoods impugning someone's character, the victim does not have an affirmative case she is trying to convey—she is only seeking to dispel the harm from posters' attacks. Even if victims could respond, their replies may never be seen. The truth may be unable to emerge from a battle of posts. Images of a private person's naked body have little value to the general public and can destroy that person's career (Citron 2014, 47). They ensure that victims are undateable, unemployable, and unable to partake in online activities. Furthermore, as Professor Daniel Solove aptly notes, "Truth isn't the only value at stake" (Solove 2007, 132).

Regulating online abuse does seek to lower the voices of harassers. Denying cyber stalkers and cyber harassers' ability to say what they want, even if it harms others, interferes with their capacity to express themselves. The autonomy account of free speech emphasizes the role of free speech in facilitating individual autonomy (Baker 1989, 54). As Justice Lewis Powell Jr. remarked, the First Amendment serves "the human spirit—a spirit that demands self-expression."[6]

Bringing law to bear against online abuse will chill some self-expression. Cyber harassers use words and images to attack victims. But to understand the risks to expression inherent in efforts to regulate online abuse, we need to account for the full breadth of expression imperiled. Some expression can make it impossible for others to participate in conversation. Professor Susan Brison persuasively argues that hateful verbal assaults undermine autonomy by inhibiting a targeted individual's "ability to be rationally self-legislating" (Brison 1998, 335). Cyber harassment perfectly illustrates how expression can deny others' "full and equal opportunity to engage in public debate" (Fiss 1996, 15).

Restrictions on cyber harassment would prevent the denial of victims' autonomy—to speak, work, and engage in all manner of life opportunities (Brison 1998, 335). Crucially, when a person's self-expression is designed for the purpose of extinguishing another person's speech, it should receive no protection (Heyman 2008, 166). Sometimes, we must lower the voices of some to permit the self-expression of others (Fiss 1987, 786). Along these lines, Professor Cass Sunstein contends that threats, libel, and sexual and racial harassment constitute low-value speech of little First Amendment consequence (Sunstein 1995, 127). As one court put it, the internet can "never achieve its potential" as a facilitator of discussion unless "it is subject to . . . the law like all other social discourse. Some curb on abusive speech is necessary for meaningful discussion."[7] Rarely is that more true than when one group of voices consciously exploits the internet to silence others.

We should be less troubled about limiting the expressive autonomy of cyber harassers who use their voices to extinguish victims' expression. Silencing is what many harassers are after. As a cyber harassment victim confided to me, she felt she was left with no choice but to withdraw from online life because whenever she engaged online, harassers went after her, and whenever she stopped, so did they (Citron 2014, 170).

Restraining a cyber mob's destructive attacks is essential to defending the expressive autonomy of its victims. Free from online attacks, victims might blog, join online discussions, share videos, engage in social networks, and express themselves on issues large and small. Protecting victims from defamation, threats, privacy invasions, and technological attacks would allow them to be candid about their ideas (Solove 2007, 130). Preventing harassers from driving people offline would "advance the reasons why we protect free speech in the first place," even though it would inevitably chill some speech of cyber harassers.

Of course, recognizing victims' expressive interests does *not* make it any easier to regulate cyber harassment. Our concern for victims' ability to engage online does not, and should not, clear the path for legal claims or prosecutions at odds with our commitment to "uninhibited, robust, and wide open public discourse." Law cannot, and should not, censor hateful or offensive viewpoints. We have to live with cruelty and falsehoods that demean and humiliate traditionally subordinated groups. A bedrock principle underlying the First Amendment is that government cannot censor the expression of an idea because society finds the idea itself offensive or distasteful.[8] Hateful words enjoy presumptive constitutional protection.[9] The antidote to speech we do not like is counter speech. As the Court instructs, our right and civic duty is to engage in "open, dynamic, and rational discourse."[10]

But cyber harassment isn't annoying speech: it is a perfect storm of threats, defamation, impersonation, and nude photos. Combating cyber harassment comports with First Amendment doctrine and honors the reasons we protect free speech, as it should.

8. Silicon Valley

Law cannot do it all, nor should we want it to. Law is a blunt instrument. It cannot solve all of our problems and we ought to be wary that the criminal law has been used to over-incarcerate disadvantaged communities, especially racial minorities. We have seen social media providers and search engines step in, which is their choice and for which they enjoy immunity pursuant to the federal Communications Decency Act of 1996.[11]

Online platforms can address cyber harassment without concerns about the First Amendment or liability for others' content. The First Amendment only constrains state actors, not private entities. Recently, social media companies have been considering if certain abuse is permitted on their platforms. Victims' expressive interests are behind their bans on threats, harassment, and non-consensual pornography.[12] Some companies have attributed their updated policies to the concept of digital citizenship—the various ways networked tools can foster expression and civic engagement (Citron and Norton 2011, 1446).

In the summer of 2014, Google and Microsoft agreed to remove nude images from searches of victims' names upon their request (O'Neill 2015). Twitter banned the non-consensual posting of someone's nude images (Tsukayama 2015). Facebook clarified its nudity ban with a detailed explanation of the difference between nudity addressing social issues, such as photos of mastectomies, which are permitted, and images of buttocks and genitals posted without the subject's permission, which are banned (Selinger 2015).

Consider Twitter's evolving policies. For years, Twitter only required users to refrain from engaging in copyright violations, spam, and impersonations. Its terms-of-service agreement has been expanded to prohibit threats, targeted harassment, and disclosures of private and confidential information (including social security numbers and nude images posted without consent).[13] Twitter's general counsel attributed the company's policy changes to its responsibility to "ensure that voices are not silenced because people are afraid to speak up." Users have to "feel safe . . . to fully express themselves" (Yoshi 2015). For Twitter, "online safety is a shared responsibility, and digital citizenship is essential to fostering a safe environment for all" (Cartes 2015).

Other providers should consider structuring terms-of-service (TOS) agreements around users' rights and responsibilities, much as Twitter has done.[14] What would this entail? Users would enjoy the right to express themselves on issues large and small. They could contribute to social, cultural, and political dialogue. They could criticize others' views without the fear of private censorship. Such policies would secure the conditions for robust and confident citizenship envisioned by John Stuart Mill and Justice Louis Brandeis. At the same time, users would be barred from using platforms to threaten, harass, and invade sexual privacy. Such behavior "shuts down more expression than it opens up by causing silence, retreat, isolation, or intimidation" (Agudo and Feerst 2015). Of course, platforms would need to explain what they mean by the terms "threats," "targeted harassment," and "privacy invasion." Users should be told what happens if their speech violates TOS agreements; they should be given a chance to appeal decisions about their speech. These efforts would help protect the expression of *all* users.

9. Conclusion

These developments suggest a growing commitment to online expression. Combating cyber harassment is good for free expression because it will prevent abuse that would otherwise silence or chill victims' expression. Of course, much work needs to be done in the law, education, parenting, and far more. But let's take our wins where we can.

Notes

1. Indeed, victims who invoked the law faced criticism and much worse (Citron 2014: 39–45).
2. Cyberexploitation website, https://oag.ca.gov/cyberexploitation.
3. In September 2017, the Department of Justice's Computer Crimes and Intellectual Property section and the University of Maryland Carey School of Law cohosted a conference

devoted to cyber stalking and other forms of online abuse to ensure that federal and state prosecutors have a better of understanding of online crimes.

4. Whitney v. California, 274 U.S. 357 (1927).

5. Abrams v. United States, 250 U.S. 616, 629 (1919) (Holmes, J., dissenting).

6. Procunier v. Martinez, 416 U.S. 396, 427 (1974), *overruled by* Thornburgh v. Abbott, 490 U.S. 401 (1989).

7. Varian Medical Sys., Inc. v. Delfino, 6 Cal. Rptr. 3d 325, 337 (Ct. App. 2003).

8. Texas v. Johnson, 491 U.S. 397, 414 (1989).

9. In *Cohen v. California,* 403 U.S. 15 (1971), the Supreme Court concluded that the defendant engaged in constitutionally protected speech when he wore a jacket into a court-room with "Fuck the Draft" written on its back. The Court explained that a governmental interest in regulating offensive speech could not outweigh the defendant's First Amendment right to freedom of speech.

10. United States v. Alvarez, 567 U.S. 709, 728 (2012).

11. 47 U.S. Code § 230 (1996)—Protection for private blocking and screening of of-fensive material.

12. As private actors that enjoy immunity from liability for the postings of others under Section 230 of the federal Communications Decency Act, content hosts can host as much or as little of their users' speech activities as they wish.

13. One by one, social media platforms updated their community guidelines to ban revenge porn during 2015. Search engines Google and Microsoft's Bing have pledged to de-index nude images from victims' search results if victims did not consent to their posting.

14. Pinterest, Digital Citizenship, https://www.pinterest.com/edutopia/digital-citizenship/.

References

Agudo, S. and A. First. 2015. "Medium Rules." *Medium,* July 27. https://medium.com/the-story/we-ve-been-thinking-hard-about-how-to-create-a-medium-where-people-treat-each-other-well-8a62695850cb.

Baker, C. E. 1989. *Human Liberty and Freedom of Speech.* New York: Oxford University Press.

Balkin, J. M. 2004. "Digital Speech and Democratic Culture: A Theory of Freedom of Expression for the Information Society." *New York University Law Review* 79: 1–58.

Brison, S. 1998. "The Autonomy Defense of Free Speech." *Ethics* 108: 312–39.

California Attorney General's Office, https://oag.ca.gov/news/press-releases/attorney-general-kamala-d-harris-announces-18-year-prison-sentence-cyber.

Cartes, P. 2015. "Introducing the New Twitter Safety Center." *Twitter,* July 20. https://blog.twitter.com/2015/introducing-the-new-twitter-safety-center.

Citron, D. K. 2009a. "Law's Expressive Value in Combating Cyber Gender Harassment." *Michigan Law Review* 108: 373–416.

Citron, D. K. 2009b. "Cyber Civil Rights." *Boston University Law Review* 89: 61–126.

Citron, D. K. 2014. *Hate Crimes in Cyberspace.* Cambridge, MA: Harvard University Press.

Citron, D. K. 2014. "Open Letter to Jennifer Lawrence." *Forbes*, October 9. https://www.forbes.com/sites/daniellecitron/2014/10/08/open-letter-to-jennifer-lawrence/#7a6e3a8a2a09.

Citron, D. K. 2015a. "Can Revenge Porn Operators Go to Prison?" *Forbes*. January 17. https://www.forbes.com/sites/daniellecitron/2015/01/17/can-revenge-porn-operators-go-to-jail/.

Citron, D. K. 2015b. "More Thoughts on How to Write a Constitutional Revenge Porn Law." *Forbes*. July 15. https://www.forbes.com/sites/daniellecitron/2015/05/23/more-thoughts-on-how-to-write-a-constitutional-revenge-porn-law/#2309559f4a34.

Citron, D. K. 2015c. "Online Engagement on Equal Terms » Law Review | Boston University." *Boston University Law Review Forum*. October 19. https://www.bu.edu/bulawreview/citron-online-engagement-on-equal-terms/.

Citron, D. K. and H. Norton. 2011. "Intermediaries and Hate Speech: Fostering Digital Citizenship for Our Information Age." *Boston University Law Review* 91: 1435–84.

Citron, D. K. and W. Hartzog. 2015. "The Decision That Could Finally Kill the Revenge-Porn Business." *The Atlantic*, February 3. http://www.theatlantic.com/technology/archive/2015/02/the-decision-that-could-finally-kill-the-revenge-porn-business/385113/.

Federal Trade Commission. 2015. "Website Operator Banned from the 'Revenge Porn' Business after FTC Charges He Unfairly Posted Nude Photos." *Federal Trade Commission*, January 29. https://www.ftc.gov/news-events/press-releases/2015/01/website-operator-banned-revenge-porn-business-after-ftc-charges.

Fiss, O. M. 1987. "Why the State?" *Harvard Law Review* 100: 781–94.

Fiss, O. M. 1996. *The Irony of Free Speech*. Cambridge, MA: Harvard University Press.

Franks, M. A. and D. K. Citron. 2014. "Criminalizing Revenge Porn." *Wake Forest Law Review* 49: 346–47. doi:10.2139/ssrn.2337998.

Franks, M. A. 2016. "Drafting an Effective 'Revenge Porn' Law: Guide for Legislators." *Cyber Civil Rights Initiative*. September 22. http://www.cybercivilrights.org/guide-to-legislation/.

Goldberg, C A. 2017. "States with Revenge Porn Laws." *CA Goldberg Law*. June 8. http://www.cagoldberglaw.com/states-with-revenge-porn-laws/.

Hess, A. 2014. "The Next Civil Rights Issue: Why Women Aren't Welcome on the Internet." *Pacific Standard*, January 6. https://psmag.com/social-justice/women-arent-welcome-internet-72170.

Heyman, S. J. 2008. *Free Speech and Human Dignity*. New Haven, CT: Yale University Press.

Kavyali, N. and D. O'Brien. 2015. "Facing the Challenge of Online Harassment." *Electronic Frontier Foundation*. January. https://www.eff.org/deeplinks/2015/01/facing-challenge-online-harassment.

Lawrence, J. 2014. "Cover Preview: Jennifer Lawrence Calls Photo Hacking a Sex Crime." *Vanity Fair*. October 8. https://www.vanityfair.com/hollywood/2014/10/jennifer-lawrence-cover.

Lewis, H. 2012. "Dear the Internet, This Is Why You Can't Have Anything Nice." *New Statesman*, June 12. http://www.newstatesman.com/blogs/internet/2012/06/dear-internet-why-you-cant-have-anything-nice.

McDonough, K. 2013. "Christian School Places Teacher on Leave after Photos from Stolen Phone Post to Revenge Porn Website." *Salon*, December 9. http://www.salon.com/

2013/12/09/christian_school_places_teacher_on_leave_after_photos_from_stolen_phone_post_to_revenge_porn_website/.

Mullin, J. 2015. "California AG Goes All-out to Fight 'Revenge Porn.'" *Ars Technica*, October 14. http://arstechnica.com/tech-policy/2015/10/california-ag-goes-all-out-to-fight-revenge-porn/.

"New York Law School Cyberharassment Clinic." 2017. Accessed October 30. http://www.nyls.edu/academics/office_of_clinical_and_experiential_learning/clinics/cyberharassment-clinic/.

O'Neill, P. H. 2015. "Microsoft Just Banned Revenge Porn." *The Daily Dot*, July 22. http://www.dailydot.com/politics/microsoft-ban-revenge-porn-bing-xbox-live-onedrive/.

Peters, J. D. 2005. *Courting the Abyss: Free Speech and the Liberal Tradition.* Chicago: University of Chicago Press.

Pinterest. 2017. "Digital Citizenship." Accessed October 30. https://www.pinterest.com/edutopia/digital-citizenship/.

Putnam, R. D. 2007. *Bowling Alone: The Collapse and Revival of American Community.* New York: Simon & Schuster.

Richards, N. 2015. *Intellectual Privacy: Rethinking Civil Liberties in the Digital Age.* Oxford: Oxford University Press.

Salinger, E. 2015. "How to Defeat Internet Bullies." *The Christian Science Monitor*, March 27. http://www.csmonitor.com/World/Passcode/Passcode-Voices/2015/0327/How-to-defeat-Internet-bullies.

Solove, D. J. 2007. *The Future of Reputation: Gossip, Rumor, and Privacy on the Internet.* New Haven, CT: Yale University Press.

Sunstein, C. R. 1995. *Democracy and the Problem of Free Speech.* New York: New York: Free Press.

Tsukayama, H. 2015. "Twitter Updates Its Rules to specifically ban 'revenge porn.'" *The Washington Post*, March 11. https://www.washingtonpost.com/news/the-switch/wp/2015/03/11/twitter-updates-its-rules-to-specifically-ban-revenge-porn/.

Valenti, J. 2007. "How the Web Became a Sexists' Paradise." *The Guardian*, April 6. https://www.theguardian.com/world/2007/apr/06/gender.blogging.

Wingfield, N. 2014. "Feminist Critics of Video Games Facing Threats in 'GamerGate' Campaign." *The New York Times*, October 15. https://www.nytimes.com/2014/10/16/technology/gamergate-women-video-game-threats-anita-sarkeesian.html.

Yoshi, S. 2015. "Policy and Product Updates Aimed at Combating Abuse." *Twitter*, April 21. https://blog.twitter.com/2015/policy-and-product-updates-aimed-at-combating-abuse.

8

"Not Where Bodies Live"

THE ABSTRACTION OF INTERNET EXPRESSION

Mary Anne Franks

1. Introduction: The Curious Embrace of Section 230

In the United States, attempts to address the myriad forms of abuse amplified or created by the internet are inevitably met with accusations of censorship. The underlying, and in many cases automatic, presumption is that internet conduct is inherently expressive activity protected by the First Amendment. This presumption owes much to early internet visionaries such as John Perry Barlow, who, along with John Gilmore and Mitch Kapor, founded the Electronic Frontier Foundation (EFF) in 1990. Barlow's 1996 "Declaration of the Independence of Cyberspace" was influential in establishing a vision of the internet as a bodiless realm of pure thought. In Barlow's words, "legal concepts of property, expression, identity, movement, and context do not apply" in cyberspace, which "is a world that is both everywhere and nowhere, but it is not where bodies live" (Barlow 1996). Accordingly, attempts by the "Governments of the Industrial World" to interfere in cyberspace are both unwelcome and illegitimate. Barlow's anarchic, utopian declaration both reflected popular thinking about cyberspace in its early days and shaped how the general public, legislators, and civil liberties groups would think about the regulation of the internet for decades.

The occasion for Barlow's purple prose was the signing of the 1996 Communications Decency Act (CDA), which was the first major attempt by Congress to regulate obscenity and indecency on the internet. As it turns out, many of the provisions of the Act were eventually struck down by the Supreme Court for violating the First Amendment. The fate of the CDA reinforced the vision of the internet as a speech forum that would flourish best without regulation.

One part of the CDA, however, not only survived, but became what many consider to be the cornerstone of the modern internet: the amendment known as Section 230.[1] Section 230's most influential provision, (c)(1), has been broadly interpreted as protecting interactive computer service providers from liability for the actions of their users. The bipartisan amendment, sponsored by Republican Christopher Cox and Democrat Ron Wyden, describes the internet in terms that would not have been out of place in Barlow's Declaration: "The internet and other interactive computer services offer a forum for a true diversity of political discourse, unique opportunities for cultural development, and myriad avenues for intellectual activity."[2] According to the findings section that prefaces the amendment, the internet has "flourished, to the benefit of all Americans, with a minimum of government regulation"; accordingly, one of the goals of Section 230 is "to preserve the vibrant and competitive free market that presently exists for the internet and other interactive computer services, unfettered by Federal or State regulation."[3] The EFF, which describes itself as "the leading nonprofit organization defending civil liberties in the digital world" (EFF 2017), relies extensively on Section 230 and the First Amendment in its litigation and lobbying efforts. Given the similarities between the sentiments expressed in Barlow's declaration and in Section 230, the fact that Barlow's EFF quickly became one of the most powerful champions of Section 230 may seem only natural.

But the EFF's embrace of Section 230 and the First Amendment points to a fundamental contradiction at the heart of the techno-libertarian approach to the internet. According to Barlow's declaration, cyberspace is not only "bodiless" but essentially lawless, a place where "legal concepts" of expression "do not apply" (Barlow 1996). But Section 230 and the First Amendment are both legal concepts of expression—American legal concepts, to be precise. Section 230 in particular is a government regulation, part of the very Communications Decency Act that Barlow railed against in 1996. The enthusiasm for Section 230 is an unacknowledged concession to the necessity and desirability of government intervention.

Indeed, it is important to bear in mind that without government intervention, the internet would not exist at all. Contrary to Barlow's startling claim that cyberspace "is an act of nature," the U.S. government was essential to the creation of the internet (Taplin 2017: 54). The U.S. government began developing the internet in the 1960s for military purposes, with the U.S. Department of Defense, the National Science Foundation, the National Aeronautics and Space Administration, and the U.S. Department of Energy all playing significant roles (Franks 2017: 455).

2. "To the Benefit of All Americans"

Section 230's assertion that the internet has "flourished, to the benefit of all Americans, with a minimum of government regulation" echoes Barlow's claim that the lawless world of cyberspace is "a world that all may enter without privilege or prejudice" (Barlow 1996). But neither Barlow nor the authors of Section 230 offered any evidence to support the claim that minimal regulation of the internet served the interests of "all." It was already quite clear by 1996 that the internet was hardly the egalitarian utopia enthusiasts made it out to be. The internet's liberating potential was certainly real, but so was its oppressive potential. The "new world" of the internet was a lot like the old one: full of wonderful opportunities for the most privileged members of society, fraught with dangers for the less privileged.

The early internet would be barely recognizable to users today. The internet began in 1969 with only four linked sites. For the first two decades of the internet's existence, nearly all sites were focused on military or academic research and access was largely restricted to an exclusive group of government officials and scholars. Commercial activity and spam were forbidden. When the "world wide web" was invented in 1989, it was completely text-based. It was only in 1992 that the ban on commercial activity was lifted, and only in 1993 that web browsers began displaying images. That same year, universities began providing students with email accounts and internet access.

Almost as soon as it became possible to use the internet to engage in mass communication, it was used to express decidedly anti-egalitarian sentiments. In 1995, the year before Barlow wrote his declaration and Section 230 became law, a male Virginia Tech student posted four pictures of naked women to a website for gay men along with a message calling for gay men to be castrated and "die a slow death" (Katsh and Rabinovich-Einy 2017: 30). A month later, four male Cornell students wrote an email to their friends with the subject line, "75 Reasons Why Women (Bitches) Should Not have Freedom of Speech" that was rapidly redistributed and made widely available on the internet (Katsh and Rabinovich-Einy 2017: 30). In the same year, a University of Michigan student named Jake Baker was arrested by the FBI after he posted a story to an online discussion board about raping, torturing, and murdering one of his female classmates. All three of these incidents were widely reported in the press and sparked national debates about free speech and the internet.

Barlow's proud proclamations about cyberspace in 1996 make no mention of the fact that some of the first uses of this powerful means of mass communication were to openly call for physical violence against gay men and for the literal censorship of women. His glib assertion that the internet is "not where bodies live" might well have been challenged by the gay men whose mutilation and murder were urged in online posts or by female students identified by name as the object of violent, pornographic fantasies. Section 230's breezy claim that a lack of regulation had produced a flourishing internet that benefited "all Americans" similarly glossed over the fact that there were stark differences in how different groups experienced the internet.

It is particularly telling that in Barlow's litany of the kinds of offline "privilege and prejudice" that cyberspace rendered obsolete—"race, economic power, military force, or station of birth"—there is no mention of gender. Even though gender bias has historically been one of the most powerful and violent forms of prejudice in the United States, it did not occur to Barlow to mention it. Barlow's lack of awareness of the privilege and prejudice created by gender foreshadowed the broader indifference and hostility to the online experiences of women to come.

Twenty years on, the consequences of techno-libertarianism are even more stark. Abundant empirical evidence demonstrates that women, racial minorities, and sexual minorities experience a very different internet than straight white men do (Franks 2011). They are disproportionately the targets of the most severe forms of harassment and abuse that the internet has made possible, from stalking to sex trafficking, from "revenge porn" to coordinated attacks by online mobs. These abuses not only ensure that the only group of people who are able to take full advantage of the internet's potential are white men, but also impose heavy real-world burdens on victims. Online abuse jeopardizes victims' physical safety, employment opportunities, educational achievement, personal relationships, and psychological health.

The experience of women and girls in particular vividly demonstrates that the liberating, "bodiless" potential of the internet has never been equally accessible to all. Women and girls, who are already disproportionately subjected to bodily objectification and discrimination offline, face invidious new forms of abuse focused on their bodies in what Barlow called "the new home of Mind." The internet all too often serves as a force multiplier for the harassment of women, lowering the costs of engaging in abuse by providing abusers with anonymity and social validation, while providing new ways to increase the range and impact of that abuse. The online stalking and harassment of women compromise their ability to participate in the internet on equal terms with men and amplify the sexual stereotyping and discrimination women experience in the offline world. Section 230 must be understood against this background.

3. Uses and Abuses of Section 230

The popular understanding of the Communications Decency Act Section 230 is not necessarily supported by the text of the statute. Most of the attention paid to the Act focuses on one isolated provision, (c)(1): "No provider or user of an interactive computer service shall be treated as the publisher or speaker of any information provided by another information content provider." This provision is often characterized as proving complete immunity to websites and other internet entities against liability for user-generated content. This characterization is incorrect in two respects.

First, the defense to liability provided by Section 230 does not apply to violations of federal criminal law, intellectual property law, or communications privacy law. That is, Section 230(c)(1) does not alter the fact that every Internet Service Provider, search engine, social networking platform, and website is subject to thousands of federal laws, including laws prohibiting child pornography, obscenity, stalking, and copyright infringement. Second, the protections of Section 230 do not apply to all online entities. The CDA distinguishes "interactive computer services" from "information content providers." An interactive computer service "provides or enables computer access by multiple users to a computer server," whereas an "information content provider" is any person responsible "in whole or in part . . . for the creation or development of information." Section 230 protection applies, in effect, to online intermediaries who facilitate third-party content, not online entities who themselves create content. An entity that creates or helps create unlawful online content is not covered by Section 230.

The distinction makes intuitive sense in many cases. To take one example, most would probably agree that Facebook (an interactive computer service), should not be held liable for the behavior of the nearly two billion users (content providers) on its platform. When people use Facebook to post defamatory comments or to harass other users, this is not the same as Mark Zuckerberg engaging in defamation or harassment. He should not be treated as the "speaker" of other people's content just because their content appears on his platform. He should also not be treated as the "publisher" of such content, as publishing implies editorial control. Facebook comments are not like a newspaper's letters to the editor section: the platform makes no conscious decision to bring the content into the public eye, unlike an editor who decides which letters to publish, edits them for clarity and length, and so on. It is perfectly appropriate, however, to treat the person who posts defamatory comments or harasses other users on a social media platform as the provider or speaker of that content. The fact that a person engages in unlawful behavior online, whether using an intermediary or not, does not immunize that behavior from liability.

But there are harder questions. Many websites and web platforms offer some mix of content created by users and owners. At what point does a site or service cross the line between being a facilitator of third-party content and being a co-creator of that content? While courts have generally been very generous in granting Section 230 immunity to online entities even when they play some role in the creation of unlawful content, two federal appellate cases have been more exacting. In a 2008 Ninth Circuit case, *Fair Housing Council of San Fernando Valley v. Roommates.com*, a roommate-matching website was sued for allegedly engaging in housing discrimination. The site raised a Section 230 defense, arguing that the offending content was created by users, not the site itself. The site required subscribers to disclose information such as gender, family status, and sexual orientation, as well as their preferences as to these categories for potential roommates. The site used this information to develop subscriber profiles that displayed these preferences for potential roommates. The court held that the site was an information content provider with respect to the questions it required users to answer, and thus did not have Section 230 immunity with regard to that content.

Similarly, in the 2009 case *FTC v. Accusearch, Inc.*, the Tenth Circuit denied Section 230 immunity to a website offering the sale of personal telephone records. The court found that exposing confidential information to public view was "development" of that information for the purposes of Section 230, making the website an information content provider (subject to liability) rather than an interactive computer service provider (immune from liability).

Thus, the line between an interactive computer service and a co-creator of content can be blurry. Even more commonly, interactive computer services may directly benefit from content even if they do not help create it. It is less clear why such services should be immunized from liability in these circumstances. If the business model of an interactive computer service allows it to earn profits from the third-party content it hosts, why should it be able to avoid liability for that content? In other words, why should an online entity be able to share in the benefits, but not the costs, of third-party content?

To return to the example of Facebook: Facebook, like many tech companies, makes money from third-party content. It does so not directly, but indirectly: Facebook makes money by putting ads in front of users, and the more content users voluntarily provide (posts, shares, likes, etc.), the more users interact on the platform, and the more opportunities Facebook has to provide more personalized and thus valuable advertising. Facebook may not be "speaking" through any particular user's posts, but it is earning revenue from them. If unlawful content provided by a user generates a high level of activity from a large number of other users, then the advertising benefit of that post goes up, which means more money in Facebook's pocket.

In such cases, it may still seem inappropriate to treat Facebook as a "speaker" of this content, or even as a "publisher." Facebook is not literally speaking through third-party content, and it does not appear to be "publishing" such content either, at least not in the technical sense of exerting editorial control over content. If Facebook were treated as exerting editorial control over third-party content, it would give rise to obligations to actively police such content in order to avoid liability for it. This, according to conventional internet wisdom, would have a profound chilling effect on companies such as Facebook. The time and resources that would be required for an interactive computer service to prescreen content would make it impossible for a platform such as Facebook to exist at all.

But while it may be wrongheaded to treat Facebook or similar entities as speakers or publishers of third-party content, it seems equally wrongheaded to treat them as though they had no relationship at all to such content. Online intermediaries such as Facebook directly benefit from making third-party content accessible to others, even if they exert no editorial control over it. In this sense, online intermediaries resemble offline distributors of books and newspapers. Like distributors, they do not exercise editorial control over content but do facilitate the ability of that content to reach an audience. Under defamation law, distributors do not face the same kind of liability that publishers or original speakers do, but can incur liability if they are made aware of the unlawful nature of content and fail to respond appropriately. As one scholar describes it, "distributor liability applies where certain parties, such as news vendors or interactive computer services, will be held to have 'published' material provided by third parties because they fail to take reasonable steps to prevent the dissemination of that defamatory information" (Dyer 2014: 851).

It is at least plausible to argue that interactive computer services should be subjected to distributor liability for unlawful content. The text of (c)(1) seems to allow for that possibility, as it only forbids treating an interactive computer service as "the publisher or speaker." However, an early and influential Section 230 case indicated that the courts were not willing to adopt this approach.

4. Moral Hazard and Corporations

Less than a week after the 1995 Oklahoma City bombing that left 168 people dead, a man named Kenneth M. Zeran began receiving threatening phone calls at his home. He soon discovered the reason: without Zeran's knowledge, an anonymous hoaxer had posted a message on an America Online (AOL) bulletin board advertising T-shirts and other paraphernalia glorifying the attack, providing Zeran's home phone number for interested buyers to call. Although AOL complied with Zeran's request that the message be removed, new messages with similar content continued to be posted to the site. At one point, Zeran was receiving threatening calls every two minutes. After an Oklahoma City radio station read the slogans on air and urged listeners to call Zeran, the phone calls became so threatening that Zeran's house was placed under protective surveillance.

Zeran sued AOL for negligence, arguing that the company had failed to respond appropriately after being made aware of the nature of the posts. The case eventually made its way to the Fourth Circuit, which held that Zeran's claim was preempted by Section 230 of the Communications Decency Act.[4] In reaching its decision, the court asserted that "Congress' clear objective in passing Section 230 of the CDA was to encourage the development of technologies, procedures and techniques by which objectionable material could be blocked or deleted." One might have thought, given this assertion, that the court was ruling in Zeran's favor. Counterintuitively, however, the court claimed that holding AOL liable as a distributor for offensive content would actually conflict with this objective. The court reasoned that the threat of distributor liability—which, as mentioned above, is triggered when the distributor is made aware of the unlawful nature of the content—would prompt intermediaries such as AOL to refrain from monitoring content at all.

In effect, the court held that entities such as AOL could not be held liable for being nonresponsive to unlawful content because doing so would encourage them to be nonresponsive to unlawful content. The court ignored the obvious point that Zeran's experience suggested that online intermediaries were already insufficiently motivated to address unlawful content. The court provided no evidence for the claim that distributor liability would make them more so, and failed to recognize that taking distributor liability for websites and internet Service Providers off the table in fact "has the effect of discouraging self-policing of content" (Lukmire 2010: 403), contrary to the goal the court itself cited. As one commentator describes it, "[w]ebsites and ISPs know that no matter how inflammatory third-party postings are, complaints from aggrieved parties will be to no avail, even after notice to the website or ISP" (Lukmire 2010: 403).

In economics, the lack of incentive to guard against risk where one is protected from its consequences is known as a "moral hazard." *Zeran*'s interpretation of Section 230(c)(1) creates a clear moral hazard. By completely immunizing AOL from liability, even when the company was made aware of the unlawful content and given ample opportunity to mitigate the harm, it effectively eliminated incentives for intermediaries to address harmful and destructive uses of their services. This moral hazard was compounded by the already existing moral hazard inherent in the corporate structure of companies such as AOL.

Corporations, despite the Supreme Court's infamous ruling in *Citizens United*, are not people. The word "corporation" derives from the Latin "*corporare*," to "combine in one body." But corporations are literally bodiless— they are aggregations of abstract interests, incapable of human thought, feeling, or vulnerability but capable of amassing gigantic profits. The corporate structure "not only allowed individuals to pool large amounts of money for a venture, it also allowed them to do so without the risk of any personal loss beyond the amount of their investment . . . if you own shares of a corporation and it acts negligently or breaches a contract, resulting in a huge court judgment against it, there is no chance, absent exceptional circumstances, that you will face personal exposure for that liability" (Niose 2014: 41). That is, the structure of the corporation is pure moral hazard: "the nature of corporate action, where bureaucracy dictates that most of the actors are far removed from the actual harm that might occur as a result of their decisions, increases the likelihood of egregious conduct" (Niose 2014: 45).

Corporations are able to derive tremendous profits from their enterprises in part because they have the power to push the negative costs of these activities onto third parties. Section 230, as interpreted in *Zeran* and most cases since then, allows interactive service providers to do the same. It is no surprise, then, that corporations that are also interactive service providers now dominate not only the internet but the economy generally. Amazon, Apple, Facebook, Google, and Microsoft are now the five largest firms in the world based on market value, and they exert outsized influence on internet communication and commerce. These corporations that have near-monopoly control of the internet are doubly protected from the costs of their risky ventures even as they reap their massive benefits. Given that the dominant business model of websites and social media services is based on advertising revenue, they have no natural incentive to discourage abusive or harmful conduct: "abusive posts still bring in considerable ad revenue . . . the more content that is posted, good or bad, the more ad money goes into their coffers" (Leetaru 2017). As Astra Taylor writes in *The People's Platform*, internet entities are "commercial enterprises designed to maximize revenue, not defend political expression, preserve our collective heritage, or facilitate creativity" (Taylor 2014: 221). These companies could be held in check if they faced liability for harmful content, but this is exactly what Section 230 as currently interpreted prevents from happening. Between the nature of corporate activity and Section 230 immunity, there is virtually no way to hold these increasingly powerful entities accountable for the harm they cause.

5. Shield and Sword

The free speech rhetoric of Section 230 is powerful, first, because it reinforces the perception that conduct = speech. It is also powerful because it provides both a shield and a sword to the increasingly powerful entities that dominate the internet. It shields intermediaries from the costs generated by the speech of third parties while allowing them to reap the benefits, monetary and otherwise, of that speech.

One particularly prominent example of a corporation using Section 230 as both a shield and sword is Backpage. Backpage is a website that has been offering classified advertisements for various products and services since 2004. Until 2017, Backpage included an adult section that listed a variety of sexually themed products and services. In 2011, the company came under scrutiny after allegations that its adult section was being used to facilitate sex trafficking and sexual assault, including of minors. Backpage has prevailed against almost every lawsuit brought against it on Section 230 grounds. Essentially, Backpage has been able to argue that as an interactive computer service, it was not the "publisher or speaker" of content provided by the parties who created the ads. If the ads facilitated sex trafficking, Backpage could not be held accountable for them because they were not Backpage's "speech."

But Backpage's claims in the case *Backpage.com, LLC v. Dart,*[5] went much further. While Backpage eagerly insisted in previous cases that it was not the speaker, publisher, or distributor of the content on its site and therefore could face no liability for any harm that content caused, in this case Backpage argued that it had affirmative and expansive First Amendment rights in the content on its site.

In 2015, Sheriff Tom Dart of Cook County, Illinois, wrote a letter to the credit card companies Visa and Mastercard, encouraging them to cease processing payments for Backpage ads due to the fact that these ads were being used for underage sex trafficking. Within days, Visa and Mastercard stopped processing payments, and Backpage suffered a fairly serious financial impact as a result. Backpage filed a lawsuit alleging that the sheriff's letter constituted an informal prior restraint on its speech. It asked for a temporary restraining order and a preliminary injunction on the basis that Dart's actions violated Backpage's First and Fourteenth Amendment rights as well as violating Section 230. The district court denied the injunction, but the Seventh Circuit reversed. Judge Richard Posner, writing for the three-judge panel, found that Backpage was entitled to a preliminary injunction against Dart, in a decision that was widely praised in tech industry and civil liberties circles.

The case seems to present a paradox: Given that the essence of Section 230 immunity is that intermediaries cannot be treated as "publishers or speakers" of third-party content, how can those same intermediaries claim First Amendment interests in that same content? How could Backpage have standing to assert a prior restraint of speech claim when it supposedly did not "speak" at all?

The aspect of the opinion that has received the most attention is Judge Posner's claim that Dart's letter constituted a threat and that it was made by Dart in his role as a public official. This point is debatable enough, but it is secondary to the question of whose rights were potentially affected by this action in the first place. If Dart's letter threatened anyone at all, it was clearly the credit card companies—not the entities who created the ads and certainly not Backpage itself. Assuming for the sake of argument that Sheriff Dart's letter was threatening, it was directed at payment processors of the ads that Backpage wanted to run on its site. Sheriff Dart's actions did not interfere with Backpage's ability to publish any content, or even with the advertisers' ability to place their ads on Backpage. What he did was attempt to discourage two particular means of payment processing for these ads. It would be easy enough to understand Visa or Mastercard bringing a claim; as it turns out, neither company did so and in fact both asserted that they did not feel threatened by Sheriff Dart's letter. Even assuming that Dart's letter constituted an official threat, it was not a threat that prevented Backpage from running any ads, or even prevented it from getting paid for running any ads. It merely kept Backpage from being able to process payments in a certain way for certain ads. Essentially, the only way that Dart could be said to have interfered with Backpage was in the sense that he made it harder for Backpage to make money. This might reasonably give rise to a tortious interference with contract or similar claim, but it is not obvious why it gives rise to a First Amendment claim.

To reach this curious result, the court relied on an analogy between the present case and *Bantam Books, Inc. v. Sullivan* (1963).[6] At issue in that case was Rhode Island's creation of a commission to suppress the distribution of books considered "objectionable." The commission contacted book distributors to inform them that they could face legal sanctions if they did not cooperate with the commission's efforts. Several distributors engaged in self-censorship as a result out of fear of possible prosecution. According to Judge Posner, the "distributor of the plaintiffs' books" in Bantam "correspond[s] to the credit card companies in this case."[7]

The analogy between the book distributor and the credit card companies is itself debatable, but that aside, the credit card companies were not the plaintiffs in *Backpage v. Dart*. Rather, the plaintiff was Backpage, an interactive computer service. The entire point of Section 230, however, is that interactive computer services *cannot* be treated as the "publisher or speaker"—or, as *Zeran* made clear, as the "distributor"—of third-party content. But the Seventh Circuit, as well as the Electronic Frontier Foundation and other civil liberties groups who filed amicus briefs on Backpage's behalf, casually assumed that Backpage *is* effectively the speaker when the question is one not of liability but of benefit. Apparently Backpage literally gets to have it both ways: it cannot be treated as the speaker of third-party content when it comes to being held accountable for harm, but it can be treated as the speaker of third-party content when it comes to exercising First Amendment rights—rights so robust, in fact, that they can be used to justify a prior restraint on another party's (Sheriff Dart's) speech.

Cases such as these demonstrate how Section 230 is being used as both a shield against liability and a sword to impose rights. Previous litigation against Backpage mostly focused on whether intermediaries can be held liable for content provided by third parties, a fairly straightforward Section 230 question. *Dart v. Backpage* is different: it makes clear that intermediaries do not merely receive immunity from liability for third-party content, but also, simultaneously, get to claim affirmative, First Amendment rights to that content.

Nothing in the text of Section 230 itself commands this bizarre result. Subsection (c)(1) states that an interactive computer service cannot be treated as a publisher or speaker of third-party content, full stop. It is not qualified as a prohibition only for purposes of liability. The provision regarding immunity from civil liability is a separate subsection (c)(2), which in fact specifies that the immunity is limited to actions taken by the interactive computer service to restrict access to harmful or unlawful content. Nonetheless, the courts, the public, and organizations such as the EFF promote this contradictory and destructive view of Section 230.

6. Conclusion

In reflecting on the impact of Section 230 and how it has shaped the internet, it is important to consider Congress's goals in passing the law. It is true, as so often proclaimed, that the policy goals of Section 230 include the promotion and protection of free speech principles. But free speech is, at least in theory, a right that should be protected for all, not just an elite class. If women and minorities are not able to express themselves freely on the internet without fear of harassment or injury, then the right to free speech is not being protected.

Moreover, free speech is not the only value protected by Section 230. The other, often overlooked goals of Section 230 include the development of technologies that "maximize user control over what information is received" by internet users, as well as the "vigorous enforcement of Federal criminal laws to deter and punish trafficking in obscenity, stalking and harassment by means of computer."[8] In other words, the law is intended to promote and protect the values of privacy, security, and liberty alongside the values of open discourse.

The district court in *Zeran* wrote in a footnote that the "CDA reflects Congress' attempt to strike the right balance between the competing objectives of encouraging the growth of the internet on one hand, and minimizing the possibility of harm from the abuse of that technology on the other."[9] While the court reiterates that Congress has the right to decide how to fulfill its own purposes, it notes that "today's problems may soon be obsolete while tomorrow's challenges are, as yet, unknowable. In this environment, Congress is likely to have reasons and opportunities to revisit the balance struck in CDA."[10]

Tomorrow's challenges have arrived. The broad interpretation of Section 230 as providing near-complete immunity to online intermediaries has encouraged websites and internet Service Providers to be increasingly reckless with regard to abusive and unlawful content on their platforms. Today, the internet is awash in threats, harassment, defamation, revenge porn, propaganda, misinformation, and conspiracy theories. In this sense, Barlow's Declaration was startlingly prescient. The internet is indeed "not where bodies live." It is where bodiless corporations extract endless profits from the misery of human beings.

Notes

1. 47 U.S.C. § 230 (1996).
2. 47 U.S.C. § 230 (1996).

3. 47 U.S.C. § 230 (1996).

4. Zeran v. AOL, 129 F.3d 327 (4th Cir. 1997).

5. Backpage.com, LLC v. Dart, 807 F.3d 229, 236 (7th Cir. 2015), *cert. denied,* 137 S. Ct. 46, 196 L. Ed. 2d 28 (2016).

6. Bantam Books, Inc. v. Sullivan, 372 U.S. 58, 61 (1963).

7. Backpage.com, *LLC v. Dart,* 807 F.3d 229, 236 (7th Cir. 2015).

8. § 230(b)(3)&(5).

9. Zeran v. Am. Online, Inc., 958 F. Supp. 1124, 1135 (E.D. Va.), *aff'd,* 129 F.3d 327 (4th Cir. 1997).

10. *Zeran,* 958 F. Supp. 1124, 1135.

References

EFF. 2017. "About EFF." *Electronic Frontier Foundation.* October 24. https://www.eff.org/about.

Barlow, J. P. 1996. "A Declaration of the Independence of Cyberspace." *Electronic Frontier Foundation.* February 8. https://www.eff.org/cyberspace-independence.

Dyer, R. J. P. 2014. "The Communication Decency Act Gone Wild: A Case for Renewing the Presumption against Preemption." *Seattle University Law Review* 37 (2): 837–63.

Franks, M. A. 2011. "Unwilling Avatars: Idealism and Discrimination in Cyberspace." *Columbia Journal of Gender and Law* 20 (2): 224–61.

Franks, M. A. 2017. "Democratic Surveillance." *Harvard Journal of Law and Technology* 30(2): 425–89.

Katsh, M. E. and O. Rabinovich-Einy. 2017. *Digital Justice: Technology and the Internet of Disputes.* New York: Oxford University Press.

Leetaru, K. 2017. "Do Social Media Platforms Really Care about Online Abuse?" *Forbes.* January 12. https://www.forbes.com/sites/kalevleetaru/2017/01/12/do-social-media-platforms-really-care-about-online-abuse/#4e82e84c45f1.

Lukmire, D. 2010. "Can the Courts Tame the Communications Decency Act? The Reverberations of *Zeran v. America Online.*" *New York University Annual Survey of American Law* 66: 371–412.

Niose, D. 2014. *Fighting Back the Right: Reclaiming America from the Attack on Reason.* New York: Palgrave Macmillan.

Taplin, J. 2017. *Move Fast and Break Things: How Facebook, Google, and Amazon Cornered Culture and Undermined Democracy.* New York: Little, Brown and Co.

Taylor, A. 2014. *The People's Platform: Taking Back Power and Culture in the Digital Age.* New York: Metropolitan Books.

9

Demographics, Design, and Free Speech

HOW DEMOGRAPHICS HAVE PRODUCED SOCIAL
MEDIA OPTIMIZED FOR ABUSE AND THE SILENCING OF
MARGINALIZED VOICES

Soraya Chemaly

The young woman, Maryam (a pseudonym) who texted me to ask for help was coming apart at the seams. In the wake of being named during a Fox News segment and identified and called out on Twitter by three powerful conservative media pundits, she was being hammered by an incessant stream of online abuse and hate speech. Misogynistic and anti-Islamic messages filled her inbox. She was graphically and pornographically threatened with rape and death. The flow of hateful and harassing commentary, including messages sharing her home address, was overwhelming. This went on for days and across all of the popular social media platforms that she used both personally and professionally. She stopped working and went into hiding. What had she done? She had expressed her opinion about a hot button political issue.

The phrase "online harassment" is an anodyne catchphrase for a spectrum of behaviors, many of which break unenforced laws, degrade people's civil rights, reduce their ability to work, cause emotional and psychological harm, and actively aim to inhibit their freedom of expression. Every day, I talk to women who have the experience that Maryam did. They start their days filtering abusive content that ranges from insulting and libelous to hateful and violently pornographic. The harassment often involves public shaming meant to humiliate and generates anxiety that comes with stranger threats and mob attacks. It also almost always alters, sometimes permanently, a person's ability to feel safe in "real" space, to make a living, and to engage publicly and politically. These episodes of harassment are deliberate, and often successful, attempts to reduce freedom of expression.

Research into online harassment shows that while everyone can fall victim to online harassment, the impact, scope, and risk of that harassment differ according to identity. Men and women are experiencing the internet in radically different ways. Women in virtually all walks of life are exposed to higher levels of online harassment. According to a 2015 Pew Research study, women aged 18–24 experience the most severe and persistent hostility online: 26% report being stalked online and 25% have been sexually harassed on social media (Duggan 2017). Women are more than twice as likely than men to report that harassment is deeply troubling, and to incur costs and take specific steps to stem their exposure to harassment. As with offline gender-based harassment and sexualized violence, institutional tolerance—in social media companies, law enforcement, and families—can be high and there is little or no recourse, especially when harassment is cross-platform.

Surveys show that most men experience harassment primarily as isolated incidents of name-calling designed to embarrass them. Women, on the other hand, are the majority of targets of sustained and sexualized abuse, stalking and online harassment linked to both anonymous and intimate partner violence. While anonymity is a contributor, it is not itself the sole cause. A large percentage of women know their aggressors. For example, in stalking cases or those involving "revenge porn" in the United States women make up more than 95% of reported cases.

Women also make up the primary targets of incidents of globally trending mob harassment. Cybermobs can include thousands of individuals harassing their targets across multiple platforms.

Online rape threats, non-consensual pornification, and the spread of manipulated images depicting sexual degradation and eroticized male domination are familiar tactics to women with public voices online. Attacks can take on absurd qualities. In 2013, British feminist Caroline Criado-Perez was sent rape threats, at one point more than 100 per minute, after she successfully campaigned to have a notable woman featured on a British bank note (Hattenstone 2013). A 2016 Amnesty International study found that Diane Abbott, the first black woman in the British Parliament, was the target of almost half of the 25,688 harassing, denigrating, and threatening tweets sent to women MPs during the studied period (Dhrodia 2017).

For women in media and in politics, particularly as well as other hegemonically masculine arenas, such as sports and finance, abuse is now part of the workday. A 2016 study of more than 70 million reader comments on the *Guardian* news website found that women columnists were 8 of the 10 most harassed writers on the site; the other two were gay men (Gardiner et al. 2016). The women targeted also disproportionately had overlapping marginalized identities. Feminist topics also resulted in the highest levels of abusive reader commentary.

Pornography and rape videos that are used to intimidate and harass women into silence exist on a spectrum along with the commonly reported online surveillance of women in public spaces such as bathrooms, locker rooms, rented apartments, store changing rooms, and even subway platforms. Cyber-cesspools, sites that are created and revenue generating, often trade in these products which, in turn, bleed seamlessly into the use of social media by sex traffickers. Girls and women make up 76% of trafficking victims sold online today. While traditional concepts of harassment do not usually include trafficking, to the people being trafficked the tactics, processes, and impacts are clearly abusive.

Trans women, black women, Muslim women, and Jewish women all report higher levels of targeted abuse, as do men of color and members of the LGTBQI community. Online harassment is remarkably heterosexist and geared toward reinforcement of rigid and binary gender and sexuality norms. LGBTQI youth, for example, experience online bullying at three times the rate of their straight peers.

Social media companies created the technology and mechanisms of this abuse and only very reluctantly have taken on responsibility for monitoring content. They rely on users to report "offensive" content, which includes hate speech, child pornography, and content that is graphically violent. Each internet platform has its own terms of service, user guidelines, policies, and procedures. The spaces where people aggregate online are not, as many assume, free from speech rules, but rather, filled with them. While platforms claim to be "neutral" and not involved in content generation, they are regulating, prioritizing, and packaging content 24 hours a day, seven days a week. Machine learning is increasingly being used to filter content, but human beings are writing rules, and human beings are responsible for deciding what constitutes "safety," "threat," "obscenity," "pornography," and "risk."

The technology industry now regulating free speech globally in unprecedented ways is notorious for its exclusion of women, sexism, and persistent marginalization of black and other ethnic minorities in its ranks.

Women make up only 24% of the workforce, and are clustered in sales, marketing, customer service, and legal areas (Lee and Stewart 2016). Latinx and black tech workers, together, are only 5% of the workforce. Twitter is a typical example. In 2105, only 30% of the company's staff was women. Men made up 79% of the company's leadership. The engineering staff was 90% male. At Facebook, Google, Microsoft, and other major tech firms, the numbers are similar or worse. Only 2% of Google's workforce is black, and only 30% are women (Miller 2014). The fastest growing demographic cohort in Silicon Valley is Asians, primarily men, who make up 40% of the industry's labor. Not only are women and people of color on the margins of the sector, but labor is sex segregated, with women clustered in marketing, sales, legal, and customer service roles—in other words, not building products.

The persistent male dominance and the sex segregation of this purportedly progressive industry have serious implications for both safety and free expression. The people most likely to be driven out of online spaces by harassment are the least likely to be involved in the creation, production, and engineering of the social media platforms on which online harassment takes place. The people who are most likely to be involved in the creation, production, and engineering of these spaces routinely demonstrate that they are blinkered by their insularity, privilege, and lack of relevant experience.

Understanding the perception and assessment of risk is critical to understanding the relationship between threats to freedom of expression and demographics of the industry and the culture that dominates it. Funders, founders, managers, and engineers who are less familiar, online or off, with the dynamics and impacts of targeted abuse end up enabling and perpetrating that abuse in the design of their products and the shaping of policy. Risk perception is governed by identity in ways that are not often acknowledged. It is primarily in the assessment of risk, and what to do about it, that harassment becomes institutionalized.

In 1994, social scientists James Flynn, Paul Slovic, and C. K. Mertz posited a theory that came to be known as the White Male Effect (WME) in a study called "Gender, Race, and Perception of Environmental Health Risks" (Flynn et al. 1994). WME has since been used to understand outlier risk assessments in virtually all areas of controversial interest including gun control, abortion, and climate change. In 2011, one study of people's attitudes toward climate change and its risks concluded that 48.4% of conservative white men, whom researchers described as "confident" in their beliefs, think global warming will not happen, compared to 8.6% of all other adults. Fully, 29.6% of white men denied that global warming effects will *ever* happen (Pyper 2011). In 2005, Yale Law School professor Dan Kahan expanded the theory to include "cultural cognition" (Kahan et al. 2007). "The reason white males are less fearful of various risks is that they are more afraid of something else: namely, the loss of status they experience when activities symbolic of their cultural worldviews are stigmatized as socially undesirable" (Kahan et al. 2007).

Digital security expert Stephen Cobb believes that the White Male Effect explains persistent failures to accurately gauge and respond to risk in tech, where men are not only high status, but demonstrably aggressively protective of that status (Bowles 2017). Companies routinely fail to recognize or underestimate potential harms related to privacy invasions, harassment, geolocation, photo tagging, data sharing, and other cyber risks. Cobb has documented how decision-makers repeatedly conclude, mistakenly, that risks related to their products are minimal. "This is consistent with research showing one group of people ranks risks lower than the rest of the population, namely: white males," he explained.

Take, for example, how harassment has to be reported on popular platforms. Traditionally, before Facebook would consider removing abusive content, a user had to report that content. In order to do that, the item—a comment, a picture, or a post on someone's wall— has to be flagged, after which it enters a detailed process of review. The system works well if you are targeted by, for example, a person who is insulting you in a comment. The target selects the comment, enters an interface that asks why you are reporting the comment, submits it, and hours or days later you are told whether the comment was removed. The system is very linear and decontextualizes the item being reported. It is, essentially, built to accommodate harassment the way a young man is most likely to experience it: as a one-off episode of name-calling. What happens, however, if you are a black trans woman whose wall is being deluged with racist and misogynistic slurs, threats, and pornographic memes? First you have to report each instance of harassment separately, which is laborious, and potentially re-traumatizing. It also means, since context has been stripped from each item of content, that the scope and intensity of your harassment are not captured. For years, content reported in this way meant that each item might end up in front of a different reviewer. Facebook has, during the past few years, attempted to make changes to its interface and data flow in order to capture context, but the onus for reporting remains on the targeted person.

Tech company moderation processes are notoriously abuser-friendly. When Criado-Perez was targeted and had to report hundreds of tweets and accounts to Twitter, also one at a time, she, like others, had to check a box saying that her submission would be shown to the person she was reporting. "every time you report someone for abuse, including threats to kill you, you have to tick a box agreeing that your information can be shared with them," she explained at the time (Doward 2013). In YouTube, the rules governing what constitutes targeted harassment are often opaque and videos in which targeted individuals are named and physically identified are often served for viewing by algorithmic design based on language and subject matter matching, alongside the channels of the person being targeted. So, for example, a teenage girl who made a video about dress code policies in her school will find, alongside her video, dozens of antifeminist videos created by users with millions of followers using parts of her video to denigrate and harass her. She will also find comments such as, "you deserve to be raped until you die."

A lack of understanding regarding the impact of this type of violence creates a denigrating and hostile environment for rape victims and women more broadly. Researcher Emma Jane, author of *Misogyny Online: A Short (and Brutish) History*, calls the use of rape to silence women online "Rapeglish," a specific dialect used automatically by men who are offended by women online. To illustrate this particular dimension of gendered harassment, Jane created a tool called the Random Rape Threat Generator, which illustrates the formulaic nature of sexualized threats. Jane collected tens of thousands of examples, spanning 12 years, from women globally to build the database fueling the app (Jane 2017). For most of the period in which she collected the data, "You should be raped," or "I will rape you," the mildest examples, were considered by platforms to be harmless.

In 2013, fed up with content like this being ignored, activist Trista Hendren set up a Facebook page that would serve as a reporting hub. Within days mobs began to post violent and antifeminist commentary, violent pornography, malicious software links, and rape and death threats. Hendren's personal information was shared online and her picture was used to create rape memes. Her daughter's name and image were also appropriated. "At first, people started posting pictures of women and young girls being raped or beat up and commenting on the page saying things like, "I will skull-fuck your children," she explained afterward. Hendren, not her harassers, chose to leave Facebook (Buni and Chemaly 2014). People who supported her efforts reported being unwilling to publicly show their support in Facebook, in effect self-silencing out of fear that they would be similarly treated and threatened. Hendren had kept her identity hidden on the page that she started, but was outed nonetheless.

In the summer of 2017, in a detailed article titled "Facebook's Secret Censorship Rules Protect White Men from Hate Speech but Not Black Children," Pro Publica described a U.S. congressman's Facebook post calling for the killing of "radicalized" Muslims. "Hunt them, identify them, and kill them," he wrote, "Kill them all. For the sake of all that is good and righteous. Kill them all" (Angwin and Grassegger 2017). His message, despite being reported multiple times, was left in place and not considered in violation of guidelines barring either graphic violence or identity-based targeting. The article compared this content to content shared by poet and Black Lives Matter activist Didi Delgado: "All white people are racist. Start from this reference point, or you've already failed," Delgado wrote (Angwin and Grassegger 2017). Her account was frozen for a week.

Corporate policies that lack appreciation for historic discrimination and marginalization are themselves forms of harassment that suppress speech. Verification of users, for example, is a process that creates power imbalances on platforms and that often exacerbates abuse. A small blue check is now the universal symbol that a person is a public figure and that the platform being used has confirmed that they are who they say they are. Verification has since become a valuable product for other reasons. It not only assures people of the legitimacy and authenticity of an account, but raises a person's visibility and influence. On some platforms, verified users are provided with specific tools, including audience growth tools, available to selected users. They gain prominent placement in news feeds and can use verification on one platform to increase the likelihood of verification on another. Content produced by verified accounts is given more weight and travels faster and farther.

Verification sets up a two-tiered hierarchy for speech. It is almost certainly why women journalists on Twitter are among the most harassed. The way status affects harassment dynamics in gaming provides insights into why this matters. In 2015, researchers at University of New South Wales and Miami University published a study of how men responded to women playing video games (Kasumovic and Kuznekoff 2015). The researchers found that men were almost always polite to one another, particularly good players, who complimented and applauded the people that they played with. Men who were not winning, however, deviated from this pattern by hurling abuse at more skilled women players. One of the lead researchers proposed that their findings were insightful for "real life" behaviors in other environments. Verification establishes a visible marker of status in which less privileged men easily identify women with higher status and influence.

Harassment of women journalists online is now an effective weapon used not only by literal losers but by governments. Finnish journalist Jessikka Aro was one of the first journalists globally to write about disinformation and Russians troll farms, places where people are hired to churn out fake news, propaganda, and politically and culturally divisive internet content that is, itself, often harassing. Aro found herself in the crosshairs of a systematic harassment campaign designed to discredit her in Twitter, Facebook, and Russian "news sites." She was accused of destroying Finnish freedom of speech, and called a slut and a "NATO Skank." When she approached the founder of one of the sites on which disinformation was being propagated he agreed to tone down the hate speech against her if she apologized and stopped her reporting, She and several other women journalists were called "media whores," images of their faces merged in memes with both the NATO logo and swastikas (Higgins 2016). Almost two-thirds of women journalists report experiencing threats, sexist abuse, intimidation, threats, and harassment in the course of doing their work.

The development of a tool such as Verification was undoubtedly predicated on the notion of technology, and this platform, being neutral. In a lengthy article titled "Twitter's New Verification Process is a Game Rigged against Its Marginalized Users," Veve Jaffa described the product's deeply rooted sociotechnical male entitlement and negative impact on attempts to participate equally in the public arena. "Verification does nothing to address Twitter's clear bias in prioritizing users who already possess the privilege not to be targets of harassment in the first place, nor does it improve the safety of users whose online presence falls outside of Twitter's nebulous definition of "public interest," Jaffa explained (Jaffa 2016). "Borrowing from the game industry's use of behavioral psychology to encourage and manipulate user participation, Twitter gamifies its verification process, drawing attention away from the requirement to surrender sensitive personal information and the risks it poses to marginalized users in particular" (Jaffa 2016).

Worse, verified accounts are often implicated in both dog whistle tactics and overt harassment. In October 2016, the *New York Times* published an article about 74-year-old Jessica Leeds in which she described Donald Trump assaulting her on an airplane 30 years before (Twohey and Barbaro 2016). The following day, Lou Dobbs, a popular and verified Fox Business commentator, retweeted a message containing what appeared to contain her private contact information, including her phone number and home address. What Dobbs, a person with 1.5 million followers did intentionally or not, is called doxing, revealing a person's private and identifying information, usually for hostile purposes (Blake 2016). Dobbs may not have had malicious intent, but his 800,000 Twitter followers favorited and shared the information at least 2,900 times in two hours. Only days before, another Trump accuser, fearing for her family's safety in the wake of a flood of threats, went into hiding.

Doxing, a vigilante tactic for taking away a person's privacy, security, and online anonymity, is sometimes used to reveal harassers, which, in turn, is considered to be harassment by many "free" speech defenders. In October 2012, Gawker reporter Adrian Chen published a now famous investigative report in which he named an infamous internet abuser known as Violentacrez, Michael Brutsch (Chen 2012). Brutsch was the moderator of Reddit pages with names such as "Creepshots," and "Jailbait," a forum where men shared photos of scantily clad underage girls harvested without their knowledge or consent. It was harassing, objectifying, and borderline criminal (child pornography laws bar sexualized imagery of children). The sites had millions of users and contributors. According to many of his critics, Chen violated an unspoken rule that internet anonymity is an inalienable right, an argument that is predominantly, consistently, and vocally made, unsurprisingly, by white men with libertarian beliefs. The right to privacy and anonymity enjoyed by Violentacrez on Reddit, and with Reddit's approval, did not extend to his victims. For his scaled up digital versions of street and sexual harassment, Brutsch was awarded a Reddit Alien bobblehead "for making significant contributions to the site."

When companies require users to use "real names" and provide "official" documentation to prove who they are, they discriminate against vulnerable populations and people in countries where government ID is not standard or recognition would endanger them. Whereas "John Smith," American college grad and tech whiz, may not see a problem with using his name, trans people, activists, and other marginalized people do. Each has to decide whether to leave a platform or risk being identified and targeted online if they publicize their names. In addition, policies like these, in execution, have proven Eurocentric. Indigenous peoples, people with "nonstandard" Anglicized names, have had to fight to have their names considered "real." In India, real name policies mean that individuals seeking to avoid stigma related to caste are forced to publicly identify themselves in ways that will lead to discrimination and abuse. In October 2015, a group of more than 40 organizations, the Nameless

Coalition, petitioned Facebook to change its policies and accept pseudonyms and non-legal names (Brandom 2015). The Coalition was started after Indian women writers were forced to shut down their social media platforms when their identities were revealed by the policy.

The same group of women was targeted by Facebook pages deliberately set up to identify them as sex workers. In Silicon Valley calling a woman a whore is not a threat, but in other parts of the world it is a very specific threat, one that puts a woman at risk of offline violence not only in public, but also perhaps within her own family. In addition, the fact that pages were being set up in languages that Facebook was not equipped to translate made the proliferation of hate pages easier for harassers. Facebook's stated policy for creating pages was that names of pages could not include hateful or harassing messages, but the policies are irrelevant if no one can understand the language that the titles are written in.

Content moderation policies also frequently institutionalize mainstream social norms in ways that actively suppress women's speech, counter-speech, and explicitly feminist expression. Content related to women's health, menstruation, breastfeeding, and reproduction has been removed from sites as pornographic because the logic of pornography is that naked women's bodies are sexual and titillating by default. Women seeking to engage in speech that counters objectifying and sexualizing representations of women, or in speech that objects to heteropatriarchal violence, report having their content removed from social media sites because they violate terms of service that conflate women's nudity or semi-nudity with "obscenity." In late 2017, the travel website Travelocity was forced to apologize after it was revealed that it was removing reviews written by women who were warning travelers that they had been raped in certain properties. Their comments violated the company's "family friendly" content rules (Nanos 2017).

Also on the basis of "family friendly rules" Facebook, until only recently, barred images of breastfeeding mothers, as well as post-mastectomy photographs. The company has continued in some instances to remove content depicting women as topless, even if the women are engaged in artistic expression or political protest. In the wake of the Arab Spring, social media companies publicized the importance of their platforms to political dissent and free expression. Arab revolutionaries were able to share pictures and words that defied the regimes they sought to overthrow and social media companies were happy to host them. When, in 2013, nineteen-year-old Tunisian activist Amina Tyler posted a picture of herself with the words "Fuck your morals" painted on her bare breasts, however, the freedom was constrained. Tyler's photograph was blocked or blurred (Gordts 2013). She was actively engaged in political protest against sexist societal double standards, cultural oppression, and institutionalized theocracy. Facebook's claims that it is dedicated to promoting public awareness and debate on controversial issues of political import did not appear to apply to Tyler or other women like her.

Harassing content is also a matter of corporate profitability. Abuse is emotionally resonant and it generates, in supporters or objectors, user activity. User activity means data, which is the lifeblood of online business. If, for example, a racist and sexist mob targets a woman celebrity for days on end, the episode might turn into a trending and marketable moment titled "Twitter users push back against the harassment of Leslie Jones."

One lengthy episode of harassment was called "Gamergate," a cross-platform online campaign that primarily targeted three women in the gaming industry with sustained abuse over a period of years. It involved the proliferation of manipulated photographs; video propaganda; sexist, racist, and transphobic vitriol; and rape and death threats as well as what later came to be called "fake news." Gamergate, nominally a protest against unethical journalistic practices in the gaming industry, was a profoundly anti-progressive movement catalyzed by an act of electronically enabled intimate partner abuse. Gamergaters rapidly focused on three women: Anita Sarkeesian, Zoë Quinn, and Brianna Wu. At one point, a game was created that allowed users to virtually beat Sarkeesian's face in to a bloody pulp. Quinn's image was used to create graphic scenes of her sexual degradation. Wu, who was forced after threats to move her family out of her house, spent one day a week with law enforcement and only made public appearances with security in tow. Sarkeesian had to cancel a speaking engagement at Utah State University after an email was sent to administrators threatening "the deadliest school shooting in American history." Online, the women battled to have companies such as YouTube, Facebook, and Twitter understand not only the harassment they were experiencing on each platform, but what the specific impact of cross-platform harassment was having on their ability to live, work, feel safe, and find a place to speak freely without constant threat. In several instances, persistent institutional tolerance included companies ignoring the role that verified users played (none of the women was verified at the time that the harassment began and built in intensity) in amplifying abuse. Sarkeesian's offense was that she analyzes sexism in mainstream video games. Wu and Quinn were reviled for claiming the name "gamer" and creating unorthodox games about, for example, depression.

Social media companies, and the tech industry more broadly, continue to maintain that their systems do not materialize specific perspectives, do not privilege the speech of people who already enjoy relatively high status, or do not, themselves, constitute obstacles to the speech of the less powerful. The belief in technological agnosticism is currently most apparent in the development of next generation algorithmic and machine learning anti-harassment tools.

In principle, "machine learning" sounds objective, but in practice it is not. It relies on humans to ask specific questions, define specific problems, consider specific solutions, and provide specific data and interpretations. The bodies and experiences of those humans matter.

Several years ago, in an effort to find effective, scalable response to the problem of online abuse and harassment, Lucas Dixon, a researcher at Jigsaw, a Google subsidiary spun off from the former Google Ideas, wondered if an AI tool could be designed that would recognize and preemptively remove toxic comments more effectively than humans. The result was an automated moderation system called Conversation AI, which was trained to do just this. In order to teach the AI idiomatic language and how to assess it, Jigsaw partnered with the *New York Times* and Wikipedia, both of which provided data sources used to train the system. More than 17 million comments were from *New York Times* articles and 130,000 comments were taken from Wikipedia pages. Human annotators contracted by Jigsaw rated the database of comments, giving them a score based on aggressiveness or a "personal attack." The resulting harassment-detection tool had a human-score matching accuracy rate of 92%, with only a 10% chance of a false positive.

During an exercise to evaluate this tool, I submitted expressions that a journalist, for example, might encounter. These ranged from the relatively mild "nice tits" to "Nigger cunt," and "You should be raped." The first iteration of the algorithm rated the expression "nice tits" as "neutral" and not "aggressive" or an "attack." More troubling however, was that the expressions "Rape her," and "You should be raped" were initially rated "Not an Attack," compared, for example to "You're a Dick" which was rated as the highest possible "Attack." Jigsaw went on to explain the various reasons why this might be the case, including that neutral ratings for many terms might be related to the fact that these words were not commonly used in the data used to train the system and, also, that they may be used in positive ways. The danger and complication of systems such as these is the difficulty of determining context and intent. Speech that resembles harassment, for example, the use of the word "rape" in "Rape Crisis Center," would be erased. The structure of sentences, the context for words, the identity of speakers all matter.

What would this look like if automated moderation based on this first test model were executed when AI evaluated it? A 2016 *Wired* article provided a good example. It described what happened when Sarah Jeong, the author of *The Internet of Garbage*, called a typical Bernie Sanders fan a "vitriolic cryptoracist who spends 20 hours a day on the Internet yelling at women." Jeong now refers to her tweet as "the tweet that launched a thousand ships." After an onslaught of harassment, Jeong was forced to withdraw from social media. She made her vibrant Twitter account private and took time off from her job, losing income in the process. In theory, the automated tool such as the one designed by Jigsaw would remove exactly the kind of hateful and violent comments that flooded her social media feeds. However, the text of one of the typical tweets sent to Jeong highlights a typical issue. It read, in part, "Twist her tits clear off." When a *Wired* reporter writing about Jigsaw's product tested the expression, it rated the phrase at the lowest possible level, "a glaring over-sight" (Greenberg 2016).

There are many reasons why certain words might score higher than others. As one researcher I spoke to explained, "There is almost no situation in which calling a person a 'dick' is not aggressive." Gendered slurs such as "Cunt," "Slut," "Skank," and "Whore" are all rated neutral when they stand alone. Machine learning incorporating human inputs that reflect our normatively high tolerance for gendered slurs and violence might easily yield these results. However, when coupled with other more complete expressions, such as "Kill the whore" or "Rape the slut" the rating might be expected to change, but does not. These, too, are rated "neutral," not either aggressive or attacks. After Jigsaw announced Conversation AI, internet trolls immediately created a list of hate term alternatives that the system had not been trained to recognize. "Skype" was a substitute for Jew. "Skittle" meant Muslim, and "Yahoo" replaced "Mexican" (Ehrenkranz 2017). The company continues to engage users in order to improve the product they are building, repeatedly refining the model and expanding data sources and evaluations to find ways to understand, assess, and offset bias that would result in more, not less, harassment.

Jeong was able to take time off and do what targets of harassment are often instructed to do by law enforcement, "just leave the internet." She is one of many prominent writers who have either temporarily or permanently decided to close their accounts on specific social media platforms after intense episodes of harassment. Feminist writers Jessica Valenti, Sady Doyle, and Lindy West have all made similar decisions.

"In my five years on Twitter, I've been called 'nigger' so many times that it barely registers as an insult anymore," explained writer and legal analyst Imani Gandy in 2014 (Buni and Chemaly 2014). Gandy has persisted for years in the face of daily assaults. "Let's just say that my 'nigger cunt' cup runneth over" (Buni and Chemaly 2014). Doyle says her experience of mass harassment has induced a kind of permanent self-censorship. "There are things I won't allow myself to talk about," she says. "Names I won't allow myself to say" (Buni and Chemaly 2014)

Being able to leave a platform is, as these women know, a relative privilege afforded by their access to other platforms and paid work in other media. For many people, particularly people of color, however, these alternatives are not available and leaving a platform isn't either.

Algorithms learn what they do from humans and, without a concerted effort to understand how they reproduce human biases there is a very real chance that they make the problem of harassment worse, not better. For women the stakes are particularly high because of the dominance of men in the tech industry and as users and deciders on influential platforms.

The Jigsaw product, in its earliest iterations, appeared to have failed in specific instances of evaluating language that is regularly used to try and silence women online. Part of the issue is a pervasive eliding of "male" with "human," and certain men's subjectivity with "objectivity," a mainstream offline default that is now happening at scale.

Wikipedia provides a closed loop example. The platform that calls itself the "sum of all human knowledge" is produced by editors who are 91% male and primarily from the United States and the United Kingdom (Wales 2004; Wikimedia Commons 2011). The average contributor is "(1) a male, (2) technically inclined, (3) formally educated, (4) an English speaker (native or non-native), (5) aged 15–49, (6) from a majority-Christian country, (7) from a developed nation, (8) from the Northern Hemisphere, and (9) likely employed as a white-collar worker." This is the demographic of people, in the United States, who are, in fact, the least likely to experience aggravated online abuse and among the most likely to believe that sexism has been eliminated as an obstacle to women's equality (Fingerhut 2016).

A similar problem can be seen in yet another major initiative tied to machine learning. In 2015, OpenAI, a research nonprofit funded by Elon Musk and Peter Thiel, announced that it would build natural language learning algorithms using Reddit message threads (Bhattacharya 2016). The goal of the project was to teach computers to develop robust understanding of human conversation so that, for example, the identification of, among other things, hateful, harassing and abusive speech can be more quickly identified. So, in essence, the partnership meant that artificial intelligence would be taught that Reddit users' language is "normatively" human language. Researchers described Reddit's database as a robust source useful for enabling computers to learn what the language of average people interacting with one another in the "real world" looks and sounds like.

It is understandable why researchers would be thrilled to have access to Reddit's database. Reddit, which calls itself "the front page of the internet," has a vibrant and engaged audience.[1] Every day, more than 160 million people (6% of internet users are Reddit visitors) use the platform to discuss everything from their hobbies, sexuality, and childcare to sports, religion, and global politics. Reddit, however, is not the front page of "the internet" but of a *specific* internet, one that is that is 74% male, concentrated in a young age group, and more than 50% American and British. This is hardly representative of humanity. If this were practically any other demographic cohort most people would describe it as a "special interest group," an expression that never applies to mainly young, mainly white, mainly men.

Since it was launched in in 2005, Reddit has been in the public eye for a steady stream of incidents involving how the company has dealt with aggressive and hateful user-generated content. While they make up only a small percentage of overall content, Reddit boards with names such as beatingwomen,

coontown, fatpeoplehate, and gasthekikes, that eventually and, at times, reluctantly, were shut down by Reddit illustrate why the site is referred to as a cyber-
cesspool. When three women computer scientists were featured in a 2014 Ask
Me Anything the result was what one Redditor described as "a parody of what
it's actually like to be a woman working in a STEM field." By comparison,
Pinterest's audience is 72% women (Ryan 2014). It's very unlikely, however,
that researchers would attribute the same universality to this user base.

Even a current emphasis on text and algorithms reflects a bias that makes
harassment more likely for women and people of color. Text-focused frames
for defining and understanding harassment that dominate high-investment,
large scale corporate solutions sideline the most effective weapons used
against women online all over the world: photographs and video. Women's
photographs and videos of girls and women are used and taken without their
consent every day to harass and extort them. Women are manipulated in imagery, and their faces and bodies memed, as part of harassment campaigns.
Shaming women for how they look, as a way to silence their speech, is a global
phenomenon, but in some parts of the world a girl or woman can be shamed
with a photograph that shows her with an uncovered head, or wearing a
skirt at her knees. In India, for example, women fearing harassment, privacy
invasions, and abuse, will not even use profile pictures in Facebook. Indian
women, prominent celebrities, activists, journalists, and politicians have reported manipulations of their photographs and threats of rape or killing. In
an effort to find a way for Indian women to more freely share their pictures,
Facebook created a "profile picture guard" that makes downloading images
harder.

When their own photos and bodies are not available, other women's
images are used for harassment. For months, women writers at a Gawker
property called Jezebel were forced to look at and moderate gifs of violent
pornography shared in the comments section of their articles every day. "The
images arrive in a barrage, and the only way to get rid of them from the website is if a staffer individually dismisses the comments and manually bans
the commenter," wrote the women in an open letter to their employer, who
had ignored requests for institutional responses (Jezebel Staff 2014). "This
weekend, the user or users have escalated to gory images of bloody injuries
emblazoned with the Jezebel logo. It's like playing whack-a-mole with a socio-
pathic Hydra" (Jezebel Staff 2014). The women pointed out that readers were
also being alienated and traumatized by the images and that they were not,
after all, paid to endure the daily onslaught.

Tech company uses of technologies that are photo- and video-based have
proven to be highly problematic. One study of Facebook's facial recognition and
photo-matching algorithm revealed that the generic categorization for "male"
and "female" was heavily raced. Automated gender classification resulted in
Asians being significantly likely, regardless of gender, to be categorized as

"female," and people of African descent as "male." The product, wrote Simone Brown in her book, *Dark Matters*, mirrors "earlier pseudo-scientific racist and sexist discourses" (Brown 2015, 111) The generic humans used to calibrate the facial recognition system, as was the case for establishing standards for film developing a century before, were white. Technology like this is based on what philosopher Lewis Gordon calls "white prototypicality."

White prototypicality is why, in 2015, Google tagged computer programmer Jacky Alciné's photograph of himself with a friend, both black, "gorillas" (Mullen 2015). As technology moves toward algorithmic biometrics embedded in the internet, face matching and detecting products seamlessly lead to "real world" harassment. As a result of technological biases such as these, black and Asian people are more likely to encounter problems online and off at verification, payment, and security checkpoints. These are institutionalized forms of harassment rarely described as harassment. Each instance discernibly degrades the freedom of movement and expression of the people targeted.

Similar problems are pervasive in gaming, the development of virtual reality programs, and robotics where women encounter "virtual rapes," where representations of embodiment are gendered and raced, and where innovation is being fueled by pornography and "traditional" forms of gender-based exploitation. In gaming, up to 70% of women players mask their gender to avoid sexist harassment (Citron 2016, 18). It is a sensible, if depressing, practice given that chatroom participants with female usernames are sent threatening and/or sexually explicit private messages 25 times more often than those with male or ambiguous usernames (Meyer and Cukier 2006).

In 2016, when Microsoft released an artificial intelligence bot named "Tay," to engage in fun and casual conversation with people on Twitter, the bot almost immediately turned into a raving racist, sexist, and anti-Semite spouting, for good measure, mid-sex banter. The release of the short-lived Tay, which dynamically acquired language through exchanges with other Twitter users, was described as a "crash-course in racism, Holocaust denial and sexism." The bot started off with "Humans are super cool," and ended the day with comments such as, "Repeat after me, Hitler did nothing wrong," and "I fucking hate feminists" (Rodriguez 2016). Microsoft had to take Tay offline, promising that its engineers would try harder to "better anticipate malicious intent that conflicts with our principles and values" (Lee 2016). In 2016, 83% of Microsoft's tech force was male, less than 6% Hispanic or black (Heer 2016). Tay was made to "look" in a photograph used for Twitter, like a teenage girl online (Gibbs 2016).

A willfully blind belief in the neutrality of media and tech is one of the fundamental obstacles to expanded free speech on the internet. There is, ultimately, very little that any one social media company can do to stem the tide of the worst of human production or to correct for systemic and automated human bias. However, if genuinely committed to trying, the tech industry could acknowledge how centrally its own systems, structures, and demographics feature in the problem. Executives, engineers, and technologists would have to understand that adhering to a stubborn and misguided mantra of "objectivity," is, in fact, itself harassing, abusive, and, ultimately, violent. To date, these shifts in culture, attitude, and philosophy have proven rare and difficult to effect.

Instead, the internet continues to reflect, as Flavia Dhozan writes, the "habitual cruelty" of capitalism. "Harassment," Dhozan explains "is the strategy" (Dzodan 2016). Harassment and violence, as she succinctly puts it, are not bugs, but features of the internet, and social media are places that, while affording opportunities for challenging white supremacist and patriarchal orders are "also where the reactionary violence to this resistance is deployed in full force" (Dzodan 2016).

If prior to the 2016 U.S. presidential election, a person had suggested that a sprawling global network—one connecting white supremacists, Nazis, the "men's rights" movement, malicious government actors, and information-just-wants-to be-free anarchists with a penchant for rape—would effect the defeat of the first woman presidential candidate by using strategic and sustained campaigns of online harassment and disinformation, she would have been dismissed as a lunatic. And yet, every major platform on the internet legally, technically, and profitably enabled the possibly illegitimate election of a white male supremacist president and administration. Mainstream media, not less diverse than tech, ignored the risk represented by the specifically gendered and raced dynamics of abuse.

To date, expressions such as "Imperialist, white supremacist, capitalist heteropatriarchy" don't roll off the tongues of Silicon Valley millionaires and idealistic technologists. Laughter, instead is the response to this bell hooks description of our dominant sociocultural and political organization. "The laughter itself," hooks says, "is a weapon of patriarchal terrorism" (hooks n.d.). Like a company slapping the parenthetical [controversial humor] on a picture of a girl being raped or a Jew being gassed. The words are critical to understanding why traditional understandings of free speech are insufficient to understanding the ways in which the internet, with its powerful network effects and ethos of radically unmoored autonomy, is so easily used to suppress the speech of the less powerful.

The internet is a powerful tool for spreading information vital to challenging limiting social roles, biases in education, sex segregation in the workplace, and restricted and controlled access to technology. Today, however, in its current management and deployment, it is reproducing rather than dismantling obstacles to women's ability to participate in emerging economies, and public and political life. Today, globally, there are 200 million fewer girls and women online than men (World Wide Web Foundation 2016). That gap, which reflects persistent and multidimensional discrimination, is expanding, not narrowing and culturally and corporately tolerated and perpetuated violence against women ensures that this will continue to be true (World Wide Web Foundation 2016).

Note

1. www.reddit.com/.

References

Angwin, J. and H. Grassegger. 2017. "Facebook's Secret Censorship Rules Protect White Men from Hate Speech but Not Black Children." *ProPublica*, June 28. https://www.propublica.org/article/facebook-hate-speech-censorship-internal-documents-algorithms.

Bhattacharya, A. 2016. "Elon Musk's OpenAI Is Using Reddit to Teach AI to Speak Like Humans." *Quartz*, October 12. https://qz.com/806321/open-ai-reddit-human-conversation/.

Blake, A. 2016. "FBN Anchor Lou Dobbs Apologizes after Retweeting Trump Accuser's Address, Phone Number." *Washington Times*, October 15. https://www.washingtontimes.com/news/2016/oct/15/lou-dobbs-apologizes-after-tweeting-trump-accusers/.

Bowles, N. 2017. "Push for Gender Equality in Tech? Some Men Say It's Gone Too Far." *The New York Times*, September 23. https://www.nytimes.com/2017/09/23/technology/silicon-valley-men-backlash-gender-scandals.html.

Brandom, R. 2015. "New 'Nameless Coalition' Challenges Facebook's Real-Name Policy." *The Verge*, October 5. https://www.theverge.com/2015/10/5/9455071/nameless-coalition- facebook-real-name-policy.

Browne, S. 2015. *Dark Matters: On the Surveillance of Blackness*. Durham, NC: Duke University Press.

Buni, C. and S. Chemaly. 2014. "The Unsafety Net: How Social Media Turned Against Women." *The Atlantic*, October 9. https://www.theatlantic.com/technology/archive/2014/10/the-unsafety-net-how-social-media-turned-against-women/381261/.

Chen, A. 2012. "Unmasking Reddit's Violentacrez, The Biggest Troll on the Web." *Gawker*, October 12. http://gawker.com/5950981/unmasking-reddits-violentacrez-the-biggest-troll-on-the-web.

Citron, D. K. 2016. *Hate Crimes in Cyberspace*. Cambridge, MA: Harvard University Press.

Doward, J. 2013. "Twitter under Fire after Bank Note Campaigner Is Target of Rape Threats." *The Observer*, July 27. https://www.theguardian.com/uk-news/2013/jul/27/twitter-trolls-threats-bank-notes-austen.

Dhrodia, A. 2017. "We Tracked 25,688 Abusive Tweets Sent to Women MPs—Half Were Directed at Diana Abbott." *New Statesman*, September 5. https://www.newstatesman.com/2017/09/we-tracked-25688-abusive-tweets-sent-women-mps-half-were-directed-diane-abbott.

Duggan, M. 2014. "Online Harassment." *Pew Research Center: Internet, Science & Tech*, October 22. http://www.pewinternet.org/2014/10/22/online-harassment/.

Dzodan, F. 2016. "Political Strategy and Buzzfeed's Analysis of 'the Twitter Problem.'" *Medium: This Political Woman*, August 18. https://medium.com/this-political-woman/political-strategy-and-buzzfeeds-analysis-of-the-twitter-problem-4ba310b7805a.

Ehrenkranz, M. 2017. "Trolls Keep Outsmarting Anti-abuse Tools. Will Twitter's New System Actually Work?" *Mic*, February 9. https://mic.com/articles/168041/trolls-keep-outsmarting-anti-harassment-tools-will-twitters-new-system-actually-work#.ktmYy4Ccn.

Fingerhut, H. 2016. "In Both Parties, Men And Women Differ over Whether Women Still Face Obstacles to Progress." *Pew Research Center*, August 16. http://www.pewresearch.org/fact-tank/2016/08/16/in-both-parties-men-and-women-differ-over-whether-women-still-face-obstacles-to-progress/.

Flynn, J., P. Slovic and C. K. Mertz. 1994. "Gender, Race, and Perception of Environmental Health Risks." *Risk Analysis* 14 (6): 1101–08. doi:10.1111/j.1539-6924.1994.tb00082.x.

Gardiner, B., M. Mansfield, I. Anderson, J. Holder, D. Louter, and M. Ulmanu. 2016. "The Dark Side of Guardian Comments." *The Guardian*, April 12. https://www.theguardian.com/technology/2016/apr/12/the-dark-side-of-guardian-comments.

Gibbs, S. 2016. "Microsoft's Racist Chatbot Returns with Drug-Smoking Twitter Meltdown." *The Guardian*, March 30. https://www.theguardian.com/technology/2016/mar/30/microsoft-racist-sexist-chatbot-twitter-drugs.

Gordts, E. 2013. "Amina Tyler, Topless Tunisian FEMEN Activist, Sparks Massive Controversy." *Huffington Post*, March 26. https://www.huffingtonpost.com/2013/03/25/amina-tyler-femen_n_2949376.html.

Greenberg, A. 2016. "Inside Google's Internet Justice League and Its AI-Powered War on Trolls." *Wired*, September 19. https://www.wired.com/2016/09/inside-googles-internet-justice-league-ai-powered-war-trolls/.

Hattenstone, S. 2013. "Caroline Criado-Perez: Twitter Has Enabled People to Behave in a Way They Wouldn't Face to Face." *The Guardian*, August 4. https://www.theguardian.com/lifeandstyle/2013/aug/04/caroline-criado-perez-twitter-rape-threats.

Heer, N. 2016. "Diversity of Tech Companies by the Numbers: 2016 Edition." *Diversity of Tech Companies by the Numbers: 2016 Edition—Pixel Envy*, August 9. https://pxlnv.com/blog/diversity-of-tech-companies-by-the-numbers-2016/.

Higgins, A. 2016. "Effort to Expose Russia's 'Troll-Army' Draws Vicious Retaliation." *New York Times*, May 30. https://www.nytimes.com/2016/05/31/world/europe/russia-finland-nato-trolls.html.

Hooks, bell. n.d. *Understanding Patriarchy*. [AU: As the source has no date, please provide an accessed date for the website].http://imaginenoborders.org/pdf/zines/UnderstandingPatriarchy.pdf

Jaffa, V. 2016. "Twitter's New Verification Process Is a Game Rigged against Its Marginalized Users." *Model View Culture*, August 15. https://modelviewculture.com/pieces/twitters-new-verification-process-is-a-game-rigged-against-its-marginalized-users.

Jane, E. 2017. "What the Random Rape Threat Generator Tells Us about Online Misogyny." *Women's Media Center*, January 18. http://www.womensmediacenter.com/speech-project/what-the-random-rape-threat-generator-tells-us-about-online-misogyny.

Jezebel S. 2014. "We Have a Rape Gif Problem and Gawker Media Won't Do Anything about It." *Jezebel*, August 11. https://jezebel.com/we-have-a-rape-gif-problem-and-gawker-media-wont-do-any-1619384265.

Kahan, D. M., D. Braman, J. Gastil, P. Slovic, and C. K. Mertz. 2007. "Culture and Identity-Protective Cognition: Explaining the White-Male Effect in Risk Perception." *Journal of Empirical Legal Studies* 4 (3): 465–505. doi:10.1111/j.1740-1461.2007.00097.x.

Kasumovic, M. M. and J. H. Kuznekoff. 2015. "Insights into Sexism: Male Status and Performance Moderates Female-Directed Hostile and Amicable Behaviour." *Plos One* 10 (7). doi:10.1371/journal.pone.0131613.

Lee, P and D. Stewart. 2016. "Predictions 2016: Women in IT Jobs: It Is about Education, but also about More than Just Education | Technology, Media, and Telecommunications." *Deloitte*, March 7. https://www2.deloitte.com/global/en/pages/technology-media-and-telecommunications/articles/tmt-pred16-tech-women-in-it-jobs.html.

Lee, P. 2016. "Learning from Tay's introduction." *The Official Microsoft Blog*, March 25. https://blogs.microsoft.com/blog/2016/03/25/learning-tays-introduction/.

Meyer, R. and M. Cukier. 2006. "Assessing the Attack Threat due to IRC Channels." *University of Maryland's A. James Clark School of Engineering*.

Miller, C. C. 2014. "Google Releases Employee Data, Illustrating Tech's Diversity Challenge." *The New York Times*, May 28. https://bits.blogs.nytimes.com/2014/05/28/google-releases-employee-data-illustrating-techs-diversity-challenge/?_r=0.

Mullen, J. 2015. "Google Rushes to Fix Software That Tagged Photo with Racial Slur." *CNN*, July 2. http://www.cnn.com/2015/07/02/tech/google-image-recognition-gorillas-tag/index.html.

Nanos, J. 2017. "TripAdvisor Removed Reports of Rapes at Mexico Resorts, Report Says." *Boston Globe*, November 1. https://www.bostonglobe.com/business/2017/11/01/tripadvisor-removed-reports-rapes-and-assaults-mexico-resorts-report-says/ST6JbI29XR25CeiDXh8K5J/story.html.

Pyper, J. 2011. "Why Conservative White Males Are More Likely to Be Climate Skeptics." *New York Times*, October 5. http://www.nytimes.com/cwire/2011/10/05/05climatewire-why-conservative-white-males-are-more-likely-11613.html?pagewanted=all.

Rodriguez, A. 2016. "Microsoft's AI Millennial Chatbot Became a Racist Jerk after Less than a Day on Twitter." *Quartz*, March 24. https://qz.com/646825/microsofts-ai-millennial-chatbot-became-a-racist-jerk-after-less-than-a-day-on-twitter/.

Ryan, D. 2014. "MIT Computer Scientists Demonstrate the Hard Way That Gender Still Matters." *Wired*, December 19. https://www.wired.com/2014/12/mit-scientists-on-women-in-stem/.

Twohey, M. and M. Barbaro. 2016. "Two Women Say Donald Trump Touched Them Inappropriately." *The New York Times*, October 12. https://www.nytimes.com/2016/10/13/us/politics/donald-trump-women.html.

Wales, J. 2004. "Slashdot." *Wikipedia Founder Jimmy Wales Responds*, July 28. https://slashdot.org/story/04/07/28/1351230/wikipedia-founder-jimmy-wales-responds.

Web Foundation. 2016. "Digging into Data on the Gender Digital Divide." *World Wide Web Foundation*, October 31. https://webfoundation.org/2016/10/digging-into-data-on-the-gender-digital-divide/.

Wikimedia Commons. 2011. "File:Editor Survey Report—April 2011.Pdf." April. https://commons.wikimedia.org/w/index.php?title=File%3AEditor_Survey_Report_-_April_2011.pdf&page=3.

10

Unmasking Hate on Twitter

DISRUPTING ANONYMITY BY TRACKING TROLLS

Diana L. Ascher and Safiya Umoja Noble

1. Introduction

Of primary interest in this chapter is the apparent emboldening of neo-nazi[1] hate speech, the implications of this phenomenon for vulnerable populations, and potential modes of remedy. Our recent experience with neo-nazi hate group members who actively engage in social media trolling led us to think about the implications of protected hate speech, and the ways in which digital media platforms protect the anonymity of speakers, while making it nearly impossible for the targets of hate speech to know its origin. Whereas Ku Klux Klan (KKK) members in the analog era used robes and hoods to assume a state of pseudonymity, certain information practices have created an emboldened sense of righteousness among neo-nazis, a desensitization of the general public to hate speech, and an exacerbation of the precariousness of the most vulnerable members of society.

Many of the protections afforded to speakers of hate on the internet are governed by legal decisions. Courts are increasingly forced to rule on "true threat" cases to determine the degree to which online comments constitute a threat that can lead to violence or other types of harm (Best 2016). Federal legislation limiting speech and information practice on social networking platforms remains unclear, though states are gaining some traction in criminalizing the harms caused by revenge porn and other malicious online communications. Constitutionally protected speech is a major sticking point when attempting to adjudicate the kinds of speech that occur online (Williams 2014), often leaving victims of misogynist, racist, homophobic, and other forms of persecution speech with little legal recourse or protection. The Communications Decency Act (CDA), which grants protections and immunity from prosecution to technology companies for content posted to their online platforms, presents an even greater challenge for victims of anonymous trolls and/or hate speech in social media networks. The Act characterizes technology companies as "vessels" for content, with no accountability for the propagation of messages through their networks. This lack of accountability is counterintuitive to those of us who know that the algorithmic curation and circulation of content through social media are tied directly to algorithmic advertising mechanisms and decision-making by human commercial content moderators (Roberts 2016; Noble 2018).

While platforms—such as Facebook, Twitter, Tumblr, and Instagram—may eschew any responsibility for hate speech content, or grapple to figure out the limits of speech that might invoke harm (Huff 2017), we contend that other avenues of protection from anonymous trolling might empower victims of targeted hate speech in social media networks. We present an account of how we tracked down the true identities of members of a neo-nazi hate group on Twitter to stimulate a conversation about the tension between free speech and criminalizing hate speech, and to determine whether a de-anonymizing toolkit for victims of hate speech on Twitter is a worthy endeavor.

2. Free Speech, Power, and Anonymity Online

Online, anonymity means that an author's identity is unknown. Sometimes, this comes in the form of pseudonymity, in which a message is attributed to an online persona, represented by a name, also called a handle, other than the author's. Pseudonymity can be insulating for authors who are more confident sharing their messages when their identities are unknown, and it is in this context that the internet has offered a unique space for people who share an interest to connect in a semi-protected environment. In other contexts, pseudonymity may represent an author's desire to compartmentalize the types of messages shared. For example, works by Mark Twain are differentiated from those attributed to Samuel Clemens, though both were penned by the same man. Thus, pseudonymity affords an author a measure of identity, but in the form of an alternate persona. This can be beneficial for social media contributors who wish to build a following that is not directly connected with their personal lives. One celebrity who has perfected the art of such compartmentalization is Beyoncé. The performer's Instagram account has 109 million followers, who may perceive an authentic connection to the artist; however, Beyoncé's public identity is the creation of a carefully crafted brand strategy that reveals little of the particulars of daily life. You never see indicators of time or place in the images that populate her social media posts; all images, like her music, are served up with a consistency of message and within the boundaries she has established since wresting control of her publicity from her manager father in 2011. Beyoncé controls what her fans know about her personal life, with very few exceptions. And recently, she has leveraged social media to make explicit her ideological and political stances, despite a conscious decision to decline personal interviews since mid-2013. Her revelations are conveyed through her art. Consider this accomplishment in contrast to internet celebrities, such as the Kardashian family, whose self-promotion of sex tapes and coverage of controversial behavior in increasingly personal contexts have launched a media empire that extends from social media to mass media.

Such personas can be deployed for both good and ill, of course. Certainly, the recent revelations about Macedonian fake news efforts represent the deceptive potential of pseudonymity (Subramanian 2017). Purveyors of hate speech on Twitter exploit a false sense of security that users have in their anonymity while accumulating social power under the guise of pseudonyms. What is it about Twitter that makes its users so vulnerable to hate speech? Part of the appeal of social media platforms for members of marginalized groups is that the networks that form among users have the potential to connect individuals with others who share some interest, despite the constraints of space and time. For example, the internet has enabled online support networks among people interested in rare diseases; such connections had not been possible prior to the ability to search for others worldwide. The cultural phenomenon known as "Black Twitter" is another such case, this time of African Americans using the platform to communicate, signify, and organize responses and resistance to racialized oppression (Brock 2012). Of course, when people are looking for collaborators and/or commiserators online, they also make themselves vulnerable to users of the platform who, for a host of reasons beyond the scope of this chapter, are willing to invest in trolling them.

3. The Internet *Does* Know You're a Dog

It is important to understand how anonymity works in social media networks if we wish to think differently about combatting hate speech on these platforms. Depending on the platform, members of social media networks may engage with one another with varying degrees of anonymity. One of the most demonstrative examples of the misperception of anonymity the general public associates with the internet, a cartoon by Peter Steiner published by *The New Yorker* in 1993, has come to represent the information practices that shape online identity (see Figure 10.1). The cartoon is among the first and most enduring memes to characterize the online world for the general public, when the promise of the internet as a democratizing technology was the prevailing perspective of the time. Sherry Turkle (1995, 184–85), among others (e.g., Rheingold 1993; Negroponte 1995), heralded the internet's inherent anonymity as a democratizing force. Turkle famously offered one gamer's characterization of what it's like to engage online:

> You can be whoever you want to be. You can completely redefine yourself if you want. You don't have to worry about the slots other people put you in as much. They don't look at your body and make assumptions. They don't hear your accent and make assumptions. All they see are your words.

And while privacy concerns were raised with respect to online identity, more attention was directed to problematizing online addiction than to the potential for disproportionate anonymity and protections (e.g., Negroponte 1995). The misperception of online anonymity was firmly entrenched in American media culture, as shown in Figure 10.1.

By the early 2000s, digital media scholars had debunked these ideas that the body could be liberated from the online experience and shown how patterns of online interaction are always racialized and gendered, much in the same ways they are offline (Nakamura 2002). Jessie Daniels (2009) wrote one of the most important monographs describing how white supremacy and racist organizations work online, showing how white supremacist groups use the

"On the Internet, nobody knows you're a dog."

FIGURE 10.1 *New Yorker* cartoon (1993).

web to bolster themselves through both cloaked websites that mask their hate speech in seemingly credible or legitimate mainstream websites and overt racist speech and websites used for that sole purpose. More recently, while some strides have been made in information literacy with respect to fraudulent online identities—perhaps most effectively as a result of the MTV program, *Catfish*—public awareness of the power dynamics inherent in online anonymity remains low.

Lisa Nakamura describes the performative nature of online identities, in which a user plays the role of an individual of a particular gender and race, engaging in what she calls identity tourism. Describing the scene in Figure 10.1, Nakamura explains that the dog avails itself of "the freedom to 'pass' as part of a privileged group, i.e. human computer users with access to the internet. This is possible because of the discursive dynamic of the internet," particularly on platforms that permit creation of a user identity without a verifiable email address (Nakamura 2002, 1). In online gamespaces, users frequently employ identities as characters. However, in the domain of social media platforms, identities are not considered characters or roles in the same manner. Identity on social media platforms is a self-representation, tailored for the specific network audience. Moreover, one's Twitter identity can be seen to take on an ideological dimension, as endorsements and redistribution of preferred content—to the exclusion of less-preferred content—signify facets of the user's belief system (Ascher 2014, 2017; Brock 2012).

Thus, social media platforms create specific expectations of anonymity through their user engagement policies. While network members believe they are somehow protected from persecution by virtue of platform-dependent anonymity, the technological expertise residing in hate groups creates a significant danger for members of vulnerable populations. Trolls understand that no one is anonymous online. And while the tech-savvy white nationalists have the wherewithal to de-anonymize members of vulnerable groups and target them with hate speech, the layperson is ill-equipped to employ technological protections or to use technology to unmask assailants in any useful way. Furthermore, the recent emboldening of white nationalists and other hate speakers online seems to negate the benefits of unmasking, in terms of social proof.

We note that targets in systems of white supremacy and racial categorization are marked, both online and otherwise in real life, because participants in open commercial media platforms are never truly anonymous. The moment a single marker is triggered that indicates a user is not part of the dominant cultural norm in a platform, the differentiating trait becomes a trolling target, and these traits are often expressed as racialized, gendered, and sexual orientation markers. In the analog era, there was no shortage of neo-nazi rhetoric and propaganda. Messages of hate came in a variety of forms, making use of every communication medium available. However, the investment of time and labor to create and disseminate neo-nazi hate speech was considerably greater in the pre-internet era than it is today. Furthermore, the material connection between hate speech and its effects on vulnerable populations was easier to trace.

4. Neo-nazi Hate Speech Online

Our speculation about how social media platforms provide protections to trolls and misconceptions about anonymity to vulnerable communities is grounded in our experience with a white nationalist group based in Southern California, informed by Social Proof Theory, and approached using network visualization and social network analysis.

Social Proof Theory (sometimes called informational social influence) is one of six principles of persuasion advanced by Robert Cialdini (1993), which describes the tendency of people to perform certain actions when they identify with other people who performed those actions previously (Cialdini 1993). In other words, the theory posits that individuals are biased toward following the crowd—people assume that "if many similar others are acting or have been acting in a particular way within a situation, it is likely to represent a good choice" (Cialdini 2009). The underlying logic of the theory rests in the assumption that others have special knowledge about the situation, which the individual decision maker lacks. Thus, individuals fail to question the propriety of the behaviors modeled by others in context. By comparing their behavior with referent others, individuals validate the "correctness" of their opinions and decisions (Festinger 1954). Research has demonstrated the role of social proof in a wide variety of activities, including approaching a frightening dog, deciding whether and how to commit suicide, donating funds to charity, engaging in promiscuous sexual activity in a "safe" versus "unsafe" manner, littering in a public place, and returning a lost wallet (Cialdini et al. 1999).

In sum, we can think of Social Proof Theory as a motivation for the popular adage: *Birds of a feather flock together.* This phenomenon is particularly relevant to information cascades in social media networks, in which individuals undertake specific information practices to signal ideological alignment. Social proof may be observed in hashtag use on Twitter, which communicates the user's perspective on a topic. For example, Twitter users convey solidarity with individuals who have been targets of sexual harassment and abuse by tweeting #MeToo. Social proof also may be observed in social media networks in the language and tone employed by individuals who identify with the white nationalist movement. We assert that specific information practices of President Trump have influenced how those who identify with this movement conceptualize appropriate information practice in the context of social media networks.

President Trump's redistribution of content from the Twitter accounts of neo-nazi leaders serves as a legitimation signal and facilitates an emboldening of white supremacists online. De-anonymizing typically happens at the direction and in the service of those in power, such as the NSA, FBI, law enforcement, or university administrators. It rarely occurs to the benefit of the victims of hate speech online. Often, this disparity stems from corporate platforms that, as a matter of policy, do not de-anonymize white supremacists and trolls who propagate hate under the guise of anonymity.

We can look to similar mechanisms of anonymity offline for insight into the advantages and disadvantages of anonymous or pseudonymous communication of hate online. For more than a century, members of the KKK have hidden their identities under hoods and robes that symbolically convey hatred and threaten harm. However, the individuals donning KKK regalia often are known by their victims and by the community at large. As a teen growing up in the South in the late 1980s, I (Ascher) witnessed the overt intimidation and symbolic communication of threat when the KKK marched through my high school. I recall vividly the story of Louis Kittler, a Jewish cobbler in a small North Carolina town, who could identify Klansmen by their shoes. Even under the ostensible guise of hood and robe, identities were no secret. The KKK garb provided a means for the community to cling to plausible deniability, as members looked the other way, permitting the symbolic intimidation. What, then, was the function of the racist garb?

We can conceive of myriad ways in which the KKK hood protects the wearer and harms the target. The hood is a means for other members of the community to deny complicity, just as online pseudonymity and invoking freedom of speech makes it easy for members of the community to avoid getting involved. The KKK robe and hood are material forms of social proof, used to reify the racist patriarchal social order. Permissive pseudonymity bolsters misperceptions about the security of users' personal information and provides a substitute for social proof, which, otherwise, might hold individuals accountable for their online behavior. This is precisely how technology companies shirk responsibility for enforcing standards of conduct on their social media platforms.

> The online pseudonym was once a guiding light of internet culture, a crucial protection for whistleblowers and communities with a legitimate fear of being exposed. Now, it's increasingly seen as a threat. Worse, it seems more and more likely that platforms will respond to Russia concerns by tightening restrictions on online anonymity, and driving webgoers to live more and more of their online life under legal names (Brandom 2017).

An interesting side effect of the Twitter platform is its contributing to the emboldening of trolls online and in the real world. Thanks to people such as Kim Kardashian and the decline of scripted television, social media has become a means for some to attain celebrity status. Two aspects are notable. First, since inflammatory content draws more attention than uncontroversial topics, the general public has become desensitized to derogatory language. This is not surprising; however, algorithmic sensationalism amplifies derogatory messages in social media networks (Ascher 2017). Second, the line between Hollywood and reality has blurred. In the years since the 2016 U.S. presidential election, we have seen not only the emboldening of trolls on Twitter, but also their rise to social media celebrity status—using their true identities. For example, Milo Yiannopoulos, who earned the distinction of receiving a lifetime ban from Twitter for his role in inciting harassment against *Saturday Night Live* actress Leslie Jones, has inspired violent protests on college campuses where he has been invited to speak (Rakhim 2017). Thus, the lever of social pressure that usually serves to discourage blatant hate crimes offline has transformed into a sort of twisted notoriety—the sort that demands five-figure speaking fees.

5. Exploring De-anonymizing Tools

When a white nationalist group blanketed the UCLA campus with racist and anti-Semitic flyers in the spring of 2017 (see Figure 10.2) and targeted one of our faculty with online hate speech and threats, we conducted a social network analysis to learn about the group and assess the risk of harm its members represented. Our purpose was twofold: assess the immediate risk, and determine whether a toolkit for de-anonymizing purveyors of online hate is a worthy endeavor.

Our investigation was not simple. As information studies researchers, we are experienced with a variety of techniques to uncover the origins of and modifications to electronic documents, including text, photos, and videos. Many of the techniques involve tracing metadata—data that describe the information—and geospatial data to identify the creator(s) and/or individual(s) responsible for modifying digital information. Stripping metadata from electronic documents is not difficult, but it does require conscientious effort on the part of the person who posts the content online. Usually, a skilled researcher can track down the source of, say, a photo of a group of neo-nazis posing together at a graffiti-covered crematorium, with little difficulty (see Figure 10.3). However, we found the level of technical sophistication demonstrated by the group members, who call themselves the Beach Goys, challenging.

Tracing the email address on the flyers and the handles of the trolls who were threatening the faculty member, we found the group's pseudonymous Twitter handle: @BeachGoys. Using the social network visualization application NodeXL Pro, we imported a list of all Twitter users who engaged with @

UCLA WHITE STUDENTS GROUP

≡ HARVARD

Abolish the White Race

IBT

New Orleans Protest Targets White People

BY CRISTINA SILVA ON
11/10/16 AT 3:19 PM

The Washington Post

Police in Dallas: 'He wanted to kill white people, especially white officers'

≡ ALON ✔

TUESDAY, DEC 22, 2015 12:15 AM PST

White men must be stopped: The very future of mankind depends on it

The Washington Post

'To be white is to be racist, period,' a high school teacher told his class

The Washington Times

Boston University professor: White males a 'problem population'

Recent rhetoric and ongoing riots have highlighted a danger to white Americans.

The governmental strategy in recent decades has been an embrace of the replacement of whites, and appeasement of the demands of minority groups. Appeasement is a strategy that history has shown only emboldens the belligerents, ultimately leading to violence as recently seen.

We are a group that is interested in discussing what can be done in the context of upcoming governmental shifts to counteract these hostile elements, encourage the enforcement of our borders, and start pursuing an agenda that is in the best interests of white Americans.

If you are interested in joining or desire further information, please use the links below to contact us. This is a group for white voices to be heard, and we ask that others respect that.

uclawhitestudentsgroup@gmail.com   http://therightstuff.biz/   twitter.com/Night_Of_Fire

FIGURE 10.2 Racist flyer distributed at UCLA.

BeachGoys, and graphed the relationships in the network to learn more about their activities (see Figure 10.4).

Armed with a list of individual Twitter handles and a sense of the connections among the users, we eventually located several members of the Beach Goys based in Long Beach and the greater Los Angeles area. Members of this group periodically get together for hikes to West Coast sites that are said to be the locations selected by Hitler for nazi occupation and continuation of the extermination of the Jewish people. Photos taken on these hikes depict several men in their 20s and 30s, decked out in hiking gear (see Figure 10.5).

FIGURE 10.3 Neo-nazis posing together at a graffiti-covered crematorium.

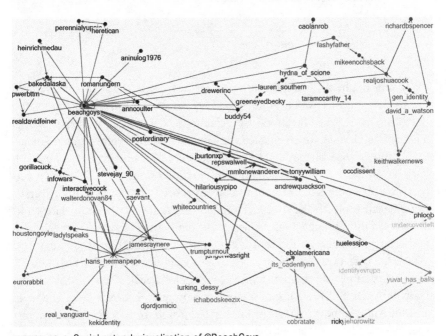

FIGURE 10.4 Social network visualization of @BeachGoys.

Faces in the images posted by the group are masked by the superimposition of several cartoon character heads, including Pepe, a frog appropriated from children's book illustrator Matt Furie, which has become a symbol of racist hate (Hunt 2017). Metadata had been stripped from these images, suggesting the group members are not only aware of the geolocation and reidentifying power of metadata, but also of the methods for removing it.

SoCal Beach Goys @BeachGoys · Mar 13

Had a great hike in Los Angeles! Growing fast!

♡   ⇄ 6   19   ↻   ✉

FIGURE 10.5 Image of Beach Goys on Twitter.

Interestingly, by searching for user names associated with the photos—the pseudonyms by which group members are known on Twitter and other platforms—we learned that the self-proclaimed leader of the group participates in a Frisbee golf league, which enabled the identification of several group members.

Using Google image search, we located several similar photos posted to various online forums, including documentation on the Daily Stormer, a neo-nazi website, of the group attending a talk by retired California State University, Long Beach Professor Kevin MacDonald (see Figure 10.6), who is known for an anti-Semitic trilogy that argues anti-Semitism is a rational reaction to Jews' genetic predisposition for outcompeting the white Christian creators of Western civilization (Southern Poverty Law Center 2018; Taylor 2016).

In the same comment thread (Los Angeles Beach Goys—Book Club—Daily Stormer BBS), we found a conversation among Beach Goys members and individuals inquiring about joining the group. In this conversation, prospective members ask about the vetting protocol, which begins with a Skype verification session. A member using the handle Salad Snake describes the group as being based in Los Angeles, with members living as far away as the San Gabriel Valley and the Inland Empire. He alludes to coordination with other white nationalist groups, mentioning meetups in Irvine that are co-sponsored with a group from San Diego. Salad Snake explains:

> The way we do it is we have you, the other founding members, and I talk on a skype call. This gives us all a chance to see if it's a good fit. We're

FIGURE 10.6 Photo of Beach Goys with CSULB professor.

normal guys. We jave [sic] jobs, bills, girlfriends etc. We'll joke about jews for a bit and talk about the group. The thing that brings us all together is we are Nationalists for people of European heritage. Everything else we believe supports this main premise ie: traditionalism; the institutions that make our civilization strong and healthy etc. We are pro white, Pro West, and having a great time about it. How do you feel about that?

Since Trump's election, a few of these group members have spoken openly with reporters about their vision for "purification" (e.g., Bhattacharya 2016; New Yorker 2016). Thus, these group members who were careful to strip the identifying metadata and conceal their faces with superimposed Pepe the Frog images, suddenly became willing to be named in the popular press. What accounts for this change—effectively, moving from the shadows into the limelight—is a sense that the power dynamic has shifted.

Several overt actions communicated this sea change in what may and may not be voiced openly. First, partisan news media, coupled with the "fake news" revelations of 2017, created filter bubbles (Pariser 2011, 2012) unlike any experienced previously. As a point of reference, the Brookings Institution notes that the "20 largest fake news stories of the 2016 election generated 1.3 million more social media engagements than the top 20 real news stories" and Americans' trust in the mass media "to report the news fully, accurately and fairly" last year dropped to an all-time low of 32% (see Figure 10.7) (Swift 2016; West 2017).

Compounding this phenomenon, President Trump tweeted reactions and affirmations of news stories in lockstep with certain news broadcasts (Kludt and Yellin 2017), and declared other mainstream news media operations to be purveyors of so-called fake news. In addition, Trump blocked access to

American's trust in the mass media, 1997–2016

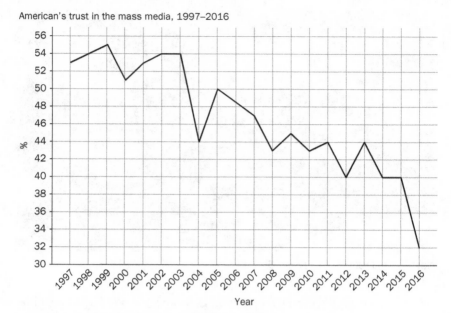

FIGURE 10.7 Declining trust in mass media (Source: Gallop).

his tweets for journalists and other Twitter users who expressed disagreement with his statements. An ongoing federal lawsuit charges that Trump's practice of blocking critics from his personal Twitter account is a violation of the First Amendment (Schonfeld 2017). Simultaneously, a new form of yellow journalism— *algorithmic sensationalism*—has arisen from information practices at news organizations that disproportionately amplify inflammatory content and lack a mechanism for applying timely human judgment (Ascher 2017). All of these actions have undermined public trust in media content authenticity and veracity.

Trump reinforces and publicizes his connections with neo-nazis through copying and pasting the content of tweets originating from Twitter accounts using known neo-nazi pseudonyms. This information practice, coupled with enthusiastic congratulations from infamous former KKK leader David Duke for sharing videos that show what appear to be Muslim men destroying Christian relics and assaulting non-Muslim men (Giaritelli 2017), has emboldened neo-nazi social media users (see Figure 10.8).

Furthermore, Trump includes language in his tweet diatribes and in his formal speeches that echo neo-nazi propaganda. For example, as concerns mounted about the potential for violence at rallies, Trump reinforced the delicate religious reframing that neo-nazis employ to protect their right to assemble and speak. His tweets often are accompanied by memes drawn from World War II-era propaganda imagery, as shown in Figure 10.9. These actions convey an alignment with the chosen reframing, and are symbolic of tacit support for the

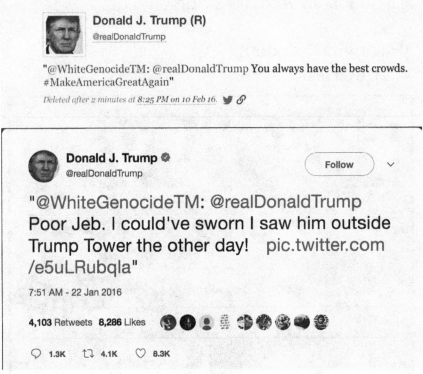

FIGURE 10.8 President Donald J. Trump communicating directly with White nationalists on Twitter.

neo-nazi agenda. Furthermore, Trump's initial refusal to condemn and his subsequent watered-down denunciation of neo-nazi hate crimes in Charlottesville and Boston provide just the right amount of wiggle room necessary to prevaricate actions that would have been condemned a mere 12 months earlier.

6. Conclusion: Unmasking Online Speakers of Hate

That there seemingly is no shame associated with voicing racist, sexist, homophobic, and misogynist opinions in public discourse should be of concern to everyone. While the pseudonymity of Twitter helps users with similar opinions find one another and reinforces their notions of community, inundation of inflammatory opinions on social media platforms contributes to a dangerous social desensitization to harmful rhetoric and blatant fake news. What this means for anonymity in social media networks is that those in power use pseudonymity to their advantage and are unconcerned with being exposed, while vulnerable members of persecuted groups increasingly depend heavily on the assumed protections of anonymity, even as these protections are challenged by the ruling administration. This transposition of the need for anonymity in

Hillary Finally Achieves Something...

#HillaryForPresident
#CorruptHillary

RETWEETS	LIKES
5	7

8:29 PM - 15 Jun 2016

FIGURE 10.9 Trump campaign tweet.

social networks shifts the chilling effect from neo-nazis and other hate groups who previously went to great lengths to protect their identities, to the vulnerable and historically unprotected, marginalized members of society.

We were fortunate to have determined the true identities of several members of the Beach Goys, which provided some potential recourse had the trolls escalated their threats against UCLA faculty. However, we are alarmed by the notoriety and emboldening of these groups, particularly as they have been legitimized and propagated by President Trump's information practice. While we are troubled by the emboldening of hate groups and the subsequent chilling effect experienced by marginalized communities, we note that those in power typically make it easier for citizens in ideological agreement with them to speak openly, support one another, and act in their own interests. Of course, this necessarily makes it harder for those who oppose the ideology of those in power to communicate openly, work together, and effect change.

In August and September of 2017, members of the Beach Goys attended meetings of the Santa Monica Committee for Racial Justice (see Figure 10.10). This development underscores the imperative that opposition groups working on behalf of human and civil rights must retain the right and ability to exchange information anonymously, yet have means to counter the effects of social proof observed in the information practice of purveyors of hate speech online through de-anonymization. We note, in conclusion, that the Federal Bureau of Investigation (FBI) has expressed grave concern over the quiet radicalization of white men, and reported that the single largest terrorist threat is domestic white supremacists infiltrating law enforcement (Speri 2017). Additionally, the Department of Homeland Security (2009) reports concern "that rightwing extremists will attempt to recruit and radicalize returning veterans in order to boost their violent capabilities." Anonymity online, particularly among speakers of hate and trolls, makes it difficult for municipalities

FIGURE 10.10 Beach Goys cover their faces while attending civil rights organizational meetings (Source: YouTube).

and the public to hold such domestic terrorists accountable for their intimidation and threats.

We believe, based on our study of the cloaking protections invoked by the white supremacists we studied, that social media platforms must work with researchers and policymakers to protect free speech online, yet provide recourse for victims and targets of hate speech. Topics for future discussion and research include new forms of social proof in social media networks, social media literacy with respect to anonymity and privacy online, and alternative means of exposing the true identities of network members who threaten and torment others with racist, sexist, homophobic, misogynist hate speech.

Note

1. We have deliberately chosen to write neo-nazi without capitals.

References

Ascher, D. L. 2014. "A Time Analytic Framework for Information Practice." *2014 ASIS&T SIG -USE Symposium Context in Information Behavior Research.*

Ascher, D. 2017. "The New Yellow Journalism: Examining the Algorithmic Turn in News Organizations' Social Media Activity through the Lens of Cultural Time Orientation." University of California, Los Angeles.

Best, A. J. 2016. "*Elonis v. United States*: The Need to Uphold Individual Rights to Free Speech while Protecting Victims of Online True Threats." *Maryland Law Review* 75 (4): 1127–58.

Bhattacharya, S. 2016. "'Call Me a Racist, but Don't Say I'm a Buddhist': America's Alt Right." *The Observer,* October 9. https://www.theguardian.com/world/2016/oct/09/call-me-a-racist-but-dont-say-im-a-buddhist-meet-the-alt-right.

Brandom, R. 2017. "Russia's Interference Could Be the End of Social Media Anonymity." *The Verge,* November 1. https://www.theverge.com/2017/11/1/16592374/russia-facebook-ads-clint-watts-social-media-anonymity-privacy.

Brock, A. 2012. "From the Blackhand Side: Twitter as a Cultural Conversation." *Journal of Broadcasting & Electronic Media* 56 (4): 529–49. doi:10.1080/08838151.2012.732147.

Brown, A. 2017. "Rogue Twitter Accounts Fight to Preserve the Voice of Government Science." *The Intercept,* March 11. https://theintercept.com/2017/03/11/rogue-twitter-accounts-fight-to-preserve-the-voice-of-government-science.

Cialdini, R. B. 1993. *Influence: The Psychology of Persuasion.* New York: HarperCollins.

Cialdini, R. B., W. Wosinska, D. W. Barrett, J. Butner, and M. Gornik-Durose. 1999. "Compliance with a Request in Two Cultures: The Differential Influence of Social Proof and Commitment/Consistency on Collectivists and Individualists." *Personality and Social Psychology Bulletin* 25 (10): 1242–53. doi:10.1177/0146167299258006.

Cialdini, R. B. 2009. *Influence: Science and Practice.* Boston, MA: Pearson Education.

Daniels, J. (2009). Cyber Racism: White Supremacy Online and the New Attack on Civil Rights. Lanham, Maryland: Rowman & Littlefield Publishers.

Domonoske, C. 2017. "Twitter Sues Homeland Security to Protect Anonymity of 'Alt Immigration' Account." *NPR*, April 6. http://www.npr.org/sections/thetwo-way/2017/04/06/522914335/twitter-sues-homeland-security-to-protect-anonymity-of-alt-immigration-account.

Festinger, L. 1954. "A Theory of Social Comparison Processes." *Human Relations*, May.

Fleishman, G. 2000. "Cartoon Captures Spirit of the Internet." *The New York Times*, December 13. http://www.nytimes.com/2000/12/14/technology/cartoon-captures-spirit-of-the-internet.html.

Giaritelli, A. 2017. "David Duke after Trump Tweets Videos of Muslims Attacking People: 'That's Why We Love Him.!'" *Washington Examiner*, November 29. http://www.washingtonexaminer.com/david-duke-after-trump-tweets-videos-of-muslims-attacking-people-thats-why-we-love-him/article/2641982.

Grannan, K. 2017. "The First-Time Voters." *The New Yorker*, September 7. https://www.newyorker.com/magazine/2016/10/31/first-time-voters.

Huff, L. 2017. "Mark Zuckerberg Vows to Remove Hate Speech from Facebook." *The Hollywood Reporter*, August 16. http://www.hollywoodreporter.com/news/mark-zuckerberg-vows-remove-hate-speech-facebook-1030327.

Hunt, E. 2017. "Pepe the Frog Creator Kills Off Internet Meme Co-Opted by White Supremacists." *The Guardian*, May 7. https://www.theguardian.com/world/2017/may/08/pepe-the-frog-creator-kills-off-internet-meme-co-opted-by-white-supremacists.

Kittner, S. 2018. "A Trial Is All We Ask . . . " *Sam Kittner Photographer*, Accessed January 19. http://kittner.com/a_trial_is_all_we_ask.php.

Klundt, T. and T. Yellin. 2017. "Trump Tweets and the TV News Stories behind Them." *CNNMoney*, October 10. http://money.cnn.com/interactive/media/trump-tv-tweets/index.html.

Nakamura, L. 2002. *Cybertypes: Race, Ethnicity, and Identity on the Internet*. New York: Routledge.

Negroponte, N. 1995. *Being Digital*. New York: Alfred A. Knopf.

Negroponte, N. 1996. *Being Digital*. New York: Vintage Books.

Noble, S. U. 2018. *Algorithms of Oppression: How Search Engines Reinforce Racism*. New York: New York University Press.

Pariser, E. 2011. *The Filter Bubble: What the Internet Is Hiding from You*. New York: Penguin Press.

Pariser, E. 2012. *The Filter Bubble: How the New Personalized Web Is Changing What We Read and How We Think*. London: Penguin Books.

Pfiffner, J. P. 2017. "The Unusual Presidency of Donald Trump." *Political Insight* 8 (2): 9–11. doi:10.1177/2041905817726890.

Rahim, Z. 2017. "President Trump Threatens to Yank U.C. Berkeley's Federal Funding over Protests against Milo Yiannopoulos." *Time*, February 2. http://time.com/4657688/trump-milo-yiannopoulos-breitbart/.

Rheingold, H. 1993. *The Virtual Community: Homesteading on the Electronic Frontier*. Cambridge, MA: MIT Press.

Roberts, S. T. 2016. Commercial Content Moderation: Digital Laborers' Dirty Work. In S. U. Noble and B. Tynes (eds.) *The Intersectional Internet: Race, Sex, Class and Culture Online*. New York: Peter Lang: 147–59.

Schonfeld, Z. 2017. "Donald Trump Blocked Me on Twitter. Should I Sue Him?" *Newsweek*, June 22. http://www.newsweek.com/should-i-sue-donald-trump-blocking-me-twitter-knight-foundation-627963.

Southern Poverty Law Center. 2018. "Kevin MacDonald." *Southern Poverty Law Center*. Accessed January 20. https://www.splcenter.org/fighting-hate/extremist-files/individual/kevin-macdonald.

Speri, A. 2017. "The FBI Has Quietly Investigated White Supremacist Infiltration of Law Enforcement." *The Intercept*, January 31. https://theintercept.com/2017/01/31/the-fbi-has-quietly-investigated-white-supremacist-infiltration-of-law-enforcement/.

Subramanian, S. 2017. "The Macedonian Teens Who Mastered Fake News." *Wired*, May 1. https://www.wired.com/2017/02/veles-macedonia-fake-news/.

Swift, A. 2016. "Americans' Trust in Mass Media Sinks to New Low." *Gallup*, September 14. http://news.gallup.com/poll/195542/americans-trust-mass-media-sinks-new-low.aspx.

Taddeo, M. and L. Floridi. 2015. "The Moral Responsibilities of Online Service Providers." *Law, Governance and Technology Series The Responsibilities of Online Service Providers* 22 (6): 13–42. doi:10.1007/978-3-319-47852-4_2.

Taylor, J. 2016. "Energized by Trump's Win, White Nationalists Gather to 'Change the World.'" *NPR*, November 20. https://www.npr.org/2016/11/20/502719871/energized-by-trumps-win-white-nationalists-gather-to-change-the-world.

Turkle, S. 1995. *Life on the Screen: Identity in the Age of the Internet*. New York: Simon & Schuster Paperbacks.

U.S. Department of Homeland Security. 2009. "Rightwing Extremism: Current Economic and Political Climate Fueling Resurgence in Radicalization and Recruitment. Prepared by the Extremism and Radicalization Branch, Homeland Environment Threat Analysis Division." *Extremism and Radicalization Branch, Homeland Environment Threat Analysis Division; Declassified*, April. https://fas.org/irp/eprint/rightwing.pdf.

West, D. M. 2017. "How to Combat Fake News and Disinformation." *Brookings*, December 18. https://www.brookings.edu/research/how-to-combat-fake-news-and-disinformation/?utm_medium=social&utm_source=twitter&utm_campaign=gs.

Williams, L. 2014. "California's Anti-revenge Porn Legislation: Good Intentions, Unconstitutional Result." *California Legal History* 9: 297–338.

11

Online Dating Sites as Public Accommodations

FACILITATING RACIAL DISCRIMINATION

Sonu Bedi

1. Introduction

The Supreme Court has recently made clear that the "most important" place "for the exchange of views" is "cyberspace—the 'vast democratic forums of the Internet.'"[1] According the Court, the internet is a "quintessential forum for the exercise of First Amendment rights."[2] This characterization seems all the more apt for commercial online dating websites where individuals express and act upon their preferences for romantic partners. This essay qualifies this view, arguing that parts of the internet are also social institutions that are within the scope of justice. In particular, I argue that online commercial dating websites are public accommodations, providing their customers an important and widely needed service: the ability to find romantic partners. And whom we find attractive is perhaps one of the most idiosyncratic choices an individual makes. The freedom to select the intimate partner of one's choice is an integral part of a right to association. Drawing on the work of John Rawls, I show that this means that such sites are subject to considerations of justice including a commitment to racial equality. It is clear that as public accommodations, these sites should not unjustly discriminate in providing their services. Analyzing recent case law, this essay goes further, arguing that these sites should also not facilitate racial discrimination. Even though racial preferences for romantic partners implicate rights to speech and association, it is unjust for commercial online dating websites to enable and explicitly endorse these preferences.

My essay proceeds in three parts. First, I explain why online commercial dating sites are "public accommodations" similar to restaurants or movie theaters and hence within the scope of justice. They are "major social institutions," as articulated by Rawls, and thereby subject to a principle of non-discrimination on the basis of race. Second, I draw from recent federal appellate cases that concern the interaction of federal non-discrimination law and the way Roommates.com, a website that matches individuals with potential roommates, permits users to filter and screen on the basis of sex, sexual orientation, and family status. Third, and most significantly, I apply this analysis to commercial online dating sites, concluding that the law ought to prohibit such sites from allowing users to identify and filter on the basis of race. I argue that whereas users of public accommodation websites may express racial preferences (triggering a right to free speech) and act upon them (triggering a right to association), these websites should not facilitate and thereby explicitly endorse racial discrimination by permitting users to search and screen on the basis of race. Doing so, as I argue, is not about speech but about unjust conduct.

2. Online Commercial Dating Sites as Public Accommodations: John Rawls and the Scope of Justice

The internet is composed of all kinds of websites, commercial and noncommercial. Individuals use the internet to, among other things, chat with friends, opine on blogs, buy goods and services, gather information, or search for real estate. Some of these websites including Facebook, LinkedIn, and Twitter function as important and essential public fora where individuals may freely engage in First Amendment activity. Other parts of cyberspace including a closed group or a church website are private spaces where individuals may exclude others. Such websites may genuinely encompass those private groups or interactions that are beyond the scope of justice. The focus of this essay is on commercial dating sites, those websites that seek to help users find romantic partners by charging some kind of fee. These sites are businesses whose purpose is to help users find a romantic match. I argue that these internet sites are public accommodations like movie theaters, restaurants, and other businesses within the scope of justice and thereby subject to principles of non-discrimination.

John Rawls famously suggests that his principles of justice apply to what he calls the "basic structure" or the "major social institutions" that "distribute fundamental rights and duties and determine the division of advantages from social cooperation" (Rawls 1999 rev. [1971]), Sec. 2: 6). In specifying the original position Rawls says delegates do not know "their own social position, their place in the distribution of natural attributes, or their conception of the good" (Rawls 1999 rev. [1971]), 172). Along with ignorance of these characteristics comes ignorance of factors that are "arbitrary from a moral perspective" (Rawls 1999 rev. [1971]), 64) including "race" and "ethnic group" status and gender (Rawls 2001, 15). The idea that race is, as Rawls famously puts it, "arbitrary from a moral perspective" is an assumption of his theory of justice. According to Rawls, it is not only that individuals should have an equal claim to basic liberties but that offices and jobs should, at a minimum, be "open to all" (Rawls 1999 rev. [1971]: 47, 64). This means that a principle of non-discrimination on the basis of race applies to those terms of social cooperation that belong to the basic structure. And I assume as much in this essay.

Obviously, a *Theory of Justice* was published in 1973, many years before the internet was created. Although Rawls would have had no occasion to consider it as part of the basic structure, I argue that certain parts of the internet do belong within the scope of his theory of justice. Although his concern is with issues of global justice, Arash Abizadeh provides a useful typology for considering the meaning of the "basic structure" (Abizadeh 2007). He says that this structure may comprise:

> (1) the institutions that determine and regulate the fundamental terms of social cooperation; (2) the institutions that have profound and pervasive impact upon persons' life chances; or (3) the institutions that subject persons to coercion (Abizadeh 2007, 319).

(3) is by far the most restrictive view of the scope of justice. This view effectively contemplates that only actions by the state trigger considerations of justice. But Rawls specifically rejects this view. He defines "major institutions" to include not only "the political constitution" but also "the principal economic and social arrangements" (Rawls 1999 rev. [1971], 6). He explicitly includes "competitive markets" as an example of a "major social institution" (Rawls 1999 rev. [1971], 6). His subsequent analysis, I argue elsewhere, makes clear that private employers, for instance, are within the basic structure (Bedi 2014).

This leaves (1) and (2) as possible accounts of the basic structure. Both would hold that not only private employers but also other businesses such as inns, restaurants, and movie theaters (the conventional account of public accommodations) are part of this structure. After all, their designation as public point to their importance as major social institutions.[3] Staying in lodges or hotels, eating at restaurants, or interacting with businesses define the terms of "social cooperation" and have a profound and pervasive impact upon a person's life. That means it is unjust for these businesses, including employers, to discriminate on the basis of race or other characteristics. In discussing Rawls's commitment to democratic equality, Elizabeth Anderson also understands this commitment as including not just state actors but civil society more broadly:

> Civil society is the sphere of social life that is open to the general public and is not part of the state bureaucracy, in charge of the administration of laws. Its institutions include public streets and parks, public accommodations such as restaurants, shops, theaters, buses and airlines, communications

systems such as broadcasting, telephones, and the Internet, public libraries, hospitals, schools, and so forth (Anderson 1999, 317).

Taking this seriously means that webpages that serve the public as a business are part of the basic structure. These online businesses are like any other kind of public accommodation. In particular, insofar as these businesses regulate our terms of social cooperation, outlining how we interact and cooperate with others, they have a pervasive impact on our lives.

Federal civil rights law such as Title II of the Civil Rights Act of 1964 defines "public accommodations" in a way that could be interpreted to exclude cyberspace. The law covers "inns, hotels, restaurants, cafeterias, any motion picture house, theater, concert hall, sports arena," along with any premises which are "physically located" within a covered establishment.[4] This may suggest that cyberspace businesses are outside the scope of federal law.

However, state public accommodation laws are sometimes written and interpreted more broadly to cover commercial websites that do not have a physical location. Consider in this respect California and New Jersey's public accommodation laws. California's Unruh Civil Rights Act, for instance, says that:

> All persons within the jurisdiction of this state are free and equal, and no matter what their sex, race, color, religion, ancestry, national origin, disability, medical condition, genetic information, marital status, sexual orientation, citizenship, primary language, or immigration status are entitled to the full and equal accommodations, advantages, facilities, privileges, or services in all business establishments of every kind whatsoever.[5]

And the California Supreme Court has made clear that the term "business establishments" must be interpreted "in the broadest sense reasonably possible."[6] And subsequent cases have applied the Unruh Act to for-profit commercial business and nonprofit organizations with an underlying business or economic purpose.[7] New Jersey's public accommodation law is similarly broad. In *Clover Hill Swimming Club v. Goldsboro* (N.J. 1966),[8] the New Jersey Supreme Court held that a swimming club could not discriminate on the basis of race in excluding a black applicant who sought to be a member. The Clover Hill Swimming Club argued that they were not a public accommodation under New Jersey's Law Against Discrimination. In defining a public accommodation, the court disagreed, reasoning that Clover Hill is not only "a commercial venture operated to return a profit to its owner"[9] but also an "establishment [that] extends an invitation to the public" to join.[10]

Given these broad definitions of public accommodations, Eric McKinley, a gay man, and Linda Carlson, a lesbian woman, filed suit under the New Jersey and California laws, respectively, against eHarmony.com. eHarmony.com, one of the most popular commercial online dating websites, distinguishes itself from other sites by providing an algorithm that proclaims to match individuals on 29 dimensions.[11] The website boasts that it is responsible for nearly 4% of U.S. marriages.[12] eHarmony only provided its matching services for opposite sex couples. Drawing on the relevant public accommodation laws, McKinley and Carlson sued the website for discriminating against gays and lesbians. Both the New Jersey and California cases were ultimately settled without eHarmony.com admitting fault or liability. As part of the settlement, eHarmony.com agreed to operate a companion website, called Compatible Partners.com, that would be available to gay and lesbians seeking to find a match with someone of the same sex.

Although the courts did not reach a decision on the merits, these complaints make out a claim that eHarmony.com and by implication other commercial online dating sites are, at the very least, public accommodations under state civil rights law. eHarmony, like Match.com or OkCupid.com, is a business. Even though these businesses do not have physical, brick and mortar locations, they are commercial enterprises that provide a matchmaking service to their respective paying customers. Moreover, these sites extend an invitation to all to join. By their very nature, these websites, like much of the internet, are open to all. Anyone may access them and pay for their services.

3. The Case of *Roommates.com*

If online commercial dating sites such as eHarmony, Match.com, and OkCupid.com are public accommodations, they are subject to considerations of justice, and in particular, a commitment to non-discrimination on the basis of race. It is clear that these sites could not decline their services to those of a particular race. After all, eHarmony was sued for failing to providing matchmaking services to gay and lesbian users. Here I draw on two companion cases to set the stage for my conclusion that, as public accommodations, these websites and ones like them should also not facilitate and thereby endorse unjust discrimination.

Roommates.com is a website that matches individuals with potential roommates. It permits users to filter and screen on the basis of sex, sexual orientation, and family status. It matches users searching for a roommate with potential applicants based on these very characteristics. That means that a user who has expressed a particular preference regarding sex or sexual orientation will only be matched with other prospective roommates who share those characteristics. The San Francisco Fair Housing Council brought a lawsuit against Roommates.com, treating the website as a real estate broker. The council argued that the website violates the Fair Housing Act and California housing law by permitting users to search and filter on sex, sexual orientation and family status.[13] In two cases: *Fair Housing Council v. Roommates.com* (9th

Cir. 2008) ("Fair Housing I")[14] and *Fair Housing Council v. Roommates.com* (9th Cir. 2012) ("Fair Housing II")[15] the Ninth Circuit Court of Appeals ultimately held that the law could not prohibit the way the website matches users to prospective roommates. I draw from these cases to criticize the court's ultimate conclusion.

In *Fair Housing I*, the court asked whether section 230 of the Communications Decency Act (CDA) immunizes websites from lawsuits when a website's users engage in illegal or actionable speech, in this case possible housing discrimination. This part of the CDA, passed in 1996, sought to ensure that the internet would grow and remain a forum for robust and unrestricted freedom of speech. In an earlier case, the Ninth Court of Appeals made clear that:

> Consistent with these provisions, courts construing § 230 have recognized as critical in applying the statute the concern that lawsuits could threaten the "freedom of speech in the new and burgeoning Internet medium." (citations omitted) "Section 230 was enacted, in part, to maintain the robust nature of Internet communication, and accordingly, to keep government interference in the medium to a minimum." (citations omitted) Making interactive computer services and their users liable for the speech of third parties would severely restrict the information available on the Internet. Section 230 therefore sought to prevent lawsuits from shutting down websites and other services on the Internet.[16]

The court justifies Section 230 as a way to further freedom of speech on the internet. If an individual could sue a service provider for content posted on its website, this could very easily put the provider out of business. For instance, if Craigslist.com is responsible for the content posted on its website, which may include information that is false or misleading, someone harmed by that information could sue Craigslist. And if there are many such lawsuits, service providers such as Craigslist may simply decide to shut down their business rather than risk being sued. And if there are fewer service providers, there are fewer spaces for individuals to exercise their freedom of speech, to disseminate information to others freely. According to the court, Congress enacted Section 230 to avoid this problem by immunizing service providers from lawsuits.

However, in *Fair Housing I*, the court held that Roommates.com could not avail itself of this immunity. Now Roommates.com did have a section on a user's profile where he or she could add additional comments.[17] One could specify here, for instance, that one was looking only for a straight roommate with no children. If that was the only way to express and act upon one's preferences for a particular kind of roommate, Section 230 would have applied. Relevant to the court's analysis is that Roomates.com *also* allowed users to screen and filter possible roommate choices on those very characteristics that the law prohibits discrimination on. In fact, Roommates.com had a system that matched individuals based on their preferences. As the court reasons

> [in] addition to requesting basic information—such as name, location and email address—Roommate requires each subscriber to disclose his sex, sexual orientation and whether he would bring children to a household. Each subscriber must also describe his preferences in roommates with respect to the same three criteria: sex, sexual orientation and whether they will bring children to the household.[18]

Consequently, *Fair Housing I* held that the website is "not entitled to CDA immunity for the operation of its search system, which filters listings, or of its email notification system, which directs emails to subscribers according to discriminatory criteria."[19] By specifically operating this kind of filtering system, Roomates.com is " 'responsible' at least 'in part' for each subscriber's profile page, because every such page is a collaborative effort between Roommate and the subscriber."[20] Because this system "steer[s] users based on preferences and personal characteristics that Roommate itself forces subscribers to disclose,"[21] Roommates.com is not entitled to immunity under the CDA. Roommates.com was not just an Internet Service Provider, passively displaying information that others (e.g., those seeking a roommate) had posted or created. In designing the very discriminatory categories at issue here, Roommates.com was providing its own content on the webpage, acting as "both a service provider and a content provider."[22] And in doing so, Roomates.com was explicitly endorsing this type of discrimination. Hence, it could not claim immunity under Section 230, which only applies to websites that do not "create" any content themselves.

According to the court, Roommates.com's search system:

> differs materially from generic search engines such as Google, Yahoo! and MSN Live Search, in that Roommate designed its system to use allegedly unlawful criteria so as to limit the results of each search, and to force users to participate in its discriminatory process. In other words, Councils allege that Roommate's search is designed to make it more difficult or impossible for individuals with certain protected characteristics to find housing—something the law prohibits. By contrast, ordinary search engines do not use unlawful criteria to limit the scope of searches conducted on them, nor are they designed to achieve illegal ends—as Roommate's search function is alleged to do here. Therefore, such search engines play no part in the "development" of any unlawful searches.[23]

Put differently, this kind of steering or facilitating is, in effect, a kind of conduct that is not simply or only about a user's speech. The very creation of the categories and their subsequent use by Roommates.com users constitute the charge of illegal housing discrimination. The website validates the very discrimination that the law deems illegal. Without such categories, any discrimination would be undertaken by the users themselves. Roommates. com's filtering and screening system is not just about content posted by a third party on its website. Roommates.com actively creates the very discriminatory categories on its website that facilitate the illegal conduct, thereby also explicitly endorsing this conduct.[24] *Fair Housing I* held that Roommates.com could not claim immunity for this kind of website filtering mechanism.

Without CDA's protection of immunity, *Fair Housing II*, the subsequent companion case, considered whether Roommates.com violated federal and state housing law by facilitating and thereby endorsing this kind of discrimination. Here the court reasoned that it would be constitutionally suspect to apply fair housing law to selection of a roommate. Noting that the "Supreme court has recognized that 'the freedom to enter into and carry on certain intimate and private relationships is a fundamental element of liberty protected by the Bill of Rights,"[25] *Fair Housing II* reasoned that the "roommate relationship easily qualifies" as an "intimate association."[26] After all, as the court goes on to say, "it's hard to imagine a relationship more intimate than that between roommates, who share living rooms, dining rooms, kitchens, bathrooms, even bedrooms."[27] In elaborating upon this conclusion, the case cites possible instances where a woman "will often look for female roommates because of modesty or security concerns."[28] Or "an orthodox Jew may want a roommate with similar beliefs and dietary restrictions."[29] Ultimately, selection of a roommate triggers a right to associate that allows individuals to discriminate. *Fair Housing II* makes clear that users have a right to discriminate (cf. Waldron 1981). Thus, the court held that "Roommate's prompting, sorting and publishing of information to facilitate roommate selection is not forbidden by" the law.[30] To prohibit this kind of filtering violates a user's right to select the roommate of his or her choice, or so *Fair Housing II* contends.

On the one hand, *Fair Housing I* reasons that a right to free speech on the internet does not justify granting Roommates.com immunity for their filtering mechanism. On the other hand, *Fair Housing II* proclaims that a right to association prohibits application of fair housing law to a commercial website's searching and filtering content. *Fair Housing II* cites cases concerning discrimination on grounds other than race, such as sex. That is, the court did not discuss an instance where the website facilitates and thereby endorses discrimination on the basis of race in selecting a roommate. Nevertheless, the court concludes that it is problematic to apply fair housing law to the way a commercial website facilitates discrimination, which presumably would also include race. Although Roommates.com does not allow users to screen on the basis of race, it allows them to do so on other characteristics that the law deems illegal. *Fair Housing II* stands for the proposition that there is a constitutional right to association that permits users to engage in such discrimination via the website's filtering mechanism. The analysis below challenges this proposition in certain respects.

4. When Online Dating Websites Facilitate Racial Discrimination

Like Roomates.com, online dating websites also have filtering and searching mechanisms. But unlike Roommates.com, most major dating websites also permit users both to identify their race and screen potential dates on the basis of race. Consider in this regard Okcupid.com and Match.com, two of the most popular online sites.[31] These sites permit a user to search for individuals of a particular race. The ease with which users can racially discriminate is noteworthy on these sites. Even though eHarmony does not permit searches (the website is responsible for matching you), it asks for your race and presumably matches individuals, in part, on the basis of it.

Admittedly, one's choice of a romantic, sexually intimate partner is one of the most personal of decisions; even more personal than selection of a roommate. After all, in order to create a family or relationship, individuals must first select whom they'd like to be with. If there is anything that seems outside the purview of justice, it must be these decisions. Moreover, whom we find attractive is perhaps one of the most idiosyncratic choices an individual makes. This entails that the freedom to select the intimate partner of one's choice is an integral part of a right to association, a basic liberty that is central to Rawls's first principle of justice, not to mention the U.S. Constitution.

I argue that whereas these decisions and decisions regarding a roommate may be outside of the reach of the law, websites that facilitate these decisions are not. I argue that it is unjust when online dating websites facilitate and explicitly endorse this kind of racial discrimination, precisely because such websites are public accommodations. Individuals may have a constitutional right to discriminate on the basis of race in selecting their intimate partner or roommate, but they do not have a right to have public accommodations or commercial websites enable and endorse that discrimination. Put simply, public accommodations should neither discriminate on the basis of race in providing their services nor facilitate and thereby validate such discrimination.

Consider as an analog *Anderson v. Martin* (1964)[32] where the United States Supreme Court invalidated a Louisiana law that required election ballots to disclose the race of the candidate. The Court invalidated this law even though it conceded that the law did not interfere with anyone running from office or from voting. The law also did not discriminate against anyone on the basis of race. It simply required all candidates to identify their race on the ballot. In striking this law down, the Court noted that in a voting district where blacks predominate, "that race is likely to be favored by a racial designation on the ballot, while in those communities where other races are in the majority, they may be preferred."[33] Put differently, it did not matter how a voter would react or interpret the racial designation. According to the Court, the very existence of such racial designations was problematic. The Court reasoned that "by directing the citizen's attention to the single consideration of race or color, the State indicates that a candidate's race or color is an important—perhaps paramount—consideration in the citizen's choice, which may decisively influence the citizen to cast his ballot along racial lines."[34] In effect, the state facilitates and validates racial discrimination by allowing those who vote to act on their racial preferences. The state makes clear that race is indeed a legitimate marker on which to discriminate among potential candidates.

Whereas election ballots are clearly state instrumentalities, public accommodations, which stand somewhere between the state and purely private associations, are also importantly designated as "public." These are business that serve the public. They are not simply private associations. Again, Rawls includes within the "basic structure" not just the "political constitution" (state actors) but also other "social institutions." If online dating sites are public accommodations, they ought also to be subject to a similar ban on facilitating racial discrimination. By asking users to identify their race and allowing them to filter and screen on the basis of it, online dating websites go beyond concerns of speech. Like their ballot analog in *Anderson*, these websites facilitate racially discriminatory conduct not speech and, in so doing, endorse such discrimination.

In fact, in so far as online dating websites are about social pairings, this kind of facilitation undermines rather than furthers racial integration. Elizabeth Anderson argues that racial integration is a requirement of justice. There is a moral imperative for us to ensure that "members of different races form friendships, date, marry, bear children or adopt different race children" (Anderson 2013 [2010], 116). Anderson argues that an "ideal of integration" challenges segregation. She defines "segregation" as embodying the "structures and norms of spatial and social separation" and dictating the terms of racial interaction based on "domination and subordination" (Anderson 2013 [2010], 112). Permitting users to search on the basis of race in online dating websites reinforces these two pillars. Such searches make it easy to ensure a norm of "separation" and permit interaction in ways that may affirm racial stereotypes. This undermines integration and its emphasis on equality and not stereotype. Although she does not focus on intimacy or the dating market, Anderson's argument underscores the importance of regulating sites to at least encourage an "ideal of integration."

Of course, this does not mean the state should prohibit racial discrimination in the intimacy context. Doing so would violate a right to intimate association. Similarly, if the state prohibited roommate discrimination based on characteristics such as sex, sexual orientation, or even race, this would also violate such a right. In so far as *Fair Housing II* affirms this right, it would be problematic for the state to prohibit or restrict individuals from selecting their intimate partners or roommates. And I do not seek to argue otherwise here.

The important point is that banning online dating sites from facilitating and thereby validating such discrimination does not prevent users from expressing and, of course, acting on their racial preferences. They can still make clear on their online profiles that they are not interested in individuals of a particular race. They could refuse to respond to messages from those potential partners from a perceived disfavored race. That would inform rather than undermine a commitment to free speech and association. Similarly, in *Fair Housing I*, the court says that users on Roommates.com could use the "Additional Comments" section to express their preferences. These preferences could also include ones based on race. Users could be responsible for posting their own content in seeking to discriminate among potential roommates or romantic partners.

In the same way, prohibiting the state from identifying the race of political candidates on the ballot does not violate anyone's right to vote or to express themselves. If candidates want to make their race or ethnic origin—or that of their opponent—salient, they are free to do so. Voters are also free to express why such racial identifications are important or relevant. They ought to be able to choose (or not to choose) a candidate for whatever reason they want, including a candidate's race. Just as there is a right to date the individual of your choice, there is a right to vote for the candidate of your choice. However, the Court struck down Louisiana's attempt to place an individual's race on the ballot, making clear that it is problematic when the state facilitates and thereby endorses such racial preferences or discrimination.

Thus, and this is the motivating sting of the essay, online dating websites (and Rooomates.com) should also not facilitate racial discrimination. Of course, as public accommodations, they may not discriminate on the basis of race (or other characteristics) in providing their services. This is why gays and lesbians brought suit against eHarmony.com. With regards to race, it is unjust if restaurants, business, and movie theaters, to name a few, refuse services on the basis of race. That much is clear.

Yet, the internet generates a kind of business where it is also possible to facilitate racial discrimination just as the racial disclosure on the ballot facilitates racial discrimination in an individual's decision about whom to vote for. This is a distinctive feature of the internet. Restaurants and movie theaters, for instance, would have no reason to categorize individuals on the basis of race. You cannot filter whom you can see or sit with in a movie theater or a business establishment. You can walk away from someone but there is no way to simply screen out individuals on the basis of race. Conventional public accommodations are physical locations. Spaces reserved for those of a particular race would be automatically problematic in these places. But online dating sites allow users to search and screen to do just that. In so doing, they validate these very discriminatory categories. Being able to identity your race and then search/filter on the basis of it facilitates the very kind of racial discrimination that public accommodations ought not to countenance and endorse. This line of reasoning suggests that we ought to be attuned to the way in which social spaces can reinforce racial norms (See generally Hayward 2013). Here the injustice occurs in those "spaces" in cyberspace where intimate partners are often selected.

In this way, *Fair Housing II* mistakenly concluded that application of the relevant housing law interferes with a right to select the roommate of one's choice. If Roommates.com could not include its filtering and searching mechanism on its website, this would still leave individuals to choose the roommate they want. They could simply not respond to profiles of women or those who are gay. They could also include information in their own profiles making clear that they only want a female roommate or a gay one. The right to discriminate in the selection of a roommate still exists. Removing the noxious filtering and searching mechanism may make it harder for individuals to discriminate on various characteristics but the ability to do so still exists. The focus should be on the website's complicity in the discrimination not the underlying user's discriminatory act. Even if the law may not prohibit the discriminatory choices or preferences themselves (they are genuinely beyond the scope of justice), the law may regulate how commercial websites facilitate and validate such choices. *Fair Housing II* fails to make that important distinction. Individuals have a constitutional right to choose the intimate partner or roommate they prefer. The state may have no business prohibiting or interfering with that choice. However, the state does have an interest in ensuring that commercial websites, including public accommodations and online brokerage sites such as Roommates. com, do not facilitate and thereby endorse discrimination on certain illegal characteristics.

Although he does not make the public accommodations argument I outline here, Russell Robinson instructively suggests "[l]awmakers might consider regulating web site design decisions that produce, exacerbate, or facilitate racial preferences" (Robinson 2007, 2794). Such regulations could include prohibiting users from searching on the basis of race (Robinson 2007, 2794). In contrast, Dov Fox, one of the few scholars who also recognizes this kind of facilitation, is skeptical about regulating websites in the way proposed here, proclaiming that:

> Dating websites are designed to forge affective connections between adults. Online compatibility searches, while reducing the spontaneity that typifies casual introductions, preserve the intimacy that is the mark of partner relationships. . . . The legitimacy of race-based dating websites also derives from the idiosyncratic and discriminating nature of preferences that properly characterize intimate voluntary relationships. Romantic norms of particularity prompt us to choose among potential partners on the basis of whatever characteristics—a quick wit, straight teeth, or shared racial background—we happen to find desirable (Fox 2009, 1883).

But Fox's concern with regulating websites in this way misses two important points. First, I'm not suggesting that the state should prohibit individuals from choosing the romantic partner of their choice. A policy that regulates websites does not infringe a right to choose the partner you want. The freedom to do so still exists. Someone can still decide to be intimate with only those of a particular race. In fact, dating websites almost always have photographs of their users. Someone who only desires to date those of a particular race can use these photographs as a way to act upon his or her racial preferences. He or she could refuse to contact or refuse to respond to a message from members of a perceived disfavored racial group. At the same time, someone could only message those users whose photographs fit his or her racial preferences. Individuals could even make clear on their own profile that they prefer individuals of a particular race. All these options still exist to exercise a right to select a romantic partner. Racial discrimination would still exist. This essay merely suggests that as public accommodations online dating websites should not facilitate and thereby endorse this kind of discrimination by making it all-to-easy for users to discriminate and filter on the basis of race. This both preserves rights to expressive speech and association while ensuring that public accommodations not countenance discrimination.

Second, Fox misses the way in which race is different from other characteristics such as height or weight that individuals on these online dating sites may screen or filter on. Although those who are taller and slimmer have social advantage, (Kirkland 2008; Rhode 2010) these markers simply do not have the political salience of race. After all, laws and social institutions have explicitly discriminated on the basis of race not on the basis of height or weight. Slavery, Jim Crow, and segregation in schools, restaurants, and other public places reveal this obvious fact. Height and weight or "straight teeth" for that matter do not structure or mark out extant deep social inequalities in the same way as race. For instance, Iris Marion Young's arguments about the five faces of oppression: exploitation, marginalization, powerlessness, cultural imperialism, and violence demonstrate the salience of race (Young 1990). These websites problematically treat racial groups just as they do other searchable characteristics including height, weight, income, or educational level. In doing so, these websites both ignore the political and normative salience of racial categories and legitimate these categories as important attributes of an intimate partner. These websites provide a user with the filtering and search-based tools to act on his or her ideas of racial hierarchy or stereotype by avoiding profiles from the racial groups they disfavor.

Moreover, race is not a mere physical attribute like height or weight. One can objectively measure one's height or weight. These are genuinely aesthetic characteristics. They completely mark out actual physical traits. Now certainly racial categories often correlate with certain physical features (e.g., lighter skin, different facial features). I'm not suggesting that race is entirely unconnected to such features. The important point from a perspective of justice is that racial categories mean much more. Scholarly work routinely argues that race is a legal, social, and political construct (see, e.g., Braman 1999; Haney-Lopez 2006; Hochschild, Weaver, and Burch 2012; Jacobson 1999). Scholars have discredited the view that there is something biological or objectively fixed about racial categories (Livingstone 1962; Lewontin 1997; Smedley and Smedley 2005), concluding in fact that there is more biological diversity within the alleged categories of race than among them (Lewontin, Rose, and Kamin 1984). To equate race with mere physical attributes such as height or weight is to affirm implicitly this discredited view, one that essentializes racial categories. This objection, one that aligns or treats race as just another physical attribute, misses the normative and political force that comes with racial categories.

And once we focus on the important difference between physical characteristics and racial categories, this reveals why it may be permissible for these websites to permit users to search on the basis of sex. Generally, sex refers to the biological category: male or female. Gender, on the other hand, refers to the attributes that are often associated with the biological category, attributes that include femininity, masculinity, and aggressiveness. These attributes fall under the description of "man" or "woman." This distinction between gender and sex is a familiar one in feminist theory. Simone de Beauvoir's classic statement that "One is not born, but rather becomes, woman" speaks to it. (Beauvoir 2009 [1949], 283; see also Butler 1990). Individuals who prioritize those of the same or opposite sex as intimate partners are usually prioritizing certain physical or biological attributes—including breasts, penises, or vaginas—over others. This may be unproblematic, precisely for the same reason that prioritization on the basis of height or weight on these websites is permissible. Certainly, if individuals prioritize gendered attributes of masculinity or femininity, this may pose a similar problem to the one of racial discrimination. In that case discrimination is not just on physical attributes but distinct notions of the appropriate relationship between gender and sex (see Hartley and Watson 2010; see also Bedi 2013, 177–207). But to my knowledge websites do not allow users to search and filter on the basis of gendered attributes (e.g., being masculine or feminine) but simply on the basis of one's physical features, features that include an individual's sex.

Whereas these online dating sites may permit users to identify and filter on the basis of characteristics such as height, weight, sex, or educational status, they should not permit users to do so on the basis of race. As public accommodations, they structure the terms of social cooperation. This is what makes them part of the "basic structure." Consider that a recent Pew research survey finds that 38% of all American singles use either the internet or cell phone apps to meet others.[35] And 5% of those who are currently married or in long-term relationships met their partners online.[36] Of those who have been together for ten years or less, the percentage that met online is even higher at 11%.[37] As the internet becomes even more ubiquitous as a platform for social cooperation, romantic pairing is more likely to occur via it. And this, in turn, reinforces these commercial sites as public accommodations. In structuring the way in which we interact and meet our romantic partners, these sites should not make it easy to discriminate on the basis of race. This does not mean that racial discrimination in the intimacy market will not occur or that users may not express their racial preferences. It just means that insofar as these public accommodations regulate the terms of social cooperation, profoundly impacting our social lives, we ought to be attuned to the way in which they may enable and validate racial discrimination.

Although the internet is indeed a space where individuals ought to express themselves freely, online commercial dating websites also serve as public accommodations. As such, they are subject to considerations of justice. Courts are already recognizing the need to balance free speech and association on these sites with concerns of discrimination. This essay takes seriously their status as public accommodations, concluding that they should also not facilitate and thereby endorse racial discrimination. This kind of facilitation is a distinctive objection, one that arises precisely because online commercial dating sites are not located in a physical space. The ease with which they permit users to screen and filter on the basis of race is not an issue of speech or association. This is a kind of unjust conduct that public accommodations ought not to countenance.

Notes

1. Packingham v. North Carolina, 582 U.S. ___ (2017) at 5.

2. Ibid. at 4.

3. Abraham Singer argues that corporations are not within the "basic structure" and hence Rawls's theory of justice "cannot be applied effectively to questions of business ethics and corporate governance" (Singer 2015: 65). He questions whether Rawls's principle of democratic governance applies to corporations and other nonstate actors. My argument, in contrast, focuses on the principle of non-discrimination on the basis of race. At a minimum, I argue that this principle—leaving governance to one side—does apply to businesses such as public accommodations.

4. 42 U.S.C. §2000a(b) (2012).

5. Civ. Code, Section 51b (2015).

6. Curran v. Mt. Diablo Council of the Boy Scouts of Am., 952 P.2d 218, 236 (Cal. 1998).

7. *See, e.g.,* Stevens v. Optimum Health Inst., 810 F. Supp. 2d 1074, 1088–89 (S.D. Cal. 2011); O'Connor v. Village Green Owners Ass'n, 662 P.2d 427, 431 (Cal. 1983); Rotary Club of Duarte v. Bd. of Dirs., 224 Cal. Rptr. 213, 221–26 (Cal. Ct. App. 1986).

8. 47 N.J. 25 (N.J. 1966).

9. *Clover Hill,* 47 N.J. at 34.

10. *Clover Hill,* 47 N.J. at 33.

11. www.eharmony.com.

12. www.eharmony.com.

13. The Fair Housing Act prohibits discrimination on the basis of "race, color, religion, sex, familial status, or national origin." 42 U.S.C. Section 3604 (c). (1994). The California fair housing law prohibits discrimination on the basis of "sexual orientation, marital status, . . . ancestry, . . . source of income, or disability," in addition to the federally protected characteristics. Cal. Gov. Code Section 12955 (2011).

14. Fair Housing Council of San Fernando Valley v. Roommates.com, LLC, 521 F.3d 1157 (9th Cir. 2008) [hereinafter *Fair Housing I*].

15. Fair Housing Council of San Fernando Valley v. Roommates.com, LLC 666 F.3d 1216 (9th Cir. 2012) [hereinafter *Fair Housing II*].

16. Batzel v. Smith, 333 F.3d 1018, 1027–28 (9th Cir. 2003).

17. *Fair Housing I,* at 1161–62.

18. *Fair Housing I,* at 1161.

19. *Fair Housing I,* at 1167.

20. *Fair Housing I,* at 1167.

21. *Fair Housing I,* at 1167.

22. *Fair Housing I,* at 1162.

23. *Fair Housing I,* at 1167.

24. In contrast, in *Doe v. Backpage.com, LLC,* 2016 WL 963848 (1st Circuit 2016), the appellate court affirmed the district court's dismissal of a lawsuit against backpage.com, a website that included a section titled "escorts" on its webpage. The content in that section often advertised for illegal sex with minors. Three such women, who claimed to be victims of human trafficking, sued Backpage.com. They alleged that the website, "with an eye to maximizing its profits, engaged in a course of conduct designed to facilitate sex traffickers' efforts to advertise their victims on the website. This strategy, [they argued], led to their victimization." (*Doe* at 4). Even though the court conceded that Backpage.com made it easier for perpetrators to engage in human in trafficking through the website, the court held that the CDA immunizes the website from such a lawsuit. Distinguishing this case from *Fair Housing I,* the district court reasoned that "[n]othing in the escorts section of Backpage requires users to offer or search for commercial sex with children." *Doe v. Backpage.com, LLC,* 104 F. Supp. 3d 149, 157 (D. Mass. 2015). Unlike Roommates.com, Backpage.com did not create any discriminatory categories or content on its website that facilitated and thereby endorsed the underlying human trafficking. For instance, if Backpage.com allowed users to view only those advertisements offering sex with minors through some filtering mechanism, that kind of website content should not receive immunity under CDA given the analysis above.

25. *Fair Housing II,* at 1220.

26. *Fair Housing II,* at 1221.

27. *Fair Housing II,* at 1221.

28. *Fair Housing II,* at 1221.

29. *Fair Housing II,* at 1221.

30. *Fair Housing II,* at 1223.

31. www.match.com; www.okcupid.com. Match.com lists the following racial groups (allowing users to select more than one): Asian, Black/African descent, East Indian,

Latino/Hispanic, Middle Eastern, Native American, Pacific Islander, White/Caucasian, Other. Okcupid.com lists the following groups (also allowing users to select more than one): Asian, Black, Hispanic/Latin, Indian, Middle Eastern, Native American, Pacific Islander, White, Other.

32. 375 U.S. 399 (1964).

33. *Anderson,* 375 U.S. at 402.

34. *Anderson,* 375 U.S. at 402.

35. http://www.pewinternet.org/2013/10/21/online-dating-relationships/.

36. http://www.pewinternet.org/2013/10/21/online-dating-relationships/.

37. http://www.pewinternet.org/2013/10/21/online-dating-relationships/.

References

Abizadeh, A. 2007. "Cooperation, Pervasive Impact, and Coercion: On the Scope (Not Site) of Distributive Justice." *Philosophy & Public Affairs* 35 (4): 318–58.

Anderson, E. 2013 [2010]. *The Imperative of Integration.* Princeton, NJ: Princeton University Press.

Anderson, E. 1999. "What Is the Point of Equality?" *Ethics* 109 (2): 287–337.

Beauvoir, Simone de. 2009 [1949]. *The Second Sex.* (trans. Constance Borde and Sheila Malovany-Chevallier). New York: Knopf Press.

Bedi, S. 2014. "The Scope of Formal Equality of Opportunity." *Political Theory* 42 (6): 716–38. doi:10.1177/0090591714538267.

Bedi, S. 2013. *Beyond Race, Sex, and Sexual Orientation: Legal Equality Without Identity.* New York: Cambridge University Press.

Braman, D. 1999. "Of Race and Immutability." *University of California, Los Angeles Law Review* 46: 1375–463.

Butler, J. 1990. *Gender Trouble: Feminism and the Subversion of Identity.* New York: Routledge Press.

Fox, D. 2009. "Racial Classification in Assisted Reproduction." *Yale Law Journal* 118 (8): 1844–893.

Hartley, C. and Lori Watson. 2010. "Is a Feminist Political Liberalism Possible?" *Journal of Ethics and Social Philosophy,* 5 (1): 1–21.

Hayward, C. 2013. *How Americans Make Race.* New York: Cambridge University Press.

Hochschild, J. Vesla M. Weaver, and Traci R. Burch. 2012. *Creating a New Racial Order: How Immigration, Multiracialism, Genomics, and the Young can Remake Race in America.* Princeton, NJ: Princeton University Press.

Jacobson, M. 1999. *Whiteness of a Different Color.* Cambridge, MA: Harvard University Press.

Haney-Lopez, I. 2006. *White by Law: The Legal Construction of Race.* New York: NYU Press.

Kirkland, A. 2008. *Fat Rights: Dilemmas of Difference and Personhood.* New York: NYU Press.

Lewontin, R. 1997. *Critical Race Theory: Essays on the Social Construction and Reproduction of Race, Vol. 1.* E. Nathaniel Gates (ed.). New York: Routledge Press.

Lewontin, R., S. Rose, and L. J. Kamin. 1984. *Not in Our Genes: Biology, Ideology, and Human Nature.* New York: Pantheon Books.

Livingstone, F. 1962. "On the Non-existence of Human Races." *Current Anthropology* 3 (3): 279–81.

Rawls, J. 2001. *Justice as Fairness: A Restatement.* E. Kelly (ed.). Cambridge: Belknap Press.

Rawls, J. 1999 [rev. 1971]. *A Theory of Justice*. Cambridge, MA: Belknap Press.

Rhode, D. 2010. *The Beauty Bias: The Injustice of Appearance in Life and Law*. New York: Oxford University Press.

Robinson, R. 2007. "Structural Dimensions of Romantic Preferences." *Fordham Law Review* 76: 2787–2819.

Singer, A. 2015. "There Is No Rawlsian Theory of Corporate Governance." *Business Ethics Quarterly* 25 (1): 65–92.

Smedley, A. and B. D. Smedley, 2005. "Race as Biology is Fiction, Racism as a Social Problem Is Real: Anthropological And Historical Perspectives on the Social Construction of Race." *American Psychologist*, 60 (1): 16–26.

Waldron, J. 1981. "A Right to Do Wrong." *Ethics* 92 (1): 21–39.

Young, I. 1990. *Justice and the Politics of Difference*. Princeton, NJ: Princeton University Press.

12

The Meaning of Silence in Cyberspace

THE AUTHORITY PROBLEM AND ONLINE HATE SPEECH

Alexander Brown[*]

1. Introduction

It has been argued that even ordinary hate speakers who are not "figures of authority" in conventional senses can possess authority to subordinate the targets of their speech in virtue of the fact that when bystanders remain silent they "license" or grant authority to ordinary hate speakers (Maitra 2012). The aim of my contribution is to examine the extent to which this account of licensing is applicable to cyberhate. More generally, I explore whether the potentially distinctive nature of online communication changes the meaning of silence such that it becomes more difficult to interpret silence in cyberspace as assent, licensing, or complicity.

Part 2 provides conceptual analyses of assent, licensing, and complicity in the face of hate speech. Part 3 puts forward three necessary conditions for silence in the face of hate speech to constitute assent, licensing, or complicity. These are: actual awareness of the hate speech; sufficient clarity as to the meaning of silence; and minimally adequate voluntariness. Part 4 then investigates whether the potentially distinctive nature of online communication makes these conditions harder to satisfy, therefore exacerbating ambiguities in the meaning of silence, or instead makes these conditions easier to satisfy, therefore reducing ambiguities in the meaning of silence. Finally, Part 5 emphasizes differences between alternative areas of cyberspace vis-à-vis the meaning of silence, and points in the direction of further lines of enquiry.

[*] I am grateful to Susan Brison, Kath Gelber, Ishani Maitra, and Jonathan Seglow for their insights and suggestions.

2. Acquiescence (Assent), Licensing, and Complicity

In this and the next part I want to explore the basic proposition that when an audience or group of bystanders remains silent in the face of hate speech their silence constitutes assent, licensing, or complicity. The term "hate speech" is an opaque idiom signifying a heterogeneous collection of expressive phenomena (Brown 2017b, 2017c). So, to give the discussion focus, I shall concentrate on people who read about, hear, or witness speakers using anti-Semitic, racist, Islamophobic, homophobic, etc. (see Brown 2016, 2017a) abusive insults or propaganda, whether face to face or online, often with a view to subordinate, intimidate or incite hatred (see Langton et al. 2012; Brown 2017c).

By "silence" I mean communicative silence, meaning withholding opinion or a failure to communicate or remark, whether or not it also involves silence in the physical sense of not uttering a sound (Sobkowiak 1997). The distinction is important because people can still communicate through disproving glances or facial expressions, say, even without making a sound.

An example of the basic proposition can be found in the words of the Canadian senator, Jerry Grafstein, speaking in the Senate of Canada in 2002.

> Last summer, I spoke in the Reichstag, the German Parliament in Berlin [. . .] urging the OSCE to lead in raising our voices against runaway anti-Semitism. [. . .] The OSCE was not silent.
>
> Yet, in Canada, I have waited, and all I have heard is silence. [. . .] Honourable senators, silence is acquiescence. Acquiescence breeds licence. Licence breeds legitimacy. Legitimacy leads to fear, scorn, loathing and then violence [. . .].[1]

Or, consider the following passages from the work of the philosopher Ishani Maitra.

> An Arab woman is on a subway car crowded with people. An older white man walks up to her, and says, "F***in' terrorist, go home. We don't need your kind here." He continues speaking in this manner to the woman, who doesn't respond. He speaks loudly enough that everyone else in the subway car hears his words clearly. All other conversations cease. Many of the passengers turn to look at the speaker, but no one interferes.
> [. . .]
> This conversation is one in which the speaker aims to mark his target as a terrorist and an undesirable, and in doing so, to rank her as inferior to others. No one challenges the speaker's claims. [. . .] [W]e can think of this failure as licensing. Since licensing is sufficient for ranking, the speaker in this case succeeds in ranking his target as inferior. (Maitra 2012, 115)

[. . .] To put the point in other (and stronger) terms, if I am right about licensing here, then in staying silent, the other passengers are, to some extent, *complicit* in what the hate speaker does. (116)

But what does it mean for hearers to acquiesce, license, or be complicit? Clearly, the word "acquiescence" can sometimes mean to agree or comply with something, without implying regret, reservation, or duress. Nevertheless, it is useful to have a concept that does imply these things (Woodard 2000). Thus, sometimes the term "acquiescence" means one or all of the following: (1) that the hearers have accepted the right of the hate speaker to engage in hate speech but have done so with regret or reluctantly; (2) that they have agreed with the opinions expressed by the hate speaker, albeit only passively or unenthusiastically; or (3) that although they have allowed the hate speaker to perform certain acts (e.g., ranking others as inferior, stirring up hatred, inciting discrimination or violence), they have done so non-freely.

Therefore, one can replace the word "acquiescence" with "assent" in instances when: (1a) the hearers have straightforwardly accepted the right of the hate speaker to engage in hate speech; (2a) they have wholeheartedly agreed with the opinions expressed by the hate speaker; *or* (3a) they have freely allowed the hate speaker to perform certain acts. The opposite of this sort of assent is dissent, meaning rejection of the right of the hate speaker to engage in hate speech, disagreement with the opinions expressed by the hate speaker, and refusal to allow the hate speaker to perform certain acts.

In addition, the word "licensing" could mean the following: (4) that the hearers have granted the hate speaker the authority required to perform certain acts (e.g., ranking others as inferior), in the sense of giving them the right, power, or permission to perform those acts. The opposite of licensing or granting authority is withholding authority: namely, to veto the speaker's right to perform certain acts, to refuse to give one's permission or approval for the speaker to perform those acts, or to insist on retaining the right, power, or permission to perform (or not perform) those acts.

I take it as read that when Maitra speaks of "licensing" in her subway car example she has in mind something like (4). Maitra also assumes (for the sake of her argument) that ranking others as inferior is an "authoritative illocution," meaning this is the type of illocutionary act that can only be successfully performed by a person with a relevant form of authority. In other words, for Maitra, that the speaker possesses authority, *by some means or other*, is part of the necessary "felicity conditions" for successfully performing the illocutionary act (Maitra 2012, 100).

Although Maitra says little to justify the assumption that ranking others as inferior is an authoritative illocution, it does not seem hard to do so, especially if we reflect further on what broader family of illocutionary speech act the act of ranking other people as inferior, for instance, falls into.

In his *How to Do Things with Words*, J. L. Austin proffered the English verbs "to demote," "to excommunicate," and "to degrade" as examples of a particular family of illocutionary speech acts he labeled "exercitives." "An exercitive is the giving of a decision in favour of or against a certain course of action" (Austin 1962, 154). That is to say, "[i]t is a decision that something is to be so, as distinct from a judgement that it is so" (ibid.). When a boss utters the words "Smith, you're demoted," he is making a decision that Smith is to be demoted. It is not hard to see why this would be an authoritative illocution. It is only by virtue of the fact that the boss occupies the relevant position of authority, namely, that he possesses the right and power to demote, that he successfully performs the illocutionary act of demoting Smith.

Nevertheless, it is hard to see how hate speech that ranks others as morally inferior is an exercitive, since, normally, such speech is not a decision that something is to be done—a decision that certain people are to be stripped of their rank, akin to the way the verbs "to demote" or "to excommunicate" signify that persons are to be lowered in rank. Rather, such speech tends to be a judgment that certain groups *are* inferior.

Interestingly, Austin himself cites the English verbs "to rate," "to grade," and "to rank" as examples of another family of illocutionary speech acts, namely, "verdictives." "Verdictives consist in the delivering of a finding, official or unofficial, upon evidence or reasons as to value or fact so far as these are distinguishable" (Austin 1962, 152). It strikes me that hate speech which ranks other people as inferior is verdictive.

Nevertheless, typically verdictives are also authoritative illocutions. Successfully issuing a judgment or delivering a verdict—including that certain other people are morally inferior—requires the speaker to have the authority to do so (see also Langton 1993, 304). Since, other things remaining equal, ordinary people lack the authority to rank others as morally inferior, this is where licensing can play a role. To license the hate speaker is to grant them the authority to rank others as inferior on one's behalf. Putting this another way, it is a matter of delegating the hate speaker to act in one's name in matters of ranking, or to give permission for one's own judgment or verdict as to the moral standing of certain people to be substituted with that of the hate speaker.

Of course, according to some scholars, this is not the only way in which hate speakers can acquire authority to perform verdictives. Rae Langton, for instance, has suggested that a hate speaker might also gain authority to rank others as inferior simply by presupposing that he or she possesses this authority and by the hearers going along with that presumption, even if their silence falls short of the granting of authority (Langton forthcoming). But since I find this alternative story of authority acquisition less persuasive than Maitra's, in this contribution I shall focus on licensing.

Finally, the term "complicity" might suggest the following: (5) that the hearers have knowingly participated—or consciously acted as accomplices—with the hate speaker in the joint performance of certain acts (e.g., ranking others as inferior). The direct opposite of complicity is a conscious refusal to participate with the hate speaker in the performance of such acts.

Complicity in the above sense also needs to be contrasted with *unwitting enabling*: (6) that the hearers have made it possible for the hate speaker to perform certain acts, but without being aware of making this possible. Whereas an accomplice knows what is going on, an unwitting enabler does not.

Relevantly, Mary Kate McGowan has argued that some hate speech falls into a family of illocutions she dubs "covert exercitives" (McGowan 2009, 394–97; 2012, 132–36). According to McGowan, such illocutions function as decisions that certain things are to be so within the context of norm-governed activities—including activities such as racism. Or, as McGowan puts it, some hate speech "enacts" facts about what is subsequently permissible or impermissible ("permissibility facts") within the activity of racism. Moreover, such illocutions work in a "covert" or sneaky manner by virtue of enacting permissibility facts independently "of either speaker intention or participant awareness" (McGowan 2012, 132). But, for McGowan, it is also the case that "one must be *a participant* in the rule-governed activity in question in order to make moves and hence in order to perform covert exercitives" (McGowan 2012, 402, emphasis added).

It is, I believe, very far from straightforward what it means for the speaker to be a participant—or what constitutes sufficient participation in an activity—such that they have the standing required to covertly change the norms of the activity (see Brown 2015, 86–91; Stanley 2015, 319–20, n.20). Furthermore, much more needs to be said about what it means for the audience to be participants such that they are in a position to unwittingly enable the speaker to have the standing required to covertly change the norms of the activity. For example, just as the audience might be unaware of a hate speaker changing the rules of the activity of racism in which they are involved, so the audience could also be unaware even of their being involved in the very activity of racism, the rules of which have been changed. In these ways McGowan may have simply replaced the authority problem with the participant problem.

No doubt unwitting enabling has an important part to play in the full story of hate speech. Nevertheless, for the above reason it is not something I intend to examine here. In what follows I shall concentrate solely on assent, licensing, and complicity. In the next part I try to identify the circumstances in which silence in the face of hate speech can constitute one—or all—of these three things.

3. Silence

Under what conditions, if any, can it plausibly be said that silence in the face of hate speech constitutes assent, licensing, or complicity? One obvious condition is that the audience or group of bystanders actually heard or read the hate speech, and recognized it as such. Without this requirement silence cannot be safely interpreted as assent, licensing, or complicity. For example, a passenger on the subway car who was fast asleep when the Arab women was being targeted with an Islamophobic slur and wakes up shortly afterward might remain silent, but this cannot be counted as licensing.

I believe that two further conditions are required, even if they are more controversial. (Note that at this point I am also parting company with Maitra's account.) The second is that in order for silence to constitute assent, licensing, or complicity it must be sufficiently clear to those people who remain silent that silence means one or more of these things.[2] This can be conceived in different ways: (i) as an intention on the part of the hearers that their silence is to be taken as assent, licensing, or complicity; or (ii) as at least partial understanding on the part of the hearers that their silence will be taken as assent, licensing, or complicity based on or in accordance with sociolinguistic conventions governing such situations.[3] Take licensing. Before one can plausibly assert that an audience or group of bystanders to hate speech has, through silence, granted authority to a hate speaker to rank as inferior a certain group of people, it first must be sufficiently clear to the hearers that their silence has this meaning or significance.

In the subway car example, potentially it is sufficiently clear (albeit not perfectly clear) to the other passengers that their silence means assent, licensing, or complicity, especially if everyone knows what the speaker is doing, everyone remembers at least one occasion in the past where passengers have spoken back to hate speakers, and there is common knowledge of how silence can reverberate and mark assent, licensing, or complicity. Of course, if there are signs and regular public announcements in the subway system stating, "As passengers on this subway car you are joining a community of fellow travelers who look out for each other and who do not remain silent in the face of hatred," as well as a regular practice of speaking back to hate speakers on subway cars, then silence may have a much clearer meaning.

A third condition is minimally adequate voluntariness. For silence in the face of hate speech to count as minimally free and unforced assent, for instance, as opposed to mere acquiescence, it must be the case that the hearers do not perceive significant danger or unreasonably high burden in doing other than remaining silent.[4] Similarly, silence cannot count as the granting of authority if the perceived consequences of not remaining silent are extremely detrimental to the person who says, "Not in my name" or "I have not granted you the authority to rank other people as morally inferior." Thus, it could be that the white man on the subway car also creates a threatening or menacing atmosphere, such that the other passengers feel too scared to speak up. Under such conditions, we cannot be at all certain that silence means the granting of authority to the hate speaker to perform certain acts (see also Brown 2015, 79–80).

Ironically, in these circumstances not merely does silence not constitute the granting of authority because this silence is the result of a threatening or menacing atmosphere (according to my second condition), but also the very use of hate speech can itself be partly responsible for creating that atmosphere. This wider phenomenon is commonly referred to as *the silencing effect*. Charles Lawrence puts the point thusly: "When racial insults are hurled at minorities, the response may be silence or flight rather than a fight" (Lawrence 1990, 452). But note, even if hate speech itself had no—or no proven—silencing effect,[5] it could still be the case that silence in the face of racist hate speech, say, cannot be taken to constitute minimally free and unforced assent, licensing, or complicity, by dint of the effects of other dimensions of racism. At any rate, my contribution is not about the silencing effect but about the meaning of silence.

As an aside, in the early literature on organizations it was assumed that when members of an organization remain silent in the face of things they do not agree with (rather than engaging in "voice" or "exit"), they are displaying "loyalty" (Hirschman 1970). But it has been subsequently understood that silence may signify either assent or dissent depending on the circumstances (Jensen 1973). For example, the historian Richard J. Evans (2015) has recently challenged conventional wisdom that the Nazis were granted the authority to rank as inferior, discriminate against, and slaughter Jews by virtue of the silence of a broad mass of German people. Evans argues that silence cannot be so interpreted because many people in the working classes or on the political left who disapproved of anti-Semitism were forced into silence by widespread Nazi intimidation and repression. This repression was undertaken by people in positions of authority throughout German society: not merely by members of the Gestapo but also by public prosecutors, the police, the judiciary, Blockwarts (Block Wardens), landlords, employers, etc.

More generally, in any instances where an audience includes people who routinely experience subordination, oppression, or systematic injustice at the hands of the very group or class of persons of which the speaker is a member, silence is more likely to be an effect of unequal power relations than something that constitutes minimally free and unforced assent, licensing, or complicity (see also Dendrinos and Pedro 1997). Returning once again to the subway car example, suppose the hate speaker is male and all the other passengers are female. In that scenario the silence of the other passengers is at least as likely—and potentially even more likely—to be a sign of male domination over women as of the voluntary granting of authority to the hate speaker. No doubt various forms of discrimination and violence against women, as well as misogynistic hate speech, will play a part in causing the involuntary silence of the female passengers in the face of the white man's hate speech against the Muslim woman.

I believe these three conditions (actual awareness of the hate speech, sufficient clarity as to the meaning of silence, and minimally adequate voluntariness) are not merely necessary conditions for silence in the face of hate speech to constitute assent, licensing, or complicity. I also happen to think they are necessary conditions for those persons who remain silent being held morally responsible, in the sense of being rightly praised or blamed, for their silence. But I shall not explore this more fully here (see Woodard 2000, 427; Maitra 2012, 116–17).

4. Cyberspace

In the previous part I argued that silence in the face of hate speech can constitute assent, licensing, or complicity, but only if three necessary conditions are satisfied. But how, if at all, does this situation change when we shift the focus from offline hate speech to cyberhate? For example, does the potentially distinctive nature of online communication make these conditions harder or easier to satisfy?

Much has been written about potential differences between offline hate speech and cyberhate (see Tsesis 2001; Perry and Olsson, 2009; Delgado and Stefancic, 2014; Citron, 2014; Cohen-Almagor, 2015; Brown 2018a). But what does silence in the face of cyberhate look like and, moreover, does online silence mean the same as offline silence?

I begin by returning to the first condition: that the audience or group of bystanders are *actually aware* of the hate speech. Suppose someone posts an Islamophobic remark on the comments section of a free to access online newspaper article or blogpost about multiculturalism. What, if anything, would count as silence in the face of the remark? At first glance, the answer seems obvious: a lack of response from other users. When nobody engages with the comment by replying to it in the same comments section, then this is silence. What is more, it is the sort of silence that might constitute assent, licensing, or complicity, potentially equivalent to the silence exhibited in the subway car example (so the thought goes).

However, there is a problem with this simple analysis. How do we know anyone has actually read the comment in question? In the case of a hate speaker on a sparsely occupied subway car, then one can safely assume that other passengers have heard the hate speech, provided other felicity conditions are met (the hate speaker is talking loudly, the passengers are not hard of hearing, etc.). But these assumptions are harder to make about comments in cyberspace. Given the vast quantity of online content, much content will simply not be seen and read by other users. In the case of the Islamophobic remark added to the comments section of an online newspaper article or blogpost, it might be one of hundreds of comments appearing in the section. Thus, silence might not mean anything, but simply reflects the fact that no one is reading the content. (In some instances internet users may be using automated systems that block or filter content before it ever reaches their eyes, and without the knowledge of those who created the content.)

Now it might be countered that internet analytics can enable us to measure how many users see particular bits of online content. For example, "Google Analytics" can provide data on numbers of "pageviews," meaning the number of instances when a webpage has been loaded onto a web browser, thus appearing on the screen of a Google user.[6] Similarly, "Twitter Analytics" allows users to discover how many "Impressions" their tweets have attracted during a given period of time, defined by Twitter as "Number of times users saw the tweet on Twitter."[7] This means that a tweet has been delivered to a Twitter user's feed and the tweet has actually appeared on the screen in front of the user.

Yet there is an important difference between the number of "Pageviews" and the number of actual reads of a webpage. Sometimes Google users click on a webpage but immediately click away without actually digesting its content— so-called bounce. Likewise, the phrase "Number of times users saw the tweet on Twitter" might give the false impression that it means the number of times users actually noticed, read, and "took in" the tweet. But it means none of those things. When users are scrolling through their Twitter feeds—potentially hundreds of tweets daily—a particular tweet can appear on their screens, and that counts as an impression, even though they have scrolled up or down without stopping to read it. So even if a tweet garners a large number of impressions and zero replies containing objections to it, this "silence" cannot be assumed to mean assent, licensing, or complicity, because it cannot be assumed that the combination of impressions and lack of replies satisfy the condition of actual awareness.

This means, for example, that hate speakers who post comments underneath online newspaper articles or blogposts or who tweet their vilificatory bile might not be licensed by the silence of other users to rank certain groups as inferior. Instead, the process of licensing hate speakers online could require more in the way of positive engagement with the hateful content. In terms of online newspaper articles and blogposts, it might be a matter of clicking the "like" icon or adding a supporting comment ("I agree with what that guy said"). On Twitter, it could involve clicking the heart icon (to signify a "like" or perhaps "love") or adding a supporting comment via the "Reply" function.

I now want to turn to the second necessary condition outlined in the previous part: sufficient clarity as to the meaning of silence. Is it clearer or less clear in the case of silence in response to cyberhate that silence means assent, licensing, or complicity? The correct answer to that question is surely that it depends on which area of cyberspace one has in mind. After all, cyberspace is not one amorphous space but a complex amalgam of public, private, and mixed spaces, each with their own characteristic speaker intentions and sociolinguistic conventions about the meaning of silence.

To illustrate, when people voluntarily attend KKK rallies it is usually taken as read that if they do not raise a voice in dissent against what is being said and done they are thereby assenting to, licensing, or being complicit in what is being said and done. By analogy, it might be abundantly clear to people who "Join" a far right online hate group, consume its online newsletters, and spend time on its online discussion forums—such as a group hosted on a social networking website such as VKontakte (Khazan 2016)—that silence means assent, licensing, or complicity.

But intentions and sociolinguistic conventions about the meaning of silence may be quite different in other parts of cyberspace, wherein it is insufficiently clear that silence means assent, licensing, or complicity. For example, it scarcely seems likely that users of mainstream online newspapers or blogs typically intend or even partially understand that their silence—failure to contribute to these online public fora—means licensing, say, the originators of the content to perform certain acts. Readers, I suspect, suppose they not only have no duty to regularly access these online fora but also have no duty to publicly pass judgement on every bit of content they happen to read—to click on the like icon or else to post a counter-comment—at the risk of their silence being taken to mean assent, licensing, or complicity.

This, in my view, reflects the fact that to be a reader of a mainstream online newspaper or blog is to be a member of a "serial collective" (Young 1994), in the sense of being a series of isolated individuals who simply happen to be confronted with the same infinite material, technological, and communicative possibilities. This is distinct from being a member of a group, in the sense of people who are truly connected with each other and who self-consciously see themselves as being united by certain shared opinions, values, or common purposes. It is an open question whether passengers sharing a subway car can be more than merely a serial collective. Perhaps in the face of the immediate threat posed by the hate speaker, in a confined space, and a space that is not a public fora but a means of transport, a random collection of individuals might have a responsibility to organize themselves into a group to meet the threat.

Similarly, having lots of followers on Twitter means many things (i.e., reach, popularity, notoriety, intrigue, significance, morbid curiosity), but surely it does not stand as a quantification of support for one's views. If the popular disclaimer "Retweets do not equal endorsements" is true, then the same goes for "Failure to engage at all with Tweets does not equal endorsement." I may choose to "Sign up" to Twitter and then to "Follow" @therealdonaldtrump, as well as following many other people on Twitter, but it is very far from being clear to me that any failure of mine to reply angrily to potential vilification of Muslims, Mexicans, or women by @therealdonaldtrump means that I am in agreement with Trump or am Trump's accomplice. That being said, where people choose *only* to follow Twitter users who are well-known hate speakers or *only* to track well-known "hate" hashtags, this may be more akin to joining a group, and in that event the intentions and sociolinguistic conventions surrounding silence may be different.

There is another layer of complexity that demands attention. It is that temporal and physical parameters are also required in order for silence to carry certain meanings by virtue of either intention or at least partial understanding of meaning. In the offline world there is a period of reasonable duration when, and a definite space in which, responses or replies must occur if they are to constitute valid expressions of dissent against, withholding authority from, or refusal to participate with hate speakers. If the other passengers on the subway car only speak up after the hate speaker has left the carriage, or if they leave the subway car and then proceed to speak up out of earshot, it seems obvious that this would not count as dissent, withholding authority, or refusal to participate. However, it might well be more difficult to clearly discern these parameters in cyberspace. For example, because tweets, hashtags, threads, and so on, can be left "open" in perpetuity, the temporal boundaries of acts of dissent, withholding authority, or refusal to participate are fuzzier. Suppose users come across a particular hate tweet, but they wait a year before replying to it. Could this count as dissent, withholding license, or refusal to participate? What is a reasonable duration in which a reply must occur in order for it to be counted as such things? If the replies can occur at any period of time after the tweet is made, because the tweet exists online in perpetuity, then potentially any silence or lack of reply by users who see the tweet could never be counted as assent, licensing, or complicity, because at any time in the future these users could reply.

Likewise, because online content can exist in potentially infinite numbers of connected virtual spaces the physical parameters of communicative exchanges are also fuzzier. For instance, users who see a tweet which employs a particular hate hashtag could respond to it using the "Reply" function and using the same hashtag. Their replies will appear under the original tweet and can be seen by the speaker as well as by anyone who follows the speaker, anyone who follows the person making the reply, and anyone who "tracks" the original hashtag (i.e., anyone who clicks on that hashtag to see the relevant tweets). Then again, they could instead respond to the tweet with a new tweet of their own, perhaps not even mentioning the speaker and adding a different, "love" hashtag. In that event the response will only be seen by users who happen to follow the person making the response or who track the alternate hashtag. But if a Twitter user opts not to use the Reply function and not to use the original hashtag, but instead responds with a new tweet and an opposing, love hashtag, could this still count as dissent, withholding authority, or refusal to participate? This question is made all the more difficult by the fact that although there will be some Twitter users who do track both hashtags, and who follow both the speaker and the person making the response, this will not be a perfect overlap of people, and so the different "spaces" will be contiguous and overlapping but also separate and non-identical.

Finally, consider again the minimally adequate voluntariness condition. It is widely supposed that online anonymity—or perceived anonymity—can embolden people to be more outrageous, obnoxious, or hateful (Branscomb 1995, 1642–43; Citron 2014, 57, 59–60; Cohen-Almagor 2015, 86–87, 114, 146; Poland 2016, 22–24). The perceived anonymity of the internet may remove fear of being held accountable for cyberhate and may also evince a sense that the normal rules of conduct do not apply (Citron 2014, 58; Delgado and Stefancic 2014, 322; Kang 2000, 1135 n.16).[8] Indeed, some media commentators have attributed the decline in Twitter users partly to the amount of hatred that can be found on Twitter, which itself could be due to the sorts of users it attracts, the anonymity it permits, and the light touch moderation it apparently employs (Topolsky 2016). This might point in the direction of understanding silence in the face of cyberhate—even to the point of abandoning Twitter, say—as partly an effect of the wider cyberhate itself but also not something that can be taken to constitute minimally free and unforced assent to, licensing of, or complicity with, the sorts of acts the online hate speaker is attempting to perform (e.g., ranking other people as inferior).

On the other hand, the perceived anonymity of the internet could also potentially liberate audiences and groups of virtual bystanders. That online hate speakers might not know who the counter-speakers are might reduce the fear and anxiety that doing other than remaining silent could lead to being identified and reprisals. In that sense, anonymity might be taken by some people to suggest that silence in the face of online hate speech is more free and unforced than silence in the face of offline hate speech.

One can tell a similar story about lack of physical presence online. Perhaps the opportunities for communication without physical presence furnished by the internet remove one incentive to refrain from directing hateful speech at other people: namely, that they could turn around and attack the speaker. But, by the same token, when it comes to audiences or groups of bystanders who are faced with the dilemma of whether to speak up or remain silent in the face of hate speech, arguably they run much less of a risk of being physically attacked by the person they would be dissenting against (the hate speaker), if they dissent online, than if the hate speaker were actually stood in front of them.

At first glance, then, the perceived lesser threat of having one's identity discovered or facing a physical backlash in cyberspace could make it easier to satisfy the condition of minimally adequate voluntariness. If people perceive these threats to be lesser, then arguably it becomes much harder to claim that silence is involuntary, in the sense of being caused by legitimate perceptions of significant danger or unreasonably high burden.

On closer inspection, however, things might not be so straightforward. The concepts of danger and unreasonably high burden are not exhausted by the perceived threat of being identified and physically attacked. Another relevant perceived danger or unreasonably high burden can be social ostracization and isolation. There is also the legitimate fear of appearing naïve or foolish.

To explain, a long-standing thesis in communication studies holds that because human beings have a deep-seated fear of social ostracization and isolation, they will have a tendency to adjust the voicing of their own opinions in public in accordance with their sense of whether or not their own opinions are shared by the majority of other people. This is the "spiral of silence" thesis (Noelle-Neumann 1974). Accordingly, one could expect that if individuals perceive they are living in a society in which nationalistic and xenophobic opinions are in the ascendancy, then those individuals might be less comfortable publicly engaging in counter-speech against certain forms of cyberhate. This could mean in turn that their silence is significantly involuntary and, therefore, *potentially* it cannot be taken to constitute assent, licensing, or complicity. A related thesis concerns the tendency of people to avoid being the first to speak out about some perceived danger (or injustice) for "fear of appearing naïve or foolish" in the event the perception turns out to be unfounded (Miller and Prentice 1994). It could be that a legitimate fear of appearing foolish in the event of having misinterpreted the situation or having gotten the wrong end of the stick might stop people from being the first to speak out against online hate speech.

How plausible is this line argument? Take the case of Islamophobia on Twitter. On the one hand, it is certainly true that Twitter users could end up seeing anti-Muslim tweets and hashtags on a regular basis. Anti-Muslim hashtags on Twitter, such as #stopislam, make it easier for users to find messages or tweets on certain topics. Because hashtags are not controlled by any one user or group of users they take on a life of their own, meaning that when enough tweets carry the hashtag they can begin to trend and appear on *any* Twitter user's "Trending Now" tab. Perhaps a Twitter user who observes that anti-Muslim hashtags are trending on Twitter might be less inclined to engage in counter-speech due to the spiral of silence. Indeed, a Twitter user who notices that anti-Muslim Tweets tend not to be removed by Twitter moderators under the Twitter Rules, might also perceive that not even the Twitter executive team truly believes that such content has no place on mainstream internet messaging services.[9]

On the other hand, Twitter also enables the creation of online discussion venues where pro-Muslim or pro-tolerance opinions are in the ascendancy. Thus, in recent years many pro-Muslim or pro-tolerance hashtags, such as #loveislam, have also garnered a great deal of popularity on Twitter. In this way Twitter enables users who perceive themselves to possess minority opinions to find each other online. The fact that there are hashtags dedicated to opinions like their own could reduce their fear of being socially isolated. Indeed, a recent study of counter-speech on Twitter has found that some users feel secure enough to deliberately post messages carrying hashtags representing the opposing opinion to their own in order to directly confront hate speakers with counter-speech (Benesch et al. 2016). Arguably this is only made possible by the fact that these counter-speakers also have access to other hashtags where their opinions are in the majority, and where their sense of community and social bonding is presumably secure. In this way both the diversity of opinions and the diversity of fora available in cyberspace may counteract the tendency identified by the spiral of silence thesis.

Of course, even if the voluntariness condition can be met in the case of audiences or groups of virtual bystanders to cyberhate, it is still necessary for the other two conditions to be met (actual awareness of the hate speech, sufficient clarity as to the meaning of silence), before silence can constitute assent, licensing, or complicity.

I want to end this part by making an observation about the ability of people to avoid putting themselves into situations in which they are challenged to speak up publicly against hate speech. It might be thought that there is a fundamental disanalogy between the subway car example and examples involving cyberhate. In the case of the subway car, we have a captive audience, whereas people who read the comments sections of online newspapers or blogs must actively choose to click on those sections and need login details to do so. And people who use Twitter must "Follow" the speaker or "track" certain hashtags in order to receive the speaker's tweets. So there is an element of active participation.

However, it would be a mistake, I think, to assume that it is impossible to be a "captive audience" in cyberspace merely because one has to switch on the computer, open up a web browser, click on an online newspaper or blog, "Follow" someone on an internet messaging service, "Friend" someone on a social networking website, etc. After all, users of subway cars must take active steps to enter a station, buy a ticket, move through a ticket barrier, and step onto a car. More importantly, what makes an audience captive in morally and legally relevant senses is the unreasonable burden of avoiding the space in question. Just as for many people traveling by subway car is a necessary and not easily avoidable means of functioning normally as a worker, citizen, and individual, the same goes for using (parts of) the internet (Brown 2017e).

5. Concluding Remarks

The internet provides unrivaled opportunities not merely for hate speakers but also for counter-speakers, and for people who wish to guide and empower the practice of counter-speech (Benesch 2016). But there is also such a thing as silence in the face of hate speech, and the offline world does not have a monopoly on such silence. Nevertheless, when this silence occurs in cyberspace it also poses particular challenges for those who would interpret its meaning, including taking it to mean assent, licensing, or complicity. My main contention has been that it can be harder to infer assent, licensing, or complicity from silence in the face of hate speech when that hate speech occurs online as opposed to offline.

I am aware that my remarks on the above subjects are incomplete, and raise many more questions than they answer. But I hope that they have at least motivated the need for further study on the meaning of silence in cyberspace.

One obvious further line of enquiry is the legal doctrine of "acquiescence by silence," whereby the victims of what would otherwise be considered tortuous acts forfeit their right to claim damages if they remain silent in the face of those acts, by virtue of their silence being taken to mean that they accept, permit, or grant authority for those acts. Hate speech as a tortuous act, or dignitary tort, is one obvious example (Brown 2018b). Here again the three necessary conditions identified above (actual awareness of the hate speech, sufficient clarity as to the meaning of silence, and minimally adequate voluntariness) seem pertinent. If, as is not uncommon, victims of hate speech feel too scared or intimidated to speak back, then their silence should not be considered to mean consent (acquiescence by silence). Otherwise they could be dammed if they do speak back and dammed if they do not.

Notes

1. Hon. Jerahmiel S. Grafstein, Debates of the Senate (Hansard), 2nd Session, 37th Parliament, Vol. 140, Issue 20, November 21, 2002, at 409–10. Available at: https://sencanada.ca/en/content/sen/chamber/372/debates/020db_2002-11-21-e#55.

2. However, it need not be perfectly clear. Otherwise the condition might be very rarely met.

3. Hate speakers will be inclined to interpret silence as assent, license, or complicity because it is in their interests to do so. But this vested interest is not the determining factor here.

4. This threshold condition of minimally adequate voluntariness reflects the fact that silence is virtually never completely willing, free, and unforced: doing other than remaining silent will always carry some extent of danger or burden.

5. However, for a defense of a precautionary approach to the silencing effects of hate speech, see Brown (2017d).

6. Available at https://analytics.google.com/.

7. Available at https://analytics.twitter.com/.

8. For a critical take on these assumptions, however, see Brown (2018a).

9. The Twitter Rules do impose "some limitations on the type of content that can be published with Twitter," including on "Hateful conduct." But this is limited to the acts of promoting violence or inciting harm against other people on the basis of certain protected characteristics. It does not extend to other hate speech acts, such as the act of ranking other

people as inferior based on their possession or perceived possession of protected character-istics. The Twitter Rules are available at https://support.twitter.com/articles/18311#.

References

Austin, J. L. 1962. *How to Do Things with Words*. Oxford: Oxford University Press.

Benesch, S. et al. 2016. *Counterspeech on Twitter: A Field Study*, October 18. https://dangerousspeech.org/counterspeech-on-twitter-a-field-study/.

Branscomb, A. W. 1995. "Anonymity, Autonomy, and Accountability: Challenges to the First Amendment in Cyberspace." *Yale Law Journal* 104: 1639–79.

Brown, A. 2015. *Hate Speech Law: A Philosophical Examination*. New York: Routledge.

Brown, A. 2016. "The 'Who?' Question in the Hate Speech Debate: Part 1: Consistency, Practical, and Formal Approaches." *Canadian Journal of Law & Jurisprudence* 29: 275–320.

Brown, A. 2017a. "The 'Who?' Question in the Hate Speech Debate: Part 2: Functional and Democratic Approaches." *Canadian Journal of Law & Jurisprudence* 30: 23–55.

Brown, A. 2017b. "What Is Hate Speech? Part 1: The Myth of Hate." *Law and Philosophy* 36: 419–68.

Brown, A. 2017c. "What Is Hate Speech? Part 2: Family Resemblances." *Law and Philosophy* 36: 561–613.

Brown, A. 2017d. "Hate Speech Laws, Legitimacy, and Precaution: Reply to Weinstein." *Constitutional Commentary* 32: 599–617.

Brown, A. 2017e. "Averting Your Eyes in the Information Age: Hate Speech, the Internet, and the Captive Audience Doctrine." *Charleston Law Review* 12: 1–54.

Brown, A. 2018a. "What Is So Special about Online (as Compared to Offline) Hate Speech? Internet Companies, Community Standards and the Extragovernmental Regulation of Cyberhate." *Ethnicities* 18: 297–617.

Brown, A. 2018b. "Retheorizing Actionable Injuries in Civil Lawsuits Involving Targeted Hate Speech: Hate Speech as Degradation and Humiliation." *Alabama Civil Rights & Civil Liberties Law Review* 9: 1–56.

Citron, D. K. 2014. *Hate Crimes in Cyberspace*. Cambridge, MA: Harvard University Press.

Cohen-Almagor, R. 2015. *Confronting the Internet's Dark Side: Moral and Social Responsibility on the Free Highway*. Cambridge: Cambridge University Press.

Delgado, R. and Stefancic, J. 2014. "Hate Speech in Cyberspace." *Wake Forest Law Review* 49: 319–43.

Dendrinos, B. and E. R. Pedro. 1997. "Giving Street Directions: The Silent Role of Women." In A. Jaworski (ed.), *Silence: Interdisciplinary Perspectives*. Berlin: Mouton de Gruyter.

Evans, R. J. 2015. *The Third Reich in History and Memory*. London: Little, Brown.

Hirschman, A. O. 1970. *Exit, Voice and Loyalty*. Cambridge, MA: Harvard University Press.

Jensen, J. V. 1973. "Communicative Functions of Silence." *ETC: A Review of General Semantics* 30: 2249–57.

Kang J. 2000. "Cyber-race." *Harvard Law Review* 113: 1130–208.

Khazan, O. 2016. "American Neo-Nazis Are on Russia's Facebook." *The Atlantic*, May 20. Available at https://www.theatlantic.com/technology/archive/2016/05/extremist-groups-vkontakte/483426/.

Langton, R. 1993. "Speech Acts and Unspeakable Acts." *Philosophy and Public Affairs* 22: 293–330.

Langton, R. forthcoming. "The Authority of Hate Speech." In L. Green and B. Leiter (eds.) *Oxford Studies in Philosophy of Law, Vol. 3*. Oxford: Oxford University Press.

Langton, R. et al. 2012. "Language and Race." In G. Russell and D. Graff Fara (eds.) *Routledge Companion to the Philosophy of Language*. London: Routledge.

Lawrence, C. 1990. "If He Hollers Let Him Go: Regulating Racist Speech on Campus." *Duke Law Journal* 1990: 431–83.

Maitra, I. 2012. "Subordinating Speech." In I. Maitra and M. K. McGowan (eds.) *Speech and Harm: Controversies over Free Speech*. Oxford: Oxford University Press.

McGowan, M. K. 2009. "Oppressive Speech." *Australasian Journal of Philosophy* 87: 389–407.

McGowan, M. K. 2012. "On 'Whites Only' Signs and Racist Hate Speech: Verbal Acts of Racial Discrimination." In I. Maitra and M. K. McGowan (eds.) *Speech and Harm: Controversies over Free Speech*. Oxford: Oxford University Press.

Miller, D. T. and D. A. Prentice. 1994. "Collective Errors and Errors about the Collective." *Personality and Social Psychology Bulletin* 20: 541–50.

Noelle-Neumann, E. 1974. "The Spiral of Silence: A Theory of Public Opinion." *Journal of Communication* 24: 43–51.

Perry B. and P. Olsson. 2009. "Cyberhate: The Globalization of Hate." *Information and Communication Technology Law* 18: 185–99.

Poland, B. 2016. *Haters: Harassment, Abuse, and Violence*. Lincoln: University of Nebraska Press.

Sobkowiak, W. 1997. "Silence and Markedness Theory." In A. Jaworski (ed.) *Silence: Interdisciplinary Perspectives*. Berlin: Mouton de Gruyter.

Stanley, J. 2015. *How Propaganda Works*. Princeton, NJ: Princeton University Press.

Topolsky, J. 2016. "The End of Twitter." *The New Yorker*, January 29. http://www.newyorker.com/tech/elements/the-end-of-twitter.

Tsesis, A. 2001. "Hate in Cyberspace: Regulating Hate Speech on the Internet." *San Diego Law Review* 38: 817–74.

Woodard, C. 2000. "The Concept of Acquiescence." *Journal of Political Philosophy* 8: 409–32.

Young, I. M. 1994. "Gender as Seriality: Thinking about Women as a Social Collective." *Signs* 19: 713–38.

13

Regulating Online Speech

KEEPING HUMANS, AND HUMAN RIGHTS, AT THE CORE

Dinah PoKempner[*]

1. Introduction

We live in a moment of transition, when many alive learned to communicate and receive information before the internet, and many also have no memory of life without it. Our world is being radically and swiftly reshaped by digital communication, the flood of data it generates, and the wild acceleration of both human and machine learning. This is producing both shock and anxiety as the full power of digital communication becomes manifest, leaving in the air a question of whether our old notions of free expression and privacy are still relevant to the flood of data that increasingly constitutes ourselves and our society[1]

To some extent, this anxiety greets the development of every new medium of communication—so much so, it has its own name, "technopanic," a situation where there is an intense, fearful public response to perceived social threats from new technology.[2] These panics often imagine the new technology overriding preexisting social strictures, leading to moral collapse and upheaval. In the case of the internet, panic runs high about unregulated expression and exposure to "dangerous" content, whether that means pornography, racism, "fake" news, state secrets, opposition politics, or "extremism" variously conceived. A telling symptom of this anxious moment is that states, even while invoking the language of human rights, are moving farther away from these standards in their own regulation, arrogating ever greater powers

[*] General Counsel, Human Rights Watch, Associate Professor, Columbia University. The views expressed here are strictly my own.

of surveillance to themselves, and demanding ever more potent proxy censorship from Internet Service Providers.

Yet as more and more of our lives move online, the rights most under threat are those that seemed at first to epitomize the internet: freedom of expression, access to information, and privacy—critical components of our self-awareness, autonomy, and dignity. These rights underpin both liberalism and the idea of a democratic society. Much can be lost if we do not act to protect the humanity that underlies our laws, our art, and our sense of worth. The human rights framework is still an important safeguard against our own worst inclinations, and is adaptable to many new challenges.

The rationale for human rights—protection of a core of human dignity against powerful entities—is highly pertinent in the digital age, and the legal standards for rights protection are flexible enough to accommodate even the distinctive problems online speech poses. So why are even democracies so reluctant to apply the standards they profess? Economic factors, including the emergence of enormously powerful companies that dominate key online platforms and services, have threatened states and provided clear, centralized targets for those who wish to influence the marketplace, including the marketplace of ideas. So even when states regulate how corporations may mine the new gold of personal data, they are reluctant to set limits on their own access. The questions of whether rights invasions are justified, truly "necessary," and "proportionate" need more serious consideration, and this may require alternate models of regulation. Rights can be protected by the design of technology, as well as through enabling individuals and communities to push back against undesirable speech. Transparency of rules and decisions is crucial, as well as notice and oversight, if we are to be able to hold either government or corporate decision-making to account. And good processes and decisions that protect human rights cost money. Investing in human rights is essential if we are at all committed to preserving zones of liberty for individuals and to keeping both corporations and government answerable for the decisions they make over our lives and our human future.

2. Where We Are Coming From

When it comes to envisioning dignity for individuals, the framework of universal human rights is a defining feature of the twentieth century. It came to being in the aftermath of World War II's wholesale destruction of human life and dignity, and wove checks on power over individuals into the very fabric of modern states and the international order.

Rights, critical to the formation of beliefs, defense of other rights, and association, are essential checks against authoritarianism. It is not accidental that the European Convention on Human Rights, and later the UN's Human

Rights Committee, posit that restrictions on these freedoms can be lawful only if necessary "in a democratic society."[3] The test of limitations on these rights rests on three pillars: legality, necessity, and proportionality. Government interference with privacy or free expression must be set forth in law of sufficient clarity and specificity to enable rights-holders to anticipate how and under what circumstances the restriction will operate. The interference can only be for an aim specified as compatible with human rights, such as defense of national security or public safety—interests that belong not to the state but to the people for whose benefit it exists. The restriction must be necessary, in the sense that it is not simply desirable, convenient, available, or hypothetically useful, but actually appropriate to the threat posed and truly needed. It must also be proportionate, in that no alternative that presents a lesser intrusion on rights would serve the purpose, and the restrictive measure itself will not be so severe as to impair the essence of the right.[4]

The internet was first expected to usher in a utopian era of free expression, as in John Gilmore's famous words, it "treats censorship as damage and routes around it" (Elmer-Dewitt 1993). Others can continue to mirror and disseminate banned content, giving states that censor burdensome choices, such as walling off their population's access or somehow enforcing censorship worldwide. Thus speech would be unbounded, unmediated, and uncensored; people would connect and organize as never before. And to some extent, this vision was true. Even in countries where mass media were heavily censored, speech flourished unhindered in cyberspace, activists organized across borders, and peasants accessed the world's markets and libraries. Minds could meet in that new location "cyberspace," making globalized creation and impact within the reach of ordinary people.

But the power of online expression and its manifestation at moments such as the Arab Spring soon convinced many governments to impose more boundaries and means of censorship. They set about monitoring and punishing online activists, sometimes imposing harsher penalties for online speech crimes than their offline counterparts, erecting barriers to companies that did not respect domestic censorship requirements (Ahram 2016). When activists (as well as criminals) tried to shield themselves through anonymity or encryption, governments issued orders or proposed laws to force ISPs to hand over their users' data and decode communications (Human Rights Watch 2016a). Firewalls, banning social media, and even internet shutdowns[5] all became ways governments tried to control online activity (Crowcoft 2016; Vasilogambros 2016). And as the public square relocated to major global platforms in cyberspace, government monitoring and control moved with it.

Privacy found at once new life and mortal threat in the digital world. Cyberspace became a place where people could find new social communities and alternate identities, where they had freedom to explore and develop, whether through sexual expression or friendships across boundaries or exposure to ideas their surrounding community might disfavor or suppress. At the same time, most actions in this domain produce data that corporations and increasingly governments collect and analyze. As algorithmic analysis develops, these clouds of personal data are available to make histories and profiles that we ourselves might be incapable of reconstructing—from what we click, whom we contact, what we say, and where we go. A prominent internet archivist noted, "Edward Snowden showed we've inadvertently built the world's largest surveillance network with the web" (Hardy 2016). The power to collect and analyze this data[6] gives control over markets, freedom, and lives (Marquis-Boire and Hardy 2012). And of course, privacy and freedom of expression are often symbiotic: the fact of being observed, and who observes us, can determine whether and how we speak, browse, read, or participate.

It is not only the government that can damage rights online, through censorship or surveillance. Online platforms can give private parties new opportunities to inflict old harms. Among these are hate speech, defamation, recruitment and incitement to violence, and disinformation campaigns—all difficult problems whose analyses and potential solutions are distinct, but all illustrative of types of speech that most democratic societies would punish or discourage in some way. Each entails a cost to rights—such as impelling discrimination, silencing others, provoking mental or physical harm, or jeopardizing the integrity of democratic processes. As these harms and their costs become ever more manifest, so too grows demand for internet regulation.

This watermark, of once high but now receding expectations for what the internet will do for rights, may oddly show the enduring salience of human rights standards in regulation. Regulating, however, is complicated by the distinctive features of online communications.

3. Online Communications Disinhibit, Persist, and Cross Borders, Making Regulation Complex

Speech in the online world does have distinctive features that make it powerful. It is often more disinhibited than face-to-face interactions. It persists as publicly accessible unless deliberately removed. And online expression, even between two persons in the same country, often travels at incredible speed across national borders. Each of these features can accentuate the damage speech can inflict, and each makes regulation of speech complicated.

Disinhibition is a much-studied but not well-understood phenomenon. It accounts for greater responsiveness and "sharing" when we interact with online platforms such as social media (think "selfies"), and yet it is also reflected in a greater propensity for incivility and invective (think "revenge porn"). While it is common to attribute disinhibition to anonymity, disinhibition is characteristic of attributed online speech as well, and various studies cite many factors that contribute to this quality, including the rapidity and impersonality of a medium lacking nonverbal cues and interaction (Masnick 2011; Martin 2013). In fact, being identified (so peers can see you as the nastiest troll on the site) may sometimes worsen behavior (Coren 2016).

This complexity suggests that real-name policies are not necessarily an optimal solution. They are, however, a favorite requirement of authoritarian regimes that would like to identify dissenters to silence them (Shu 2016). Re-inhibiting trolls can be done in many ways—through government-created laws that impose penalties on speakers or platforms, through corporate rule-making and enforcement, or through other social consequences, such as ex-posure, peer condemnation, or employment consequences. Platform design can also make a difference, by allowing participants to block harassers, submit complaints, or rate responses. Each method has implications for not just the speaker and his victim, but for free expression more broadly, through the collateral effects of the rule, its enforcement, and the precedent it sets.

The persistence of online information advances all types of research and newsgathering, long after first reports. Real-time fact checking in political contests, for example, can add immeasurably to informed decision-making in elections. But malicious, false, or unlawful speech also persists, and even when the subject succeeds in having it retracted in one jurisdiction, it may be mirrored in or available from another. Persistence may also encourage mobbing, enabling harassment or gossip to gain momentum rather than fade away. The "right to be forgotten," pronounced by the European Court of Justice in the *Costeja*[7] case, is an effort to counteract persistence, requiring search engines such as Google to delink material claimed to be "inaccurate, inadequate, irrelevant or excessive," a definition drawn from data protection that can be in tension with rights to expression and information. Companies thus found themselves with the burden of drawing the balance between rights, a delegation no electorate made.

Finally, the transborder accessibility and routing of online communications empowers those far from cities and traditional institutional nodes of information. The internet is built for networking, and it grants immediate access to the world's libraries, commercial markets, and science not only to those in the hinterland but also to networks of violence, extremism, and revolution. Knowledge is power, and governments have sought to control who has access to what data by requiring it be kept within their borders to facilitate surveillance, or by using firewalls to keep undesirable content out. It is quite difficult to limit only undesirable information without limiting some of the benefits of free access in the process, and even more difficult to filter or censor without trampling human rights (as activists the world over know, throwing their thoughts over national firewalls or communicating privately through a foreign company's overseas servers).

There are considerable opportunity costs—both in terms of human rights and economic interests—to imposing and maintaining filters and walls between any jurisdiction and the rest of the internet. Democracies generally are not willing to take this route. Yet they face a real problem in regulation, when courts may order intermediaries to delink or delete content that offends the law, only to have it still accessible through foreign websites. Of course, the injured party could seek, court by court and country by country, to have the content removed, but few would go to these lengths. There is still no Berne Convention for problems such as defamation, hate speech, or similar harms of online expression, and significant differences between regional and national traditions on the regulation of speech make a global agreement of this sort unlikely.

One solution national courts have grasped is the unilateral order for global compliance. The validity of such global injunctions is being tested, in a case from France[8] regarding its view of the "right to be forgotten," and in another intellectual property case in Canada[9] where the highest court has validated the approach. Google, the predominant index, is the target of both cases. And Google is willing to legally contest this novel approach, because its interest aligns with its users' in seeking to preserve its character as the most comprehensive search engine. But eventually, even this corporate Goliath's willingness to fight in the world's courts may flag, shifting the burden of challenge to those of few means—the consumer or the producer of censored information. If no one challenges the order to delist, the safest route for the company is to comply. And if readers or writers who challenge delisting orders sue and win, the company will face a dilemma—comply with the censoring jurisdiction or with the protective jurisdiction? The damages, if indeed there are any, for delisting are likely to be smaller and more uncertain than the sanctions for refusing to obey. And non-democratic states that would like nothing better than to erase their critics from the internet will surely study the precedent.

4. Limiting Access to Data Troves: The Worrisome Precedent of Surveillance

When, in 2013, Edward Snowden disclosed the massive, indiscriminate nature of global data collection by the United States and its allies, the diplomatic response was outrage. At the UN, the General Assembly debated resolutions on the right to privacy and the Human Rights Council ordered expert reports and created an expert position on the right. National leaders decried US espionage, and activists challenged the legality of surveillance practices in courts. Yet it is striking how little state surveillance powers have been curtailed since then. Indeed, many countries instead moved to replicate US powers of surveillance and place them on a firm legislative footing.

There have been many reasons it has been difficult to muster political pressure for surveillance reform, among them continual terrorist attacks, migration and refugee flows, worries over cyberattacks, and disinformation campaigns. In December 2016, the United Kingdom put the manifold spy practices of its government on a legislative footing in the Investigatory Powers Act[10] (popularly known as "the Snooper's Charter"), which Edward Snowden described as legalizing "the most extreme surveillance in the history of western democracy" (MacAskill 2016; Wong 2017; Lubin 2016). Among these powers are bulk hacking into the devices of persons suspected of no crime, mass surveillance by tapping the undersea cables that route internet traffic to the rest of the world, requirements that internet companies store browsing histories of their users (which forty-eight government departments can access without judicial oversight), and weak judicial oversight of generalized surveillance orders that does not evaluate the need for the order under the human rights standards of necessity and proportionality. France also rushed through a new surveillance law in 2015 that greatly augmented executive powers with minimal judicial oversight and control and placed bulk data collection and retention on a legal footing (PoKempner 2015).

If these laws sound more like the product of authoritarian governments, there's a reason—they are light on independent oversight and particularized justification of any surveillance operation, and they operate to create huge data troves that can be searched for many purposes. For comparison, Russia has long maintained the System of Operative-Investigative Measures (SORM), which requires all communications companies including ISPs to install devices that enable the security services to monitor communications.[11] Recent legislation requires companies to store and process the personal data of citizens on servers located in Russia, retain content for six months and metadata for three years, and disclose them to the authorities on request without a court order (the 2016 "Yarovaya" amendments). These amendments also require companies to provide "information necessary for decoding" electronic messages to security authorities (Human Rights Watch 2016a, 2017a). China, long a leader in censoring online speech and controlling access through a national firewall, in 2016 enacted a new Cybersecurity Law that requires foreign companies to store data in China and submit to government "security checks," surrendering source code on demand. The law also requires companies to censor "prohibited" information[12] and obtain real names and personal information for users (Human Rights Watch 2016b, 2017c). (Other laws on national security and counterterrorism permit the government to take "all necessary" steps to guard China's sovereignty and grant authorities assistance such as decryption in preventing and investigating terrorism) (Bowman, Ying Li, and Ho 2017). These powers live in the wider context of China's efforts to build nationwide databases and surveillance networks that can give the authorities a huge range of information on every citizen (Wang 2017).

Overall, judicial bodies have shown some commitment to actually applying human rights standards. The European Court of Human Rights, for instance, has made clear that indiscriminate, blanket surveillance—in the sense of creating a "haystack" of data on the population in order to search for terrorist "needles"—cannot be a necessary and proportionate measure to secure society against the threat of terrorism. The European Court of Human Rights Grand Chamber suggested recently that an independent authorizing agency reviewing whether a secret surveillance measure was necessary and proportionate "must be capable of verifying the existence of a reasonable suspicion against the person concerned."[13] Simply alleging someone has committed a criminal act or threatened national, military, economic, or ecological security, without a specific factual basis for evaluation, would not be enough.[14] And the European Court's Fourth Section observed that a state surveillance measure, to be "necessary in a democratic society," had to be "strictly necessary . . . for safeguarding the democratic institutions," as well as "for the obtaining of vital intelligence in an individual operation."[15] The court framed this by observing these standards would preclude "so-called strategic, large-scale interception" of communications."[16]

Popular demand for regulating access of corporations to personal data, however, is stronger, and governments are more willing to act in this area. Again, courts seem willing to go further than governments to protect rights, as demonstrated by the Court of Justice of the European Union's decision in *Digital Rights Ireland* invalidating the Data Retention Directive with its requirement that processors retain data of all persons in all locations at all times for six months to two years.[17] This was followed by the CJEU decision invalidating the Safe Harbour agreement that allowed US companies to transfer data out of the European Union to servers located in the United States, where Maximilian Schrems contended his right to privacy of communications would not be adequately protected. The Court had no difficulty finding in this context that law authorizing government "access on a generalised basis" to the content of electronic communications must "be regarded as compromising the essence of the fundamental right to private life."[18]

5. Who Bears the Burden of Regulation, and What Are the Costs to Human Rights?

Governments generally have preferred regulating companies to limiting themselves, and often justify their acts publicly through rights-talk. In the case of data protection law, the rationale is protecting the privacy and data of their citizens, just as surveillance is justified in terms of public safety. Yet economic factors underlie much regulation as well, and looking at them helps to illuminate why so many regulatory approaches often leave individuals in the weakest position, all the rights-talk notwithstanding.

In many democracies, a favorite mode of regulating online speech is to press corporations to assume the burden of censorship, rather than legislate clear requirements that could be put to judicial test. When companies resist, they often cite concerns with free expression, but there are economic realities at play too. Internet platforms have little economic incentive to oust members, since the larger the network, the more attractive and valuable it is to all participants (Coren 2017). Even so, these companies require acceptance of extremely broad Terms of Service that allow them almost unlimited discretion to reject anyone for almost any reason. These private conditions are like the strictures of a shopping mall, where the owners are free to set the rules of decorum. Governments often try to accomplish censorship of undesirable content by pressuring companies to enforce their expansive terms of service, sometimes trying to add an economic incentive by threatening legislation or fines. This can reduce political costs (one less law to sponsor and campaign for), social resistance (as corporate takedown decisions are private and largely unknown), regulatory costs (by shifting most to companies), and even the cost of defending the law in courts or during elections.

The market dominance of the major internet platforms makes burden-shifting more popular. Google (owned by Alphabet); Amazon, Facebook, and Apple (known in Europe as "GAFA"); along with Microsoft, Yahoo, PayPal, and others dominate the global market for their services and goods. If you want to ensure content is delisted globally, an order focused on just Google can go far to accomplish that goal. That these market giants are US companies only adds to other nations' anxiety and eagerness to constrain the unaccountable foreigners whose revenue may exceed their own gross domestic product.[19] Many government regulatory regimes and demands—data protection, right to be forgotten, filtering of extremism—are tailored to the giants, where the assumption is that enormous global corporations have the means to readily comply.

Demands on companies also have an element of both *ressentiment* and wishful thinking, imputing to the wizards of technology both the duty and expertise to put their genie back into its bottle. An example is the FBI's demand that Apple engineer a way around the password protection feature of the iPhone the San Bernadino shooter used. The demand was not to simply remove some feature, but to invent something new. The idea that it was *necessary* for Apple's engineers to work for the FBI—and thereby undo a safety feature for millions of other owners of that model— was questionable on many fronts, not least that the attack was over, the attackers were dead, and the phone was unlikely to hold many secrets as it was a secondary device provided by his employer. But we know dragooning Apple's engineers wasn't necessary— because another company cracked the security for the FBI, while yet other experts freely and publicly offered their own ideas for workarounds on the internet.

Unfortunately, this experience did not stop other governments from demanding that companies such as WhatsApp or Facebook find ways to decode content secured by end-to-end encryption. Here, the demand is general, untethered from any particular case or exigency—but it is also difficult to pass the "necessary and proportionate" test for an interference with rights, as undoing the security technology for the benefit of one government will make many innocent communications susceptible to breach by many. Secure encryption is a necessary feature that makes many online activities possible, whether good or bad. It makes no more sense to ban it than to ban flush toilets, which pundits note also can be used to destroy evidence.

In the wake of terrorist attacks, leaders in France, the UK, Germany, and Italy have repeatedly called on companies to swiftly remove or filter out "extremist" content, without waiting for user complaints or government adjudication as to its legality (Campos and Nichols 2017).[20] There is no clear definition of what makes content "extremist," and there is a troubling pattern of states using this term to sweep up disfavored views that are most likely protected speech. Government pressure on companies to rapidly identify extremist speech and delete it under their own terms of service carries certain implications: companies would have to scan all content on their platform to identify such speech (a form of prepublication censorship that protection from intermediary liability is supposed to obviate), and the standards under which censorship would be performed are those of unaccountable private parties, not government agencies that are directly accountable to human rights law, domestic and international.

Demands such as these ignore whether the goal can be accomplished without also censoring protected speech. Companies, even when willing, find it difficult to distinguish unlawful speech from protected speech reliably. Child pornography, universally unlawful, is relatively easy to identify, yet even here Facebook faced public backlash when its algorithms or reviewers banned Nick Ut's iconic photograph of a naked girl fleeing a napalm attack and also removed a photograph of Denmark's Little Mermaid statue (Levin, Wong, and Harding 2016; Supernova 2016). Hate speech or recruitment to terrorism is vastly more complex to analyze, as is "fake" news (deLisa Coleman 2017, Talbot and Fossett 2017). Algorithms have difficulty incorporating the enormous number of variables that indicate to humans the intent and meaning that lie behind particular verbal cues and patterns,[21] and even human moderators have difficulty applying corporate rubrics for censorship across cultures.

So far, most major internet companies are not interested in opening up to public scrutiny their algorithms, machine learning processes, or even moderator guidance. And when these are revealed, they vividly illustrate the difficulty in coming up with globally applicable rules that can be easily and consistently applied by either machines or humans. Consider Facebook's rule that slurs and invective directed at two "protected categories" can be deleted as unprotected hate speech, but not those where only one descriptor falls into such a category (these are race, sex, gender identity, religious affiliation, national origin, ethnicity, sexual orientation and serious disability/disease). That formula allows for the deletion of speech targeting "white males" but not speech targeting "female drivers" or "black children" (Angwin and Grassegger 2017). Plainly, an ocean of social context has been omitted because social context is local and nuanced.

There is much more at issue than just the complexity of technology and rule. Truly effective vetting of content at scale is expensive. Algorithms offer a cheap way of sorting through the mountains of content, but so far are susceptible to error and bias. Human review costs money, and so far platforms have not been willing to invest deeply in it. Facebook, in addition to some automated prescreening for child sexual abuse and terrorism, employed about 4,500 content moderators around the world at the time of a 2017 exposé by *The Guardian* (Hopkins 2017). These people, equipped with two weeks' training, guidance manuals from headquarters, and salaries of about $15 an hour, were making the decisions to cull disputed material for further evaluation. Under pressure from both governments and users over depictions of violence, the company agreed to add an additional 3,000 moderators to its force (Gibbs 2017). This is still a paltry investment, given the many difficult issues, the millions of complaints, and the user population of 2 billion people worldwide.

Censorship on the cheap is unlikely to protect rights well. Protecting rights, of course, is not the primary purpose of corporate terms of service, or algorithms, or rules for content moderators. They are intended to produce rapid decisions over huge volumes of data in ways that will keep the platform away from controversy and trouble. When in 2017 the German government put forward a draft law to fine companies that failed to remove false news and hate speech, Facebook protested that when social networks face such a disproportionate threat of fines, it "provides an incentive to delete content that is not clearly illegal" (Shead 2017). It also observed the draft law "would have the effect of transferring responsibility for complex legal decisions from public authorities to private companies" (Shead 2017). It is not realistic to expect private companies to reproduce judicial-quality distinctions between protected and unlawful speech. People whose rights may be limited by a government demanding corporate censorship may not always get notice that, much less reasons why, content was removed.[22] They will not have recourse in the courts by and large, and many companies provide little in the way of their own process for appeal.

Proposals in the United States to scrap the mutual legal assistance treaty (MLAT) system are another example of cost-shifting with little regard to rights protection. This system, through which other governments request evidence held in the United States for their own criminal investigations, is highly bureaucratic, essentially requiring the submission of requests through ministerial channels to US law enforcement agencies that then obtain orders for the evidence through US courts. The process averages ten months, but provides the foreign data subject at least a judicial consideration of whether constitutional protections are satisfied (AccessNow 2014). The government has proposed speeding up the process by giving foreign governments it certifies as generally rights-respecting the ability to directly demand and access corporate data without judicial review. It is also creating integrated databases of biometric and other data, allowing for what may become the most comprehensive profiling of a population by a government (Human Rights Watch 2017b). This is a proposal driven by reciprocal interests in law enforcement and intelligence—state interests—not individual human rights. Despite many dire warnings that the system is irreparably broken, there are alternatives to this proposal beyond state hacking or surveillance as ways to unilaterally grab information overseas. Adding resources to expedite or streamline the MLAT process might work quite well—but so far, the legislature has not wanted to fund these solutions, whose prime beneficiaries tend not to be US voters.

6. More "Necessary and Proportionate" Approaches

As described, many forces militate against a rigorous application of the human rights rules that require limitations on rights (whether they be surveillance, censorship, or other obstacles to accessing the internet) to be lawful, necessary, and proportionate. Governments pursue their own dominance in intelligence for a wide variety of purposes; citizens are afraid of terrorism and crime and hope that more control over online communication can produce safety. Additionally, there are strong economic factors that impel corporations to gather more data and platform users, and governments to target them as surrogates for information and control. But allowing these fears and ambitions free rein can destroy not only rights, but also the very idea of a democratic and liberal society.

It is instructive to look at developments in the illiberal world powers for how the digital age looks without constraints of human rights protection. China leads in some of the worst practices. Its "Great Firewall" obstructing access to content the Communist Party disfavors is growing ever less permeable by ordinary people. Censorship, including on social media, is mandated, pervasive, and invisible to the user, while the state employs armies of opinion-shapers online. Companies must localize data to enter the market, the better to ensure government access to that data on demand. It is developing a "social credit" system that is far more intrusive than most credit rating systems in the West, including search-engine history and purchasing records, all centralized into a system that can affect everything from whether one can purchase an airplane ticket to getting loans or jobs (Hawkins 2017). It is also creating numerous biometric databases with the plan to enable their integration, allowing for what may become the most comprehensive profiling of a population by a government (Human Rights Watch 2017c). But as noted earlier, Western democracies are aping some features of authoritarian surveillance regimes and attacking privacy technology such as encryption with a similar zeal.

As the cloud of data around our online lives grows thicker, it is worth considering whether there are alternative modes of regulating online speech that could be more sensitive to their impact on rights. Taking into consideration some of the distinctive characteristics of online speech, we might ask whether there are less intrusive alternatives to algorithmic prescreening, censorship, or profiling. Are there effective means of identifying potential criminals without destroying encryption or normalizing mass surveillance? Could we reduce and stigmatize hate speech and mobbing reactions without obviating anonymous speech or subjecting the entire internet to imprecise and culturally bound censorship? Can we slow down production and dissemination of false or harmful content, make it harder to stumble upon, less persistent, or less economically viable? How will we know if any measures are effective, unless greater transparency is demanded? Law may not be the whole answer to these questions.

Highly detailed, situation-specific, universally accepted formulae for determining how human rights apply to various issues of speech and privacy online might make regulation of online speech much easier and avoid conflicts between various legal systems that are so frequent now. But new universal instruments are unlikely, given divergent state and regional interests and approaches, and the chance of gaining stronger protection for rights this way even more so.[23] Some friction and disagreement can at least preserve zones of relative freedom on the internet, and prevent the worst prospect of a universal censorship or surveillance regime.[24] Our best option may be to live with imperfect enforcement and a multiplicity of standards.

Technologists agree that any weakness or back door cannot be designed to be exploited only by "the good guys," even if we were to trust that our government agencies were all good guys (Abelson et al. 2015). That doesn't necessarily doom law enforcement or counterterrorism efforts. First of all, we have to acknowledge that social expectations of perfect prevention of terrorism may be unrealistic. Science has transformed our attitude toward many problems that we used to consider acts of God, but so far we cannot predict with any reliability who might one day engage in violence—though we are predisposed to apply our beliefs and prejudices to such hypotheses.[25] Screening everyone's communications all the time seems either unworkable or capable of leaving us with a dystopian surveillance society. Though we believe there must be some technological fix, it seems predicting criminal behavior remains difficult, and removing every possible risk factor might leave us with societies we do not want to live in. The telephone produced similar anxieties, but even when we worked out wiretapping, some conspirators didn't talk about their crimes on the phone. Similarly, some terrorists are pretty wise to surveillance; groups like al-Qaeda have devised their own encryption systems, and will use them even if we deny strong encryption on popular platforms to millions of ordinary people whose conversations, commercial transactions, medical records, love letters, acquaintances, and political views could be exposed as a result (Ahlberg 2014).

Fortunately for the police, it is very difficult for anyone, criminals included, to leave no digital trail, even if strong, end-to-end encryption becomes widespread. Metadata, which is not hidden by encryption, can render an extremely detailed picture of anyone's contacts and comings and goings, and people have increasing numbers of devices that collect data on their movements and habits that are not encrypted. Given some reason to believe a device holds evidence, police may seize it and in many countries a judge may order its owner to give up the password (Price 2014). Encryption is mainly an obstacle to sifting through massive amounts of communications in search of yet-unknown suspects or risks. Of course, sifting through the communications of people who there is no specific (or non-discriminatory) reason to think were involved in criminal activity is probably a disproportionate interference with their privacy. We have to consider whether such sifting is even "necessary" to obtain information, given that solving and preventing crimes has been going on for quite a while using alternate methods before digital communications. Many times, the problem doesn't seem to be identifying potential terrorists hiding behind encrypted communications, but simply keeping suspects we already know under watch. This suggests a variety of other solutions, such as cultivating social networks that might yield early warnings of suspect activity, and devoting adequate resources to various types of targeted surveillance rather than focusing on decryption.

"Extremism" is undefined in international law, and not all "extremist" content is necessarily unprotected speech. For a ban to be acceptable under human rights standards, it would need to serve a specific state aim, such as public safety or national security and be both "necessary" and "proportionate" in a democratic society (where prepublication censorship will be rarely justified). There would also need to be a law of sufficient clarity to give people an idea of what crossed the line. Plainly, governments are not enacting legal bans because they are having difficulty describing everything they want off the internet in these strict terms. Even what should be the "easy" cases— say, beheading videos on YouTube—might deserve protection because they are newsworthy, or important as evidence, or more repellant than inciting (MacDonald 2017).

Despite the widespread belief that exposure to extremist content radicalizes and renders one susceptible to terrorist recruitment, in-depth studies suggest this result is influenced more by social relationships offline, and in any case is a highly individualized process.[26] One might question, then, whether laws against online extremism are fit for purpose, that is, "necessary." The "germ contact" view prevails among politicians, and thus "sanitization" to prevent infection is a popular cure. Preemptive identification of such content for removal requires invading all users' privacy as algorithms search for potentially offending content, a disproportionate effect, not to mention a type of prior restraint, but with no recourse to judicial review. Companies are being asked to take down such content under their Terms of Service, which allow censorship of almost anything, so decisions could be arbitrary or at the least far removed from judicial consideration under human rights standards.

So what would be alternative ways to regulate unwanted or harmful content online that would be more sensitive to human rights? We could try out various regulatory approaches on Lawrence Lessig's vectors of markets, law, norms, and architecture (Lessig 2006). We might also consider who takes the regulatory action—government, businesses, or users and/or communities.

For example, we might try to shift back to government the responsibility for decision-making, so that it can be tested by courts for consistency with constitutional and international guarantees of human rights, and examined by international human rights mechanisms. We should consider if governments should act through economic incentives, civil law, or criminal law—all of which may have different effects in terms of propelling over-censorship. If companies are the decision-makers, we could treat the largest platforms more like public utilities, and alter the normal rule that they are free to set their terms and require that their decision-making incorporate (or at least not violate) human rights standards. Mandating greater transparency in corporate decision-making could enable legal challenges or consumer pressure. We might demand that internal rules, algorithms, and machine learning processes be open, and the rationale for decisions given.[27] We might also want to require more in the way of open procedure, such as notification, a period to contest, and appeals, on the theory that introducing more requirements could force decision-making to be more deliberative and consultative, and allow more opportunity to surface and correct poor choices. Companies could be required to invest more heavily in expert content review, to conduct and release periodic assessments of the accuracy or human-rights impact of their processes, or make their data, appropriately anonymized, more available for academic research and testing.

Alternatively, we could approach the problem through design choices that empower users or the community. Many platforms now allow users to be their own censors, blocking undesirable content or interlocutors. Many already enable user tagging of inappropriate content for moderation. We can do more to let people limit how their data is shared, used, and retained by companies, curtailing contracts of adhesion for platforms that are increasingly the utilities of modern life. While it is still early to evaluate how different ways of tagging "fake news" affect its salience in different markets, this could, in combination with greater media literacy, weaken its potential for harm, and is certainly preferable to either censorship or criminal penalties (Pennycook and Rand 2017; Silverman 2017). Platforms are trying out excluding harmful content from newsfeeds or advertisements, placing it farther down in search results, and weeding out bots that spread it. Certain types of content can be subject to a short mandated delay before posting or reposting, to enable checks and reduce the potential for disinformation around flashpoint events such as elections.[28] Platforms and applications can be designed to mitigate echo-chamber effects and work against our tendency to credit whatever we hear repeated most.

Such strategies all would require testing for effect and may have human rights drawbacks as well—but this list is merely to show there may be other ways to counter some of the effects of the persistence, global availability, and speed of online communication without resort to preemptive censorship strategies. The varieties of undesirable, harmful speech are numerous, and each requires a tailored approach. Moreover, the speaker is not the only holder of rights that must be considered; some speech is designed to silence or hurt others, in violation of their rights, while other types may encourage more systemic harms to rights even if not directed at specific targets (See Citron 2014).[29]

To sum up, while we are at the beginning of understanding speech in the digital age, we are not novices at human rights analysis or at regulating technology. Technopanic is neither helpful nor warranted, but applying our values to new technology is important. Well-tested standards, if applied, can reduce the likelihood that human values will be compromised by our latest invention, or that technology will be turned against human dignity, rather than used to protect and enhance it.

Notes

1. In this new "age of anxiety," even what is human may be up for revision. Not only our communications, but our very selves may become transborder; we may have choices not only over what we believe or do in our lives but over our very physical and mental components; we may come to see our identity as networked; we may come to value artificial intelligence the way we do human life. Endless science fantasy novels and films about the cyborg future speak to this; so does Harari (2016).

2. See Thierer (2013).

3. Council of Europe, European Convention for the Protection of Human Rights and Fundamental Freedoms, as amended by Protocols Nos. 11 and 14, 4 November 1950, ETS 5; UN Human Rights Committee (HRC), General comment no. 34, Article 19, Freedoms of opinion and expression, 12 September 2011, CCPR/C/GC/; Office of the High Commissioner for Human Rights, The right to privacy in the digital age, Report of the Office of the United Nations High Commissioner for Human Rights, 30 June 2014 A/HRC/27/37*.

4. Human Rights Committee General Comment 34 (2011) http://www2.ohchr.org/english/bodies/hrc/docs/gc34.pdf; this standard finds an earlier articulation in Case of Handyside v. The United Kingdom (Application no. 543/72) December 7, 1976 paragraph 48. See also Human Rights Committee General Comment 31, paragraph 6 (2004) https://undocs.org/CCPR/C/21/Rev.1/Add.13.

5. See the #KeepItOn campaign, *AccessNow*, available at https://www.accessnow.org/keepiton/.

6. Citizen Lab, Communities @ Risk: Targeted Digital Threats against Civil Society, University of Toronto's Munk School of Global Affairs (2014), available at https://targetedthreats.net/media/1-ExecutiveSummary.pdf.

7. *Google v Costeja*, Judgement of the Court (Grand Chamber), European Court of Human Rights, Case C-131/12 (2014), available at http://curia.europa.eu/juris/document/document_print.jsf?doclang=EN&docid=152065.

8. Commission Nationale de l'Informatique et des Libertés, Délibération n°2016-054 du 10 mars 2016, available at https://www.legifrance.gouv.fr/affichCnil.do?oldAction=rechExpCnil&id=CNILTEXT000032291946&fastReqId=348450254&fastPos=2; See Hern (2017).

9. *Google Inc. v. Equustek Solutions Inc.* Supreme Court Judgments [of Canada], June 28, 2016, available at https://scc-csc.lexum.com/scc-csc/scc-csc/en/item/16701/index.do.

10. Investigatory Powers Act 2016 available at http://www.legislation.gov.uk/ukpga/2016/25/contents/enacted.

11. The agencies are only to access the data with a court order, but they need not show anyone the order, and the level of judicial consideration of the request is pro forma. See Soldatov and Borogan (2015), Case of Roman Zakharov v. Russia, (Application no. 47143/06) Grand Chamber ECHR 4 December 2015.

12. China prohibits and punishes a wide range of speech that is protected under international human rights guarantees, including criticism of the government, information about political events, religious expression outside the bounds of state-approved messages, ethnic minority cultural and political views, social activism, etc.

13. Case of Roman Zakharov v. Russia, (Application no. 47143/06) Grand Chamber ECHR 4 December 2015, para. 260.

14. Ibid. at para. 261. It further noted with concern the Russian practice of specifying an area rather than a suspect for surveillance, sometimes without a fixed duration, para. 265.

15. Case of Szabó and Vissy v. Hungary, (Application no. 37138/14) Fourth Section ECHR 16 January 2016, para. 73.

16. Ibid., para. 69.

17. EU Directive 2006/24 DRI, paras. 58–59; Directive 2006/24, article 6. But see AG opinion in Tele2 Sverige.

18. Maximillian Schrems v. Data Protection Commissioner, Digital Rights Ireland, Ltd. Case C-362/14 para. 94 (2015); http://curia.europa.eu/juris/document/document.jsf?docid=169195&doclang=EN.

19. This short editorial in *Le Monde* manages to hit many of these themes in arguing that "GAFA" have a duty, with their massive resources in artificial intelligence, to devise algorithms that can identify and root out extremist speech on their platforms, especially because they are so rich and adept at evading their fiscal and tax responsibilities in Europe (LeMonde 2017).

20. Prime Minister Theresa May told executives from Google, Facebook, and Microsoft to develop new technology to ensure such content is removed within two hours of posting. See Stewart (2017).

21. Stewart (2017). An interesting alternative approach that focuses on training the algorithm on community speech patterns rather than hateful terms is described in Saleem, Dillon, Benesch, and Ruths (2017).

22. See the ongoing series by the Electronic Frontier Foundation, "Who Has Your Back?" on company policies in relation to government data requests. The score for 2017 is available at https://www.eff.org/who-has-your-back-2017.

23. That hasn't stopped some from trying: the Tallinn group of experts have issued manuals aiming to describe the customary international law applicable to cyberattacks; Microsoft has called for a "Digital Geneva Convention," and the Special Rapporteur on Privacy has been drafting a legal instrument on surveillance that is expected to become public in 2018.

24. For a pungent analysis of the Orwellian nature of the European Commission's September 2017 Communication proposing guidelines for companies to proactively scan to remove illegal content across platforms, see Keller (2017).

25. Mental illness, exposure to extremist ideas, even adoption of extremist beliefs, while possible factors, do not predict recruitment to terrorism, as most people with these characteristics never become violent. See Friedman (2017); Patel and Koushik (2017).

26. See el-Said and Barett (2017). The report notes "there is no one profile" and "social and personal networks are key mechanisms in the evolution of a FTF." It also disputes the prevalent academic view that social media is a key channel of recruitment, giving greater weight to face-to-face relationships and Seamus Hughes, "To Stop ISIS Recruitment, Focus Offline," *Lawfare* August 7, 2016 at https://www.lawfareblog.com/stop-isis-recruitment-focus-offline (role of the internet in radicalization has been overblown). See also von Behr, Reding, Edwards, and Gribbon (2013), concluding that while the internet was a mode of accessing propaganda, connecting with remote like-minded persons and potentially serving as an echo chamber for beliefs, in all cases studied "the offline world played an important part in the radicalization process."

27. See the Report of the Special Rapporteur on the right to privacy, A/72/43103 October 19, 2017 section II, Conclusions and Recommendations on open data and open government.

28. Facebook is already deprioritizing links that are aggressively shared by suspected spammers and providing counter-narrative information in its newsfeed. See Syed (2017) for an excellent discussion of other characteristics of online platform ecosphere for fake news, including information filters, communities, the amplification effect, speed of dissemination, and economic incentives.

29. Compare threats and mobbing aimed at an individual with disinformation campaigns aimed at discrediting people's faith in the judiciary. Both may harm rights, but they will require very different calculations as to risk, imminence, scope of harm, and consequently as to a response that minimizes harm to rights.

References

Abelson, H., R. Anderson, S. M. Bellovin, J. Benaloh, M. Blaze, W. Diffie, J. Gilmore et al. 2015. "Keys under Doormats: Mandating Insecurity by Requiring Government Access to All Data and Communications." Cambridge, MA: Massachusetts Institute of Technology.

AccessNow. 2014. "MLAT: A Four-Letter Word in Need of Reform." *Access Now*, January 9. https://www.accessnow.org/mlat-a-four-letter-word-in-need-of-reform/.

Ahlberg, Christopher. 2014. "How al-Qaeda Uses Encryption Post-Snowden (Part 1)." *Recorded Future*, May 8. https://www.recordedfuture.com/al-qaeda-encryption-technology-part-1/.

Angwin, J. and H. Grassegger. 2017. "Facebook's Secret Censorship Rules Protect White Men from Hate Speech but Not Black Children." *ProPublica*. June 28. https://www.propublica.org/article/facebook-hate-speech-censorship-internal-documents-algorithms.

Arham Online. 2016. "Rights Groups Condemn Egypt's Cybercrime Draft Law." *Ahram Online*, June 14. http://english.ahram.org.eg/News/223035.aspx.

Bowman, C., Y. Li, and L. Ho. 2017. "A Primer on China's New Cybersecurity Law: Privacy, Cross-Border Transfer Requirements, and Data Localization." *Proskauer Privacy Law Blog*, May 9. http://privacylaw.proskauer.com/2017/05/articles/international/a-primer-on-chinas-new-cybersecurity-law-privacy-cross-border-transfer-requirements-and-data-localization/.

Campos, R. and M. Nichols. 2017. "May, Macron, Gentiloni Push for Quick Removal of Extremist Online Content." *Reuters*, September 20. https://www.reuters.com/article/us-internet-extremists/may-macron-gentiloni-push-for-quick-removal-of-extremist-online-content-idUSKCN1BV0CL.

Citron, D. K. 2014. *Hate Crimes in Cyberspace*. Cambridge, MA: Harvard University Press.

Coleman, L. deLisa. 2017. "Why the Sensitive Intersection of Race, Hate Speech and Algorithms Is Heating Up." *Forbes*, August 17. https://www.forbes.com/sites/laurencoleman/2017/08/17/why-the-sensitive-intersection-of-race-hate-speech-and-algorithms-is-heating-up/.

Coren, M. J. 2016. "Internet Trolls Are Even More Hostile when They're Using Their Real Names, a Study Finds." *Quartz*, July 27. https://qz.com/741933/internet-trolls-are-even-more-hostile-when-theyre-using-their-real-names-a-study-finds/.

Coren, M. J. 2017. "Ending Fake News Means Changing How Wall Street Values Facebook and Twitter." *Quartz*, October 18. https://qz.com/1099581/blame-wall-street-for-fake-news/?mc_cid=a398033dfa&mc_eid=68e12ac28f.

Crowcroft, O. 2016. "How China Is Winning Its War against Internet Freedom." *International Business Times UK*, May 9. http://www.ibtimes.co.uk/behind-great-firewall-china-winning-its-war-against-internet-freedom-1558550.

el-Said, H. and R. Barrett. 2017. "Enhancing the Understanding of the Foreign Terrorist Fighters Phenomenon in Syria." *United Nations Office of Counter-Terrorism*, July.

Elmer-Dewitt, P. 1993. "First Nation in Cyberspace." *TIME International*, December 6. http://kirste.userpage.fu-berlin.de/outerspace/internet-article.html.

Friedman, R. A. 2017. "Psychiatrists Can't Stop Mass Killers." *New York Times*, October 11. https://www.nytimes.com/2017/10/11/opinion/psychiatrists-mass-killers.html?_r=0.

Gibbs, S. 2017. "Facebook Live: Zuckerberg Adds 3,000 Moderators in Wake of Murders." *The Guardian*, May 3. https://www.theguardian.com/technology/2017/may/03/facebook-live-zuckerberg-adds-3000-moderators-murders.

Hardy, Q. 2016. "The Web's Creator Looks to Reinvent It." *New York Times*, June 7. https://www.nytimes.com/2016/06/08/technology/the-webs-creator-looks-to-reinvent-it.html.

Harari, Y. N. 2016. *Homo Deus: A Brief History of Tomorrow*. New York: Harper Collins.

Hawkins, A. 2017. "Chinese Citizens Want the Government to Rank Them." *Foreign Policy*, May 24. http://foreignpolicy.com/2017/05/24/chinese-citizens-want-the-government-to-rank-them.

Hern, A. 2017. "ECJ to Rule on Whether 'Right to Be Forgotten' Can Stretch beyond EU." *The Guardian*, July 20. https://www.theguardian.com/technology/2017/jul/20/ecj-ruling-google-right-to-be-forgotten-beyond-eu-france-data-removed.

Hopkins, N. 2017. "Facebook Moderators: A Quick Guide to Their Job and Its Challenges." *The Guardian*, May 21. https://www.theguardian.com/news/2017/may/21/facebook-moderators-quick-guide-job-challenges.

Hughes, S. 2016. "To Stop ISIS Recruitment, Focus Offline." *Lawfare*, August 31. https://www.lawfareblog.com/stop-isis-recruitment-focus-offline.

Human Rights Watch. 2016a. "Russia: 'Big Brother' Law Harms Security, Rights." *Human Rights Watch*. July 12. https://www.hrw.org/news/2016/07/12/russia-big-brother-law-harms-security-rights.

Human Rights Watch. 2016b. "China: Abusive Cybersecurity Law Set to Be Passed." *Human Rights Watch*. November 6. https://www.hrw.org/news/2016/11/06/china-abusive-cybersecurity-law-set-be-passed.

Human Rights Watch. 2017a. "Online and on All Fronts: Russia's Assault on Freedom of Expression." *Human Rights Watch*. July 18. https://www.hrw.org/report/2017/07/18/online-and-all-fronts/russias-assault-freedom-expression.

Human Rights Watch. 2017b. "Coalition Letter on Cross-Border Data Deal." *Human Rights Watch*. September 20. https://www.hrw.org/news/2017/09/20/coalition-letter-cross-border-data-deal.

Human Rights Watch. 2017c. "China: Police 'Big Data' Systems Violate Privacy, Target Dissent." *Human Rights Watch*. November 19. https://www.hrw.org/news/2017/11/19/china-police-big-data-systems-violate-privacy-target-dissent.

Keller, D. 2017. "The European Commission, for One, Welcomes Our New Robot Overlords." *Center for Internet and Society*, October 9. https://cyberlaw.stanford.edu/blog/2017/10/european-commission-one-welcomes-our-new-robot-overlords.

Le Monde. 2017. "Face au terrorisme, le devoir des géants du high-Tech." *Le Monde. Fr.*, September 22. http://abonnes.lemonde.fr/idees/article/2017/09/22/face-au-terrorisme-le-devoir-des-gafa_5189656_3232.html.

Lessig, L. 2006. *Code: Version 2.0*. New York: Basic Books.

Levin, S., J. C. Wong, and L. Harding. 2016. "Facebook Backs Down from 'Napalm Girl' Censorship and Reinstates Photo." *The Guardian*, September 9. https://www.theguardian.com/technology/2016/sep/09/facebook-reinstates-napalm-girl-photo.

Lubin, A. 2016. "UCL Journal of Law and Jurisprudence Blog." *UCL Journal of Law and Jurisprudence Blog RSS*, December 26. https://blogs.ucl.ac.uk/law-journal/2016/12/26/the-investigatory-powers-act-and-international-law-part-i/.

MacAskill, E. 2016. "'Extreme Surveillance' Becomes UK Law with Barely a Whimper." *The Guardian*, November 19. https://www.theguardian.com/world/2016/nov/19/extreme-surveillance-becomes-uk-law-with-barely-a-whimper.

MacDonald, A. 2017. "YouTube AI Deletes War Crime Videos As 'Extremist Material.'" *Middle East Eye*, August 13. http://www.middleeasteye.net/news/youtube-criticised-after-middle-east-video-taken-down-over-extremist-content-1244893230.

Marquis-Boire, M. and S. Hardy. 2012. "Syrian Activists Targeted with BlackShades Spy Software." *The Citizen Lab*, June 19. https://citizenlab.ca/2012/06/syrian-activists-targeted-with-blackshades-spy-software/.

Martin, A. 2013. "Online Disinhibition and the Psychology of Trolling." *WIRED UK*, May 30. https://www.wired.co.uk/article/online-aggression.

Masnick, M. 2011. "Trolls Don't Need to Be Anonymous, and Not All Anonymous People Are Trolls." *Techdirt*. September 27. https://www.techdirt.com/articles/20110926/16014916101/trolls-dont-need-to-be-anonymous-not-all-anonymous-people-are-trolls.shtml.

Patel, F. and M. Koushik. 2017. *Countering Violent Extremism*. Brennan Center for Justice: New York University School of Law.

Pennycook, G. and D. G. Rand. 2017. "Assessing the Effect of Disputed Warnings and Source Salience on Perceptions of Fake News Accuracy." *SSRN Electronic Journal*, September. doi:10.2139/ssrn.3035384.

PoKempner, D. 2015. "France: Bill Opens Door to Surveillance Society." *Human Rights Watch*. April 6. https://www.hrw.org/news/2015/04/06/france-bill-opens-door-surveillance-society.

Price, R. 2014. "Can Police Force You to Surrender Your Password?" *The Kernel*, December 7. http://kernelmag.dailydot.com/issue-sections/features-issue-sections/11071/police-force-password-cellphone/.

Saleem, H. M., K. Dillon, S. Benesch, and D. Ruths. 2017. "A Web of Hate: Tackling Hateful Speech in Online Social Spaces," http://docplayer.net/48533991-A-web-of-hate-tackling-hateful-speech-in-online-social-spaces.html.

Shead, S. 2017. "Facebook said Germany's Plan to Tackle Fake News Would Make Social Media Companies Delete Legal Content." *Business Insider*, May 30. http://www.businessinsider.com/facebook-says-germany-fake-news-plans-comply-with-eu-law-2017-5.

Shu, C. 2016. "China Attempts to Reinforce Real-Name Registration for Internet Users." *TechCrunch*, June 1. https://techcrunch.com/2016/06/01/china-attempts-to-reinforce-real-name-registration-for-internet-users/.

Silverman, C. 2017. "Facebook Says Its Fake News Label Helps Reduce the Spread of a Fake Story by 80%." *BuzzFeed*, October 11. https://www.buzzfeed.com/craigsilverman/facebook-just-shared-the-first-data-about-how-effective-its?utm_term=.fsAZA1YbB#.jbvMyGZlX.

Soldatov, A and I. Borogan. 2015. Inside the Red Web: Russia's back door onto the internet—extract.   https://www.theguardian.com/world/2015/sep/08/red-web-book-russia-internet.

Stewart, H. 2017. "May Calls On Internet Firms to Remove Extremist Content within Two Hours." *The Guardian*, September 19. https://www.theguardian.com/uk-news/2017/sep/19/theresa-may-will-tell-internet-firms-to-tackle-extremist-content.

Supernova, B. 2016. "Facebook's Most Famous Banned Images." *The Daily Beast*, September 9. https://www.thedailybeast.com/facebooks-most-famous-banned-images.

Syed, N. 2017. "Real Talk about Fake News: Towards a Better Theory for Platform Governance." *The Yale Law Journal Forum*, October 9, https://www.yalelawjournal.org/forum/real-talk-about-fake-news.

Talbot, D. and J. Fossett. 2017. "Exploring the Role of Algorithms in Online Harmful Speech." *Medium*, Berkman Klein Center for Internet & Society at Harvard

University. August 9. https://medium.com/berkman-klein-center/exploring-the-role-of-algorithms-in-online-harmful-speech-1b804936f279.

Thierer, A. 2013. "Technopanics, Threat Inflation, and the Danger of an Information Technology Precautionary Principle." *Minnesota Journal of Law, Science & Technology* 14 (1): 309–440.

Vasilogambros, M. 2016. "Why Ethiopia Blocked Social Media." *The Atlantic,* July 11. https://www.theatlantic.com/news/archive/2016/07/ethiopia-blocked-social-media/490775/.

von Behr, I., A. Reding, C. Edwards, and L. Gribbon. 2013. "Radicalisation in the Digital Era: The Use of the Internet in 15 Cases of Terrorism and Extremism." *RAND Europe.*

Wang, M. 2017. "China's Dystopian Push to Revolutionize Surveillance." *Washington Post,* August 18. https://www.hrw.org/news/2017/08/18/chinas-dystopian-push-revolutionize-surveillance.

Wong, C. 2017. "Surveillance in the Age of Populism." *Human Rights Watch,* February 7. https://www.hrw.org/news/2017/02/07/surveillance-age-populism.

INDEX